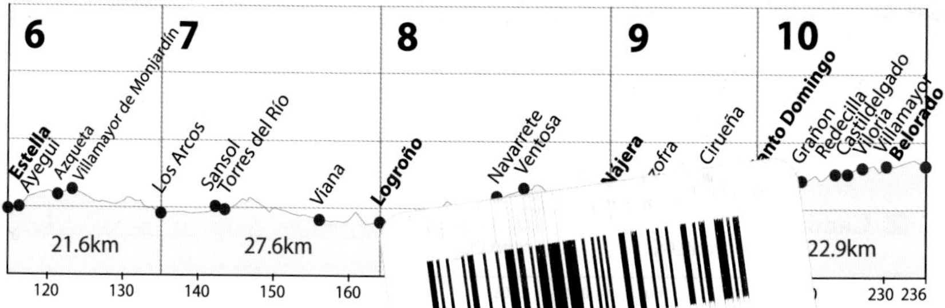

6 7 8 9 10

Estella Ayegui Azqueta Villamayor de Monjardín Los Arcos Sansol Torres del Río Viana **Logroño** Navarrete Ventosa **Nájera** Azofra Cirueña **Santo Domingo** Grañon Redecilla Castildelgado Viloria Villamayor **Belorado**

21.6km 27.6km 22.9km

120 130 140 150 160 230 236

15 16 18

Boadilla Frómista Población Villarmentero Villalcázar **Carrión** Calzada Ledigos Terradillos Moratinos San Nicolás **Sahagún** Calzada Calzadilla Reliegos **Mansilla**

24.5km 26.6km 26.4km 23.6km

350 360 370 380 390 400 410 420 430 440 447

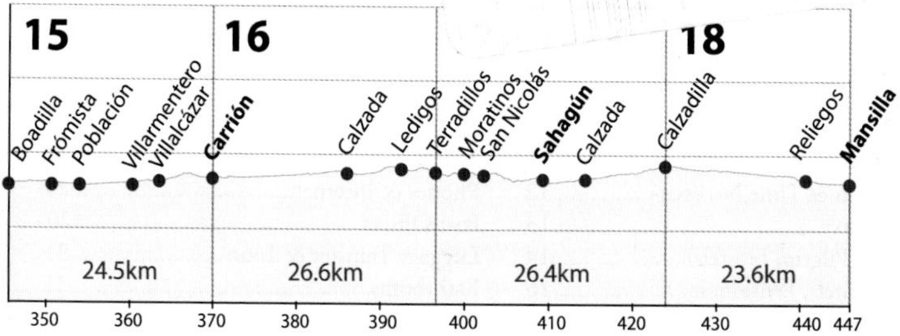

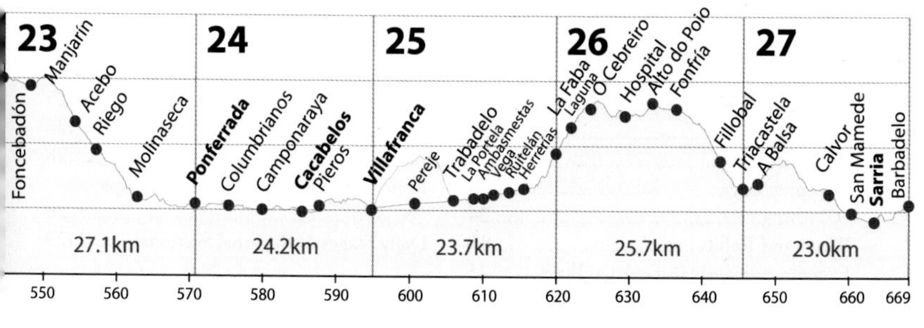

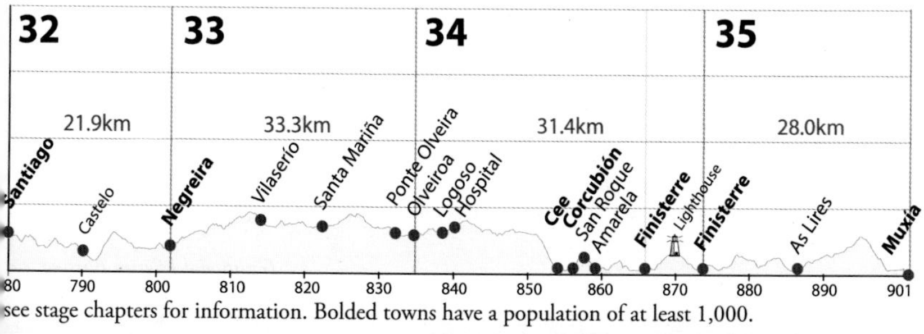

see stage chapters for information. Bolded towns have a population of at least 1,000.

Contents

Lord Jesus, as you brought your servant Abraham from the city of Ur of the Chaldeans, guard these in all their pilgrimages, and as you guided the Hebrew people through the desert, we pray that it would please you to bless these, your children that love your name, on their pilgrimage to Compostela.

Be for them companion in the journey, guide at the crossroads, shelter on the way, shade in the heat, light in the darkness, comfort in their discouragement and firmness in their purpose, so that by your guidance they would arrive intact to the end of the path and, enriched by grace and virtue, return to their houses unharmed and full of healthy virtue.

Traditional Pilgrim Blessing

Camino de Santiago, Camino Francés: St. Jean - Santiago - Finisterre
4th edition, March 2017

Village to Village Press, LLC, Harrisonburg, VA, USA
www.villagetovillagepress.com

Photographs/Diagrams
All photographs and diagrams © David Landis and Anna Dintaman except p. 87, 191 © Betsy Dintaman

Cover Photographs © David Landis
Front: Camino before Los Arcos
Back (left to right): Camino before Castrojeriz, Santiago Cathedral, Finisterre Lighthouse

Many of the images in this guide are available for licensing: www.dplandis.com

ISBN: 978-0-9843533-8-5
Library of Congress Control Number: 2014905489

Text, photographs, images and diagrams © Village to Village Press, LLC, 2017
Map data based on openstreetmap.org, © OpenStreetMap contributors (except p. 6-7)
Cover and book design by David Landis

Denis Murphy's translation is used for quotes from the Codex Calixtinus. James A. Hall's translation is used for quotes from Domenico Laffi (Suggested Reading online).

***Disclaimer**: Every reasonable effort has been made to ensure that the information contained in this book is accurate. However, no guarantee is made regarding its accuracy or completeness. Reader assumes responsibility and liability for all actions in relation to using the provided information, including if actions result in injury, death, loss or damage of personal property or other complications.*

A Note on Name Variations

Spanish and French towns in this book have a variety of names drawn from different layers of history. Many towns have more than one official name, one in Spanish and the other in the local regional language (for example, Basque or Galician). Even the more commonly known names have a variety of influences, including Iberian/Celtic, Roman/Latin, Germanic, French and Arabic. In this book, we generally refer to towns by their more common name as written on maps and road signs. When possible, we include other name(s) as legitimate alternatives. For example, we generally refer to St-Jean-Pied-de-Port (the French name), rather than the Basque name, Donibane Garazi. This is not intended to marginalize local names and minority cultures, but for practical travel purposes.

A Note on Terminology

To indicate dates, we use the commonly accepted academic terms of BCE (Before the Common Era) and CE (Common Era). For dates when the era is not specified, assume Common Era.

A Note on Text Type

Words in languages other than English are italicized, with the exception of common words, such as camino, albergue, iglesia, etc. after they are introduced (see Spanish phrasebook online). Navigational text, which describes how to navigate between towns and landmarks, is italicized while town/site descriptions are not italicized. Towns with distances shown on the map are bold in route descriptions.

A Note on Guidebooks

Each pilgrim has a different style of traveling. Some prefer light, minimalist guidebooks while other choose more thorough guides. We have tried to make this book as flexible as possible to appeal to a wide variety of travel styles. A Kindle e-book is also available for ultralight portability. We encourage those with a paper copy to remove any pages that are no longer necessary for their journey.

Visit us online for extended planning info, accommodation booking and gear recommendations at **www.caminoguidebook.com.**

CAMINO DE SANTIAGO
ROUTE NETWORK

SPAIN

1) **Camino Frances** (800km, St-Jean-Pied-de-Port to Santiago)
2) **Camino Finisterre** (90km, Santiago to Finisterre and Muxia)
3) **Camino de Norte** (825km, Irún to Santiago)
4) **Camino Portugués** (610km, Lisboa to Santiago)
5) **Vía de la Plata** (1000km, Sevilla to Santiago)
6) **Camino Aragonés** (170km, Samport Pass to Puente la Reina)
7) **Camino de Levante** (1300km, Valencia to Santiago)
8) **Camino Inglés** (110km, Ferrol to Santiago)
9) **Camino Primitivo** (320km, Gijón to Melide)

FRANCE

10) **Chemin de Le Puy** (730km, Le Puy to St-Jean-Pied-de-Port)
11) **Chemin de Paris** (1000km, Paris to St-Jean-Pied-de-Port)
12) **Chemin de Vézelay** (900km, Vézelay to St-Jean-Pied-de-Port)
13) **Chemin d'Arles** (740km, Arles to Samport pass)

Many other connecting routes exist from various locations in Europe.

Pilgrims, poor or rich, whether coming or going to the place of St. James, must be received charitably and respected by all peoples. For whoever will take them in and diligently procure hospitality for them, will be hosting not only St. James but even the Lord Himself.

Codex Calixtinus

UNITED KINGDOM
LONDON
Portsmouth
Plymouth
HOLLAND
BELGIUM
Brussels
Cologne
FRANKFURT
Luxembourg
LUXEMBOURG
GERMANY
TIC SEA
Chartres
PARIS
FRANCE
Orléans
Tours
Vézelay
Bourges
11
Poitiers
SWITZERLAND
Le Berne
12
Nevers
BAY OF BISCAY
Saintes
Limoges
GENEVA
Périgueux
Le Puy
Conques
Milan
Bordeaux
Turin
Gijón
3
Santander
10
Bilbao
Bayonne
Moissac
ITALY
Irún
St-Jean P.P.
Toulouse
13
León
Arles
Nice
Sahagún
Roncesvalles
Montpelier
Logroño
Somport Pass
Pamplona
Marseille
Toulon
1
Burgos
Puente la Reina
6
Jaca
Zaragoza
Corsica
BARCELONA
vila
MADRID
Toledo
7
Valencia
Sardinia
SPAIN
Alicante
MEDITERRANEAN SEA
Granada
Málaga
TUNISIA
ALGERIA

Pilgrims on the Way

The Camino de Santiago is often known in English as the Way of Saint James. The Spanish word *camino* can be translated as *trail*, *path*, *road* or even *journey*, but *way* serves a most accurate translation. This *way* is much broader and more expansive than any geographic track. Likewise, the Way of Saint James invites walkers not merely to a physical path, but to a way of life. The goal is not simply to arrive in Santiago de Compostela, but to be personally transformed and inspired. Charles Foster writes, "As conventional churchgoing plummets, the number of people taking to the road rises" (*The Sacred Journey*). Something draws this diverse group to leave behind the comfort of home for the unknown along the way.

To walk 500 miles across Spain sounds rather unbelievable—such a great task of endurance that only the most adventurous and inquisitive of freespirited youngsters might undertake. However, this way is growing exponentially and has almost reached the status of a rite of passage in Europe, not only for the young but for anyone with a longing for direction, renewal and challenge, a longing for pilgrimage.

The Camino is different than long-distance wilderness trails, such as the Appalachian Trail in the USA, which is often undertaken as a solitary wilderness expedition. While the Camino does pass through uninhabited wilderness, the path also traverses towns, villages and even urban centers. While it is possible to walk alone, more often the way is walked surrounded by others.

The great joy and gift of the Camino is in the people you meet along the way and the sense of connection to the millions that have gone before since medieval times. Come prepared to journey with a motley crew of pilgrims and seekers from many walks of life. Bring your burden and step into the river of people flowing to Santiago. Through the days and the miles, you will most certainly be transformed.

St. James and Spain

"*[Jesus] saw two other brothers, James son of Zebedee and his brother John. They were in a boat with their father Zebedee, preparing their nets. Jesus called them, and immediately they left the boat and their father and followed him.*" Matthew 4:21-22

In the New Testament, St. James is referred to as a disciple of Jesus who left his trade as a fisherman to follow Jesus. The Bible tells us little about him, save that he requested to be seated at the right hand of Jesus in heaven and was present at many important events such as the Transfiguration and Jesus weeping in the Garden of Gethsemane. The last biblical mention of James is of his martyrdom by Herod Agrippa in 44CE.

St. James became known as the patron saint of Spain not from biblical account, but from tradition, oral history, legend and myth. The story goes that James preached unsuccessfully in Iberia and, attracting only seven disciples. The Virgin Mary appeared to James with the pillar to which Jesus was tied to be whipped and instructed him to build a church in Zaragoza, Spain. Shortly after his encounter with Mary, James returned to Jerusalem and was martyred, and his body was transported to Spain on a stone ship without oars or sails, "carried by angels and the wind." The ship landed at Iria Flavia (present-day Padrón), and James' disciple met the ship there and transferred his body to be buried on a nearby hill.

The body of St. James was forgotten until 813CE when a Christian hermit named Pelayo saw a light that led him to the grave. The bishop authenticated these relics, and King Alfonso II built a chapel to the saint. The current cathedral was begun in the year 1075 and completed in the 1120s. The event that catapulted this modest shrine to a major pilgrimage site was the mythical Battle of Clavijo in 852, when St. James was said to have appeared to assist the Christian army against Muslim invaders. This story mirrors Muslim legends about Muhammad appearing in battle to assist the Muslim forces, who were said to carry Muhammad's relics. This image of St. James was a convenient motif to draw Christian support to the frontier of Christian-Muslim battle and to bolster interest and financial investment in maintaining Christian domination of Iberia.

Santiago, Rome and Jerusalem

Pilgrimage to Santiago continued to increase, reaching its zenith in the 11th-12th centuries, with reports of 1,000 pilgrims a day visiting the cathedral of Santiago de Compostela. Interest in relics was very high during this time, and infrastructure for pilgrims increased, including the establishment of the Spanish Military Order of Santiago to protect pilgrims. Many churches and monasteries provided accommodation for pious pilgrims. Santiago de Compostela became one of the three main Christian pilgrimage sites, along with Rome and Jerusalem. Since Jerusalem at times was a dangerous destination and the pilgrimage to Rome was mainly taken by boat, Santiago became the preferred pilgrimage site as it could be walked to from almost any site in Europe (routes on p. 6).

Early Medieval Pilgrims

For most medieval pilgrims, the journey to Santiago entailed a grueling journey of six months to one year. As today, pilgrims came with diverse motivations, such as *orandi causa*—in order to pray, to seek forgiveness, to fulfill a vow, or to petition St. James for a certain blessing, such as healing. The pilgrimage was sometimes "prescribed" by a priest or religious official as penance for a crime committed.

Codex Calixtinus: The First Camino Guidebook

The Codex Calixtinus, a collection of writings about Saint James, was written in the 12th century. The t
provides fascinating insight into the trials and joys of medieval pilgrimage. The name "Calixtinus" con
from a letter introducing the volume, supposedly penned by Pope Callixtus II but thought to be forg
The Codex is a collection of five books, including the "traveler's guide," which describes stages, towns,
commodation, the character of local people, descriptions of local shrines, warnings of bad water sources a
scams to avoid, and finally the city of Santiago de Compostela. The book was likely never used as a tra
guide considering that most medieval pilgrims would have been illiterate and few copies existed. The ent
text of book five, the traveler's guide, is available for free online.

Given the provincial lives of many peasants who rarely left their own tiny villages, the pilgrimage must have been attractive as an adventure that could be justified with pious purposes.

Pilgrims came from all strata of society, from royalty and wealthy landowners by horse and carriage, to middle class artisans and workers on horseback, to peasants, paupers and beggars on foot. Medieval pilgrims carried coins sewn into the lining of their cloaks and were often easy prey for thieves and dishonest money changers.

Medieval pilgrims had a certain style of dress that can still be noted in pilgrim depictions. Pilgrims wore short cloaks so as not to interfere with walking but to still provide warmth. A wide-brimmed hat protected from both sun and rain. Leather shoes needed frequent repair, so towns were often lined with cobblers.

Pilgrims carried several symbolic items. The ***bordón***, a wooden staff with a metal point on the bottom and a hook for hanging a drinking gourd, was symbolic of the wood of Christ's cross. The ***escarcela***, a leather bag that was flat and narrower at the top than the bottom, reminded pilgrims to carry little and rely on God's provision. The final symbolic item was the **scallop shell**. The *Codex Calixtinus* describes the shell as the fingers of an open hand, symbolizing the good deeds expected of a pilgrim. While medieval pilgrims only bore the symbol of the shell upon their return journey, today many pilgrims wear a shell on their way to Santiago.

Medieval pilgrimage was fraught with many dangers, including finding drinkable water, crossing rivers, exorbitant tolls, lice and fleas, bandits, thieves and murderers. For this reason, pilgrims traveled in groups made up almost entirely of men. Though a few women completed the pilgrimage with their husbands, the pilgrim road was not considered a wholesome place for women. Most hospices provided large straw mattresses that were shared by dozens of people. These hardships were viewed as an integral part of the pilgrim experience, identifying with the *Via Dolorosa* or 'way of suffering' undertaken by Jesus on his way to the cross.

Sacred Travel: Making your Trip a Pilgrimage

Prepare for an Inward Journey. Prepare for an Inward Journey. While outward preparations, such as packing and purchasing plane tickets, are likely foremost on your mind, you may also wish to block out some time to mentally prepare for your journey. This might include spending a few hours in silence in a natural setting. You might write in a journal, reflecting on what has drawn you to embark on a pilgrimage and what you hope to find, experience or achieve. Other ways to prepare yourself could include reading from the Bible or other inspirational books, spending time in prayer and meditation and speaking about your pilgrimage with a trusted mentor or friend.

Focus on a Theme. Pay attention to themes that emerge as you prepare for pilgrimage. Think back over the past year and identify moments which were the most life giving for you and the most challenging. Ancient pilgrims were often seeking healing, penance or an answer to prayer. If you have been going through a difficult or traumatic time, perhaps your pilgrimage will center on seeking forgiveness, direction or peace. If you feel at a good place in life, perhaps the focus of your pilgrimage can be thankfulness. It can be helpful to choose a symbol that represents your theme and carry it with you on your journey.

Be Open to New Experiences and People. As you prepare for your pilgrimage, keep your eyes open and senses alert for surprises. Things will never all turn out as planned, but the challenges and inconveniences can also be a vehicle for learning. It can be helpful to think of each person you meet as a potential teacher, and be mindful of what you might learn from him or her. Remember, too, that your kind words, encouragement or assistance may impact others far more than you may realize. At its best, pilgrimage entails a community of people willing to care for one another.

Images of St. James

In Christian art, St. James is usually portrayed as one of three images. First, James the Apostle often carries a book or scroll, and gives a sign of blessing with his right hand. James the pilgrim is portrayed wearing a pilgrim's traveling cloak with a staff, traveling hat, drinking gourd and the symbol of the scallop shell (p. 10). James the Moor-slayer is shown brandishing a sword and rearing back on a white horse, with the anguished faces of Moors beneath the horse's feet.

Pilgrim Practicalities

This information will get you started, and more extensive details are online.

Credencial (Pilgrim passport)

The *credencial* is a document that identifies the bearer as a pilgrim, with space for stamps from accommodations and sites along the Camino. A pilgrim passport is required in order to use the Camino's system of hostels (*albergues*, p. 14) and serves as proof of completing the pilgrimage (1-2 stamps per day are recommended). You may either apply for a *credencial* ahead of time via a Camino organization in your home country, or pick one up at any of the larger cities along the Camino at the pilgrim office or main albergue. As of April 2016, there is a new requirement to use an official *credencial* issued by the pilgrim office in Santiago or an affiliated organization, such as the American Pilgrims on the Camino, in order to receive the *Compostela*.

Backpacks lined up until albergue opening time

Compostela (certificate of completion)

The *Compostela* is a document of completion awarded to those who walk at least the last 100km to Santiago, or who bicycle the last 200km. Present your completed *credencial* at the pilgrim office in Santiago de Compostela in order to get your Compostela, written in Latin and personalized with your name and date of completion. A donation of €1-2 per document is requested. Those who answer that they had no spiritual motivation for the journey will be awarded an alternate unadorned certificate. Tubes for secure transport can be purchased at the pilgrim office.

When to Go and Time Necessary

When should I go? While the Camino can be walked in any season, weather and hiker volume are the main factors to consider. Refer to the average temperature and rainfall charts in each regional introduction for a better idea of typical weather. Spring and fall are generally considered the best times as temperatures are normally pleasant, most services are open and the trail is less crowded.

Summer months can be very crowded on the Camino Francés, with some competition for albergue beds. Many private albergues can be reserved in advance for those who fear not finding a bed, and a variety of hotels and other non-albergue accommodations provide options. Winter is the least popular season due to the cold and potentially rainy, snowy or icy weather. Most albergues and many other services are closed in the winter, though hearty winter pilgrims also report deep satisfaction in completing their pilgrimage under challenging winter conditions.

How much time do I need? This full itinerary from St. Jean to Santiago requires a bare minimum of four weeks (not including Finisterre), and is best experienced with at least five weeks to allow for rest days and shorter days when necessary. An extra 3-4 days to continue to Finisterre are recommended.

We have split up the journey to Santiago into 31 daily stages, with an average daily distance of 25km (15.6mi), allowing for a 5-week journey with four rest days. Most reasonably fit, determined walkers who avoid injury will be able to keep up with the stages in this book. Feel free to deviate from this pace, staying at intermediary accommodations, which are noted on maps and in the text. See our website for alternate suggested "fast" and "slow" itineraries.

Visas and Entry

Spain and France are both among the 26 *Schengen* states of the European Union (EU) that have no internal borders. Citizens of the USA, Canada, Australia, New Zealand and some South American countries are issued a free visa upon arrival with valid passport. This visa is limited to 90 days within a 180-day period, which is cumulative over multiple trips. Most African, Asian, Middle Eastern and some South American nationalities must apply for an advance visa. Visit the EU website and check with your embassy or consulate for visa-related questions.

Collecting stamps in the credencial

Sleeping A H

Albergues (Pilgrim hostels) A

One of the great achievements of the Camino's infrastructure is the *albergue* (pilgrim hostel) system, (also called *refugios*). Pronounced "al-BAIR-gay," these simple, affordable accommodations are present approximately every 5-15km (6mi) and are available only for non-motorized pilgrims (walking, by bicycle or horse) on a first-come first-serve basis. Walkers are generally prioritized over cyclists, who might need to wait until later in the day to confirm their bed. A pilgrim's *credencial* (p. 12) is needed to use most albergues, except some private albergues. The person in charge of an albergue is called a *hospitalero* (male) or *hospitalera* (female), and is often a volunteer.

Costs are minimal, between €5-15 ($5.50-17) per person per night, with the average around €9 ($10). For this price, don't expect luxury! The sleeping situation is normally bunk beds in communal mixed-gender dormitories, between 2-90 persons in a room, with an average of 15. Be prepared with earplugs for all manners of snoring, sleep talking, bag rustling, and nighttime bathroom visits past your bunk.

Unless noted in the text, all albergues have beds with mattresses (usually pillows), showers with hot water, toilets, a place to hand wash clothes and a clothesline. Many have kitchens, machine washers/dryers, and internet facilities. Amenities are shown in the text through symbols (back cover). Accommodations with their own website have a (links listed at **www.caminoguidebook.com**).

In the text, albergue prices refer to a dormitory bed. If an albergue also offers private rooms, the prices indicate dorm bed/single room/double room prices (for example, €10/30/50). For private accommodations, we list the single/double prices per room. Prices indicate approximate high season rates and are subject to change. High season is generally July/August and *Semana Santa* (the week before Easter). Outside of high season, prices may be 15-25% lower.

Most albergues are open from around April 1 to November 1, with some staying open for winter or year round. Winter walkers are highly encouraged to call ahead, as even those albergues that are open all year are not usually staffed on a daily basis for walk-ins. In winter it may be necessary to sometimes rely on private hotels.

Albergue types A

There are several types of albergues along the Camino, and we encourage trying all the types for a varied experience. Prices are similar, with private albergues being slightly higher, especially in Galicia.

- **Municipal/***municipal* (muni): Run by local municipalities and tend to be the most basic, popular and affordable. In Galicia, these are run by the governing body and known as *Xunta* hostels. They are in varying states of repair or disrepair, run by a local employee or volunteer.

A Donation/*donativos* (don): Donativo albergues do not have a fixed price, but rely on pilgrim donations to keep providing future services. Donativo does not mean free, so please be as generous as you can.

- **Parochial/***parroquial* (par): Run by church organizations, whether a parish, convent or monastery. Many are offered on a donation basis and provide an evening Mass or other religious service. They tend to have a simple, quiet and prayerful atmosphere, often staffed by nuns or volunteers.
- **Association/***asociación* (assoc): Operated by national Camino organizations, and often staffed by former pilgrim volunteers who know what a pilgrim needs.
- **Private/***privado*: Operated privately as a business, these tend to be more comfortable with a wider range of services and more flexibility. Many private albergues accept reservations, and some have private rooms along with the dormitory. Some are formed together into a network with certain standards. Private albergues range in atmosphere, to some feeling like hotels and others run by former pilgrims who maintain a homey atmosphere.

Albergue Respect and Privacy Concerns A

With the variety of exhausted pilgrims arriving in droves, its no wonder that albergues can be a frustrating place of clash between cultures and personalities. Some pilgrims have different views on modesty than others. Don't be surprised if you see men walking around in their briefs or women changing in the common area. Some albergues (particularly the *Xunta* albergues in Galicia) do not have separate gender bathrooms and have shower facilities that are not very private. With limited resources such as bottom bunks, hot water or space to hang out laundry, things can get competitive. The best advice is to go with the flow and try to be as generous and considerate as possible, even if others do not return the favor. See our list of suggested "albergue etiquette" online.

ed Bugs, or *Cimex lectularius,* a blood-sucking parasitic insect, are on the rise around the orld and have been a problem in accommodations along the Camino in recent years. While ed bugs do not carry any known diseases, bites can be very uncomfortable and cause painful ashes for some people, and the insects are very difficult to get rid of once infested. Some ways avoid bed bugs include pretreating your sleeping bag and backpack with permethrin or other nsect repellent and checking that any albergue you stay in has been fumigated recently.

Hotels and Private Rooms

In addition to pilgrim albergues, there are hundreds of private accommodations available, from 5-star hotels to simple *pensiones* in homes of local families. Some purists would say that true pilgrims only stay in albergues, but weary pilgrims took advantage of all types of lodging even in medieval times. Staying in private accommodations helps to support local business, and a good night's sleep and solitude may be just what you need to renew your pilgrim spirit.

Spain has a confusingly specific method to classify accommodations. The general hierarchy (simplest to most expensive) is *fonda*, *pensión*, *hostal*, *casa rural* and *hotel*, with various stars for each. The classification is posted on the outside of accommodations (except albergues). For example, Hs*** means a three-star *hostal*. A P signifies a *pensión* with zero stars. Cheaper rooms often have a shared bathroom. *Fondas*, *pensiónes* and *casas rurales* are usually owned and managed by an individual, while *hostales* and *hoteles* tend to be larger with en suite bathrooms and hired staff.

Camping

With inexpensive congenial albergues widely available, there is little need to camp on the Camino. Official campsites with services are not very common, often located several kilometers off-route, and usually cost more than albergues! Some people do "wild/free camp" unobtrusively along the Camino, either to really stretch their budget or to enjoy solitary nights. If you choose to free camp, check the weather and please follow Leave No Trace principles rigorously. Camping is not allowed in urban, touristic or military areas, or within 1km of official campsites.

Breakfast spread at Monte Irago albergue in Foncebadón

Eating

Typical Spanish meal times are breakfast at 10am, a large lunch around 2pm (followed by a *siesta*) and light dinner at 10-11pm. This schedule is directly opposite to the pilgrim walking schedule. Most pilgrims have been on the road several hours by 10am and are fast asleep by 10pm. Restaurants along the Camino have adapted to the pilgrim schedule and offer meals accordingly. Spanish bars (synonymous with cafés) are generally open all day, offering drinks, sandwiches, and light foods. On maps in this book, we do not distinguish between bars/cafés and restaurants, as both normally offer drinks and food.

Lunch & Snack Ideas

- Granola bars
- Chocolate
- Tuna or canned meat
- Nuts and seeds
- Dried fruit
- Olives
- Salami
- Peanut butter and jelly
- Drink mix (electrolytes)
- Fruits/vegetables

A **Spanish breakfast** usually consists of coffee with a little toast or a pastry, no full English breakfast or greasy diner to be found. Consider carrying extra food if you are accustomed to more filling breakfasts. A wedge of Spanish tortilla (a hearty egg and potato omelet) can often be found for a more substantial morning meal. A **packed grocery store lunch** is convenient, as you can stop and eat when you feel hungry. Bars and restaurants usually offer sandwiches (a lot of ham and cheese).

Snacks for the road: The ideal snacks for backpacking are calorie-dense, provide carbohydrates and protein and have light packaging. Eat fresh fruits and vegetables for nutrition and to help maintain hydration. Nuts and dried fruit make a filling snack with protein and a kick of sugar. While you'll be burning a lot of calories, keep nutrition in mind and try not to overdo it on junk food (candy, sugary drinks, simple carbs).

The typical **evening meal** on the Camino is the *menú peregrino* or pilgrim menu. These set menus typically feature a hearty appetizer, main course, dessert, wine, water and bread for €8-12. Meals tend to be ample and filling, but focus more on quantity than quality and tend to feature a hearty side of French fries/chips. *Platos combinados* (plates with various combinations of foods) provide another more economical meal choice for lunch or dinner.

Another option is to **cook your own evening meal**. Grocery prices are reasonable in Spain, and a simple pasta meal can cost very little. In albergue kitchens there is often a shelf of leftover pilgrim staples, such as pasta and rice. Most kitchens have some basic spices, oil and vinegar at least. Usually albergues with kitchens have a variety of useful pots and pans, plates, dishes and utensils. However, in Galicia the kitchens are almost always devoid of cookware, and it may be worth bringing your own on these sections if cooking for yourself is a priority.

Restaurants and supermarkets are readily available along the Camino. Some small towns do not have a shop, but almost every town with an albergue has at least one restaurant or cafe. Small village stores tend to be more expensive than in towns and cities but are locally owned and contribute to the local economy.

Vegetarian, Vegan and Celiac Options:
Awareness of vegetarian needs is increasing along the Camino, with some restaurants offering vegetarian pilgrim menu options. However, meat is ubiquitous in the Spanish menu and it may take some creativity to maintain a vegetarian diet. Salads are common and quite good, though usually include tuna so you may have to request a vegetables-only salad. If preparing your own meals, you should not have trouble finding good protein alternatives, such as nuts, beans and cheese, and in larger towns tofu and hummus. Vegan travelers may have a more difficult time, though not impossible. Larger supermarkets in Spain have gluten-free products, but awareness is not high in general. Spanish tortillas (potatoes and eggs) are a good option. Rice, fresh vegetables, meats and cheeses are widely available.

Transportation

Train:
Spain: Renfe
www.renfe.com
France: SNCF
www.sncf.com

Bus :
Alsa (major routes)
www.alsa.es

Getting to the Camino: First fly into one of the major airports near the Camino (Paris or Madrid are popular) and take local public transport to your starting point. For detailed information about getting to the Camino, including air, train and bus travel with links to major carriers within Spain and France, see our website.

To get to St. Jean, take the train from Paris to Bayonne, or bus from Madrid via Pamplona. Bayonne has several daily trains to St. Jean. Biarritz airport (near Bayonne) is also an option for local flights. The St. Jean pilgrim office is walking distance from the train station. In high season several buses per day leave from Pamplona to Roncesvalles (Artieda company). Pamplona is also a starting point that can be reach by flight, train or bus. Other popular starting points for shorter walks include Logroño, Burgos, Frómista, León, Astorga and Sarria.

Buses and **trains** are the basic modes of public transportation along the Camino. The train line connecting Santiago to Irun/Hendaye on the French border passes through major cities from Burgos west to Santiago. An extensive bus network accesses most Camino towns, with the exception of small villages and hamlets. Bus schedules change seasonally and sometimes run once daily in small towns. Ask your hospitalero or locals for advice if you can't find the correct information.

Towns and cities with daily bus and train access are labeled with respective symbols in stage chapters. **Taxis** are also an option, as well as **car rental** from major population centers. **Hitchhikers** are rarely picked up, and should assume all known risks.

Money, Costs and Budgeting

Currency:
US $1 ≈ EU €0.95
EU €1 ≈ US $1.05
EU €1 ≈ UK £0.86

The unit of **currency** in Spain and France is the euro, made up of 100 euro cents. The best way to obtain euros is to use an ATM/cash machine, which are available in all cities and most towns. Travelers' checks are a hassle to cash. You can carry dollars or other currency and change them into euros, but the exchange rate will not be as good as by ATM. Albergues almost always work on a cash basis, but some restaurants, stores and other services do accept credit cards. Remember that most credit cards charge a foreign currency conversion fee of about 3%, so consider applying for a card with no fee, such as Capital One or Chase Sapphire.

Daily costs for most pilgrims are simply lodging, food/drink and sometimes first aid supplies. By the standards of any European trip, the Camino is relatively inexpensive beyond the costs of airfare and transportation and can be adapted to a wide variety of budgets. On a strict budget, you may be able to walk the Camino for **as little as €20 per day** if you stay in the cheapest albergues, cook your own meals, hand wash your clothing and forego any luxuries. A more **comfortable daily budget of €35** gives you the freedom to eat in restaurants, upgrade to more comfortable albergues, have the occasional coffee or glass of wine in a café, use a washing machine periodically and pay entrance fees to museums. **With €60 or more a day**, you could upgrade to modest private accommodations, eat more adventurous restaurant meals and treat yourself to a few other luxuries.

Whatever your daily budget goals, make sure you have some **extra padding in case of emergency**. If you would become too injured to walk, consider transportation and accommodation costs to leave the Camino. Gear might need to be replaced. Leave room in your budget for the occasional private room, in case all albergues are full in a town or you simply need a break from communal living.

Most travelers **keep valuables in a travel wallet** (money belt or neck pouch) that can easily be concealed when in crowded places. As a precaution, make photocopies of your important documents (passport, driver's license, health insurance) and also email them to yourself so you can print them in case of theft. Write down phone numbers from credit cards in case they are lost or stolen. Call your bank and let them know you will be traveling, so they don't put a hold on or cancel your ATM card when they see "suspicious" activity in Spain.

Phones and Internet

Technology can be a point of controversy among pilgrims, with some who eschew mobile phones and internet as distractions to their journey, while others embrace them as necessary for emergencies, making reservations, contacting home, etc. Only you can decide what technology is right for you, but it is worthwhile to consider how you can minimize any distraction it may present. Two main options for having mobile phone coverage are enabling international roaming on your home mobile phone plan or purchasing a **Spanish SIM card** (which requires an unlocked GSM phone). **International roaming** on many US and Canada based plans is often quite expensive, but can be a good solution if only used in case of emergency. T-Mobile has free international data and text on some of their US plans. European plans tend to have inexpensive roaming within Europe.

The main mobile carriers in Spain are Movistar, Vodafone, Yoigo and Orange. Plans vary, and a prepaid SIM with minimal **data and minutes** starts around €10, with extra minutes costing around €0.10-0.15. Unlike most US plans, you only pay to make calls and send text messages and are not charged to receive. **Text messages**/SMS or apps like WhatsApp, Viber or Skype are an inexpensive way to let your family know you are still alive without disturbing your pilgrim zen. **Public pay phones** are becoming less common, but can still be found.

Country codes and dialing internationally

- To call Spain (+34) from the USA: 011 - 34 - 7-digit number
- To call France (+33) from the USA: 011 - 33 - 9-digit number
- To call the USA and Canada (+1) from abroad: 00 - 1 - 10-digit number
- Spanish numbers have 9 digits including the area code: landlines begin with 9, mobile numbers begin with 6, toll free numbers begin with 900/901

Wifi ("wee-fee" in Spanish) is increasingly available along the Camino; many albergues and cafés offer free access. Some albergues still have **desktop computers** with coin-operated internet while larger cities often have internet cafés, though they are both becoming more rare. Prices range from €1-4/hour. Be careful entering any sensitive personal information on public computers as some are not secure. Mobile data can be used as a personal hotspot for laptop internet access.

Post Offices

Spain has an excellent postal service, called *Correos*. Stamps can be purchased either at the post office or at an *estanco* (small convenience shop). If you have packed items you are not using, you can mail them back to your home, though postage is expensive to destinations outside of Europe.

You can also send items ahead to the post office in Santiago or another city along the Camino to be picked up later through a system called *Lista de Correos*. Address the package with your name (as it appears in your passport). A postal worker can help you correctly address the package. In order to claim the package at its destination, you'll need to show ID. Post offices hold mail for up to 15 days, then €1 for each additional day.

Example:
Your Name
Lista de Correos
15780 Santiago de Compostela
A Coruña

Luggage Transfer and Tours

Transfer services cost **€5-10 per day** to pick up luggage at one accommodations and deliver it to the next. Weight (<15kg) and distance (<30km) restrictions often apply. Usually service must be facilitated with reservation-based private albergues or hotels, not municipal or parochial albergues. Remember to still carry water, snacks and a medical kit in a daypack during your walk. Several luggage transfer companies cover different areas of the trail. Private albergues usually can arrange the transfer with the company covering their area, or you can **book transfers online** at Caminofácil (✆610-798138) and Hike-Tech. Other service providers include Jacotrans (✆610-983205, from Saint Jean to Finisterre) and Correos (Spanish post office, ✆606-618341, from Roncesvalles to Finisterre).

If you prefer to entrust your logistics to a tour company, many offer **guided or self-guided tour packages** on sections of various Camino routes. A good tour guide can help pilgrims understand and appreciate Camino history. This is the simplest option for those who prefer nicer accommodations but do not have time to make their own arrangements. For a list of tour operators, see our website.

Bathrooms, Toilets, *Servicios*, WC, the Loo

Finding a restroom when necessary along the Camino can be a challenge. Public bathrooms are few and far between. Buy a little something in a bar and use their facilities. When the call of nature comes at an inconvenient time far from any town, please be responsible with how you go in nature. In recent years the quantity of toilet paper and waste visible along the Camino has become a problem.

Walk at least 30m (100ft) from the trail and any water source. Place used toilet paper in the nearest trash can in a plastic bag. Toilet paper takes a long time to decompose, and wind often carries it out onto the trail. For solid waste, find a private spot and dig a 15-20cm (6-8in) cat hole using a stick or trowel. Cover your deposit with dirt and pack out your toilet paper.

Medical Care

Health clinics, or *Centros de Salud*, are generally open from 8am-3pm, often 24 hours in larger cities. Hospitaleros can direct you to the nearest medical resources. Citizens of Great Britain, Ireland and the EU need a European Health Insurance Certificate (EHIC). US, Canadian and other non-EU citizens are recommended to have private health and travel insurance. Carry an emergency contact card with known allergies, pertinent medical history and information that is helpful to medical staff if you are unable to communicate. In emergencies, dial ✆112 to reach the police, called *Guardia Civil* or *Policia Nacional* in Spanish, and they can connect you to the appropriate medical facility. For suggested travel medical insurance providers, see our website.

Safety Issues

Spain has very low crime rates, and the Camino is probably one of the safest walking routes in the world. Violent crime is extremely rare. However, it is always good to take certain precautions, especially for women who are traveling alone. Walking during high season, you should have no problem finding others to walk with and will likely constantly be in view of other pilgrims. In some of the more isolated areas, police vehicles make rounds throughout the day to check on pilgrims. Do not leave valuables unattended. Report any incidents to the police as soon as possible by dialing ✆112. Authorities take these reports seriously and make an effort to deal with the problem.

On some sections of the Camino, you will walk alongside or on roads with **heavy traffic**. If you are walking directly on the road, make sure you are walking on the left side, so that you can see oncoming vehicles in the lane closest to you. Exercise caution when crossing roads.

There are many **dogs** along the Camino but most are tied up or fenced and so accustomed to a steady stream of walkers that they barely notice passing pilgrims. Carrying a walking stick can enhance confidence when encountering animals. All dogs in Spain are required to be vaccinated against rabies.

Additional planning topics are available on our website.

Camino Cyclist

About 10% of pilgrims who receive a Compostela cycle the Camino rather than walking. Cycling can be a good alternative for those who have limited time, have knee or other joint issues that are exacerbated by walking, or just enjoy covering ground more quickly. Several companies offer high quality, affordable bicycle and bike bag rentals including delivery to and from the Camino. The most common setup is a mountain bike with rear rack and panniers, some basic bike tools, a tire pump, and a spare inner tube. Helmets are required by law in Spain, and a loud bell to alert walkers is essential.

Cyclists can take the same path as walkers, which is paved almost half of the time. There are often road detours that cyclists can take to avoid rocky or challenging footpaths. Cyclists need to carefully control speed and be very patient in busy areas where they are frequently overtaking walkers. You don't necessarily need bicycle touring experience to cycle the Camino, but you would want to be comfortable on a bicycle for long distances, be reasonably fit, train adequately, and be sure to rent or bring a high quality, well-fitted bicycle.

The bicycle symbol represents a bike shop in a town amenity list, in an albergue amenity list it represents a "bike-friendly" albergue that has bicycle storage and sometimes other amenities like a bike wash or tools.

Suggested itinerary for cycling the Camino Francés in two weeks (one rest day):

- 1: Saint Jean Pied de Port to Zubiri, 47.0km
- 2: Zubiri to Puente la Reina, 44.9km
- 3: Puente la Reina to Logroño, 72.0km
- 4: Logroño to Belorado, 73.4km
- 5: Belorado to Burgos, 50km
- 6: Burgos to Carrión, 84.4km
- 7: Carrion to Mansilla, 80.2km
- 8: Mansilla to Astorga, 70.9km
- 9: Astorga to Ponferrada, 53km
- 10: Ponferrada to La Faba, 47.9km
- 11: La Faba to Barbadelo, 48.7km
- 12: Barbadelo to Melide, 57.9km
- 13: Melide to Santiago, 53km

For comprehensive information about bicycling, visit **www.caminocyclist.com.**

Packing for the Road: Gear, Resupply and Navigation

He who would travel happily must travel light. -Antoine de Saint-Exupéry

A light load makes for a happy pilgrim, and weight should be a primary concern in packing. A popular guideline is to pack no more than 10% of your body weight. Resist the temptation to pack many extras "just in case." Shops are readily available in Spain and most anything lacking can be purchased along the way.

Backpacks: A 30-40L (1800-2500in^3) pack is sufficient for warm weather (40-60L for winter). Measure your torso length and choose a pack of the proper size, preferably being fitted at a knowledgeable outdoor retail store. Aim for a pack that weighs less than 3lb (1.5kg) when empty.

Footwear: Light boots or sturdy trail runners with a stiff or semi-rigid sole offer enough protection for your feet and ankles against the occasionally hard-surfaced, rocky and uneven path (trail surfaces, p. 29). Get fitted for footwear in the afternoon or evening to make sure footwear still fits after feet have expanded during the day. Bring some kind of lightweight footwear to wear in the evenings, such as flip-flops or foam sandals. ⚠ Be sure to thoroughly break in your footwear before beginning the Camino with practice hikes wearing your loaded pack. Invest in wool socks (not cotton), which wick moisture away from your skin, dry quickly, insulate when wet and manage odor better. If you're prone to blisters, experiment with liner socks (wool or polypropylene) to create an extra rubbing layer other than your skin.

Sleeping Bags: Most pilgrims prefer a lightweight, mummy-style, 1-season summer sleeping bag (rated $^{+}$40+°F/$^{+}$5+°C) for the summer season. Some opt for only a sleeping bag liner in the heat of summer. For winter and the cool edges of fall and spring, it's a good idea to have a 3-season sleeping bag (rated $^{+}$15-$^{+}$35°F/$^{-}$10-0°C. Buy the lightest bag you can afford within your temperature range.

Clothing: Consider hiking clothes as layers, with inner layers for moisture management, middle for insulation and outer for weather protection. The general rule for outdoor clothing is to avoid cotton as it does not retain insulating properties when wet and dries slowly. Synthetic materials (polyester, nylon, spandex) and wool (especially merino) are preferred, especially in cold and wet weather. In warm seasons, choose lightweight breathable clothes that provide sun protection.

Be prepared for the sun with a wide-brimmed hat and **sunglasses** and use **sunscreen** regularly. Bring a **lightweight rain jacket** with a waterproof breathable membrane, or use a poncho that can also cover your backpack. Bring a waterproof pack cover or line your pack with plastic garbage bags to keep your gear dry. Pack electronics in zippered plastic bags to protect against moisture.

Hypothermia is possible in wet, cool weather, so be prepared with a dry set of clothes (socks included) for after a rainy day and bring one insulating layer, such as a warm fleece or down sweater.

Water and refills: While water is ready available most days of the Camino, it is important to carry sufficient amounts. Always carry at least one liter, and refill often; carry more than two liters on hot days or in more remote areas. Reliable water refill sites are marked on stage maps ( ). Tap water in Spain is treated and drinkable (potable). Most historic springs are marked as undrinkable (no potable) because they have not been treated or tested. Bottled water is widely available, but less environmentally friendly than refillable bottles.

Dehydration and heat-related illness: Dehydration can lead to fatigue, headaches, heat exhaustion and heat stroke (a dangerous and life-threatening condition). Be sure to eat foods that help to replenish electrolytes and consider an electrolyte drink, such as Aquarius™, on hot days. If you become dehydrated and overheated and are unable to cool down, take a break in a cool, shady place, rehydrate with electrolytes and cool with a wet cloth or fanning until you feel better.

Fitness and Training: While the Camino is not a technically challenging hike, the length of the journey and total distance walked day after day takes a toll on the body. By taking the time to practice before beginning the pilgrimage, you will greatly reduce possible injuries. Training walks will help you get used to your hiking gear, the weight on your feet and shoulders and any other potential issues you might be able to prevent. It's wise to get used to full-day walks, taking 2-3 shorter walks per week and one full-day walk weekly with your loaded backpack. Check with your doctor if you have concerns about your health or fitness level.

Blister Prevention: The most common injury can cause an end to your trip.

- At home: choose properly fitting footwear. Try on many options before buying (foot should not move or slip when walking on various terrain types and grades). Use wool socks and liners. Break in footwear by taking hikes with a loaded pack prior to beginning the Camino.
- On the trail: keep feet cool and dry, take off shoes and socks for breaks, wash feet and socks daily, use liner socks.

Hiking Gear Essentials

- ☐ **Backpack** (30-40L)
- ☐ **Sleeping bag or bag liner**, lightweight
- ☐ **Navigation**: guidebook, GPS (optional)
- ☐ **Headlamp** or flashlight/torch
- ☐ **Sun protection**: hat, sunglasses, sunscreen and lip balm
- ☐ **Towel**, lightweight travel type
- ☐ **Water bottles** and/or **hydration system** (2L)
- ☐ **Waterproof pack cover/poncho**
- ☐ **Pocket/utility knife** (checked luggage)
- ☐ **Lighter** or **matches** (buy locally)
- ☐ **Toiletries** (list opposite)
- ☐ **Personal items** (list opposite)
- ☐ **First aid kit** (list opposite)

Take the time to visit a quality outdoor gear shop to get fitted for a backpack that is comfortable and footwear that fits properly.

Footwear & Clothing

- ☐ **Footwear** (boots or trail runners)
- ☐ **Sandals** or flip-flops
- ☐ **Hiking socks** (3 pairs wool)
- ☐ **Sock liners** (1-2 pairs wicking)
- ☐ **Pants** (1-2 pairs quick-drying, zip-offs, or shorts)
- ☐ **Short-sleeved shirts**, tank tops (1-2)
- ☐ **Long-sleeved shirts** (1-2)
- ☐ **Light fleece** or jacket
- ☐ **Waterproof jacket** or poncho
- ☐ **Underwear** (3 pairs)
- ☐ **Sports bras** (2)
- ☐ **Bandana** or Buff
- ☐ **Swimsuit** (optional)
- ☐ **Warm hat***
- ☐ **Insulating jacket***
- ☐ **Long underwear** top/bottom*

**only necessary in cold seasons*

Additional Gear (Optional)

- ☐ **Hiking poles**: Used correctly, poles can take up to 25% pressure off of your leg joints. Poles are great for stability, especially going up and down hills, and serve double-duty as a means to chase away dogs. Worthwhile for anyone with joint issues. Inexpensive poles can be purchased in Spain.
- ☐ **Sleeping mat**: A lightweight foam pad can come in handy for sitting on and for sleeping if albergues are full. You can often find left behind mats for free along the Camino.
- ☐ **Pillowcase**: Most albergues have pillows but do not change the pillowcases regularly, a spare T-shirt can also be stretched over the pillow as a makeshift case.
- ☐ **Stuff sacks** or (cloth bags with drawstrings) don't weigh much and keep you organized
- ☐ **Reusable nylon grocery bag**: Comes in handy as a laundry bag, purse and grocery bag
- ☐ **Clothespins** or safety pins for hanging laundry.
- ☐ **Travel cooking pot and utensils**: Many of the albergues in Galicia have kitchens, but no kitchen equipment whatsoever. If you are intent on cooking your own dinners, you may wish to bring a lightweight cooking pot, or purchase one when you arrive in Galicia.
- ☐ **Camping gear:** Lightweight tent (TarpTent) or bivy sack, camping stove, a pot and utensils, and extra water carrying capacity. (See Camping p. 16).

***For recommendations on specific brands and models, visit caminoguidebook.com.**

***Decathlon** is a chain of outdoor gear retailers throughout Spain with stores in Pamplona, Logroño, Burgos and Santiago de Compostela, as well as Madrid and Barcelona.

Toiletries

Don't pack too much. Bring small refillable travel bottles of shampoo and conditioner <100mL/4oz. Refill from items left behind (ask at the albergues) or buy your own refill and share.

- ☐ **Shampoo/conditioner** (100mL/4oz bottles)
- ☐ **Toothbrush** and **toothpaste** (travel sized)
- ☐ **Soap**, biodegradable bar or liquid, such as Dr. Bronner's™
- ☐ **Laundry detergent** (powder works well and weighs less) or 100mL/4 oz. bottle or solid bar
- ☐ **Toilet paper** or tissues (albergues frequently run out)
- ☐ **Deodorant** (optional, you will stink with or without it!)
- ☐ **Hand sanitizer** (optional)
- ☐ **Contact solution** (if necessary), replace at pharmacies

First Aid/Medical Kit

Supplies are available in pharmacies throughout Spain and most albergues have a basic medical kit. It's always best to be prepared with at least a few day's worth of each supply. Keep it light!

- ☐ Any **prescription medicine** you need
- ☐ Variety of **Band-Aids®/plasters, sterile gauze pads**
- ☐ Antiseptic towelettes or **wound disinfectant**
- ☐ **Antibiotic ointment**
- ☐ **Medical tape**
- ☐ **Elastic bandage** (such as ACE™)
- ☐ **Pain reliever/fever reducer** (such as acetaminophen or ibuprofen)
- ☐ **Antihistamine** (such as Benadryl®)
- ☐ **Anti-diarrheal** medicine: loperamide hydrochloride (Imodium®)
- ☐ **Blister treatment** (such as Moleskin or Compeed®)
- ☐ **Safety pins**
- ☐ **Baby powder** (helps with chafing)
- ☐ Small **scissors** and **tweezers**

Personal Items (Optional)

- ☐ **Travel wallet**: with passport/ID, health insurance card, pilgrim passport, money, credit cards, ATM card, etc. Stash an extra ATM card or wad of cash somewhere separate from your wallet.
- ☐ **Earplugs**: high quality noise-canceling earplugs are essential for a good night's sleep.
- ☐ **Mobile phone** and **charger** (see Phones and Internet p. 20)
- ☐ **Camera, charger, memory cards**, compact USB flash drive for backup
- ☐ **Journal with pen/pencil**: highly recommended for remembering the details of each day, reflecting more fully on the experience and recording contact info of new friends.
- ☐ **Tablet or e-reader:** useful for checking email and for pleasure reading without carrying heavy books. Photos of family and home are good conversation starters.
- ☐ **Book** for pleasure reading (just bring one and trade when you're done)
- ☐ **Plug/currency converter** for any electrical appliances (European plugs run on 220V with two round prongs. Most electronics run on 110-220V, labeled on device, requiring only a plug converter and not a currency converter.)
- ☐ **Zippered plastic bags or waterproof stuff sacks** for keeping electronics and other valuables dry and organized.
- ☐ **Pilgrim's shell** (p. 10) and **stone** for Cruz Ferro (p. 188)

The path is well marked with yellow arrows and cement markers.

Blister Treatment

• Take a break, remove socks to let feet cool and dry out. Check for hot spots and address by applying moleskin, Compeed®, or duct tape to create an additional rubbing surface to protect the hot spot.

• If a blister forms, use a sterilized needle to puncture its edge near the skin and drain using sterile materials. Air dry and re-dress blister with sterile bandages.

• If the blister or surrounding area becomes infected over the course of several days (increasing red appearance, tenderness, pus, red streaks), see a doctor.

For **dry and cracked feet**, consider wearing socks all the time to keep moisture in for cracks to heal. In severely painful cracks, a tiny bit of super glue can be helpful to hold the crack together, but make sure to clean the area thoroughly with soap, water and antiseptic.

Impact-related injuries are common with the large amount of paved surfaces on the Camino. If your feet and joints are taking a pounding, consider reducing your daily distance, walking on the softer shoulder near the paved path or adding walking poles and/or thicker socks.

The Trail: The paths that make up the Camino de Santiago covered in this book span over 900km (560 miles) and vary greatly in trail surface, grade, landscapes, ecosystem and climate. Proportionately, the Camino has more paved surfaces than many hikers expect, contributing to more stress on feet and joints. P Paved/ U Unpaved designations in this book refer to most obvious walking surface. There may be unpaved shoulders or faint footpaths along paved roads.

Route Finding, Trail Markings, Maps and GPS ➡ The Camino Francés is extremely well marked and among the easiest long-distance trails for navigation. The Camino is marked by a variety of official and unofficial signs, all pointing to the final destination, Santiago de Compostela. (After Santiago, the Camino Finisterre markings point to the coast, splitting for the options ending in Finisterre and Muxía). The most common waymarks are painted yellow arrows *(flechas amarillas)* ➡. Many other trail markers are used in different regions, most incorporating yellow arrows or scallop shells on posts, signs and emblems on sidewalks and walls.

The most difficult sections to navigate are through large cities, where routes are often poorly marked and Camino markers compete with other signs. For this reason, we've included a number of detailed city maps throughout this book, though note that the maps are representative and not exhaustive, without every street and name. **GPS files are on our website, as well as tips on smart phone navigation.**

Daily Stages and Regional Sections: This book organizes the Camino Francés and Finisterre into 36 daily stages averaging about 25km per day. The page spreads introducing each stage include a stage map, elevation profile, total distance, paved/unpaved (P/U) percentages, difficulty level (see below), time estimate (⏲) and a list of towns with albergues. In the albergue list in the sidebar, the destination of the stage is underlined and albergues beyond the stage that could also be reasonably walked for a longer day are present in italics with distances. This allows the reader to see at a glance the options for a shorter or longer stage, for maximum flexibility and customization.

All stage routes begin and end at the main or largest albergue in each respective town. For mid-stage towns and points of interest without albergues, measurements are taken from the town center or main church, whichever is closest to the marked route or visually prominent. Cumulative stage distances are noted on the stage maps and correspond to distances listed in stage chapter text and town amenity boxes. Distances for off-route accommodations or points of interest are indicated with a plus symbol (example: +1.3km). Town amenity boxes list resources available in each town and list all the albergues and a selection of private accommodations in varying price ranges. Names of towns that have amenity boxes are underlined with a dotted line in the text.

Distances are measured in metric units (kilometers and meters). Estimated **walking time** for each stage assumes a pace of 3-5 km/hr (1.8-3 mph) with difficulty in terrain and elevation change considered. Factor extra time for breaks and to explore points of interest. Each day's stage route is assigned a **difficulty level** from 1-3. These ratings consider an "average" walker, who is reasonably fit but not necessarily athletic.

Length:
1m = 1yd or 3ft
100m ≈ 100yd
1km = 0.62 miles
10km = 6.2 miles
1.6km = 1 mile

Easy: Slight elevation change, sturdy footing, water easily accessible
Moderate: Some elevation change, moderately challenging terrain
Challenging: Significant elevation change, possibly rocky or narrow path with less stable footing, water sources may be scarce

See p. 287 for a list of expanded planning topics available on our website.

1-7 BASQUE COUNTRY & NAVARRA

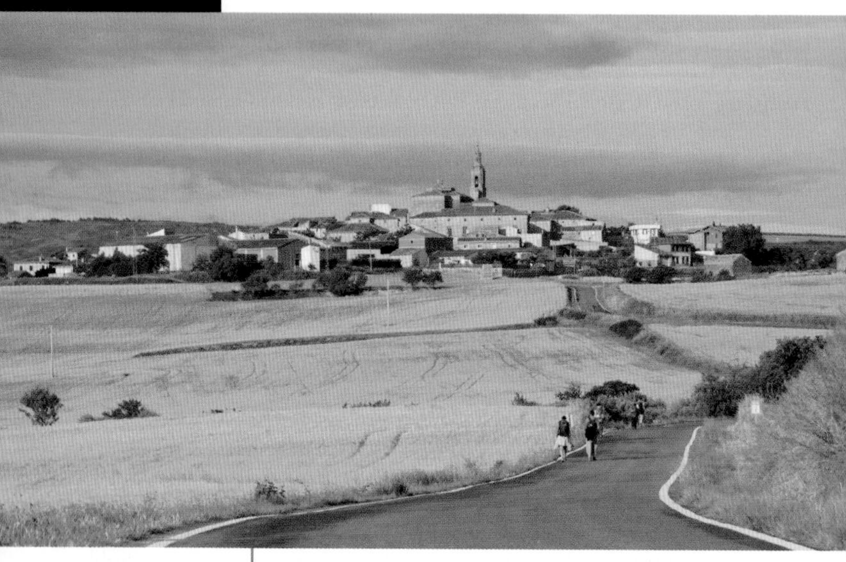

Pilgrims approach the medieval town of Sansol

Begin in the enigmatic Pyrenees, bastion of Basque culture. Enjoy hearty foods, watch a game of *jai alai* and learn a few phrases in the local language.

Useful Basque phrases:
Welcome *Ongi etorri*
Hello *Kaixo*
Good morning *Egun on*
How are you? *Zer moduz?*
Thank you *Eskerrik asko*
Goodbye *Agur*
Please *Mesedez*
How much does this cost? *Zenbat balio du?*

While the Camino Francés begins in France, within 20km the path enters the autonomous region of Spain called Navarra. This region borders Basque Country and is also home to the unique and mysterious Basque people, thought to have descended from some of the oldest European tribes. Their language, *Euskara*, is not related to any Indo-European languages and is believed to be the oldest living language in Europe (described in the *Codex Calixtinus* as "incomprehensible").

Basques have a reputation for being independent and have resisted assimilation through successive historical periods, in spite of frequent persecution. During the Inquisition, thousands of Basques were tried for witchcraft. Under Franco, Basque language and culture was repressed, which led to the formation of the ETA ("Basque Homeland and Freedom"), a separatist movement involved in violent protest. The ETA declared a ceasefire in 2011 that has been honored.

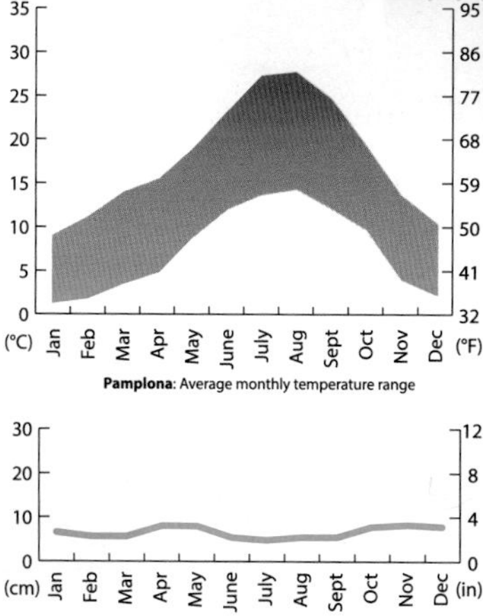

Pamplona: Average monthly temperature range

Pamplona: Average monthly rainfall

Basque culture is spread through autonomous regions in France and Spain and the surrounding areas. Most towns have courts (*frontónes*) for the fast-paced Basque sport *Jai Alai* (also called *pelota)*, reminiscent of handball. Unique pastimes include goat racing, stone throwing and competitive lawn mowing (using a scythe).

Basque areas are known for their superior cuisine. Foods are hearty, unrefined and delicious including grilled meats, fish, stews and creamy cheeses. The region produces decent wine, and it is even said that the cement of a church near Puente la Reina (p. 64) was mixed with wine rather than water. *Patxaran* is a local sweet fruit liqueur and the area is known for its cider. For the sweet tooth, the region has a strong pastry tradition—try the *Gâteau Basque*, an almond cake with fruit filling.

The Basque section of the Camino begins in the Pyrenees, with its unpredictable weather and challenging terrain. Look for birds of prey, such as Griffon Vultures and Lammergeiers. In spring, enjoy over 160 species of indigenous plants and stunning wildflowers. The forested hills of Navarra ease into the Río Ebro Valley, an area of over 85,000km through which Spain's largest river flows, filled from tributaries in the Pyrenees and Iberian mountains. Enter Navarra's central plains, characterized by fields of grain, vineyards and beech forests.

Navarra leads the way in renewable energy technologies, especially windmills, of which you will see many. Several well-known Basques are Juan Sebastián Elcana, who took over after Ferdinand Magellan died on the first expedition to circumnavigate the globe, King Sancho III of Navarra and Ignatius of Loyola, founder of the Society of Jesus.

"Around the Pass of Cize is the Basque country... The terrain is woody and mountainous with a serious shortage of bread, wine and other food supplies, except for plenty of apples and cider and milk. This region...has some truly vicious toll collectors. They come at pilgrims with weapons, and demand an exorbitant fee. Their hard faces and strange language strike terror into the heart."

Codex Calixtinus

1 ST-JEAN-PIED-DE-PORT TO RONCESVALLES

24.7km
(15.3mi)

7-9 HOURS
DIFFICULTY:

NAPOLEAN ROUTE
P 58%, 14.2km
U 42%, 10.5km

A ALBERGUES:
Honto 5.3km
Orisson 7.7km
Roncesvalles 24.7km
Espinal 31.5km

ALT. STAGE 1A:
Valcarlos Route,
24.0km (p. 42)

VALCARLOS ROUTE
P 69%, 16.5km
U 31%, 7.5km

A ALT. ALBERGUES:
Valcarlos 11.6km
Roncesvalles 24.0km
Espinal 30.8km

Idyllic mountain scenery on the Napolean Route

Cross the Pyrenees from France to Spain, take in breathtaking mountain scenery, arrive to a cozy medieval hamlet.

The Camino Francés traditionally begins in St-Jean-Pied-de-Port, which can be reached by public transport by train or bus (p. 18). This path crosses the Pyrenees on the first day of its journey from France into Spain. Various Camino routes in France converge on this historic town, channeling hikers onto one route, the Camino Francés, or the "French Way." Two-thirds of pilgrims arriving in Santiago walk the Camino Francés, of which 10% start their journey here.

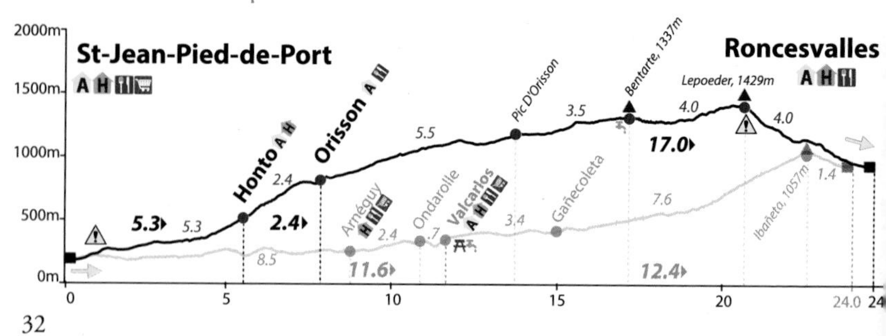

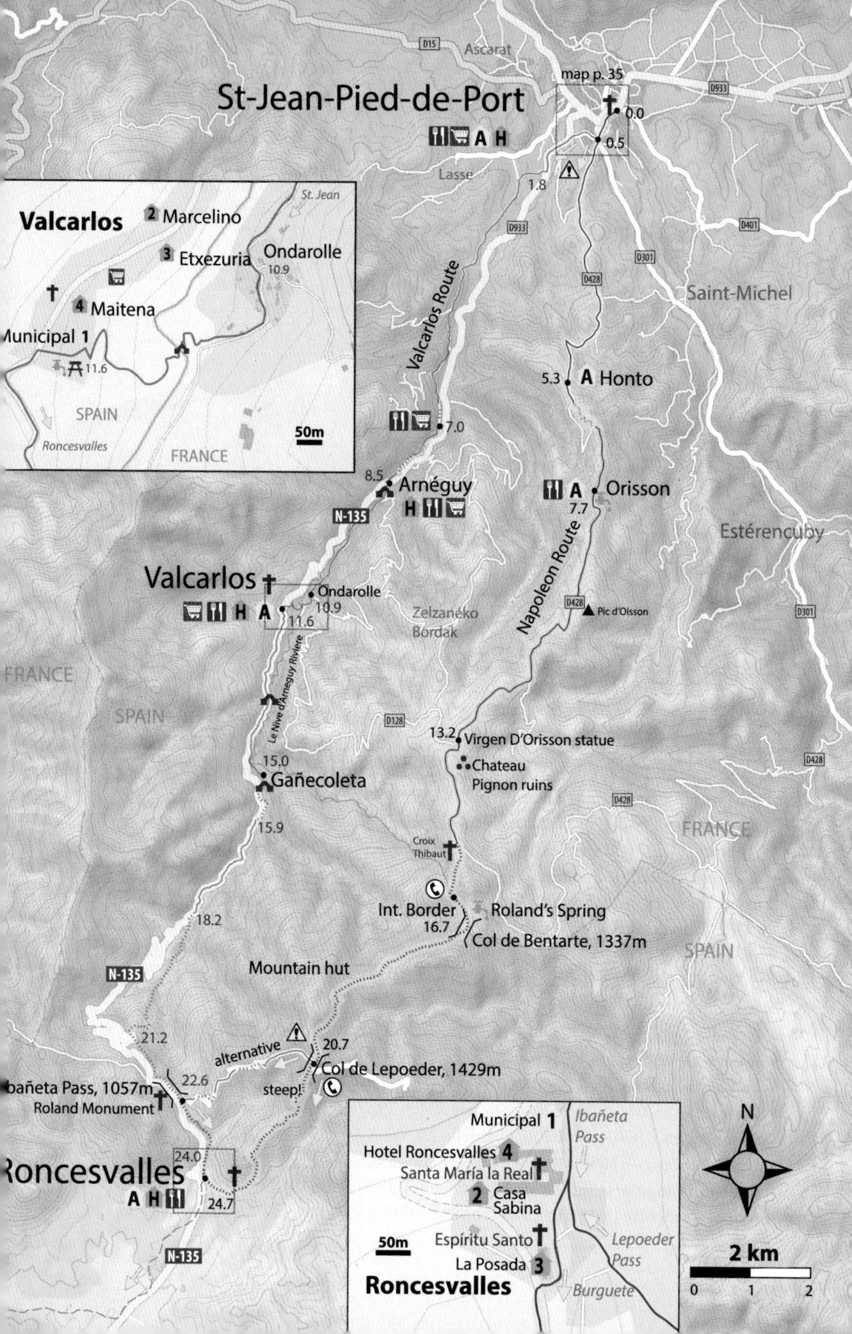
St-Jean-Pied-de-Port
map p. 35
Ascarat
Lasse
Saint-Michel
Valcarlos Route
Napoleon Route
Honto
Orisson
Arnéguy
Estérencuby
Valcarlos
Ondarolle
Zelzanéko Bordak
Pic d'Oisson
Le Nive d'Arneguy Riviere
Gañecoleta
Virgen D'Orisson statue
Chateau Pignon ruins
Croix Thibaut
Int. Border
Roland's Spring
Col de Bentarte, 1337m
Mountain hut
alternative
steep!
Col de Lepoeder, 1429m
Ibañeta Pass, 1057m
Roland Monument
Roncesvalles
FRANCE
SPAIN
0.0
0.5
1.8
5.3
7.0
7.7
8.5
10.9
11.6
13.2
15.0
15.9
16.7
18.2
20.7
21.2
22.6
24.0
24.7
Valcarlos
2 Marcelino
3 Etxezuria
4 Maitena
Municipal 1
Ondarolle 10.9
11.6
St. Jean
Roncesvalles
50m
Municipal 1
Hotel Roncesvalles 4
Santa María la Real
2 Casa Sabina
Espíritu Santo
La Posada 3
Ibañeta Pass
Lepoeder Pass
Burguete
Roncesvalles
50m
N
2 km
0
1
2

0.0 **St-Jean-Pied-de-Port** A H

Pop. 1,754, Basque: *Donibane Garazi*, French: "Saint John's at the foot of the mountain pass"

1. A **Municipal** (32, €10 w/): , Rue Citadelle 55, 05-59370509, 2pm all year
2. A **Refuge Esponda** (20, €10-14): , Place du Trinquet 9, 06-79075252, all day
3. A H **Auberge du Pélerin** (48, €16/-/45): (free), Rue Citadelle 25, 05-59491086, mid Mar-mid Oct, online booking
4. A **Azkorria** (8, €16-18): , Rue Citadelle 50, 05-59370053
5. A **Beilari** (18, €30 w/ and dinner): , Rue Citadelle 40, 05-59372468, Mar 14-Nov 1, online booking
6. A **Sur le Chemin - Au Chant du Coq** (15, €10/€30/35): Rue Citadelle 36, 06-74310283
7. A H **Gîte Ultreïa** (15, €17/-/48): , R. Citadelle 8, 06-80884622, May-Oct 15
8. A H **Compostella** (14, €12.50/-/30): , Route de D'Arneguy 6, 05-59370236
9. A **Le Chemin Vers L'Etoile** (20, €17-20 w/): , Rue d'Espagne 21, 05-59372071 Mar-Oct
10. A H **Zuharpeta** (22, €12.50/-/40): , Zuharpeta 5, 05-59373588, Mar 15-Oct 1
11. A **Kaserna** (par, 14, €15): , Rue d' Espagne 43, 05-59376517, 2pm, Apr 4-Oct 30
12. A **La Coquille Napolean** (10, €15) : , Uhart-Cize, 06-62259940
13. H **Itzalpea** (€55/65): 5 Place du Trinquet, 05-59370366
14. H **Ramuntcho** (-/€70+): , Rue Citadelle 24, 05-59373517, Old City
15. H **Les Pyrénées** (-/€165): , Place du General-de-Gaulle 19, 05-59370101
16. H **Maison Donamaria** (€60/75): , 1 Chemin d'Olhonce, 06-61902921

Municipal Campsite (tent €10): Av. Fronton, 05-59371119, , Mar 25-Nov 1

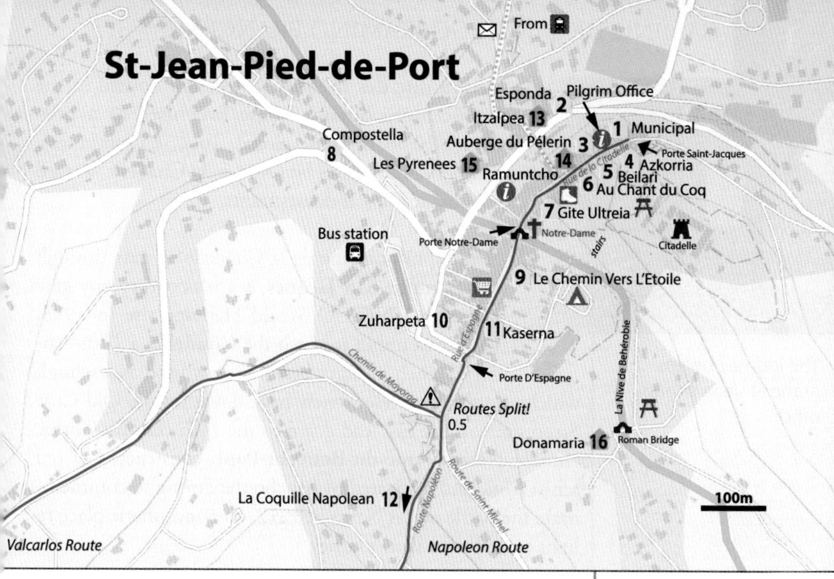

Rue de la Citadelle and Porte Saint Jacques in St. Jean (opposite)

St-Jean-Pied-de-Port has been welcoming pilgrims and "God walkers" for hundreds of years. Today, the small Old City makes for pleasant strolling along cobbled streets with views of traditional red-tile-roofed houses with colorful shutters. The main street of *Rue de la Citadelle* bustles with artisan shops, cafés, pilgrim hostels and tourists. Basque specialties can be found including bold linens, handmade *espadrilles*, and local foods such as *Gâteau Basque*, sheep cheeses, local ham and fish.

St. Jean was founded in the late 12th century and served as the capital of Navarra, the Basque kingdom, after *St-Jean-le-Vieux* ("Saint John the Old") was destroyed by the army of Richard the Lionheart. Camino routes from all over France converged in St. Jean before crossing the treacherous and demanding Pyrenees Mountains.

St. Jean provides a marvelous place to wander about and explore. First stop is the **Pilgrim Office (*Accueil des Pélerins*)** on Rue de la Citadelle, which offers *credenciales* (p. 12) for €2, as well as extremely helpful advice from multilingual volunteers. Printouts of Camino elevation charts and accommodations. Just past the pilgrim office is the

St. Jean hosts a variety of restaurants, many of which offer a pilgrim menú. Two grocery stores in the Old City offer food to prepare at your albergue. There are no more grocery stores until the next stage, so plan accordingly.

The journey begins at the St. Jean pilgrim office.

Prison dite des Evêques, a museum housed in the 13th-century bishop's house later used as a prison (10:30am-7pm, closed Tues, €3 entrance). Numerous albergues line Rue de la Citadelle, as well as tourist shops and restaurants.

Walk uphill on Rue de la Citadelle to pass through the **Porte de San Jacques**, a 15th-century city gate named a UNESCO World Heritage site in 1998. Continue uphill to reach the **Citadelle**, a 17th-century French military building now used as a school, which affords a marvelous view back down on the Old City. Steep stairs to the east lead down to the 14th-century Gothic church, **Notre-Dame-du-Bout-du-Pont**, constructed of red schist stone and dedicated by Sancho the Strong to commemorate the battle of Las Navas in 1212, an atmospheric place to light a candle for your journey.

From the church, it is possible to walk east along the river, crossing over via a **Roman bridge**, and returning via **Porte d'Espagne**, the "door to Spain" that will begin your journey over the Pyrenees. Continue north on **Rue d'Espagne**, crossing over the River Nive. Be sure to look down the river at the historic houses lining the river with their sweet balconies. Rue d'Espagne turns to Rue de la Citadelle to bring you back to the Pilgrim Office and albergues.

Monday is a lively market day in St. Jean, with traditional artisan foods and livestock sales.

Two Routes Across the Pyrenees

For medieval pilgrims, crossing the Pyrenees was one of the most treacherous parts of the pilgrimage. They feared foul weather, exorbitant tolls, bandits and exhaustion. The **Valcarlos Route** was popular among medieval pilgrims because it was not as steep or difficult, however, the **Napoleon Route** became the preferred alternative when bandits became a persistent problem on the lower route.

Private albergues accept reservations and in high season may be full far in advance. There is also a wid selection of hotels just outside of the Old City.

The Old City has a supermarket (8am-12:30pm, 4-7pm) and a gear store, Boutique du Peleri (Rue Citadelle 32, 6:30am-8:30pm daily). Place du Général de Gaulle

Roland & Charlemange

History buffs will recognize Ronvesvalles and Valcarlos as in the Battle of Roland, immortalized in *La Chanson de Roland*, "Roland's Song," one of the earliest examples of French epic poetry. The poem, likely from the end of the 11th century, recounts and embellishes the story of Roland's battle death in 778 in mythical proportions.

Monument to Roland at Alto de Ibañeta

The story goes that Charlemagne and his army were returning from six years of battling Muslims in Spain. His nephew Roland was in charge of the rear guard, and his brother-in-law/stepfather, Ganelon, in charge of relaying a message back to the Muslim king. Ganelon and Roland quarreled, and Ganelon was jealous of Roland's position with the king. So Ganelon went to the Muslim leaders and revealed Charlemagne's route back to France, suggesting that in the narrow pass through the Pyrenees the rear guard would be most vulnerable.

On August 15, 778, Charlemagne's main army passed through the Pyrenees (the Valcarlos route) without any problem. However, Roland's rear guard was attacked and mercilessly slaughtered. Roland fought bravely, refusing to sound his horn and call Charlemagne back. Deeply wounded, Roland blew on his horn (named *Oliphant*) so strongly that he burst his temples and split the horn. In his death throes, he shattered his sword (named *Durendal*) against a rock to prevent it from falling into the hands of his enemies. Charlemange returned to a bloodstained valley with all of his rear guard and his beloved nephew dead.

At the **Alto de Ibañeta**, high point of the Valcarlos route, there is a monument to Roland, supposedly where Charlemagne buried Roland's body, near the modern Iglesia de San Salvador de Ibañeta built over the site of a medieval church.

While the story may be inspiring, it is most certainly embellished, and it is now believed that it was local Basques, not the Muslims, who defeated Roland. While Charlemagne was supposedly fighting in Spain to protect Christendom, he did his fair share of looting and destruction along the way, including destroying the walls of Pamplona and accepting a bribe to return to France. While local Basques let him pass on his way in, they had their revenge on the way out.

The path can be crowded before walkers spread out.

While you need no longer fear bandits or toll collectors along the Valcarlos Route (24.0km), most pilgrims choose the higher Napoleon Route (24.7km) for the incredible views, natural paths and quiet roads.

The Napoleon Route made an appearance in the film *The Way* as the place where Emilio Estevez's character dies in a storm. The route should not be walked in winter or in foul weather, when the Valcarlos Route should be used. In recent years, several pilgrims have died or needed to be rescued from the mountain when walking in the snow.

The Valcarlos Route (p. 42), while also scenic, spends 4.6km along the N-135 highway. However, the Valcarlos Route has more intermediate services such as grocery stores, cafés, hotels and an albergue 11.6km from St. Jean and does not climb as high as the Napolean Route. For either route, start at sunrise and give yourself a good eight hours of walking time (plus breaks) to arrive at Roncesvalles.

"The Basque Country has the highest mountain on the Camino. The mountain is eight miles up, and eight miles down the other side, and seems to touch the sky. Climb it and you'll feel you could push the sky with your hand."

Codex Calixtinus

Napolean Route

Many pilgrims are intimidated by this route, which passes over the Pyrenees at a high point of 1,429m. While the route is challenging and should be planned for accordingly, the views are spectacular and the feeling of accomplishment at day's end is priceless. Weather at the pass is unpredictable, so make sure to have rain gear handy (jacket, pack cover, and a change of dry clothes). The path is marked with red/white stripes, yellow/blue shell markers and a few yellow arrows.

Mountain Wildlife

Watch the path, of course, but keep your eyes on the skies for the majestic swooping Griffon vultures, which soar above the Pyrenees on the warm updrafts. These large scavengers have white heads and dark brown wings and can weigh up to 12kg with a wingspan up to 3m. Chamois, a small goat-antelope species, can sometimes be observed with their distinctive white faces with a black stripe under the eye. Domesticated hill ponies often graze in the green fields along the route. Wild horses also roam the mountains but are not frequently seen. *Latxa* sheep can often be seen, a special Basque black-faced breed whose milk is used in the unpasteurized traditional delicacy of *Idiazábal* and *Ossou-Iraty* cheeses.

Griffon vultures soar over the Pyrenees

0.0 *Leave St. Jean on Rue D'Espagne straight through Porte d'Espagne. Follow the small, paved road straight and uphill;* ***the first 7km are the steepest****.*

Latxa sheep grazing in the Pyrenees

5.3 **Honto** is the first small hamlet on the trail with an albergue. *Shortly after Honto, leave the paved road and head straight on a wide grassy path while the road curves to the R. Rejoin the paved road in 900m at a display about the surrounding landscape, reaching Orisson 1.1km later.*

7.7 **Orisson** is a small hamlet with two albergues and a café, the last place with food until Roncesvalles and a convenient place to fill water outside of the albergue. Sandwiches and soups at Orisson cost €3-5. *Continue steeply up along the road to emerge at Pic D'Orisson.*

5.3 Honto A

A Ferme Ithurburia (22, €15/-/70): , 05-59371117

7.7 Orisson A

A Refuge Orisson (28, €35 w/ and dinner): , 0681-497956, Mar-Oct, recommended to book ahead

A Kayola (15, €15): , 05-59491303, Apr-Oct, 800m before Orisson

13.2 Pic D'Orisson

affords a marvelous view, where the Vierge d'Orisson "Virgin of Orisson," keeps her silent vigil over the spectacular valley vistas. Shepherds brought the statue from Lourdes.

Follow the road for another 1.8km, where a cross and signposts mark a R turn on a dirt footpath. Follow this footpath around the mountain top, to arrive at the ***Spanish border (16.7km)*** *and* ***Fontaine de Rolánd*** *("Roland's Fountain") at Col Bentarte. It's another 4km to the Col Lopoeder on a footpath protected by forest. The waymarking on the Spanish side is more thorough, with high, numbered poles, visible even in snow. Just 1.7km before the high point, pass a small one-room mountain hut with a fireplace (no bathroom, no services, emergency only).*

Vierge d'Orisson

Misty mountain paths

20.7 **Col Lopoeder** is the high point of the day at 1,429m. *Descend via one of two paths: 1) steep way-marked dirt path (4km) or 2) paved road (4.3km) to the R (also marked with red/white GR markings and footpaths to connect the road's switchbacks). The pilgrim's office recommends the road option. Exercise caution if taking the dirt path as it is steep and end of the day tiredness and mud could make you more vulnerable to injury. The road option affords nice valley views of the beech forest and Roncesvalles, joining the Valcarlos Route at **Ibañeta** for the last 1.6km on a peaceful forest path to Roncesvalles.*

The first pilgrim guest-house in Roncesvalles was built in 1127 and lauded in the poem *Song of the Hospital* in the document "*La Pretiosa*:"

Porta patet omnibus, infirmir et sanis, Non solum Catholicis verum et paganis, Judeis, hereticis, otiosis, vanis.

"The door opens to all, to sick and healthy, not only to true Catholics but also to pagans, Jews, heretics, the idle and vagabonds."

24.7 Roncesvalles

After a tiring day, you may be relieved to arrive in Roncesvalles, a small medieval hamlet dominated by a large abbey and several historic churches. This popular tourist spot is a second gateway to the Camino, sometimes crowded in summer.

The current albergue of Roncesvalles is new as of 2011, with excellent facilities. The previous albergue, a historic building that had over 100 beds in one large room, was shown in the 2010 film *The Way* as the place Martin Sheen's character spends his first night on the Camino. Two restaurants offer a pilgrim menú; be sure to buy a ticket and select a dinner time beforehand.

The **Iglesia de Santa María** is open to the public with a pilgrim Mass offered (8pm weekdays, 6pm weekends), and houses the 13th-century statue of **Our Lady of Roncesvalles**, made of wood covered in luminous silver. She used to be hidden behind a curtain and only viewed with great ceremony, but now she is prominently displayed on the front altar. Don't miss the ornate canopy of silver above her, known as a baldachín, a recreation of the original.

24.7 Roncesvalles A H

Pop. 30, French: *Ronceveux*, Basque: *Orreaga*; Spanish: "Valley of Thorns" or "Valley of Junipers"

1. A **Municipal** (183, €12): W D, 948-760000, group reservations 2pm, all year
2. H **Casa Sabina** (-/€55): 948-760012
3. H **La Posada** (€55/65): 948-760225
4. H **Hotel Roncesvalles/Casa de Beneficiados** (-/€80): W D, 948-760105

The **Capilla de Santiago**, a 13th-century Gothic chapel, includes bells used to guide pilgrims down from Ibañeta Pass in foul weather. Nearby, the **Capilla de Sancti Spiritus**, also known as Charlemagne's Silo, houses ossuaries (bone boxes). According to legend, the bones belong to soldiers killed with Roland in the Battle of Roncesvalles, but they are more likely the bones of unlucky pilgrims who died on the mountain pass.

Pilgrim accommodations in medieval times were called "hospitals," even though they were not specifically for sick people.

Visit the **Real Colegiata de Santa María**, one of the earliest Gothic structures in Spain, built by Sancho VII in 1219 (called Sancho the Strong perhaps because of his 2.2m/7'3" height). Some parts of the complex can be visited independently, others require a museum ticket.

To visit the following areas, a ticket to the museum is required (**Museum of Roncesvalles**, €5, 10am-2pm, 3-6pm, 948-760000). An audio guide costs €1.10 (various language options).

The cloister, containing the 14th-century chapter house, collapsed under a freak snowstorm in the 17th century and was replaced with a more plain structure. The Tomb of Sancho VII is found in the chapter house. Note the chains at the foot of the tomb, said to the be the those of Christian prisoners freed from the Muslim army by Sancho's knights at the Battle of Las Navas de Tolosa in 1212. The symbol of chains still adorns the flag of Navarra to this day. The stained glass window depicts the Battle of Navas with Sancho and his knights trampling their Muslim opponents.

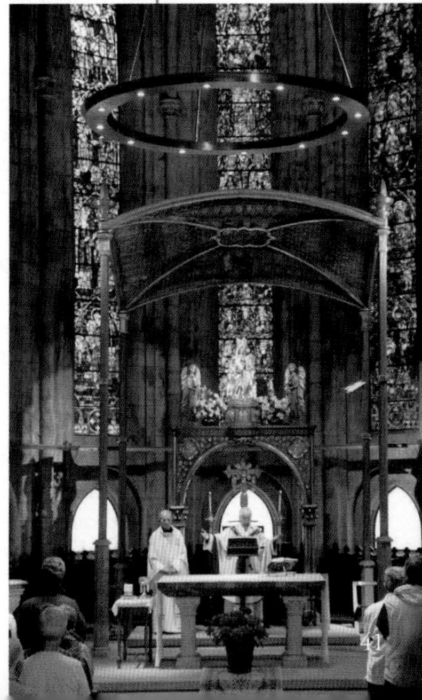

Pilgrim mass at Iglesia Santa María in Roncesvalles

The museum houses religious relics and historical items, including *Oliphant* (Roland's famed horn made of ivory), Charlemagne's chessboard (actually a 14th-century reliquary with 32 squares, each filled with a relic, such as bone fragments of a saint) and a gold reliquary said to house two thorns from the crown worn by Jesus.

View of Valcarlos

⚠ Alternate Stage 1A: Valcarlos Route

St. Jean to Roncesvalles (via Valcarlos), 24.0km

In spite of the sections of highway walking, much of this route is on pleasant quiet country roads or lovely dirt footpaths. The trail crisscrosses the Nive River and Spanish/French border. Remain vigilant for vehicles on blind corners, as this highway has no shoulder in most places.

If the 24km first day strikes as too daunting, split the day by sleeping in Varcarlos and continue up the pass to Roncesvalles in a more manageable 12.4km day.

From Valcarlos, be sure to refill water as there are not more sources until Roncesvalles.

0.0 St. Jean: *Leave via the main street over the bridge to Rue d'Espagne. Note the R turn at the road "Chemin Mayorga" (0.5km), scarcely waymarked. Continue out of town, joining the busy D933 highway before turning R onto a quiet paved country road with a sign for "Valcarlos Luzaine" (1.8km).*

7.0 Rest Stop: The first services are at a large rest stop for travelers on the nearby highway, including a supermarket and café. *Cross the parking lot and walk through the shopping area to exit behind the gas station on a dirt path (waymarked) to Arnéguy.*

8.5 Arnéguy is a small town that straddles the Spanish/French border. *From Arnéguy cross D933 and the bridge to take a waymarked quiet country road on the east side of the river, cutting out about 3km of busy road walking. Pass through* ***Óndarolle (10.9km)****, and descend steeply to cross a bridge and ascend to Valcarlos.*

8.5 Arnéguy Pop. 271
Hotel Clementenia (-/€60): , 05-2434100

11.6 Valcarlos housed a medieval hospice and church, which no longer stand. A modern church contains a life-size statue of Santiago (ask for key in Bar Iñaki). *Leave Valcarlos via the main road, and turn L (13km) on a quiet country road to pass through Gañecoleta.*

11.6 Valcarlos Pop. 30
Basque: *Luzaide*, Spanish: "Valley of Charlemange"
1. **Municipal** (24, €10 w/): , c/Elizaldea 52, 696-231809, noon, all year, key may be at municipal building
2. **Casa Marcelino** (-/€50): , c/Elizaldea 1, 948-790063
3. **Casa Etxezuria** (-/€45 w/): , c/Elizaldea 60, 948-790011
4. **Hostal Maitena** (-/€55): , c/Elizaldea, 948-790210

15.0 Gañecoleta is a small sleepy hamlet with quaint country cottages. *At the far end of town, follow waymarks to the R on a pleasant forest dirt path. After 1km, rejoin the highway (15.9km) for another 2.4km. After the "km 58" sign on the road, turn L back onto a dirt path (18.2km). The path intersects the road (21.2km), almost immediately leaving it to the L, and follows a dirt footpath. The final 3km to the pass are steep and tiring! Remember to save energy for this final challenge.*

22.6 Ibañeta Pass marks the high point of this stage, with a small chapel and monument to Roland. *A brisk downhill walk of 1.4km heads to Roncesvalles, directly to the albergue.*

24.0 Roncesvalles
Details on p. 40.

Colorful window in Gañecoleta

2

RONCESVALLES TO ZUBIRI

22.3km
(13.9mi)

5-6 Hours
Difficulty: ▬□□
P 32%, 7.2 km
U 68%, 15.1 km

A Albergues:
Espinal 6.8km
Zubiri 22.3km
Urdaníz 26.5km
Larrasoaña 28.0km

Leaving Roncesvalles: only 790km to go!

Enjoy shaded forest trails, pass rivers and small villages, explore Hemingway lore and a Romanesque bridge.

This is a beautiful day of walking, primarily on forest walking trails, occasionally crossing the main highway. The many flat sections are a welcome rest after the Pyrenees yesterday. Periodic services in charming towns pleasantly break up the stage.

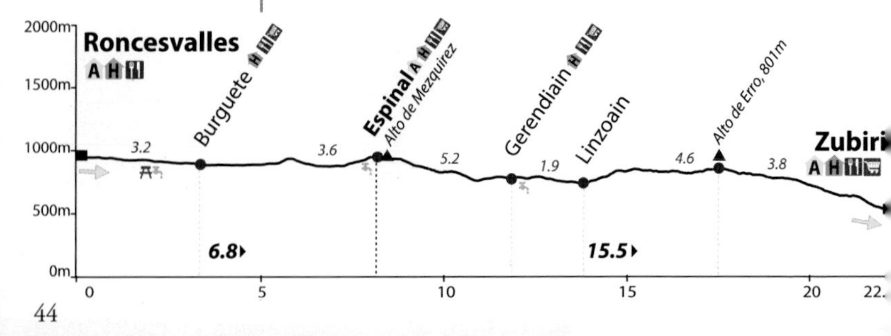

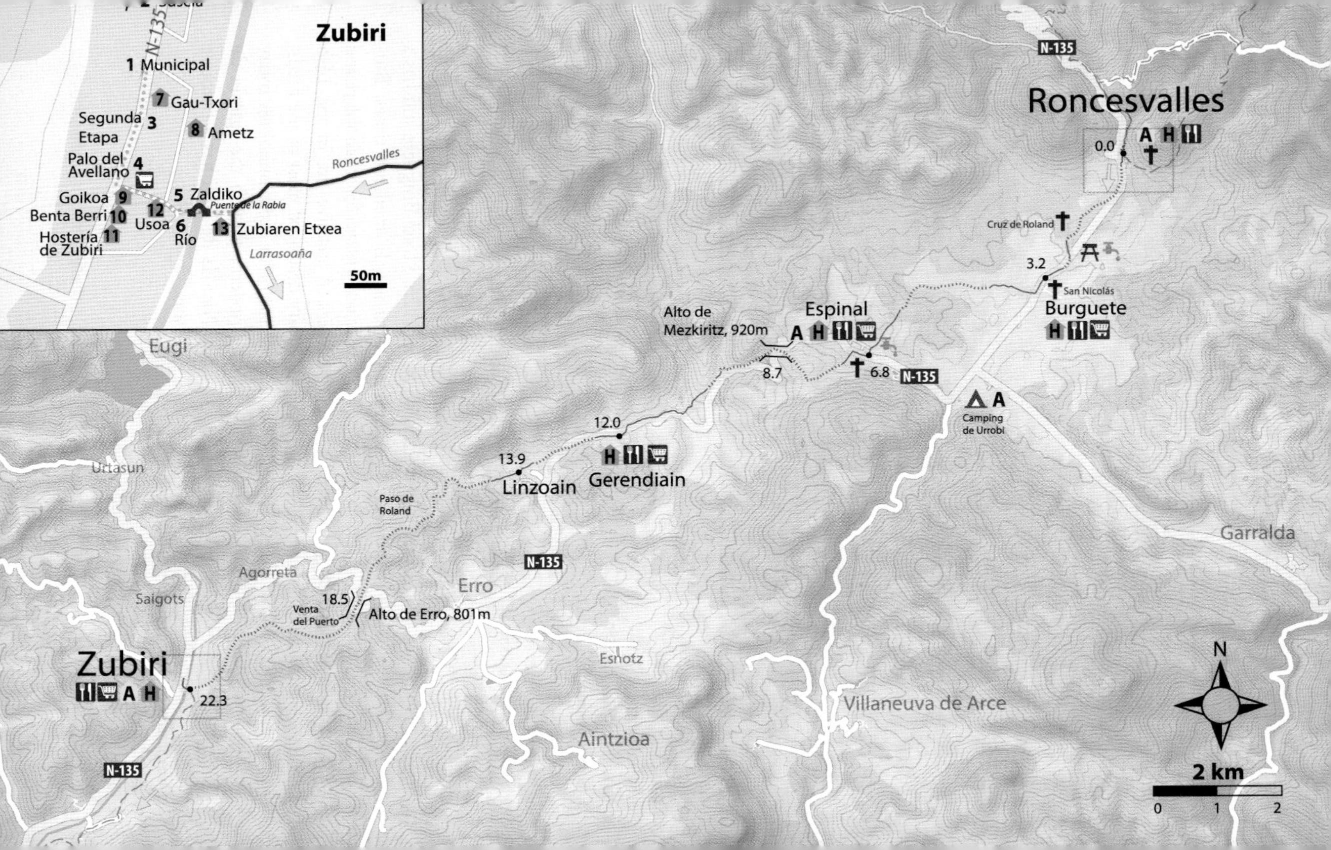
Zubiri
1 Municipal
7 Gau-Txori
Segunda Etapa 3
8 Ametz
Palo del Avellano 4
5 Zaldiko
Goikoa 9
Benta Berri 10
12 Usoa
6 Río
Puente de la Rabia
13 Zubiaren Etxea
Hostería de Zubiri 11
Roncesvalles
Larrasoaña
50m
Roncesvalles
0.0
Cruz de Roland
3.2
San Nicolás
Burguete
Espinal
Alto de Mezkiritz, 920m
8.7
6.8
Camping de Urrobi
12.0
Gerendiain
13.9
Linzoain
Paso de Roland
Erro
Garralda
Eugi
Urtasun
Agorreta
Saigots
18.5
Venta del Puerto
Alto de Erro, 801m
Esnotz
Zubiri
22.3
Villaneuva de Arce
Aintzioa
N-135
N
2 km
0
1
2

This scrubby forest full of gorse and thickets (and blackberries in summer!) was supposedly a place of witchcraft in the 16th century, when nine women were put to death by the Inquisition, accused of practicing witchcraft in the forest between Roncesvalles and Burguete.

0.0 *Leaving the Roncesvalles albergue, walk to La Posada restaurant to pick up trail markings which follow highway N-135. Leave the road for a dirt footpath (0.4km), and soon note the stone Cruz de Peregrinos, a 14th-century Gothic cross with the image of Sancho the Great and his wife.*

3.2 **Burguete**, a popular breakfast stop, is a typical Navarran town whose main claim to fame is a mention in Ernest Hemingway's famous novel, *The Sun Also Rises*, which he wrote in just eight weeks in 1926. Hotel Burguete still has a piano with Hemingway's signature. In medieval times, Burguete was known for its cobblers and barbers. A massive fire in the 14th century destroyed most of the medieval town, so most buildings today are modern, though the **Iglesia de San Nicolás de Bari** has a Baroque doorway.

3.2 **Burguete**

Pop. 290, Basque: *Auritz*

- **Iturrialdrea** (-/€25-28): W, ✆948-760243
- **Pedro Arena** (-/€38): W D, ✆948-760164
- **Hotel Burguete** (€40/56): c/San Nicolas 71, ✆948-760005, piano signed by Hemingway
- **Don Jáuregui de Burguete** (-/€50+): c/San Nicolás 32, ✆948-760031
- **Loizu** (-/€65-85): c/San Nicolás 13, ✆948-760008

Rural scenery after Burguete (above)

Watch for the Santander Bank (3.3km), where the trail turns to the R out of town on a small footpath, partly paved (10m beyond this turn, a panadería offers coffee and fresh baked goods from 8am). Cross the Río Irati and through pleasant farmland to Espinal.

6.8 **Espinal** was founded in 1269 as a place to protect pilgrims from bandits. *The trail leaves town to the L via a small country road, which becomes a paved footpath. Climb up through beech forest to cross the highway and the **Alto de Mezquirez (920m, 8.7km)**, and descend via steep paved footpath over the Río Erro through the last beech forest of the Camino to Gerendiain.*

12.0 **Gerendiain** is mentioned in the *Codex Calixtinus* as the end of the first segment from St. Jean, with the 13th-century Iglesia de San Bartolomé. On the way out of town is a mini market open daily.

*Continue on the wooded path into the hamlet of **Linzoain (13.9km)**, with a 13th-century church dedicated to San Saturnino, and several houses display lintels (coats of arm) from the 18th and 19th century. Continue steeply up through dense woodland. Look R for a boulder painted yellow, said to represent the length of **Roland's stride (Paso de Roldán)**. This shady path leads uphill to Alto de Erro.*

6.8 Espinal A H

Pop. 249, Basque: *Aurizberri*

- A H **+600m Irugoienea** (22, €10/-/40): Oihanilum 2, 649-412487, free 5km transfers to/from Roncesvalles, Apr-Oct
- A H **+1.5km Camping Urrobi** (42, €12.20): 948-760200, Apr-Oct
- A H **Hostal Haizea** (30, €12/35/60): Ctra Francia, 948-760379
- H **Errebesena** (-/€30): c/San Bartolomé 25, 948-760141, Milagros Saragüeta
- H **Gertxada** (-/€33): 948-760261

12.0 Gerendiain H

Pop. 25, Basque: *Viscarret/Bizkarreta*

- H **Corazón Puro** (€20 per person w/ and dinner): c/San Pedro 19, 948-392113, offer pickup from Pamplona
- H **La Posada Nueva** (-/€35-45): c/San Pedro 2, 699-131433

Wayside shrine near Espinal

Lambs along the Camino

18.5 **Alto de Erro** once housed an inn, the Ventas del Puerto, with a few ruins still visible in the cattle yard. *Cross the highway and a parking lot (seasonal drink/snack truck) for a steep, sometimes slippery, descent down to Zubiri. If staying in Zubiri, enter via the bridge.*

An overnight in Zubiri is slightly off route. To continue to Larrasoaña, you do not need to enter Zubiri (unless you wish to visit the grocery store as Larrasoaña has only a very small shop off route). If you're still feeling spry, continue on the 5.7km to Larrasoaña, advantages include a shorter day tomorrow to explore Pamplona, also Larrasoaña is off the highway so has a more remote feel. Larrasoaña has fewer accommodation and eating options than Zubiri.

22.3 **Zubiri**: Enter via a Romanesque bridge, known as the **Puente de la Rabia** (Rabies Bridge), named because of a tradition that if animals are led three times across the bridge, they will be protected from rabies. The tradition comes from a legend that the builders of the bridge in the 15th century dug into the rock to place the central pillar and found an

22.3 Zubiri A H Pop. 432, Basque: "village of the bridge," gear store Planeta Agu

1. A **Municipal** (80, €8): 628-324186, 10am, Mar-Oct, basic, bathrooms and kitchen in separate building, no fridge
2. A **Suseia** (22, €15 w/): c/Murelu 12, 948-304353
3. A **Segunda Etapa** (12, €12): Av. Roncesvalles 22, 697-186560, Mar-Oct
4. A H **El Palo de Avellano** (60, €16-18/-/58 w/): (free), Av. Roncesvalles 16, 666-499175, mid Mar-Oct
5. A **Zaldiko** (24, €10): (free), Puente de la Rabia 1, 609-736420, Mar-Oct
6. A H **Río Arga Ibaia** (12, €15/-/40): Puente de la Rabia 7, 948-304243
7. H **Gau-Txori** (€30/49): Av. Roncesvalles 24, 948-304076
8. H **Amets** (€45/58): c/Gerestegi 25, 618-636189
9. H **Goikoa** (€25/30): Av. Roncesvalles 12, 638-847974
10. H **Benta Berri** (-/€35): Av. Roncesvalles 10, 636-134781
11. H **Hostería de Zubiri** (€69/87 w/): Av. Roncesvalles 6, 948-304329
12. H **Usoa** (€24/36): Puente de la Rabia 4, 948-304306
13. H **Zubiaren Etxea** (€30/48): c/Camino 2, 948-304293

embalmed body. The body turned out to be Santa Quiteria, patron saint against rabies. When she was being transported to Pamplona to be buried, her body miraculously refused to budge from this spot, so her processional assumed it was a sign that she wished to be buried along the pilgrim road.

A leper hospital was once located near the bridge, though nothing remains of the structure. Zubiri is first mentioned in a 1040 document in which the area is donated to the Leyre monastery. Domenico Laffi's pilgrim account describes the bridge as treacherous, with guards of the bridge demanding a toll and brutally injuring those who refused. Today Zubiri is rather industrial, with many locals working at the magnesium factory visible along the trail on the next stage.

Zubiri
June: Día del Valle
August: Patron saint San Esteban

A standard greeting along the trail is *Buen Camino*, literally meaning "good way."

In medieval times, the greeting was *ultreia* meaning "further onward," with the response being *et suseia* "and further upward," highlighting the physical and spiritual aspects of the journey.

Enter Zubiri over la Puente de la Rabia

3

ZUBIRI TO PAMPLONA

21.1km
(13.1mi)

5-6 Hours
Difficulty:
P 43%, 9.1km
U 57%, 12.0km

A Albergues:
Urdániz 3.7km
Larrasoaña 5.7km
Zuriáin 9.6km
Zabaldica 12.9km
Trinidad 16.6km
Pamplona 21.1km
Cizur Menor 26.2km

Plaza del Castillo in Pamplona

Follow the Arga River, visit medieval churches, gaze at Pamplona's Gothic cathedral, see where the famous bulls run.

Today's path primarily follows the Arga River through rural hamlets on pleasant natural paths with plenty of places to fill water. The day ends in Pamplona, the city with the largest population on the Camino Francés, with some urban road walking to arrive to the charming walled Old City, alive with cafés and Hemingway lore.

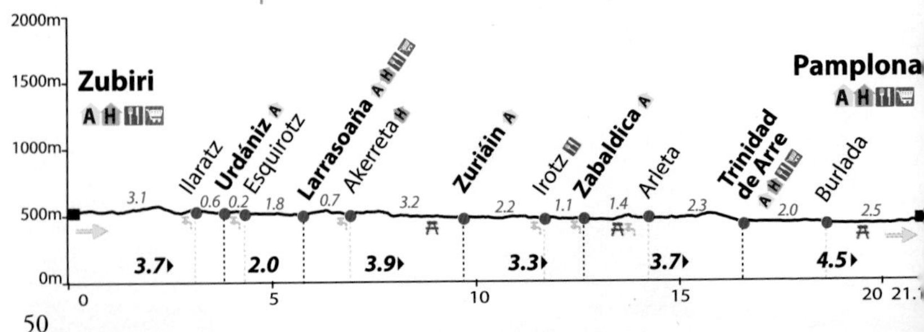

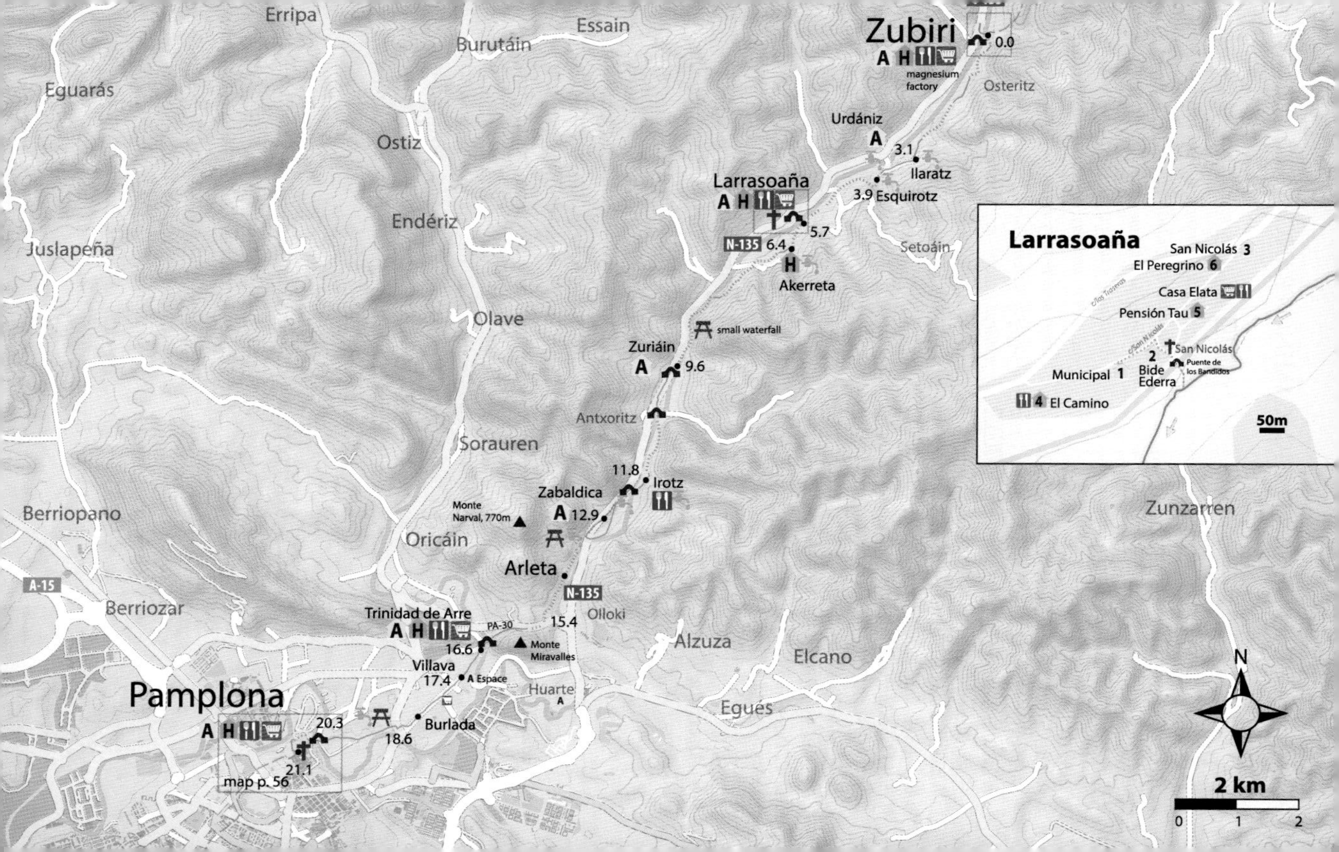
Zubiri
0.0
A H
magnesium factory
Osteritz
Erripa
Essain
Burutáin
Eguarás
Ostiz
Urdániz
A
3.1
Ilaratz
3.9 Esquirotz
Larrasoaña
A H
5.7
N-135
6.4
H
Akerreta
Setoáin
Endériz
Juslapeña
Olave
small waterfall
Zuriáin
A
9.6
Antxoritz
Sorauren
11.8
Irotz
Zabaldica
A 12.9
Monte Narval, 770m
Oricáin
Arleta
N-135
Berriopano
A-15
Berriozar
Trinidad de Arre
A H
PA-30
15.4
Olloki
16.6
Monte Miravalles
Alzuza
Elcano
Villava
17.4
A Espace
Huarte
A
Egués
Pamplona
A H
20.3
18.6
Burlada
21.1
map p. 56
Zunzarren
N
2 km
0
1
2
Larrasoaña
San Nicolás 3
El Peregrino 6
Casa Elata
Pensión Tau 5
c/Los Traseras
c/San Nicolás
San Nicolás
2
Bide Ederra
Puente de los Bandidos
Municipal 1
4 El Camino
50m

3.7 **Urdániz** A

A **Acá y Allá** (6, 15€ w/): , c/San Miguel 18, 615-257666, +0.5km

5.7 **Larrasoaña** A H

Pop. 143, Basque surname

1. A **Municipal** (36, €8): , c/San Nicolás, 605-505489, 12:30pm, mid Mar-Oct, basic
2. A H **Bide Ederra** (4, €16/-/40 w/): , c/Carmen 18, 685-735595, Feb-Nov
3. A **San Nicolás** (40, €11): , 12pm Mar-Oct, c/Sorandi 5-7, 619-559225
4. H **El Camino** (-/€60): , c/Portalcelay 12, 948-304250, Apr-Sept
5. H **Pensión Tau** (-/€40-60 w/): , c/Errotabidea 18, 948-304720
6. H **El Peregrino** (-/€50): , c/San Nicolás 50, 948-304554

6.4 **Akerreta** H

H **Akerreta** (-/€77 w/ pilgrim rate): , c/Transfiguración 11, 948-304572, makes an appearance in the film *The Way*

9.6 **Zuriáin** A

A **Parada de Zuriáin** (16, €12/-/50): , c/Landa 8, 699-556741, Mar-Oct

0.0 *Leave Zubiri on a well-marked farm track to a paved road through an unpleasant industrial stretch past a magnesium factory. Following the Río Arga valley today, pass through numerous tiny hamlets consisting of several large multi-story houses, spread in this way for defense and farming the fertile valley, such as* ***Ilaratz (3.1km), Urdániz (3.7km, +500m across river)*** *and* ***Esquirotz (3.9km)****. Arrive at Puente de los Bandidos, the 14th-century bridge where bandits were said to hide and wait for pilgrims. Cross the bridge to enter Larrasoaña or continue to the L to Akerreta.*

5.7 **Larrasoaña** has a classic Camino town layout and originates from the 12th century. Two historic hospices no longer remain, though the Clavería de Roncesvalles (storehouse) and the 13th-century **Iglesia de San Nicolás de Bari** can still be seen at the town entrance. Historic houses from the 15th and 16th centuries line the main street; some retain their coat of arms above the door. If you stay overnight, reserve your dinner at the small restaurant. Basic supplies and a café are available at Casa Elata, +350m. *Head uphill through small rolling hills on a gravel path.*

6.4 **Akerreta** is a small hamlet with an impressive hotel in a restored 1723 Basque house. Three-story houses were typical of the area, with the bottom floor for livestock, the next floor for family living space and a short upper floor for pigeons. *Continue on mostly dirt paths until the hamlet of* ***Zuriáin (9.6km)*** *and cross over the Río Arga to join busy highway N-135 for 600m. Break to the L on a smaller paved road and again to the R onto a dirt path to arrive at Irotz.*

Tunnel of green before Larrasoaña

Medieval bridge entering Villava

11.8 **Irotz** has the Iglesia de San Pedro and sometimes a seasonal snack stand. *Cross back over the Río Arga on the Romanesque Puente Iturgaiz and into the "playa fluvial" park (river beach park, 12.1km). The trail is waymarked two ways—one which turns L just after the bridge and passes through the park along the river on a cement bike path which goes all the way into Pamplona (all paved and much longer) along the banks of the river. The second and preferred option is waymarked just a little further after the bridge and follows a pleasant footpath through the hamlet of Zabaldica.*

12.9 **Zabaldica** contains the 12th-century Iglesia de San Esteban with one of the oldest bells in Spain (1377). *Continue straight through the town and out on a dirt path, crossing highway ⚠ N-135 to a* ***rest area*** ***(13.5km)****. From the rest area, the trail becomes a dirt footpath that veers steeply up the hillside of Monte Nerval and passes under highway PA-30 through a tunnel (15.4km). Enter Trinidad de Arre via a Romanesque bridge.*

A legend says that a woman was baking bread when a passing pilgrim asked her for some. She lied, saying that she had none and returned to her oven to find the bread had turned to stone.

12.9 **Zabaldica** **A**

A **Zabaldika** (par, 18, don): , c/San Esteban 8, 948-330918, Apr 15- Oct 15, communal meals

16.6 Trinidad de Arre/Villava
A H Pop. 10,487
A **Hermanos Maristas** (par, 34, €8): at the bridge, 948-332941, 2pm, Mar-mid Dec, reservations
A **Villava Municipal** (54, €9): Pedro de Atarrabia 17-19, 948-517731, 11am, mid Mar-Oct
H **Villava** (-/€46): 948-333676
H **La Buhardilla** (-/€66): c/Serapio Huici 15, 948-382872

+2.1 Huarte A Pop. 6,309, (+2.1km)
A **Municipal** (60, €10): Plaza San Juan, 948-074329, 1pm, Apr-Nov, can stay more than 1 night

16.6 Trinidad de Arre, now a suburb of Pamplona, is located on the ancient Roman road and was re-founded in 1184 by Sancho IV. The Camino enters by the historic Romanesque bridge with six arches, followed by a sharp right angle after the bridge, which was a defense point for the town. Directly to the R after the bridge is the parochial albergue, adjoined to the basilica where a pilgrim accommodation was also located in medieval times. Below the bridge are remains of medieval mills and fulling stations (for felting material). The 1057 bylaws of Arre state that villagers were to support the pilgrim hospital with a half pound of bread per year in order to feed the pilgrims. Nowadays, you'll have to buy your own bread. [From *Plaza Consistorial* (17km), there is an optional detour L off route to stay at the **Villava** Municipal albergue or the albergue at **Huarte**, another suburb of Pamplona.]

*Continue along a pedestrian path to Pamplona. Cross c/San Andreas in **Villava (17.3km)** and continue straight. After Burlada at the traffic circle with Palacete Municipal (18.6km), turn R and cross c/Bizkarmendia to walk along a garden center and pass a picnic area with water. Arrive to the historic **Magdalena Bridge (20.3km)** and follow the dirt path up to the Old City by the historic walls. Pass through the **Old City gate (20.8km, Portal de Francia)** and another gate to walk straight on c/de Carmen, passing a plaza. Turn L on c/Navarreria for the cathedral and municipal albergue, or straight to continue on the Camino.*

21.1 Pamplona is the first major city on the Camino and a worthwhile place to take a rest day if you enjoy exploring historic buildings, twisting Old City alleys and expansive green parks. If there are any items in your backpack that you haven't used yet (except rain gear & first aid kit), consider mailing them ahead (p. 21).

Puerta del Amparo on the south portal of Pamplona's cathedral

Pamplona is best known for the **running of the bulls** at the **Fiesta de San Fermín**, celebrated July 6-14 each year, in which six bulls are released daily to run a course through the city to the plaza. The festival was propelled to worldwide fame by its prominence in Hemingway's The *Sun Also Rises*. Now, locals and tourists come to run with the bulls while consuming copious amounts of wine (an estimated three million liters are imbibed during the festivities), precipitating numerous injuries. The city swells with over a million people, accommodations rates quadruple and albergues close. If you happen to pass through Pamplona during San Fermínes, just keep on walking (or run!) and look for a bed in the next town.

Pamplona was founded by the Roman general Pompeoalo, built over a previous Basque encampment, an ideal defensible location along the *Via Trajana*. Roman ruins have been excavated from under the **cathedral**, including 1st-century streets and buildings. Muslims took the city in 718 and ruled until overthrown by local Basques in 799. In 778, Charlemagne was said to have destroyed the city walls of Pamplona, leading up to the Battle of Roncesvalles (p. 37).

An influx of foreign immigrants in the 12th century led to infighting between neighborhoods, with each ethnic neighborhood fortifying themselves against the others. Pamplona was more fort than city, encapsulated within the defensive walls until the 20th century when building was finally allowed outside city walls. Today, Pamplona is a prosperous and attractive city with a number of historical buildings and museums. *Plaza del Castillo* is a great place for an evening stroll, with numerous cafés including Café Iruña, a favorite haunt of Hemingway, and historic hotels such as La Perla, which has hosted Orson Welles, Charlie Chaplin and Hemingway.

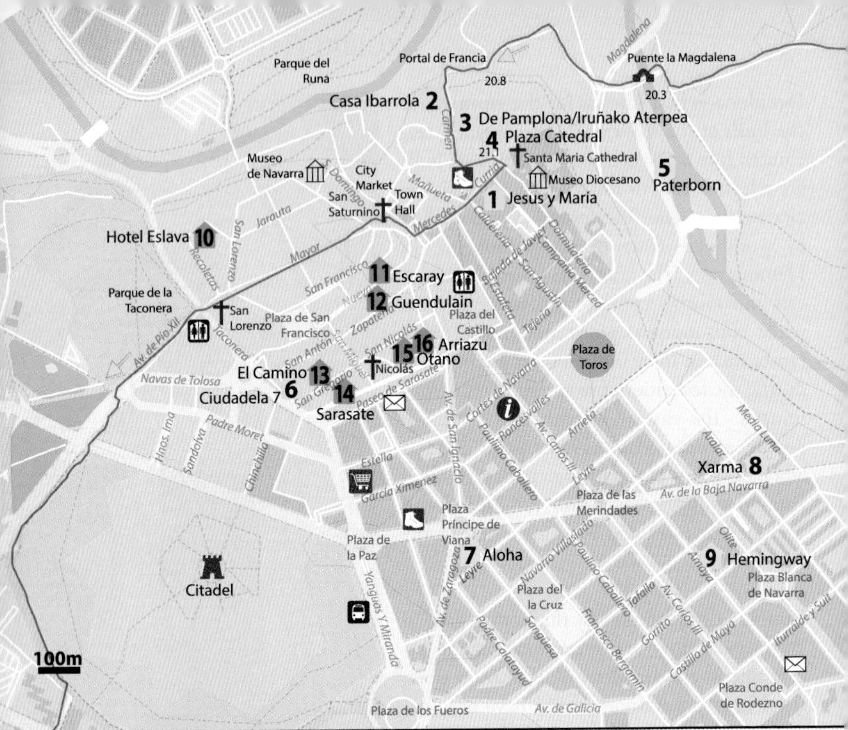

21.1 **Pamplona** A H Pop. 197,932, Named for Roman general Pompael Basque: *Iruña* "the city," c/S. Saturnino 2, 948-420700: M-F 10am-7pm; Sa 10am-2pm, 4-7p Su 10am-2pm, Caminoteca, c/Curia 5, 948-210316, 11am-7pm; all San Fermín prices higher

1. A **Jesús y María** (muni, 112, €8): c/Compañía 4, 948-222644, all year
2. A **Casa Ibarrola** (20, €18 w/): c/del Carmen 31, 692-208463, all year
3. A **De Pamplona/Iruñako Aterpea** (24, €15 w/): c/Carmen 18, 685-735595, Feb-Nov
4. A **Plaza Catedral** (46, €15-18 w/): c/Navarrería 35, 620-913968, all year
5. A **Jacobusfreunde Paderborn** (assoc, 24, €6): Playa de Caparroso 6, 948-211712, Mar-Oct, river-side albergue run by a German confraternity
6. A **Hostel Ciudadela 7** (24, €16): c/Ciudadela 7, 616-786479, all year
7. A **Aloha Hostel** (26, €15 w/): c/Sangüesa 2, 648-289403, bike rental
8. A H **Xarma** (22, €20/-/42 w/): Av Baja Navarra 23, 948-046449
9. A H **Hostel Hemingway** (€15-18/-/€40): c/Amaya 26, 948-983884
10. H **Hotel Eslava** (€35/60): Plaza Virgen de la O 7, 948-222270
11. H **Pensión Escaray** (€20/40 shared bath): c/Nueva 24, 948-227825
12. H **Palacio Guendulain** (-/€160): Zapatería 53, 948-225522
13. H **Pensión El Camino** (€29/34 shared bath): c/San Gregorio 12, 948-213567
14. H **Sarasate** (€50/60): Paseo Sarasate 30, 948-223084
15. H **Casa Otano** (€25/42): c/San Nicolás 5, 948-227036
16. H **Hostal Arriazu** (-/€55): c/Comedias 14, 948-210202

✝ Catedral Santa María el Real (€5, €3 with *credencial*, M-Sa 10:30am-5pm, 7pm summer, 948-212594) The entrance fee includes a brochure and map of the many chapels and features of this 15th-century Gothic cathedral. The main altar houses the silver-coated *Virgen de Sagrario* where the medieval Navarran kings were crowned. Visit the 13th-century cloister, one of the finest examples of Gothic style in Europe. See the *Puerta Preciosa* with a detailed tympanum depicting the life of the Virgin Mary. The north bell tower houses one of the largest bells in Spain at over 11 tons!

If you prefer to forego the hustle and bustle of cities, make a brief stop at the cathedral and continue to **Cizur Menor** (+5.1km), a peaceful village just beyond Pamplona with two excellent albergues.

Town Hall (Ayuntamiento)
This impressive Baroque facade, bedecked in striking flags, was rebuilt in 1951.

✝ Iglesia de San Saturnino
Dedicated to San Saturnino, whose main pilgrimage church is located in Toulouse, showing French influence in Pamplona. Look on the right wall for a stone figure of Santiago Peregrino helping a small child.

Museo de Navarra (€2 or free with *credencial*, Tu-Sa 9:30am-2pm, 5-7pm Su 11am-2pm, closed Mon, *c/Santo Domingo* 47) This museum was once a pilgrim hospital and now houses impressive artifacts from throughout Navarra, including Roman mosaics, the Romanesque capitals from Pamplona's cathedral, an intricately carved ivory chest from Córdoba and Gothic murals.

Citadel/Ciudadela
This star-shaped fortress on the south side of the city dates from the 16th century and was transformed into a park in 1964.

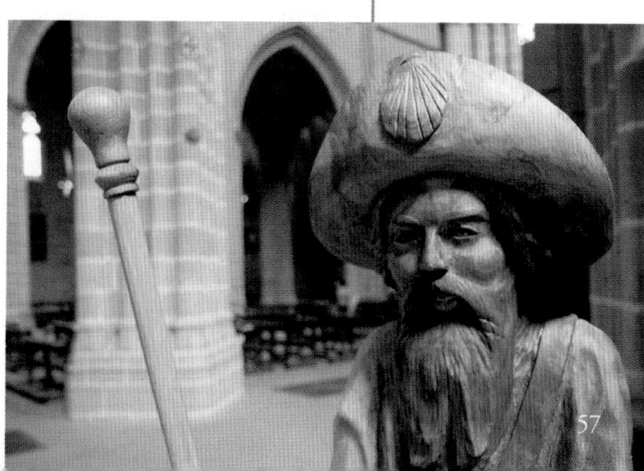

Image of Santiago Peregrino in the Pamplona Cathedral

4

PAMPLONA TO PUENTE LA REINA

23.8km
(14.8mi)

6-7 Hours
Difficulty:
P 40%, 9.4 km
U 60%, 14.4 km

A Albergues:
Cizur Menor 5.1km
Zariquegui 11.2km
Uterga 17.2km
Muruzábel 19.7km
Óbanos 21.5km
Puente la Reina 23.8km
Mañeru 29.0km
Cirauqui 31.6km

Alt. Route:
Eunate Church
+2.8km, (p. 64)

Pilgrim statue at Alto de Perdón

Climb the wind-whipped Alto de Perdón, detour to the mysterious church at Eunate, ponder the mystery of Óbanos and marvel at the famous bridge of Puente la Reina.

This stage leaves Pamplona by way of the Citadel park and climbs to the small town of Cizur Menor. The steep climb to Alto de Perdón affords wonderful views. A worthwhile detour leads to the enigmatic church of Eunate. Be prepared for less shade today as you enter a more temperate climate with fields of wheat and grapes.

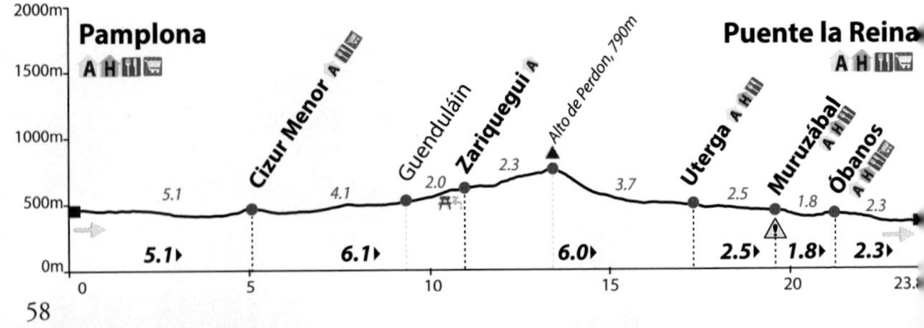

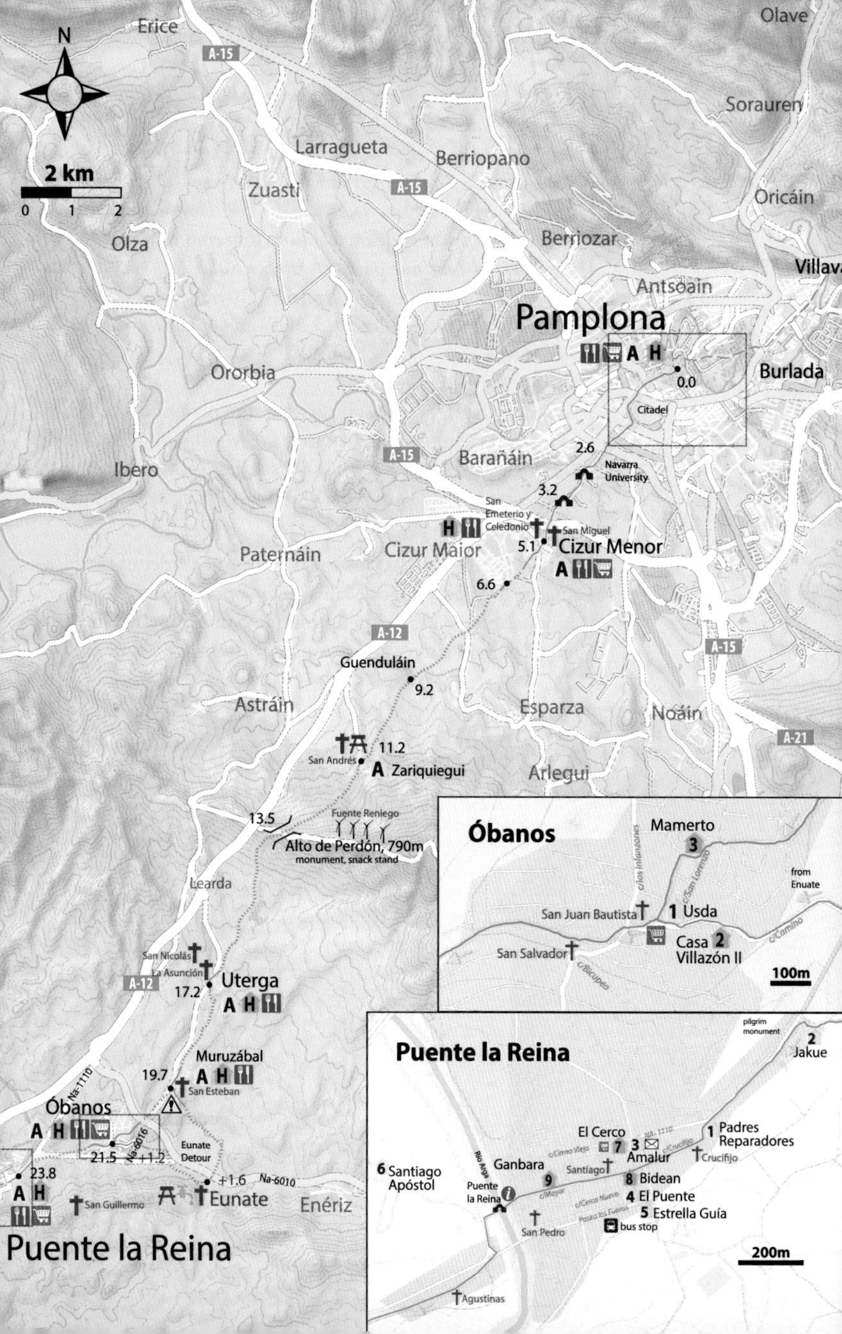
N
2 km
0 1 2
Erice
A-15
Olave
Sorauren
Larragueta
Berriopano
Zuasti
Oricáin
Olza
Berriozar
Villava
Antsoain
Pamplona
A H
0.0
Burlada
Ororbia
Citadel
2.6
A-15
Barañáin
Ibero
Navarra University
3.2
San Emeterio y Celedonio
San Miguel
H
5.1
Cizur Menor
Paternáin
Cizur Maior
A
6.6
A-12
A-15
Guenduláin
9.2
Astráin
Esparza
Noáin
A-21
11.2
San Andrés
A Zariquiegui
Arlegui
13.5
Fuente Reniego
Alto de Perdón, 790m
monument, snack stand
Learda
San Nicolás
La Asunción
A-12
17.2
Uterga
A H
Muruzábal
19.7
A H
San Esteban
Na-1110
Óbanos
A H
21.5
Na-6016
+1.2
Eunate Detour
23.8
A H
+1.6
Na-6010
San Guillermo
Eunate
Enériz
Puente la Reina
Óbanos
Mamerto
3
c/los Infanzones
c/San Lorenzo
from Enuate
San Juan Bautista
1 Usda
Casa 2
Villazón II
c/Camino
San Salvador
c/Bicupea
100m
Puente la Reina
pilgrim monument
2
Jakue
El Cerco
7 3
Na-1110
1 Padres Reparadores
c/Cerco Viejo
c/Crucifijo
Amalur
Crucifijo
6 Santiago Apóstol
Río Arga
Ganbara
Santiago
9
8 Bidean
Puente la Reina
c/Mayor
c/Cerco Nuevo
4 El Puente
Paseo los Fueros
5 Estrella Guía
San Pedro
bus stop
200m
Agustinas

If you get stuck for a bed or want to visit the 14th-century **Iglesia de San Andrés**, walk or take a bus 2km west to Cizur Mayor.

Cizur Menor's mini market "Dividi": 8:30am-2pm, 4:30-8:30pm/8pm weekends

0.0 *Leaving the Pamplona municipal albergue (map p. 56), take c/de Curria to c/Mercaderes to c/Mayor, following Camino signs and passing the Ayuntamiento on Plaza Consistorial and the Iglesia de San Saturnino. Pass the Iglesia de San Lorenzo (0.7km) and walk on footpaths in the Parque de Taconera, around the edge of the Citadel. Turn R to cross c/de la Vuelta del Castillo and continue on c/del Hierro Kalea (1.7km) and stay straight through Navarra University (2.6km). Cross the Río Sadar via the Puente de Accela (3.2km) and follow the road to Cizur Menor.*

A famous battle was fought here on the plains between Pamplona and Cizur Menor, between the Muslim king Aigolando and Charlemagne. Over 100,000 soldiers gathered from each side. After bloody battle, the Crusaders emerged victorious.

5.1 **Cizur Menor** is the base for the Order of the Hospitalers of Saint John of Malta (*Sanjuanistas*), who established a monastery in 1135. The **Iglesia de San Miguel** is all that is left of the monastery and was used to store grain for over 100

A storm brews at the approach to Cizur Menor

years until it was restored in the 1980s. Above the door on the tympanum notice the simple *crismón* (a rosette containing the Greek symbols of the cross, *Chi Rho*, and an *Alpha Omega*). Fortified churches set upon hills in strategic military positions were often named for San Miguel (Saint Michael, the archangel), guardian of the church. The 12th-century Romanesque Iglesia de San Emeterio y Celedonio has also been restored. In 1508, the pilgrim hospital in Cizur Menor was recorded as having 8 beds; there are almost 10 times that now with two appealing albergues. Several restaurants offer a pilgrim menú.

5.1 Cizur Menor A Pop. 2,113

Basque: *zintzur* "narrow mountain pass"

A Orden de Malta (assoc, 27, €4): , 616-651330, May-Sept, stocked with food for a donation, run by the Sanjuanista Order of Malta with the feel of a parochial albergue

A ☆ De Maribel (52, €10): , 948-183885 , noon in summer, closed Nov, owner Maribel Roncal often graciously helps to treat pilgrim's blistered feet

Follow the main road out of Cizur Menor, exiting the town on a dirt footpath that soon skirts a housing development of Cizur Mayor to the north and enters fields on mixed gravel/paved paths (6.6km). Continue to the hamlet of Guenduláin off-route on your R, where the ruins of 16th-century Guendeláin palace and church once housed a pilgrim hospital (9.2km). Note the view of Pamplona behind as you arrive in Zariquiegui.

Iglesia de San Miguel in Cizur Menor at sunrise

11.2 **Zariquiegui** A Pop. 179

A **De Zariquiegui** (18, €10): , c/San Andrés 16, 948-353876, Mar-Oct

A **San Andrés** (18, €11): , c/Camino de Santiago 4, 948-353876

11.2 **Zariquiegui** is a hamlet housing the 13th-century Romanesque **Iglesia de San Andrés**, which you might recognize from a scene in the film *The Way*. The village was almost wiped out by Bubonic plague in the 14th century. *The grade increases steadily onwards and upwards as the ridge of the Alto de Perdón lined with windmills looms ahead.*

Alto de Perdón Pilgrim statue (right above)

Fields of wheat below Alto de Perdón (right below)

Just below the ridge of the Alto del Perdón, to the L is a (now dry) fountain known as **El Fuente Reniega (13.2km)** "Fount of Renunciation" because of a pilgrim legend. A pilgrim was extremely thirsty, and the devil came to him in the form of a wanderer and offered to give him water if he would just renounce God. The pilgrim stayed strong in the faith and refused. Having passed the test, the devil disappeared and Santiago appeared to the pilgrim and offered him water to drink from a scallop shell.

13.5 **Alto de Perdón** housed both a basilica with a pilgrim hospice and a hermitage in medieval times, though nothing remains of them, and today the view is dominated by a row of some 40 windmills providing electricity. The energy company has erected a pilgrim statue depicting a band of medieval pilgrims walking, pressed forward against the wind. The inscription reads: *"Donde se cruza el Camino del viento con el de las estrellas"* ("Where the way of the wind meets the way of the stars").

View of the path from Alto de Perdón

From the ridge, upcoming villages can be seen including Puente la Reina. Note the changes to a more Mediterranean climate as you leave the Pamplona basin behind, with cereals, oak and Mediterranean brushwood ahead. Enjoy the gentle descent as the wheat and wine-growing valley spreads out before you, and enter the town of Uterga.

17.2 **Uterga** contains the **Iglesia de La Asunción,** featuring a retablo including scenes from the life of Santiago Peregrino. One medieval hermitage remains (of Uterga's five original), San Nicolás, near the cemetery. *Leave town via a dirt footpath, continuing to the nearby Muruzábel.*

19.7 **Muruzábel**: The Iglesia de San Esteban features a chromatic retablo in Hispano-Flemish style with a number of saints including Santiago. [⚠ *After the church, watch for signs to turn L to take the detour to Eunate church (closed Monday), which adds about 1 hour/2.8km to the day. Otherwise, continue straight to Óbanos where the detour rejoins.]*

21.5 **Óbanos** is a lovely historic Camino town, best known for a murderous 14th-century pilgrim legend. Duke William (Guillermo) of Aquitane and his sister Felicia undertook the Camino de Santiago. On the return journey, Felicia was overwhelmed with piety and went to become a hermit in Amocain rather

17.2 Uterga A H Pop. 205

A H **Camino del Perdón** (16, €10/-/50): , c/Mayor 61, 948-344598, Mar-Oct

A H **Casa Baztán** (26, €10/-/45): , c/Mayor 46, 948-344528

19.7 Muruzábel A H Pop. 271

Basque surname

A H **El Jardín de Muruzábel** (26, €15/-/40): , c/Monteviejo 21, 696-688399

A **Mendizabal** (10, €18 w/): , c/Mayor 7, 948-344169, can borrow a bicycle to visit Eunate

H **Casa Villazón I** (€25/35): , c/Rebote 5, 620-441467

21.5 Óbanos A H Pop. 800

1. A **Albergue Usda** (36, €8): , San Lorenzo 6, 676-560927, 1:30pm, Apr-Sept
2. H **Casa Villazón II** (€25/35): , San Sebastián 5, 620-441467
3. H **Mamerto** (-/€45): , c/San Lorenzo 7, 948-344344

than returning to her life of luxury. Her brother tracked her down and tried to convince her to return to her court duties. When she refused, he became enraged and stabbed her to death. He was then overcome by remorse and walked to Santiago again and returned to Óbanos to mourn his sister for the rest of his life. He built a hermitage on Arnotegui (a southern hilltop) to serve pilgrims and the poor. Guillermo's silver-covered skull is kept in **Iglesia San Juan Bautista**. The town puts on a play called *The Mystery of Óbanos* every year, retelling the legend with a cast of most of the 800 villagers!

Puente la Reina
July 24-30: Patron saint Santiago festival
Sept: Competition using pitchforks as stilts (*carrera de layas*)

Pimientos de Piquillo (roasted red peppers) are a Puente la Reina specialty with a special pepper market in Sept.

Pass through an arch and past Ermita de San Salvador on the way out of town and down through olive groves and vineyards. Cross NA-6010 (22.7km) and turn L along NA-1110 after Albergue Jakue (23.3km). Follow this road into Puente la Reina.

23.8 Puente la Reina: In the 11th century, Sancho el Fuerte's wife (or perhaps his successor's wife) financed a beautiful **6-arched Romanesque bridge** over the Río Arga, so pilgrims and other travelers on the Roman route could avoid expensive ferrymen and treacherous boat rides. The town of Puente la Reina grew up around the queen's bridge, providing services and commerce for the pilgrims. The middle of the bridge used to have a niche, which held a statue of the Virgin

Unique octagonal church of Eunate

⚠ Alternate: Eunate Church, +2.8km

After leaving the main route in Muruzábel, follow paved roads to the edge of town, continuing on dirt roads until crossing NA-6010 to arrive at the Eunate church. The Camino Aragonés passes here, which returns to the Camino Francés in Óbanos. From Eunate, leave via a dirt track, past a picnic area, and back to the cross Na-6010 and Na-6016 up the hill into Óbanos where it joins the main route at the church.

La Ermita Santa Maria de Eunate
From Basque, meaning "house of 100 doors," call to confirm open hours: 628-872835

The beautiful setting and fascinating mystery of the **Ermita de Santa María de Eunate**, a 13th century octagonal stone church, is well worth the detour of 2.8km. The origins of the church are unknown, though it is thought to be related to the Templars who had an affinity for octagonal churches. The former parochial albergue at Eunate has closed.

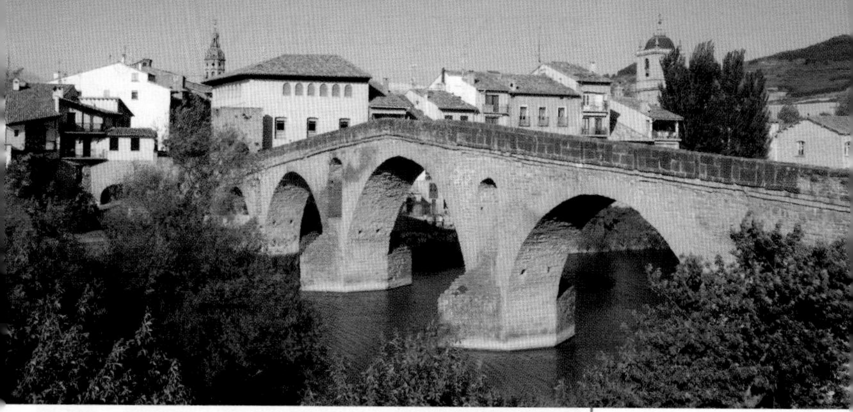

Mary. Legend has it that a *Txori* ("little bird" in Basque) used to come clean the statue's face and was considered a good omen by the town. One story tells that during the Carlist Wars, a count laughed at the *Txori* and made fun of the town's devotion to the bird. Two weeks later, he was defeated in battle and locals believed it to be divine punishment.

23.8 Puente la Reina

Pop. 2,877, Basque: *Gares* "grain," Spanish: "the queen's bridge"

1. **A Padres Reparadores** (par, 96, €5): , Crucifijo 1, 948-340050, noon, all year, nice green yard/garden, credenciales available
2. **A H Albergue Jakue** (46, €12/-/40): , c/Irunbidea 34, 948-341017, noon, Mar 15-Oct, located in hotel
3. **A Amalur** (20, €10): , Cerco Nuevo 3, 696-241175, 11:30am all year
4. **A H Puente** (36, €12/-/34 w/): , Paseo de los Fueros 57, 661-705642, Apr-Nov 15
5. **A Estrella Guía** (6, €12 w/): , Paseo de Los Fueros 34, 622-262431, 1pm Feb-Nov
6. **A Santiago Apostól** (100, €10): , 948-340220, 11am, Apr-Oct, **Camping El Real** at same establishment (€6)
7. **H El Cerco** (-/€75): , c/Rodrigo Ximenez de Rada 36, 948-341269
8. **H Bidean** (-/€55): , c/Mayor 20, 948-340457
9. **H Ganbara** (€25/40 w/): , c/Mayor 86, 948-341186

La Iglesia del Crucifijo was founded in the 12th century by Templars and still displays a 14th-century Y-shaped crucifix brought by a German pilgrim in the Middle Ages. The church was used as barracks during the Carlist wars.

La Iglesia de Santiago demonstrates Mudéjar influence and features a Baroque retablo, which recalls scenes from the life of Santiago, along with a famous statue from Gothic times known as the *beltza Santiago* ("black Santiago" in Basque). Pilgrims were entitled to one night at the Templar's hospital on their way to Santiago, and two nights on the way back. Nesting storks can often be seen on the belfry.

Romanesque bridge of Puente la Reina

5

PUENTE LA REINA TO ESTELLA

21.8km
(13.5mi)

5-6 Hours
Difficulty: ▬□□
P 28%, 6.0km
U 72%, 15.8km

A Albergues:
Mañeru 5.2km
Cirauqui 7.8km
Lorca 13.4km
Villatuerta 18.1km
Estella 21.8km
Ayegui 23.4km
Villamayor 31.0km

Alt. Routes:
Split to Villatuerta (6A Villatuerta to Los Arcos, p. 78)

Scenery after Cirauqui on the way to Estella

Revel in marvelous rolling agricultural views, enter history on a Roman road, discover a wealth of churches in "Estella la bella."

A stage primarily on dirt paths with gently rolling ups and downs, passing through picturesque medieval towns. Authentic stretches of Roman road and a Roman bridge invite walkers to step back in time. Be prepared for little shade and some road noise from A-12 highway around Lorca. A day of beautiful scenery with fields and vineyards.

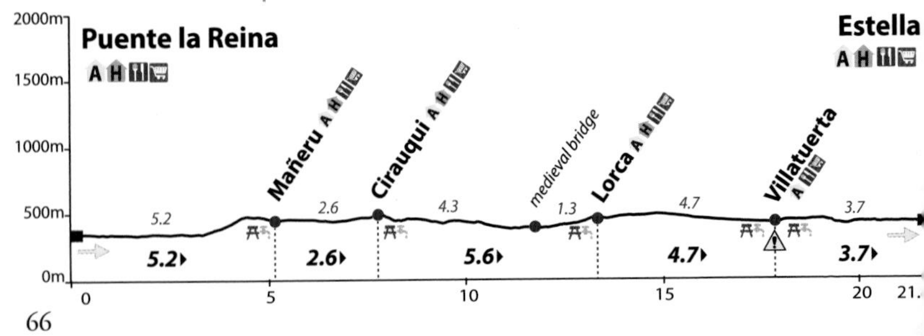

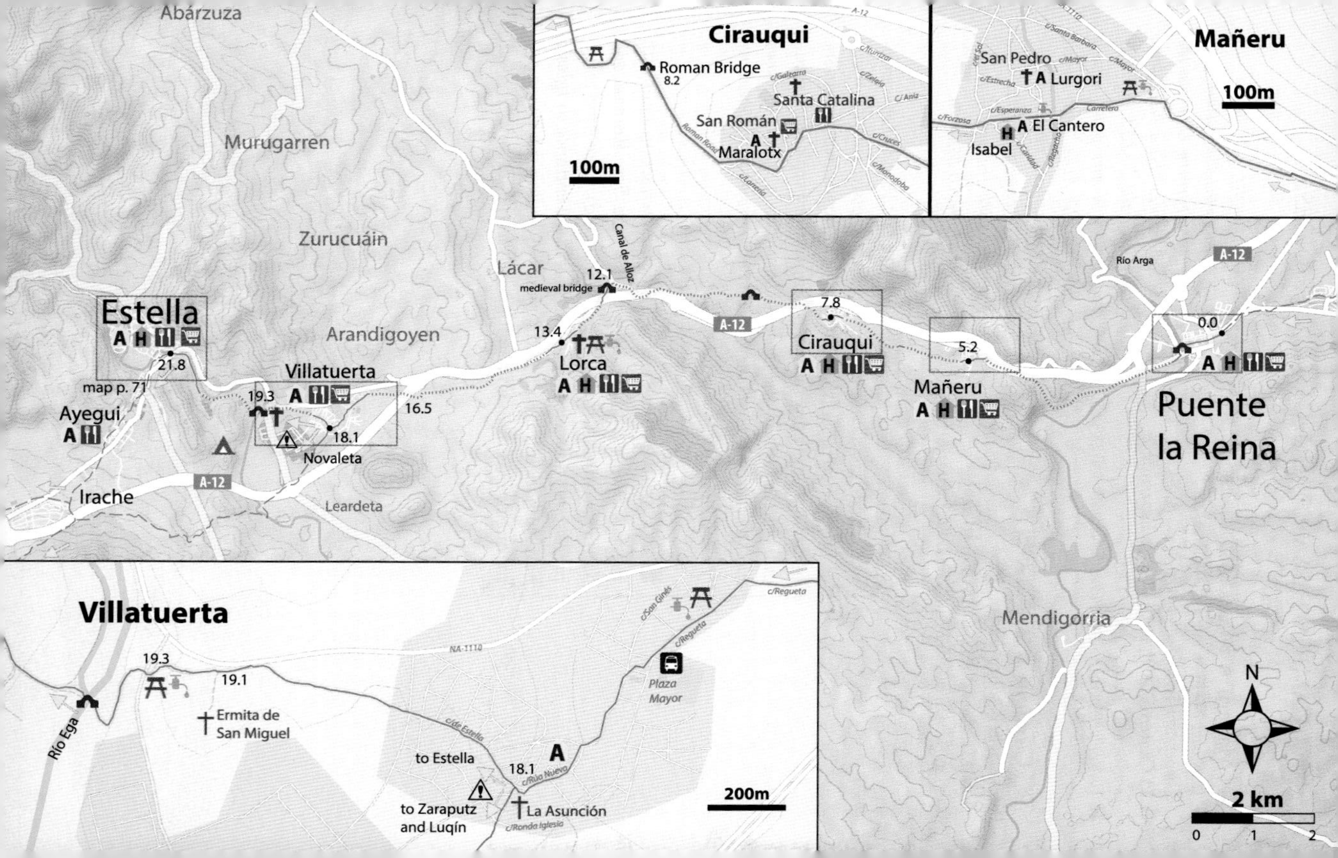

Abárzuza
Murugarren
Zurucuáin
Lácar
Canal de Alloz
12.1
medieval bridge
Estella
A H
21.8
map p. 71
Arandigoyen
Ayegui
A
Villatuerta
A
19.3
16.5
18.1
Novaleta
Irache
A-12
Leardeta
13.4
Lorca
A H
A-12
7.8
Cirauqui
A H
5.2
Mañeru
A H
0.0
A H
Puente
la Reina
Río Arga
Mendigorría
N
2 km
0
1
2
Cirauqui
Roman Bridge
8.2
Santa Catalina
San Román
A
Maralotx
Roman Road
100m
Mañeru
San Pedro
A Lurgori
A El Cantero
H
Isabel
100m
Villatuerta
19.3
19.1
Ermita de
San Miguel
Río Ega
NA-1110
Plaza
Mayor
A
to Estella
18.1
to Zaraputz
and Luqín
La Asunción
200m

5.2 Mañeru A H Pop. 427

A Lurgorri (12, €11): (free), c/Esperanza 5, 686-521174, Apr-Oct

A El Cantero (26, €11): , c/Esperanza 2, 948-342142, May-Oct

H Isabel (-/€38): , c/Caridad 5, 948-340283

7.8 Cirauqui A H

Pop. 505, Basque: "nest of vipers"

A H Maralotx (32, €11/-/40): , c/San Román 30, 678-635208, Mar-Oct

0.0 *Leave Puente la Reina on c/Mayor, crossing over the historic pilgrim bridge, then turning L to pass the Barrio de los Monjas (Nun Neighborhood). Cross over the N-111 highway to leave town on a dirt path, which winds along the Río Arga. After about 1km the track passes a factory and veers uphill to the R through fields and past the ruins of the 13th-century Monasterio de Bargota to reach Mañeru.*

5.2 Mañeru: Pass a 16th-century roadside cross coming into town. Impressive historic houses line the streets displaying coats of arms above the doors. Iglesia de San Pedro from the 18th century replaced a medieval church built by the Order of San Juan (p. 60). *Leave town on a footpath through vineyards and olive groves to the medieval town of Cirauqui.*

7.8 Cirauqui is a quaint medieval town set on a hill with the fascinating 13th-century **Iglesias de San Roman** and **Santa Catalina** (7pm Mass often offered). Take time to appreciate the ornate Mudéjar portal over the entrance to **Iglesia San Roman** and its organic capitals, including the image of a mermaid. Pass through a Gothic arch in the historic city wall

Picturesque Cirauqui perched on a hill

with a self-service stamp under the arch. *Leaving Cirauqui descend via a Roman road to a restored Roman bridge (8.2km). Continue along a dirt path passing under the raised cement aquaduct Canal de Alloz (11.9km) and then over the Río Salado on a medieval bridge (12.1km). The trail then passes under both highways (A-12 and N-111) to enter Lorca.*

Traditional door in Mañeru

13.4 Lorca: The 12th-century **Iglesia de San Salvador** features an 18th-century retablo including a Santiago Peregrino image. The *Codex Calixtinus* says that at Lorca hapless pilgrims would unknowingly water their horses in the poisonous Río Salado. Navarran men would lie in wait to skin the horses once they died. *From Lorca, follow the dirt path parallel to the highway until passing underneath (16.5km) and descending into Villatuerta.*

13.4 Lorca A H

Pop. 135, Arabic: *al-aurque* "battle"

A H **La Bodega del Camino** (36, €8/-/€25-40): W D, c/Placeta 8, 948-541162, May-Oct, groups all year

A H **Albergue de Lorca** (14, €7/-/20): W, c/Mayor 40, 948-541190, Apr-Oct

18.1 Villatuerta: In Villatuerta, the beautiful 14th-century **Iglesia La Asunción** is worth visiting, the retablo illustrates a battle between Moors and Christians. *[Just after the church the ⚠ alternate stage 6A via Zaraputz and Luquín veers to the L, marked by a small sign (p. 78).]*

18.1 Villatuerta A Pop. 1,122

Latin: *vilatorta* "twisted village"

A ☆ **La Casa Mágica** (40, €12): W D, c/Rebote 5, 948-536095, Apr-Oct, beautifully restored building, massage therapy, no bunk beds

Leaving Villatuerta, there is an optional detour to the **Ermita de San Miguel (19.1km, +200m)**, normally open, and the table overflows with handwritten prayers to the saint in many languages. *After a picnic area, an underpass at the highway (19.3km) was precipitated by the death of a Canadian pilgrim in 2002 who was struck by a car (above the underpass there is a memorial made by her husband). Follow a dirt path, which will cross over the Río Ega and enter Estella through a park along the river's shores. Continue straight for the municipal albergue, or cross the stone bridge for other albergues.*

If taking the full alternate stage 6A via Luquín, you'll want to stay overnight in Villatuerta as there are no accommodations until Los Arcos.

21.8 Estella A H Pop. 14,251 Basque *Lizarra:* "old church" Latin *stellae:*

1. A **Municipal** (96, €6): c/de la Rúa 50, 948-550200, all year except Dec/Jan, crowded rooms, outdoor patio area
2. A **San Miguel** (par, 36, don): Mercado Viejo 18, 948-550431, 12:30pm, Apr-Oct, communal meals
3. A **ANFAS** (34, €7): (free), c/Cordeleros 7, 639-011688, noon, May-Sept, employs adults with intellectual disabilities
4. A H **Capuchinos Rocamador** (par, 54, €13-16/-/40): c/Rocamador 6, 948-550549, 11am summer, Jan 7-Dec 23, adjoined to Capuchin convent
5. A H **Oncineda** (youth hostel, 95, €10/-/28): c/Monasterio de Irache 11, 948-555022, Mar 15-Oct 31
6. H **Fonda Izarra** (-/€35): c/Calderería 20, 948-550678
7. H **San Andrés** (-/€32-40): Plaza Santiago 58, 948-554158
8. H **Apartamentos Gebala** (-/€88): Plaza de los Fueros 31, 609-099422
9. H **Cristina** (-/€45): c/Baja Navarra 1, 948-550450
10. H **Chapitel** (€75/95 w/): c/Chapitel 1, 948-551090, massage available
11. H **Hostal El Volante** (€35/59): c/Merkatondoa 2, 948-553957

A H A **Camping Lizarra** (dm €9.80/tent €16.50): Paraje Ordoiz, 948-551733, off rou

"Estella [is] full of good bread and the best wine and meat and fish, and plenty of all good things."

Codex Calixtinus

21.8 Estella: Development began under King Sancho Ramírez in the early 11th century, after a shooting star led to a Virgin Mary statue in a cave (Basílica del Puy houses the statue). Sancho encouraged French settlement and the town flourished with vibrant pilgrim business and agriculture, and textile industries of wool and leather. The town grew wealthy and important religious and civic institutions were built, giving the nickname *Estella la bella* ("Estella the beautiful").

As in Pamplona, ethnic neighborhoods grew up, separating Navarros, Francos and Jews. By the 14th century, Jews made up 10% of the population. In 1328 much of the Jewish community was massacred in a riot, and the rest were forced to convert in the 15th-century Inquisition. The Black Plague halved the population of Estella in the 14th century.

Houses line the Ega River in Estella

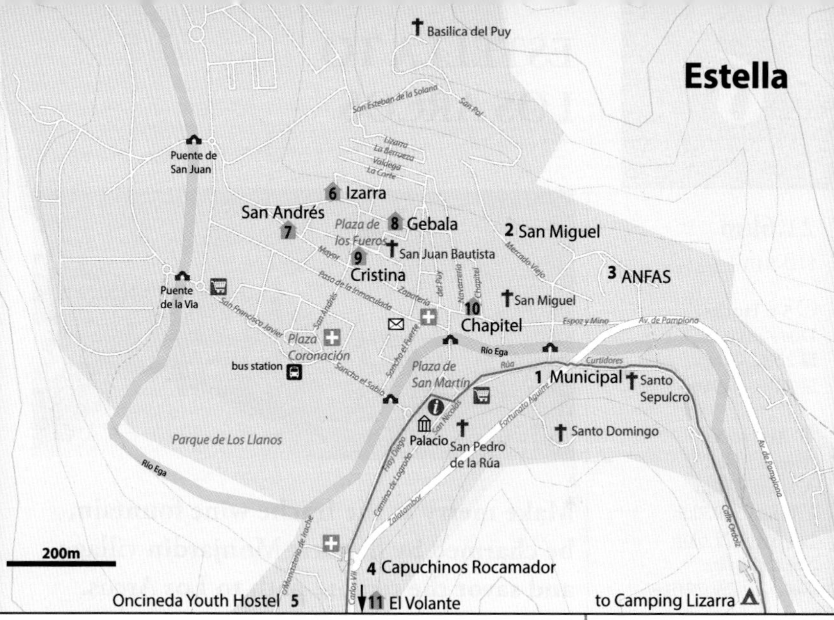

Historic Churches and Buildings:

- **Iglesia de Santo Sepulcro**: On the R as you enter town, this façade shows Santiago among the apostles.
- **Palacio de los Reyes de Navarra/Museo Gustavo de Maeztu**: Tu-F 9:30am-1pm, S/Su 11am-2pm Interesting example of civil Romanesque architecture, note the fine capitals that depict deadly sins and the battle of Roland and Ferragut (p. 92).
- **Iglesia de San Pedro de la Rúa**: An impressive 12/13th-century fortified church that contains important relics, such as a piece of the true cross and Saint Andrew's shoulder bone.
- **Iglesia de San Miguel**: A fortress-like 12th-century church with a spectacular north portal.
- **Iglesia de San Juan Bautista**: Built by Sancho el Fuerte and containing images of Santiago Peregrino.
- **Basílica del Puy**: Built on the spot that legend holds a Virgin was found in 1085; the wooden silver-covered statue is still on display within.

Estella
Aug: Patron saint San Andrés with running of the bulls
May 25: Virgen del Puy with traditional dances
Thursday is market day.
Suckling pig is a local delicacy (*gorrín asado*).

6

ESTELLA TO LOS ARCOS

21.6km
(13.4mi)

5-6 HOURS
DIFFICULTY:
P 22%, 4.7km
U 78%, 16.9km

A ALBERGUES:
Ayegui 1.6km
Azqueta 7.4km
Villamayor 9.2km
Los Arcos 21.6km
Sansol 28.4km
Torres del Río 29.3km

ALT. STAGE 6A:
Villatuerta or Irache to Los Arcos, 23.4km (p. 78)

6A ALTERNATE:
P 8%, 1.9km
U 92%, 21.5km

A ALT. ALBERGUES:
Los Arcos 23.4km

Fuente de los Moros outside of Villamayor

Make merry at the Irache wine fountain, be charmed by historic Monjardín village and savor the remote path to Los Arcos.

More rolling red hills and vineyards lead to a place of Camino legend, the Irache wine fountain. Villamayor de Monjardín provides a welcome halfway stop, with an imposing castle on the hilltop above and a historic fountain at the entrance. The last 12km are remote and beautiful, but be prepared for no services and little shade. The alternate route via Luquín offers a more remote but demanding path with hilltop views, which rejoins the main trail after Villamayor.

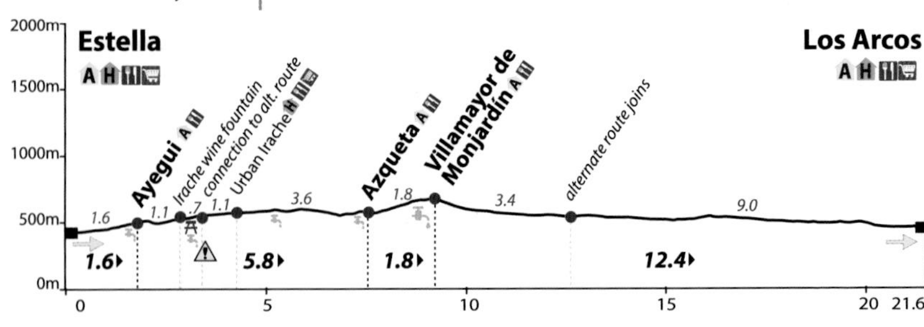

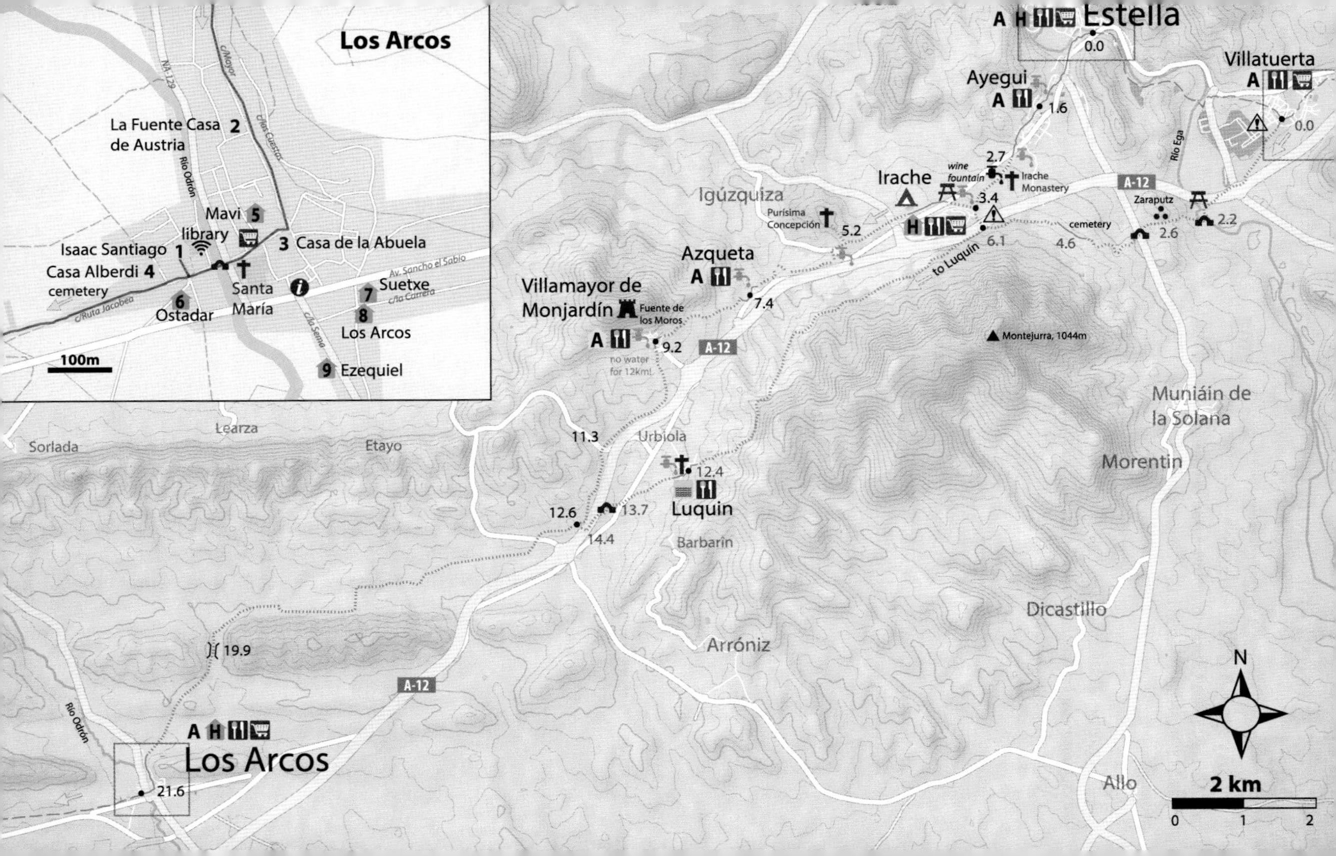
Los Arcos
La Fuente Casa de Austria 2
Mavi 5
library
Isaac Santiago 1
3 Casa de la Abuela
Casa Alberdi 4
cemetery
Santa María
6 Ostadar
7 Suetxe
8 Los Arcos
9 Ezequiel
NA-129
Río Odrón
c/Mayor
c/las Cuestas
Av. Sancho el Sabio
c/la Carrera
c/Ruta Jacobea
c/la Sema
100m
A H Estella
0.0
Villatuerta
0.0
Ayegui
1.6
2.7
wine fountain
Irache Monastery
Irache
3.4
Igúzquiza
Purísima Concepción
5.2
6.1
cemetery
4.6
Zaraputz
2.6
2.2
Río Ega
A-12
to Luquin
Azqueta
7.4
Villamayor de Monjardín
Fuente de los Moros
9.2
no water for 12km!
Montejurra, 1044m
Muniáin de la Solana
Morentin
Learza
Sorlada
Etayo
11.3
Urbiola
12.4
Luquin
12.6
13.7
14.4
Barbarín
Dicastillo
Arróniz
19.9
Los Arcos
21.6
Río Odrón
Allo
N
2 km
0
1
2

1.6 Ayegui Pop. 1,932
Albergue San Cipriano (muni, 80 mats, €6): , 948-554331, 1pm all year

3.8 Irache Pop. 426
Camping Iratxe (cabins €28-95): , Av. Prado de Irache 14, 948-555555

0.0 *The way out of Estella is well-marked along c/Rúa to c/San Nicolás, straight through the first roundabout, and to the R at the next roundabout. Take c/Camino uphill toward* ***Ayegui (1.6km)*** *near the albergue, and as you descend out of town the impressive Irache monastery looms ahead.*

2.7 The Irache monastery dates back to the year 958, with a pilgrim hospital added in the 11th century and cloisters added in the 16th and 17th centuries. The historic buildingwas scheduled to become a luxury Parador hotel before the economic downturn. *Leave town and cross N-1110 onto a dirt path, which will lead you to* ***Irache Winery (2.7km)****, where a free wine fountain delights visitors 8am-8pm, and festivities can even be watched via webcam. Wine museum is open 10am-2pm. [Just after the winery, there is an opportunity to cross over to the Luquín alternate route (p. 78) or to return from that route to the main route. The main route turns R, while*

The plaque on the wall at the wine fountain reads: *"Pilgrim, if you wish to arrive at Santiago full of strength and vitality, have a drink of this great wine and make a toast to happiness."*

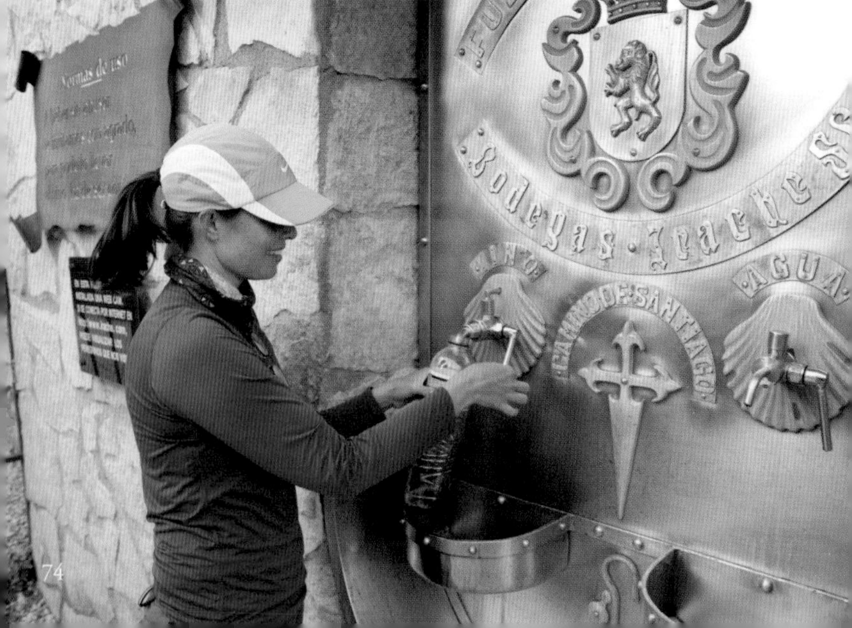

Irache Wine Fountain

the alternate route continues straight. Anticipate this junction as the intuitive turn is the more remote alternate route 6A described on p. 78.]

Re-cross N-111a and pass by ***Camping Iratxe (3.8km)*** *before walking through lovely shaded forests on a dirt path. Pass through* ***Azqueta (7.4km)****, and continue on dirt road through expansive agricultural land past the* ***Fuente de los Moros (8.8km)****, a Gothic fountain associated with the moors (rebuilt from an earlier fountain or simply misattributed).*

9.2 Villamayor de Monjardín is a picturesque small town with a popular café for a pick-me-up afternoon coffee or snack. Romanesque **Iglesia de San Andrés** contains a processional cross from the year 1200. Legend has it that Charlemagne battled for the town and wrested it from the Muslim army. Charlemange asked God which of his soldiers would die in the battle, and a red cross marked the heads of 150 soldiers. Charlemagne had all the ill-fated men stay back at their encampment, but he returned to find they had all died in a fire.

Fuente de los Moros near Villamayor

7.4 Azqueta A

A La Perla Negra (7, €27 w/ and dinner): , c/Carrera 18, 627-114797

9.2 Villamayor de Monjardín A H

Pop. 139, Latin: "Mount García" for Sancho Garcés, first king of Pamplona

A Hogar de Monjardín (assoc, 25, €8): , across from San Andrés church, 948-537136, 2pm Apr-Oct, fireplace, run by Dutch Christian association

A H Villamayor de Monjardín (20, €15/-/40 w/): (free), c/Mayor 1, 677-660586, 2pm, Mar-Nov

H Casa Rural Montedeio (€35/45): , c/Mayor 17, 676-187473

Cyclists on the path between Villamayor and Los Arcos

Leaving Los Arcos

On the way out of town, the large warehouse visible below is Castillo de Monjardín winery, known for its whites. The **Castillo de San Esteban** looming over the town can be visited via a small road (ask at the bar for the key to the castle if you have the energy to make the trek). ⚠ Be sure to rest and fill up water in Monjardín, as the next 12km have little shade and no services. While the terrain is not very challenging, the town of Los Arcos is tucked away in a valley and not visible until arriving, this section can feel interminable!

Continue on dirt paths, crossing a paved road (11.3km), and meet the junction of the ***alternate from Luquín (12.6km)*** *near a highway underpass. Take dirt paths through the beautiful valley to cross a small pass (19.9km). At the entrance to Los Arcos (20.7km) is a rest stop with shelter and extensive vending machines. The municipal albergue (21.6km) is just beyond the church across the river.*

21.6 Los Arcos A H

Pop. 1,244, Spanish: "the bows"

Plaza Fueros, ✆948-640077, at library

1. A **Isaac Santiago** (muni, 70, €6): c/San Lázaro, ✆948-441091, 12pm, Apr-Oct, garden, crowded rooms
2. A H **La Fuente Casa de Austria** (54, €9-11/-/30): W D, Travesía del Estanco 5, ✆948-640797, 1pm, Feb-Dec 15
3. A H ☆ **Casa de la Abuela** (32, €10/-/35-45): W D (free), Plaza de la Fruta 8, ✆948-640250, 12pm Mar-Oct, restored house of owner's grandmother
4. A H **Casa Alberdi** (30, €10/-/36): W, c/Hortal 3, ✆650-965250, 2pm all year
5. H **Pensión Mavi** (€30/50): c/del Medio 7, ✆608-934222
6. H **Pensión Ostadar** (€35/50): c/San Lázaro 9, ✆649-961440
7. H **Suetxe** (€49/55): c/Carramendavia, ✆618-724437
8. H **Pensión Los Arcos** (€40/50): W D, c/la Carrera 8, ✆608-585153
9. H **Hostal Ezequiel** (-/€50-70): c/La Serna, ✆948-640107

21.6 **Los Arcos** occupies an ideal location by the Río Odrón and at the crossroads of two ancient trade routes, and was once a Roman city (Curnonium). The current name comes from a battle in 914 when three Sanchos (the kings of Navarra, Castilla and Aragon) fought over the town. The Navarran army won with the help of their excellent archers, therefore the coat of arms of the city contains bows (*arcos*) and arrows. In medieval times, the city was a place for toll collection and changing money. Los Arcos flourished as a market town, becoming quite wealthy with all this pilgrim commerce.

Luminous retablo of Iglesia de Santa María de Los Arcos

The main historical site is the **Iglesia de Santa María de la Asunción**, which contains one of the most ornate retablos on the entire Camino Francés. *Santa María de los Arcos* occupies the central position; look also for Santiago (with crystal eyes) as well as a pelican (a symbol of Jesus' sacrifice often seen in religious art). A shaft of sunlight naturally illuminated the retablo once a year in the summer.

Pilgrims eating together at Casa de la Abuela

Los Arcos
Spring: Small bull-running festival
August 14-20: Santa María patron saint day
Saturday is market day.
Rosquillos de Los Arcos are a local specialty of small donuts made with orange juice.

⚠ Alternate Stage 6A: Luquín Route

Villatuerta to Los Arcos (via Irache & Luquín), 23.4km

This waymarked alternate route follows an earlier pilgrim way, which later was routed through Estella as pilgrim services developed there. This route is more remote with fewer walkers and services. A short path (+350m) connects this route to the main route near the Irache Monastery (p. 74), and so it is possible to switch back to the main route there, or to sleep in Estella and take the Luquín detour from Irache. If starting this route from Villatuerta, there are no accommodations for 23.4km until Los Arcos, unless you return to the main route at Irache. Distances noted are cumulative from the split in Villatuerta.

This alternate route via Luquín is 1.8km longer than stage 6 from Estella to Los Arcos with more elevation change.

The only chances to refill water between Villatuerta and Los Arcos are near Irache (6.2km, slightly off-route) and Luquín (12.3km).

Maps for this route are primarily on the stage 6 map, with the first junction in detail on the Villatuerta map (p. 67).

0.0 Villatuerta: *In Villatuerta, turn L at the church toward Zarapuz (note the split shown on the blazes on the building after the church). Leave town through an industrial area on dirt paths through agricultural fields fed by cement canals. After two underpasses, cross a bridge over the* ***Río Ega (2.2km)****; turn R to cross the bridge (not well marked), and R again immediately on a dirt path directly after the bridge. The path will lead by agricultural fields and uphill to the ∴ ruins of Zarapuz.*

2.6 Zarapuz was a 15th-century medieval pilgrim albergue. *From the ruins, the trail continues upward to offer a remarkable view of Estella. Cross the highway on a* ***bridge (3.3km)****, and curve R on 4X4 tracks through vineyards. At a paved road by a cemetery, continue straight (4.6km, not marked), then turn L on a dirt path (5.0km, well marked) and take a quick R toward the silver water tower. Turn R at the next trail marker and pass between the line of trees on L and wheat field on R. Cross a paved road (5.4km) and enter a forested area. At the* ***signpost for Irache and Los Arcos (6.1km)****, either continue to the L to Los Arcos or take the underpass down to Irache to join the more traditional route (and visit the wine fountain, +1km).*

Medieval pilgrim hospital ruins at Zarapuz

Continue following waymarks toward Los Arcos through forest. After leaving the forest, turn L on a dirt road (7.7km) and note the view of Monjardín castle ahead. When the dirt road curves to the R, continue straight on smaller dirt 4X4 (8.1km). Turn L on dirt one-lane road and leave the forest to walk along the line of trees for open valley views (8.9km). Continue uphill to a ridge with some miscellaneous ruins (10.8km), and follow the footpath straight ahead downhill to the village of Luquín.

The winding trail of the Luquín route

12.4 Luquín Pop. 138

Luquín is home to the medieval Iglesia de San Martín Obispo and 18th-century Basílica de Nuestra Señora de los Remedio. The basilica houses two images of the Virgin Mary that, according to legend, were found by a farmer plowing his field. The images were initially split up in order to house one in Luquín and one in nearby Villamayor. However, the second virgin kept reappearing in Luquín with a drop of blood, so the towns decided the two must remain together.

Pass by the Plaza de los Fueros past a natural spring, the municipal pool and a café. Cross the paved road leaving town (c/Carretera) and go straight on a cement road, which turns to dirt as you leave town. Turn R at the sign for "10.2km to Los Arcos" (13.1km), follow markings across a paved road and over a small ***bridge (13.7km)****. Turn L on a gravel road parallel to the highway and use the underpass to the R (14.3km). Rejoin the main trail at* ***signpost "9km to Los Arcos" (14.4km)*** *and turn L to continue for the remaining 9km to Los Arcos on the main route on stage 6, p. 74.*

7

LOS ARCOS TO LOGROÑO

27.6km
(17.1mi)

7-8 Hours
Difficulty:
P 41%, 11.4km
U 59%, 16.2km

A Albergues:
Sansol 6.8km
Torres del Río 7.7km
Viana 18.4km
Logroño 27.6km
Navarrete 40.2km

A pilgrim approaches the picturesque medieval town of Sansol

Wander through vineyards and fields of golden wheat, visit medieval villages and sample the wine of la Rioja.

Endless fields of golden wheat lead to the hilltop medieval towns of Sansol and Torres del Río. The rolling hills to Viana have a remote feel with little shade and no services. From Viana to Logroño the trail passes through a bird-watching area and enters into the autonomous region of La Rioja, best known for its superlative red wine.

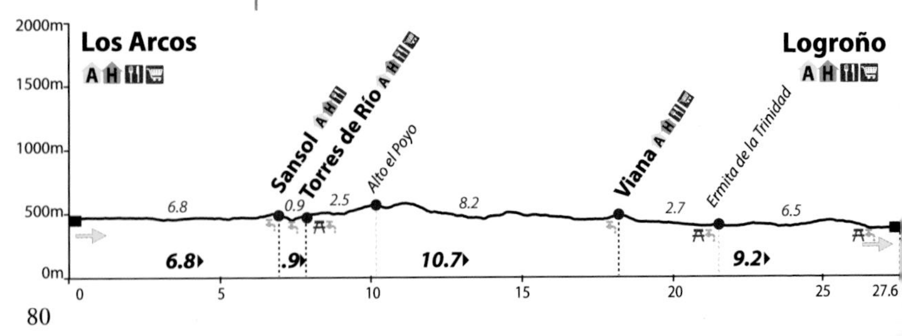

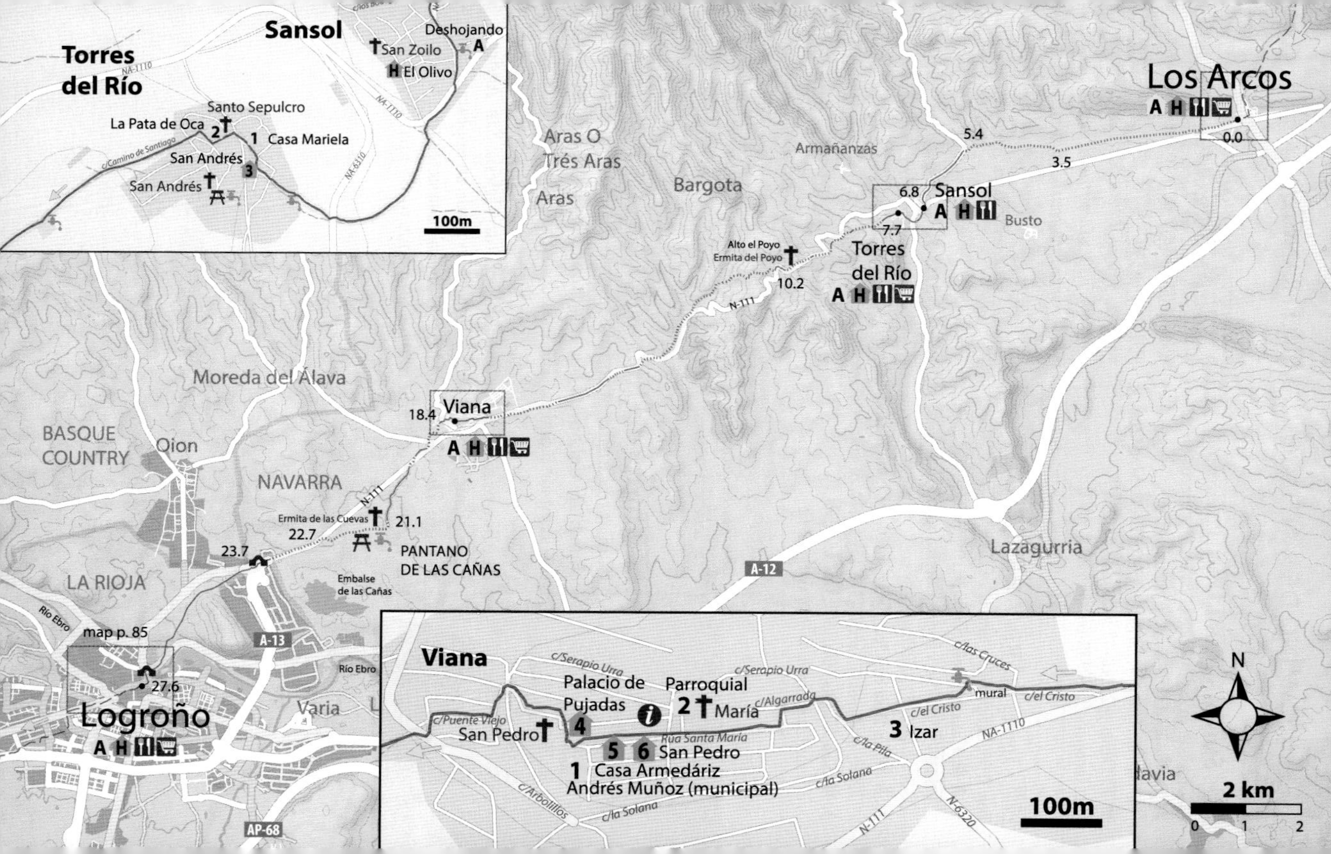

Torres del Río
Sansol
Deshojando
San Zoilo
El Olivo
Santo Sepulcro
La Pata de Oca
Casa Mariela
San Andrés
San Andrés
c/Camino de Santiago
NA-1110
NA-6310
100m
Los Arcos
0.0
5.4
3.5
Armañanzas
Aras O Trés Aras
Aras
Bargota
6.8
Sansol
7.7
Busto
Alto el Poyo
Ermita del Poyo
Torres del Río
10.2
N-111
Moreda del Álava
Viana
18.4
BASQUE COUNTRY
Oion
NAVARRA
Ermita de las Cuevas
21.1
22.7
23.7
PANTANO DE LAS CAÑAS
Embalse de las Cañas
Lazagurria
A-12
LA RIOJA
Río Ebro
map p. 85
A-13
Río Ebro
27.6
Logroño
Varia
AP-68
Viana
c/Serapio Urra
c/Serapio Urra
c/las Cruces
Palacio de Pujadas
Parroquial María
c/Algarrada
mural
c/el Cristo
c/el Cristo
c/Puente Viejo
San Pedro
Rúa Santa María
San Pedro
3 Izar
NA-1110
c/la Pila
1 Casa Armedáriz
Andrés Muñoz (municipal)
c/la Solana
c/Arbolillos
c/la Solana
N-111
N-6320
100m
N
2 km
0
1
2

6.8 Sansol Pop. 112, S. Zoilo, a Cordoban martyr under Diocletian persecution

- **A Deshojando** (24, €10), c/Barrio Nuevo 4, 948-648473, Mar-Oct
- **H El Olivo** (€25/40-45 w/): c/Taconera 9, 948-648345

7.7 Torres del Río
Pop. 156, Spanish: "towers of the river"

1. **A H Casa Mariela** (50, €10/-/35): Plaza Padre Valeriano Ordóñez 6, 948-648251, 10am, all year
2. **A H La Pata de Oca** (32, €10/-/60): c/Mayor 5, 948-378457, all year
3. **H San Andrés** (€40/60): c/Jesús Ordoñez 6, 948-648472

0.0 *From the municipal albergue of Los Arcos, turn R and leave town on wide dirt path past a cemetery (note cryptic inscription, "I once was what you are, you will be what I am,") and through vast vineyards. Turn R at a well-marked footpath (3.5km) before turning L on a paved road (5.4km) into the village of Sansol.*

6.8 Sansol has the simple Iglesia de San Zoilo, with a marvelous view of Torres del Río. *Cross the paved road outside of Sansol, and turn R to walk along the road. Turn L off of the main road (7.0km) onto a smaller road, then take a quick R onto a paved footpath, which later becomes dirt. Enter the outskirts of adjacent Torres del Río, where a natural spring beckons pilgrims to refreshment.*

Iglesia del Santo Sepulcro in Torres del Río

7.7 Torres del Río: Visit the unusual octagonal church (similar to Eunate) of **Santo Sepulcro** (€1). The origins of the church are unknown, but it is thought to be associated with the Templar Knights. The outside corbels show animals and plants, while the interior altar niche resembles a *mihrab*, or Muslim prayer niche. The 16th-century Iglesia San Andres has a picnic area and water. Torres also made an appearance in the film *The Way*, where Martin Sheen's character tries to stay in the house of Ramón, who turns out to be mentally ill (a

true story adapted from Jack Hitt's Camino memoir *Off the Road*). *Leaving town, pass a cemetery with water, and the trail becomes unpaved with no shade. Continue on dirt paths near a paved road, past the hermitage at Alto el Poyo (10.2km).*

10.2 **Alto el Poyo**: **Capilla de la Virgen del Poyo** contains a statue of Mary that was said to continue returning to this spot even after being relocated many times. *Follow mostly dirt paths through rolling hills and vineyards, eventually along N-111 into Viana, passing a mural of the pilgrimage road. Take c/Algorrada through an arch to Rúa de Santa Maria and to the café-lined Plaza de Fueros.*

Hikers between Torres del Río and Sansol

18.4 **Viana**, a delightful walled town with a bustling downtown and many attractive cafés, is best known as the final resting place of Navarran hero Cesare Borgia who died at the siege of Viana. Visit **Iglesia de Santa María de la Asunción**, with a retablo of Santiago in the ambulatory. Ruins of 13th-century **Iglesia de San Pedro** have been turned into an interesting municipal park with Gothic architecture. *Leaving Viana on c/Fuente Vieja, the trail continues through the pleasant wetlands of Pantano de las Cañas.*

18.4 **Viana** A H Pop. 4,018

1. A **Andrés Muñoz** (muni, 54 in triple bunks, €8): K W D @, c/Ruinas de San Pedro, 948-645530, Mar 15-Oct, call in winter
2. A **Parroquial de Viana** (par, 15 mats, don): K, Plaza de los Fueros, 948-645037, communal meals, simple and caring, June-Sept
3. A H **Izar** (44, €8-10/-/30): K W D @, c/El Cristo 6, 660-071349, noon Mar-Nov
4. H **Palacio de Pujadas** (€60/80 w/, pilgrim rate): @, c/Navarro Villoslada 30, 948-646464
5. H **Casa Armendáriz** (-/€40): c/Navarro Villoslada 19, 948-645078
6. H **San Pedro** (€30/40): , c/Medio San Pedro 13, 948-645927

21.1 **Pantano de las Cañas** is an important bird migrtion area well known for bird watching. Pass the inviting chapel of the **Ermita de la Trinidad de las Cuevas (21.1km)** with picnic area. *The natural path soon turns to asphalt and joins N-111 (22.7km) through an industrial area. Pass the sign "2km to Logroño," which is also the boundary of entering* ***La Rioja region (23.7km)****. On the outskirts of Logroño, a classic Camino character named Doña Felisa used to set up a table by the Camino that offered "higos, agua y amor" ("figs, water and love"—the inscription on her stamp) to passing pilgrims. She died in 2003, but her daughter carries on the tradition. Cross the long 19th-century* ***Puente de Piedra (27.3km)*** *over the Río Ebro to enter Logroño. The bridge was originally built in the 11th century by Santo Domingo de la Calzada (p. 96) and rebuilt by his disciple San Juan de Ortega (p. 108).*

Just before the bridge, on the L is a **pilgrim information office** w/lockers and maps. (Nov-Mar M-Sa 12-4pm, Apr-Oct 9am-2pm)

Logroño
Sept: Fiesta de San Mateo, a wine festival featuring grape crushing exhibitions

27.6 **Logroño** is the capital of the winemaking region of La Rioja. With its strategic location on the banks of the Río Ebro and right along the border between Aragón, Navarra and Castile y León, it's no wonder why Logroño was a much fought-over commodity. Constant warfare may be a reason that practically nothing remains of the many medieval pilgrim hospitals. Logroño is mentioned in pilgrim records as a place where a duty of two *reales* was collected.

The main churches to visit are **Iglesia de Santa María la Redonda** ("Saint Mary the Round"), with Baroque façade and stork-topped spires. **Iglesia de San Bartolomé** from the 13th century and **Iglesia de Santiago el Real**, with an impressive 17th-century Santiago Matamoros above the entrance and numerous Santiago images within. On the sidewalk just before Iglesia de Santiago, there is a large game called *Juego de Oca,* which is similar to Chutes and Ladders. *Calle Laurel* is the nightlife zone with over 60 bars and restaurants, locally known as

Santiago Matamoros at Iglesia de Santiago in Logroño

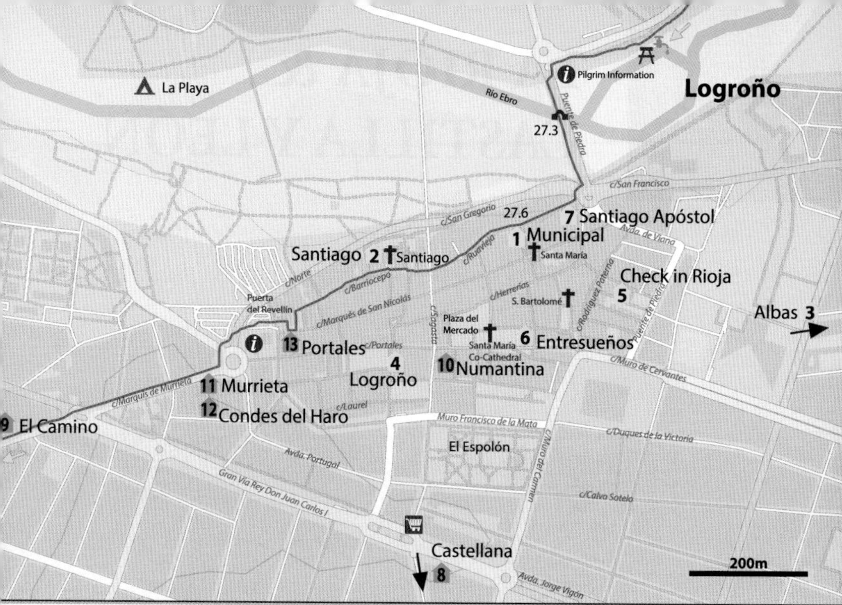

7.6 **Logroño** A H Pop. 152,641, Celtic-Latin, *ilo Gronnio*: "ford/pass"

A **Municipal** (68, €7): Ruavieja 32, 941-248686, Mar-Oct, crowded & stuffy, courtyard with foot pool

A **Iglesia de Santiago** (par, 30, don): c/Barriocepo 6, 941-209501, all year, comm. meals

A **Albas** (22, €12): Pl. Martínez Flamarique 4, 941-700832, 11am all year

A H **Logroño** (48, €10/30/40): c/Capitán Gallarza 10, 941-254226

A **Check In Rioja** (30, €12): c/Los Baños 2, 941-272329, 1pm Mar-Oct

A H **Hostel Entresueños** (youth hostel, 90, €10/-/38): c/Portales 12, 941-271334

A H **Santiago Apóstol** (78, €10/-/30): c/Ruavieja 42, 941-256976, all year

H **Castellana** (-/€35): c/San Anton 17, 941-251369

H **El Camino** (€20/40): Industria 2, 618-655000

H **Numantina** (€36/59): c/Sagasta 4, 941-251411

H **Hotel Murrieta** (-/€60): Marqués de Murrieta 1, 941-224150

H **Condes de Haro** (-/€60): Saturnino Ulargui 6, 941-208500

H **Sercotel Portales** (-/€60): Portales 85, 941-502794

H **La Playa** (bungalows, dbl €50, tent €12): Av. de la Playa 6, 941-252253, +850m

"*la senda de los elefantes*" (the elephant walk), since sampling wine in too many establishments may have you walking out on all fours. The town of Clavijo, where the mythical Battle of Clavijo took place, is located about 16km from Logroño and makes an interesting side trip by bus.

8-12 LA RIOJA & CASTILLA Y LEÓN

El Cid
Rodrigo Díaz de Vivar was a medieval Spanish military leader born near Burgos in 1043, now considered the national hero of Spain. His nickname, El Cid, means "the master." Many legends tell of his exploits in battle along with his trusty warhorse Babieca and his sword, Tizona. His exploits are extolled in *El Cantar de Mio Cid*, one of the earliest examples of Spanish epic poetry.

Highlights include beautiful vineyards, superlative wine and extensive sections of Roman road.

Shortly after Viana, the Camino enters the autonomous region of La Rioja and its capital, Logroño. The climate becomes more Mediterranean in La Rioja, and the deep red earth is ideal for the cultivation of wine grapes. The region has produced wine since the time of the Romans, and was improved by French immigrants who relocated here after their vines were devastated by the Phylloxera blight.

While white and rosé wines are also produced, of the 250 million liters (66 millions gallons) produced annually, 85% are reds, especially from the Tempranilla grape. La Rioja has one of the highest per capita incomes in Spain, in part thanks to its successful wine industry, with over 500 wineries in commission.

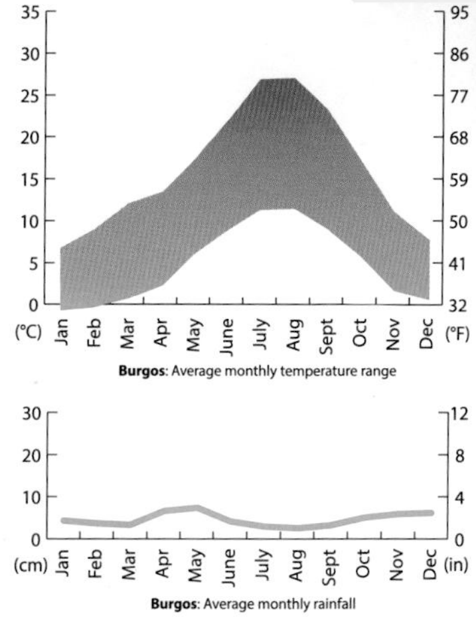

Burgos: Average monthly temperature range

30
20
10
0
(cm)
12
8
4
0
(in)
Jan Feb Mar Apr May June July Aug Sept Oct Nov Dec

Burgos: Average monthly rainfall

There are four classifications of Riojan wine: *Rioja* is the youngest and aged less than one year; *Crianza* is aged at least 2 with at least 1 in oak barrels, *Rioja Reserva* is aged at least 3 years with 1 in oak barrels, and *Rioja Gran Reserva* is aged at least 2 years in oak and 3 in the bottle.

The climate is also amenable to wheat, olives and vegetables, particularly the plump stalks of white asparagus common to the region. In spring and summer, huge storks seem to make their nest on every available church spire. Local culinary specialties include potato stew with spicy *chorizo* sausage, and *cordero lechal*, thick slices of young lamb roasted over a fire with grapevine in the fire for a smoky flavor. Baked apples and peaches in wine sauce are both popular desserts.

Shortly after Grañon, the trail enters Castilla y León, the largest autonomous region in Spain in which almost exactly half of the Camino Francés is located. With its large size of over 94,000km² and population of over 2.5 million, the region is very diverse. In this geographic section, the Camino climbs the scrubby Oca mountains by historic San Juan de Ortega monastery and passes by the prehistoric site of Atapuerca to enter Burgos. The Camino stays in Castilla y León until crossing into Galicia just before O Cebreiro (p. 208).

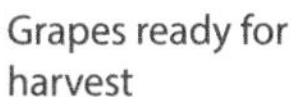
Grapes ready for harvest

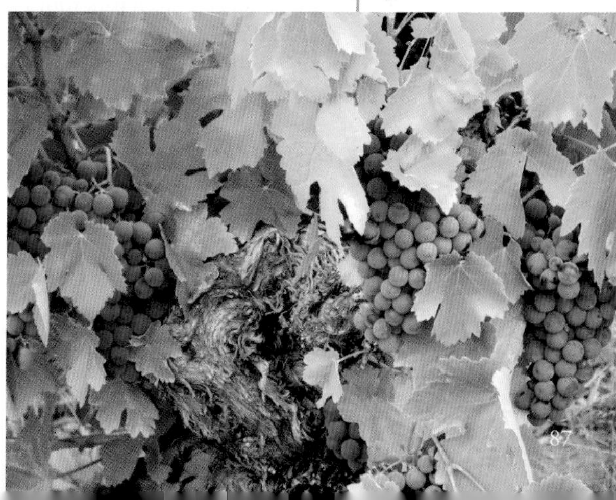

Red earth vineyard views in La Rioja (opposite)

8

LOGROÑO TO NÁJERA

29.6km
(18.4mi)

7-9 Hours
Difficulty:
P 40%, 11.9km
U 60%, 17.7km

A Albergues:
Navarrete 12.6km
Ventosa 19.4km
Nájera 29.6km
Azofra 35.4km

Golden wheat between Navarrete and Ventosa

Stroll through a pleasant reservoir park, peek in the church of Navarrete with its spectacular golden retablo, lounge by the river of Nájera.

A rolling stage with a mix of natural walking paths and sections on or close to roads. After Logroño, there is a pleasant stretch through a green park with a reservoir lake. The path is close to the highway between Navarrete and Ventosa and the approach to Nájera is decidedly industrial, but before Nájera some classic Rioja red earth vineyards can be seen.

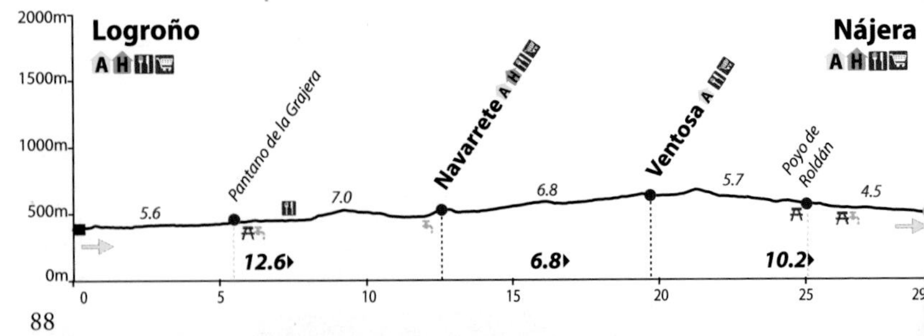

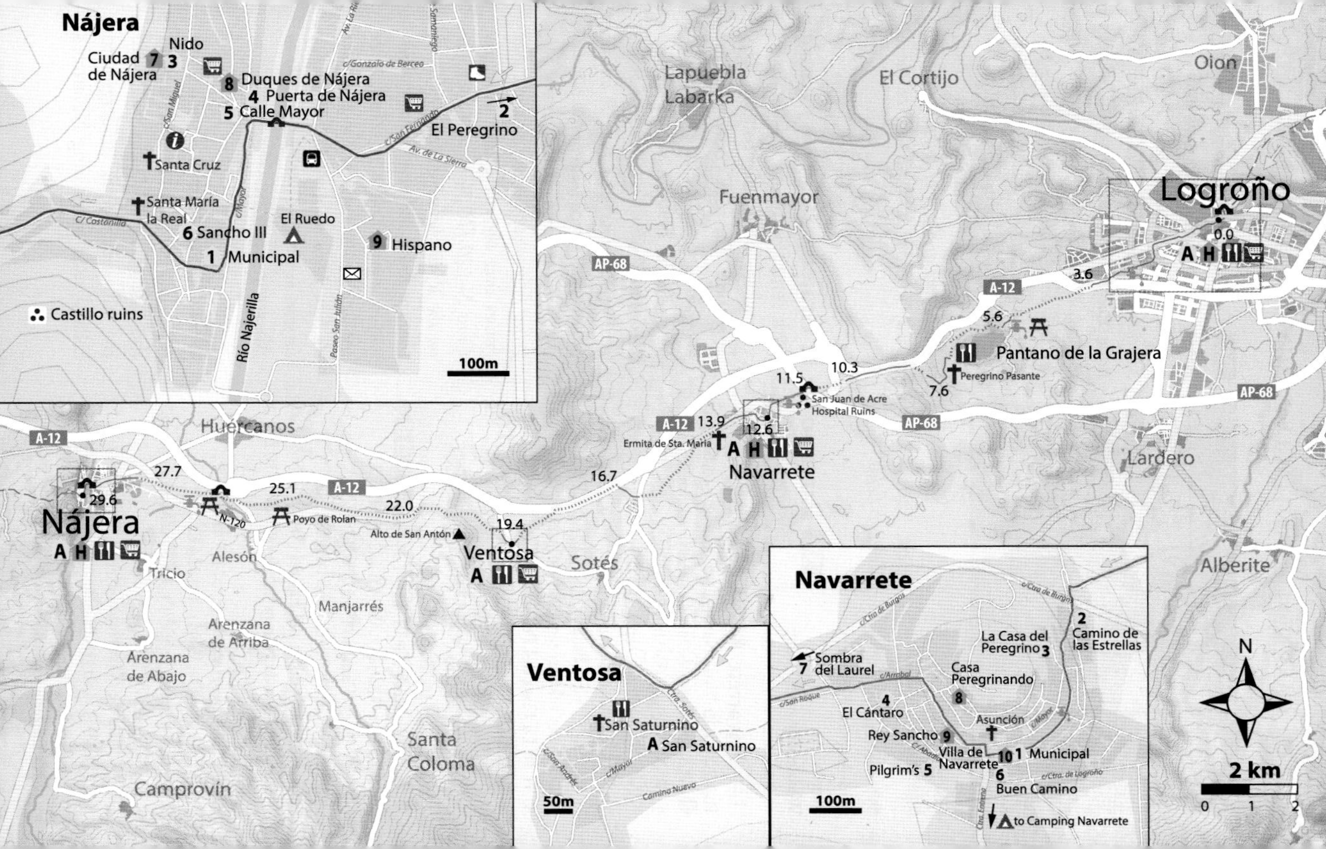
Nájera
Ciudad de Nájera 7
Nido 3
8 Duques de Nájera
4 Puerta de Nájera
5 Calle Mayor
El Peregrino
2
Santa Cruz
Santa María la Real
6 Sancho III
1 Municipal
El Ruedo
9 Hispano
Castillo ruins
Río Najerilla
c/Gonzalo de Berceo
c/San Miguel
c/San Fernando
Av. de La Sierra
c/Mayor
C/ Costanilla
Paseo San Julián
100m
Lapuebla Labarka
El Cortijo
Oion
Fuenmayor
Logroño
0.0
3.6
5.6
7.6
10.3
11.5
12.6
13.9
16.7
19.4
22.0
25.1
27.7
29.6
A-12
AP-68
N-120
Pantano de la Grajera
Peregrino Pasante
San Juan de Acre Hospital Ruins
Ermita de Sta. María
Navarrete
Lardero
Alberite
Huércanos
Nájera
Poyo de Rolan
Alto de San Antón
Ventosa
Sotés
Alesón
Tricio
Manjarrés
Arenzana de Arriba
Arenzana de Abajo
Santa Coloma
Camprovín
Ventosa
San Saturnino
A San Saturnino
Ctra. Sotés
c/Mayor
c/San Andrés
Camino Nuevo
50m
Navarrete
2 Camino de las Estrellas
La Casa del Peregrino 3
7 Sombra del Laurel
Casa Peregrinando
8
4 El Cántaro
Asunción
Rey Sancho 9
Villa de Navarrete 10
1 Municipal
Pilgrim's 5
6 Buen Camino
to Camping Navarrete
c/Ctra. de Burgos
c/Arrabal
c/San Roque
c/Mayor
c/Ctra. de Logroño
100m
N
2 km
0 1 2

Golden retablo in Iglesia de la Asunción

Navarrete:
Mid-August: Fiesta del Virgen
Wednesday market day.

0.0 *Leave Logroño (map p. 85) by following brass inlaid scallop shells along the sidewalk on c/Ruavieja past Iglesia de Santiago and leave the Old City via the stone Puerta de Revellín arch (0.4km), the only remaining original entryway to the Old City. Walk L across the parking lot to the roundabout, and go R on c/Marqués de Murrieta. Turn L on c/Duques de Nájera (1.6km). Cross over the train tracks (2km) and out of town through a park. Pass under the highway (3.6km) and split off to the L through fields.*

5.6 Pantano de la Grajera: Soon enter a wetland park centered around a water reservoir where locals often fish on a lazy afternoon. The park contains picnic areas, an inexpensive café and public WC. *Reach **Ermita del Peregrino Pasante (7.6km)**, "Hermitage of the Passing Pilgrim," and turn R on the paved road, which leads out to parallel the highway for a stretch, where pilgrims have woven crosses of sticks and grasses into the chain link fence.* ⚠ *Cross N-120 (10.3km) and continue on the R side before splitting to the R through fields and over another highway on a green bridge (11.2km). After the bridge, the ruins of the **Hospital de San Juan de Acre (11.5km)** can be seen to the L. Continue straight to Navarrete.*

12.6 Navarrete A H

Pop 2,865, "little Navarra" or "gateway to Navarra"
c/Cuesta Caño 941-441062 in summer

1. A **Municipal** (50, €7): c/San Juan, 941-440722, 1pm, Mar-Oct
2. A H **Camino de las Estrella** (40, €10/-/40): Crta Burgos 9, 618-051392, all year, bike storage and workshop
3. A H **La Casa del Peregrino** (20, €10/-/25): c/las Huertas 3, 630-982928, Easter-Oct 15
4. A H **El Cántaro** (22, €10/-/30): c/Herrerías 16, 941-441180, all year
5. A H **Pilgrim's** (38, €10-12/-/30): (free), c/Abadía 1, 941-441550
6. A H **Buen Camino** (10, €9/25/35): La Cruz 2, 681-252222
7. A H **A la Sombra del Laurel** (30, €15/30/40): Crta de Burgos 52, 639-861110, all year
8. H **Casa Peregrinando** (€35/45): c/Mayor Alta 34, 941-441324
9. H **Rey Sancho** (€50/70): c/Mayor Alta 5, 941-441378
10. H **Villa de Navarrete** (-/€40): c/La Cruz 2C, 941-440318

Navarrete (cabin €105, tent €16): Crta Entrena km 15, 941-440169

12.6 Navarrete is an attractive town, laid out semi-circularly around the base of a hill. Doors built into the hill are *bodegas* (underground cellars) used for storing Navarrete's specialties: wine and mushrooms. Navarrete is also known for its excellent pottery made with local red clay. Enter **Iglesia de La Asunción**, one of the most impressive Baroque retablos in Spain! Spring the €1 to illuminate and prepare to be dazzled by the golden masterpiece.

Cyclists along the red earth path near Logroño

*Wind through Navarrete clockwise, emerging on the paved highway (13.1km). At **Ermita de Santa María de Jesús (13.9km)**, which has a lovely Romanesque façade taken from the historic pilgrim hospital, the trail turns to dirt and heads to the L through agricultural fields. Soon the trail parallels the highway again (16.7km), until a dirt path to the L (18.2km) leads to Ventosa.*

19.4 Ventosa A

Pop. 169, Spanish: "windy"

A San Saturnino (42, €10): , c/Mayor 33, 941-441899, 1pm all year, fireplace, shop with basic food

19.4 Ventosa has a church dedicated to **San Saturnino**. *From Ventosa, walk through agricultural fields. To the R, the ruins of a monastery stand on the Alto de Antón. Re-cross the highway (22.0km) to the **Poyo de Roldán picnic area (25.1km)** and monument of the famous battle with Ferragut (p. 92). Cross two small bridges and N-120 (27.7km) before entering the industrial outskirts of Nájera past a large pilgrim poem painted on the side of a building. The main albergue is located on the far side of the city, so you may wish to get groceries or anything else you need from the center before crossing the bridge (29.2km). Turn L along the Río Najerilla for the Nájera municipal albergue.*

Friendly local on horseback outside of Navarrete

29.6 Nájera A H

Pop. 8,452, Arabic: "between the rocks"

1. A **Municipal** (90, don): , 941-360041, all year, 1pm summer, crowded
2. A **El Peregrino** (20, €10): , c/San Fernando 90, 640-072753
3. A H **Nido de Cigüeña** (20, €10-15/-/30): , Cuarta San Miguel 4, 941-896027, 1pm, Apr-Oct
4. A H **Puerta de Nájera** (32, €10-15/-/40): , c/Ribera del Najerilla 1, 941-362317, Mar-Oct
5. A H **Calle Mayor** (17, €9/-/30): , c/Dicarán 5, 941-360407, Apr-Oct
6. A **Sancho III - La Judería** (10, €8): , c/San Marcial 6, 941-361138, Easter-Oct
7. H **Ciudad de Nájera** (€50/60): , Calleja San Miguel 14, 941-360660
8. H **Duques de Nájera** (-/€50): , c/Carmen 7, 941-410421
9. H **Hispano** (€32/48): , c/la Cepa 2, 941-363615

Camping El Ruedo: , Paseo de San Julián 24, 941-360102, Apr-Sept

29.6 Nájera city is bisected by the Najerilla river, with the historic center built into the jutting red rock. The pleasant grassy banks of the river are perfect for an afternoon picnic or snooze. The main site to visit is the **Monasterio de Santa María la Real** €4, Tu-S 10am-1pm, 4-7pm, Su 10am-12:30pm, 4-6pm, closes early in winter, 941-361083), an 11th-century church built by King Garcia III after a most unusual hunting trip. The story goes that as Garcia hunted partridge along the riverbank, his falcon flew into a nearby cave. Garcia followed and was amazed to find a beautiful statue of the virgin with a vase of fresh lilies and a burning oil lamp. He saw this as a blessing on the Reconquista, and used some of the money he plundered from the Moors to build a church here for the icon. The statue wore a crown of jewels, which was later stolen and divided; the Black Prince Ruby made its way to England's coronation crown!

Virgin Mary statue discovered in 1044 by Navarran king

Visit the arresting virgin statue still in the original cave (in the church), with a statue of a kneeling García outside. The church also serves as a burial place for Navarran royalty, including Garcia III as well as a particularly nice tomb of Sancho III's wife, Doña Blanca. Don't miss the fine filigree work in the arches of the cloister.

The story of **Roland and Ferragut** took place near Nájera, which closely mimics the story of David and Goliath; Ferragut is even described as a descendant of Goliath. The story goes that the giant Ferragut was sent along with 20,000 soldiers from Turkey to fight against Charlemagne's army. Ferragut came out from Nájera, challenging any of the opposition to fight him one-on-

Río Najerilla in Nájera

one. Many tried and failed. Finally, Roland insisted on having his turn and fought with the giant for three days. In between spurts of fighting the two conversed about their respective faiths, and Ferragut revealed that his one weak place (his Achille's heel if you will) was his belly button. A final battle ensued, having both agreed that the winner would be the one espousing the true faith. Ferragut tried to fall on Roland to crush him to death, but Roland stabbed him in the belly and won. Artistic renderings can be found in churches along the way, including San Pedro de Rúa in Estella.

Nájera is an interesting town to explore and has good amenities, but if you have it in you to continue 5.8km of pleasant walking to Azofra, the municipal albergue has rooms for two for €7 per person. Worth the extra walk for a night without bunk beds or snorers!

Nájera
Late June: San Juan y San Pedro festival
Sept 15-18: San Juan Mártir y Santa María la Real festival

Ornate windows in the cloister of Santa María la Real in Nájera

9

NÁJERA TO SANTO DOMINGO

20.9km
(13.0mi)

5-6 Hours
Difficulty:
P 37%, 7.7km
U 63%, 13.2km

A Albergues:
Azofra 5.8km
Cirueña 15.1km
S. Domingo 20.9km
Grañon 28.1km
Redecilla 32.1km

Live chickens in the Santo Domingo Cathedral

Wander vineyard vistas, pass a 15th-century stone boundary marker, find out why live chickens dwell in Santo Domingo's cathedral.

Much of this day is on wide farm tracks through fields of grain and grapes, far from the busy highway. Prepare for little shade and few places to get water on this more remote day with fewer services. A golf course and ghost town in Cirueña feel strangely out of place.

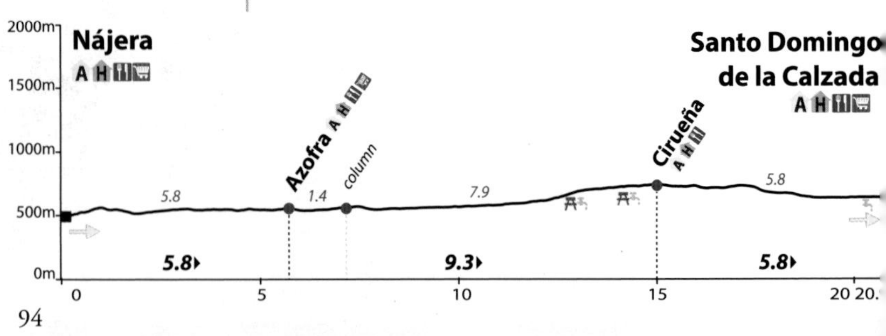

Villalobar de Rioja
San Torcuato
Bañares
Hervias
N-120
A H
20.9
Santo Domingo de la Calzada
Ciriñuela
13.1
15.1
Cirueña
A H
column
7.2
5.8
Azofra
A H
A-12
Torrecilla sobre Alesanco
Alesanco
Canillas de Río Tuerto
0.0
Nájera
A H
Tricio
Badarán
Cárdenas
N
2 km
0
1
2
Ciriñuela
LR-409
LR-204
Camino Cirueña
15.4
Av La Rioja
Urb. Camp de Golf Cirueña
1 Virgen de Guadalupe
Ctra. Santo Domingo
2 Casa Victoria
3 Victoria
200m
Cirueña
Fuente de los Romeros
50m
A Municipal
H Real Casona de las Amas
c/Mayor
c/Magdalena
H
La Plaza
Los Ángeles
c/Antonio Pérez
Azofra
6 El Molino de Floren
Santo Domingo de la Calzada
Virgen de las Abejas
Río Oja
Av Burgos
Medieval Walls
Av. de la Rioja
c/Mayor
Cathedral
Av. Calahorra
1 Cofradía del Santo
Parador 7
3 El Corregidor
Abadía 2 Cisterciense
c/Isidoro Salas
c/Piñar
9 Parador Bernardo
San Francisco
Rey Pedro
5
Av. Juan Carlos I
4 Hospedería Cistercience
8 Miguel
c/Doce de Mayo
c/San Roque
100m

0.0 *Leave Nájera heading west away from the river on c/Costanilla, past Iglesia de Santa Maria la Real to climb up out of town and turn R on a dirt road through the small pass of Najera's western rocky hillside (0.6km). Follow pleasant dirt tracks through vineyards to arrive in Azofra via the main street.*

5.8 Azofra A H
Pop. 251, Arabic: *as-suxra* "tribute"
- A ☆ **Municipal** (60, €7): , c/Las Parras 7, 941-379049 all year, 2 beds per room
- H **Real Casona de las Amas** (-/€140+): , c/Mayor 5, 941-416103, spa, luxurious
- H **Pensión La Plaza** (€30/45): , Plaza de España 7, 629-828702

15.1 Cirueña A H Pop. 131
1. A **Virgen de Guadalupe** (35, €7): , c/Barrio Alto 1, 638-924069, 1:30pm, Mar 15-Oct 15
2. A H **Casa Victoria** (15, €25/42): , Plaza del Horno 8, 941-426105
3. A H **Victoria** (12, €10/-/40-44): , c/San Andrés 10, 941-426105, Mar-Oct

5.8 Azofra's Iglesia de Nuestra Señora de los Angeles houses a wooden statue of Santiago Peregrino. *Leaving town, follow the sidewalk along the main road briefly, turning R and then L on a small paved road (6.1km) just before the Fuente de los Romeros. The path soon becomes dirt and follows beautiful tracks through fields. Note the wayside* ***15th-century columna justicia (7.2km)****, a stone boundary marker. Cross a paved road near the highway (9.0km) and pass a rest area with water (13.1km) before arriving to Cirueña.*

15.1 Cirueña is basically a ghost town other than the ritzy golf club, sadly demonstrating Spain's housing bubble. *Leave Cirueña by turning R on the main road and soon L on a gravel track (15.4km). Follow rolling hills through wheat fields and sheep flocks, down toward the main road and industrial outskirts of Santo Domingo (19.3km). Stay straight on the main street to reach the main Santo Domingo albergues, just before the Cathedral.*

Wildflowers and wheat along the path to Santo Domingo

20.9 Santo Domingo de la Calzada takes its name from Saint Dominic, born in nearby Viloria de la Rioja, who developed sections of the Camino in this area in the 11th century including building bridges and clearing the path. A famous legend associated with Santo Domingo is the "hanged innocent." A German family were on the pilgrimage to Santiago who stayed with a farmer's family in Santo Domingo. The farmer's daughter tried to seduce the German son but, as a pious pilgrim, he refused her. For revenge, she hid silver items in his backpack and accused him of theft, for which he was found guilty and hanged. His parents continued to Santiago, and stopped on the return journey to see his body. They were delighted to find him still alive, hanging in the noose, claiming that the saint held him up so he did not die. They hurried to the magistrate to demand the boy be cut down since he was clearly innocent. The magistrate shouted, "Why, he is no more alive that this roasted chicken I'm about to eat." At this, the chicken stood up on his plate, miraculously brought back to life feathers and all, and crowed.

A shepherd tends his flock near Cirueña

In remembrance of this story, live chickens are kept in the **Cathedral** (€3 w/*credencial*, M-F 9am-8:30pm, Sa 9am-7:10pm, Su 9am-12:20pm, 3:45-7:10pm earlier in winter, audioguide €1, 941-340033), which are said to be the descendants of the resurrected fowl in the story. The cathedral tower is curiously not attached to the cathedral, but across the street, and can be climbed for €2 or on a combined ticket with the cathedral for €4.

Santo Domingo
May 10-15: Fiesta del Santo
Sept 18-19: Fiestas de Gracias y Hermosilla with traditional Riojan potato dishes

Ahorcaditos (little hanged men), a popular local snack, are sweet almond cream pastries shaped like a shell.

20.9 Santo Domingo de la Calzada

A H Pop. 6,694, "Saint Dominic of the Causeway" after the town's founder

1. A **Cofradía del Santo** (assoc, 211, €7): , c/Mayor 38, 941-343390, 11:30am all year, modern facilities, laundromat next door, chickens!
2. A **Abadía Cistercience** (par, 33, €5): , c/Mayor 31, 941-340700, 12pm May-Sept
3. H **El Corregidor** (€40/60): , c/Mayor 14, 941-342128
4. H **Hospedería Cisterciense** (€40/60): c/Pinar 2, 941-340700, run by same nuns as albergue
5. H **Rey Pedro I** (€40/50): , c/San Roque 9, 941-341160
6. H **El Molino de Floren** (-/€59): , c/Margubete 5, 941-342931
7. H **Parador de Santo Domingo de la Calzada** (-/€95+): , Plaza del Santo 3, 941-340300, former pilgrim hospice, historic building
8. H **Hostal Miguel** (€30/42 shared bath): , c/Juan Carlos I 23, 941-034325
9. H **Parador Bernardo de Fresneda** (-/€80+): , Plaza de San Francisco 1, 941-341150

Bañares camping (bungalow, €60-115, tents €7): , 2km east on N-120, 941-340131

10

SANTO DOMINGO TO BELORADO

22.9km
(14.2mi)

5-6 Hours
Difficulty:
P 31%, 7.1km
U 69%, 15.8km

A Albergues:
Grañon 7.2km
Redecilla 11.2km
Castildelgado, 12.8k
Viloria 14.7km
Villamayor 18.0km
Belorado 22.9km
Tosantos 27.8km
Villambistia 29.7km
Espinosa 31.3km
Villafranca 34.8km

A cross adorns the expansive fields of the Meseta.

Relish agricultural vistas of lush wheat fields, visit the birthplace of Santo Domingo, cross into Castilla y León.

About half of this day consists of paths right next to the busy highway N-120. Luckily, there are frequent small villages that offer some respite and services. Vast corn fields characterize the landscape as the trail enters Castilla y León, the largest autonomous region of the Camino.

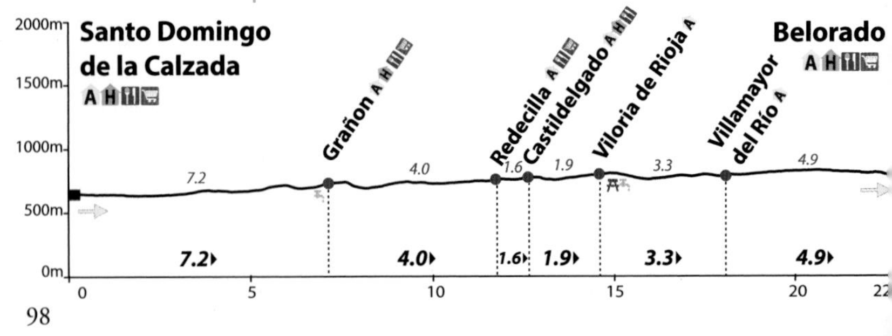

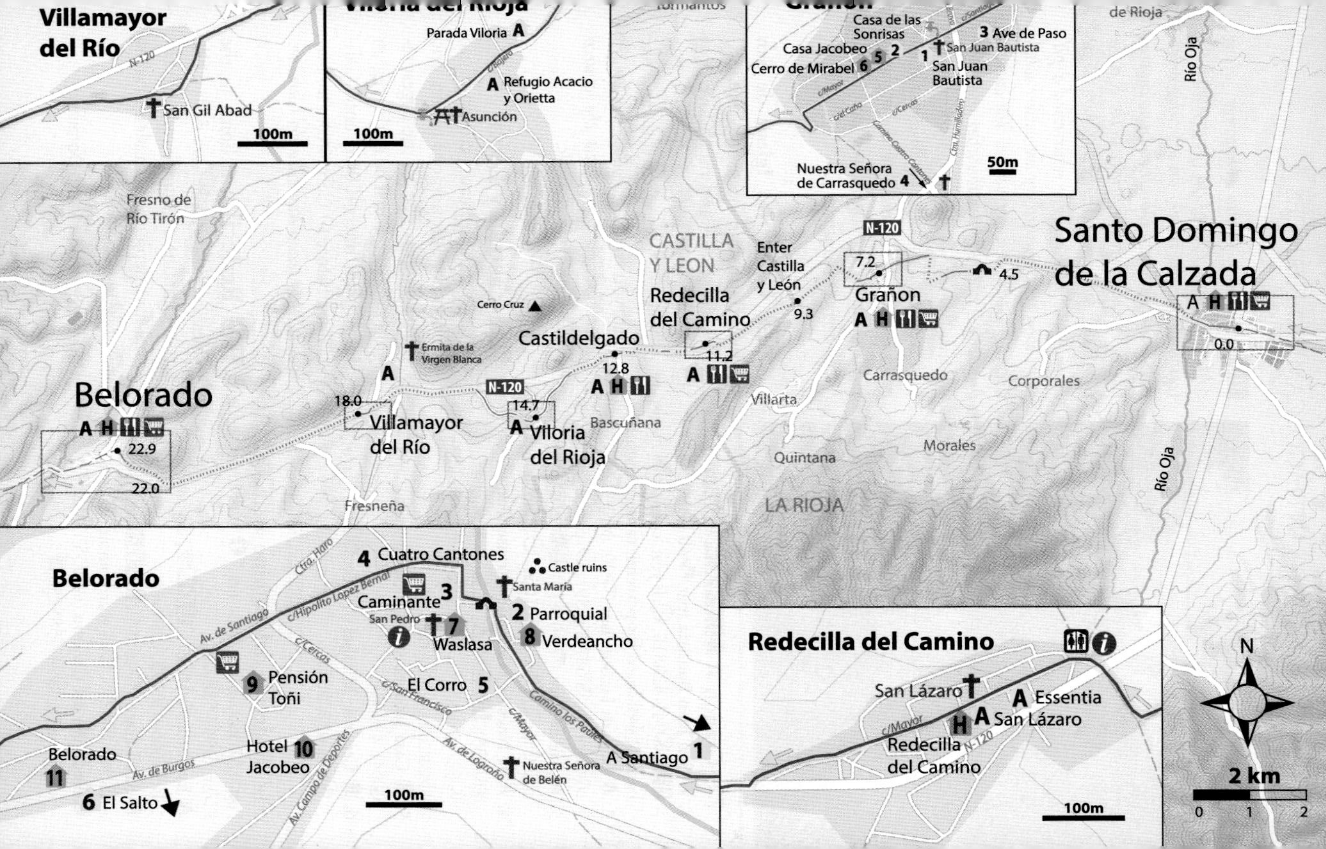
Villamayor del Río
N-120
San Gil Abad
100m
Viloria del Rioja
Parada Viloria A
A Refugio Acacio y Orietta
Asunción
100m
Casa de las Sonrisas
3 Ave de Paso
San Juan Bautista
Casa Jacobeo 5 2
Cerro de Mirabel 6
1 San Juan Bautista
c/Mayor
c/Cercas
Nuestra Señora de Carrasquedo 4
50m
de Rioja
Río Oja
Fresno de Río Tirón
CASTILLA Y LEON
Enter Castilla y León
N-120
Santo Domingo de la Calzada
7.2
4.5
Redecilla del Camino
9.3
Grañon
Cerro Cruz
Castildelgado
11.2
0.0
Ermita de la Virgen Blanca
12.8
Carrasquedo
Corporales
Belorado
18.0
14.7
Villarta
Villamayor del Río
Viloria del Rioja
Bascuñana
22.9
Morales
Quintana
Río Oja
22.0
Fresneña
LA RIOJA
Belorado
4 Cuatro Cantones
Castle ruins
Ctra. Haro
Santa María
c/Hipolito Lopez Bernal
Caminante 3
Av. de Santiago
2 Parroquial
San Pedro
7
Waslasa
8 Verdeancho
c/Cercas
9 Pensión Toñi
El Corro 5
c/San Francisco
Camino los Paules
c/Mayor
Belorado 11
Hotel 10 Jacobeo
Av. de Burgos
Av. Campo de Deportes
Av. de Logroño
Nuestra Señora de Belén
A Santiago 1
6 El Salto
100m
Redecilla del Camino
San Lázaro
A Essentia
A San Lázaro
c/Mayor
N-120
Redecilla del Camino
100m
N
2 km
0 1 2

7.2 **Grañon** A H Pop. 307

1. A **San Juan Bautista** (par, 40 mats, don): , ©941-420818, all year, communal meals, basic & well-loved for peaceful, caring atmosphere
2. A **Casa de las Sonrisas** (20, don): , c/Mayor 16, ©687-877891, 1pm all year
3. A **Ave de Paso** (10, €10): , c/El Caño 18, ©666-801051, 11am, all year
4. A H **Nuestra Señora de Carrasquedo** (42, €6/-/35): , Camino Ermita 45, ©627-341907, all year, historic building, about 1.5km off-route
5. H **Casa Jacobeo** (-/€50): c/Mayor 34, ©941-420684
6. H **Cerro de Mirabel** (-/€50): , c/Mayor 40, ©941-420798

11.2 **Redecilla del Camino** A

Pop. 137, Spanish: "little net," with internet for €1/hr, ©947-588078

A **Essentia** (10, €7): , c/Mayor 34, Re©606-046298, all year

A **San Lázaro** (46, €5): , c/Mayor 24, ©947-580283, all year, communal meals

H **Redecilla del Camino** (€40/55): , c/Mayor 12, ©947-585256

0.0 *Leaving Santo Domingo along c/Mayor, cross the* ***Río Oja*** *(from which the region derives its name) on a bridge originally built by Santo Domingo (now covered in concrete). Before the bridge to the R is the Ermita de la Puente (0.7km), where Santo Domingo is said to have resurrected a pilgrim who was crushed by an oxcart while sleeping outside the hermitage. The current building is a 1917 creation after the original was flooded. In summer, stork nests on high poles abound along the bridge. Follow paths adjacent or parallel to the highway, leaving it to the L (4.5km) and ascending a hill to arrive in Grañon.*

7.2 **Grañon's** **Iglesia de San Juan Bautista** houses some nice retablos. Its simple and much-loved parochial albergue has a donativo box that reads, "give what you can, take what you need." *Follow the main street through town past the church and leave on gravel roads.*

9.3 Castilla y León

A large sign indicates crossing into yet another autonomous region, and the map shows that, as the largest region in Spain, you'll be in this region for a long time (400km until Galicia just before O Cebreiro). *Pass over N-120 to reach Redecilla del Camino.*

11.2 **Redecilla** is home to the Iglesia de Nuestra Señora de la Calle that contains a Romanesque baptismal font depicting Jerusalem. *Follow N-120 to Castildelgado.*

The path leaving Santo Domingo

12.8 Castildelgado was once home to a monastery and pilgrim hospital. Today there is not much to see other than the 16th-century Gothic Iglesia de San Pedro. *Leave the town along N-120, turning L (13.6km) on a smaller paved road into Viloria de Rioja.*

14.7 Viloria de la Rioja is the birthplace of Domingo de la Calzada (p. 96), who was born in 1019. Sadly, his house has been demolished. A rundown church remains, which houses the font in which he was baptized. *Leave town on a small paved road and turn L to rejoin the side of N-120 (16.1km), following it to Villamayor del Río.*

18.0 Villamayor del Río has the 18th-century neoclassical Iglesia San Gil Abad. The tiny village is sometimes known as the "place of three lies," as the name Villamayor del Río suggests a large town on a river, and the actuality is a tiny hamlet along a creek. *Rejoin N-120 to the outskirts of Belorado, finally leaving the busy road by turning R on a dirt path (22.0km). This path leads to Belorado's center and most of its albergues and services.*

12.8 Castildelgado H
Pop. 54, Named for the 16th c. bishop of Burgos
A H **Bideluze** (16, €10/-/30): W D, c/Mayor 8, 616-647115, all year
H **El Chocolatero** (€25/50): 947-588063, along noisy N-120 highway

14.7 Viloria de la Rioja A Pop. 50
A **Refugio Acacio y Orietta** (10, €5): W D (€2), c/Nuevo 6, 947-585220, Apr-Oct, communal meals, sponsored by Coelho
A **Parada Viloria** (16, €5): K W D, c/Bajera 37, 639-451660, Mar-Oct

18.0 Villamayor del Río A Pop. 52
A **San Luis de Francia** (26, €5): W D, 947-580566, Easter-Oct, slightly off route

Camino symbols on the door of the parochial albergue in Grañon

22.9 **Belorado** Pop. 2,140
local surname Plaza Mayor 947-580815,
10am-2pm, 4-8pm

1. **A Santiago** (98, €5-10/30/40): , Camino Redoña, 677-811847, all year, call in winter, located just before town
2. **Refugio Parroquial** (24, don w/): , Barrio de El Corro, 947-580085, May-Oct, run by volunteers
3. **Caminante** (26, €6/-/40-50): , c/Mayor 36, 947-580231, Mar-Oct
4. **Cuatro Cantones** (62, €7-11): , c/Hipólito López 10, 696-427707, Mar-Oct
5. **El Corro** (muni, 40, €7/-/25): , c/Mayor 68, 947-580683, all year
6. **El Salto** (24, €15): , bike shop and rentals, c/Los Cauces, 669-415639
7. **Casa Waslasa** (€25/42): , c/Mayor 57, 647-102254
8. **Verdeancho** (-/€56): , c/El Corro 11, 659-484584
9. **Pensión Toñi** (€31/40-50): , c/Redecillo del Campo 7, 947-580525
10. **Hotel Jacobeo** (-/€59): , Av. de Burgos 3, 947-580010
11. **Belorado** (€30/45): , Av. de Burgos 30, 947-580684

22.9 **Belorado** has been settled since Roman times and was known as *Bilforado* by the 10th century. After being granted a charter in 1116 that allowed for an annual fair, the town grew in commerce and had eight churches in the 13th century. Belorado had pilgrim hospitals on either side of town, while today most albergues are concentrated around the historic center. The **Iglesia de Santa María** has a stone retablo with both Matamoros and Peregrino images of Santiago.

Behind the church, caves were once occupied by hermits, most famously San Caprasio the patron saint of the *Vía Francigena*, and have been known to provide shelter for wandering pilgrims as well. At the top of the cliff, the ruins of a medieval castle can be seen. In modern times, Belorado was well known for its high-quality leather products, but has fallen on hard times economically, though leather goods are still for sale in many local shops.

Belorado
Early Sept: Thanksgiving celebration with parade
Jan 25: Virgen de Belén festival
Aug 26: Patron saint festival for San Vitores

Belorado central plaza and Iglesias de San Pedro (above) and Santa Maria (right)

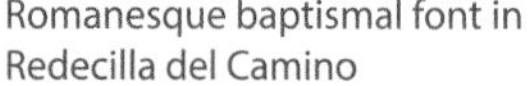

Romanesque baptismal font in Redecilla del Camino

11 BELORADO TO AGÉS

27.7km
(17.2mi)

7-8 Hours
Difficulty:
P 12%, 3.2km
U 88%, 24.5km

A Albergues:
Tosantos 4.9km
Villambistia 6.8km
Espinoso 8.4km
Villafranca 11.9km
San Juan 24.1km
Agés 27.7km
Atapuerca 30.2km

Ermita Virgen de la Peña near Tosantos

Tread earthen paths through the Oca hills past the monastery of San Juan de Ortega with a remote forest landscape.

This is a lovely day mostly on earthen paths and passing through frequent villages. The trail crosses through the remote Oca hills, infamous in medieval times as a dangerous route rife with thieves and ne'er-do-wells. Legend credits San Juan de Ortega, disciple of Santo Domingo, with cleaving this path through the thick oak and pine forest with its dense undergrowth. Be extra careful with traffic in Villafranca, where trucks barrel through at full speed.

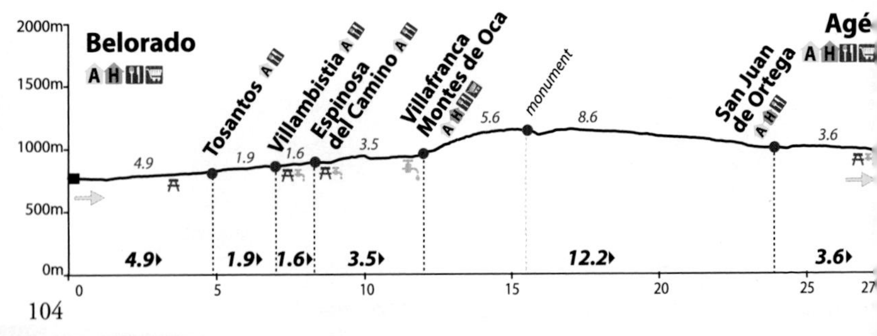

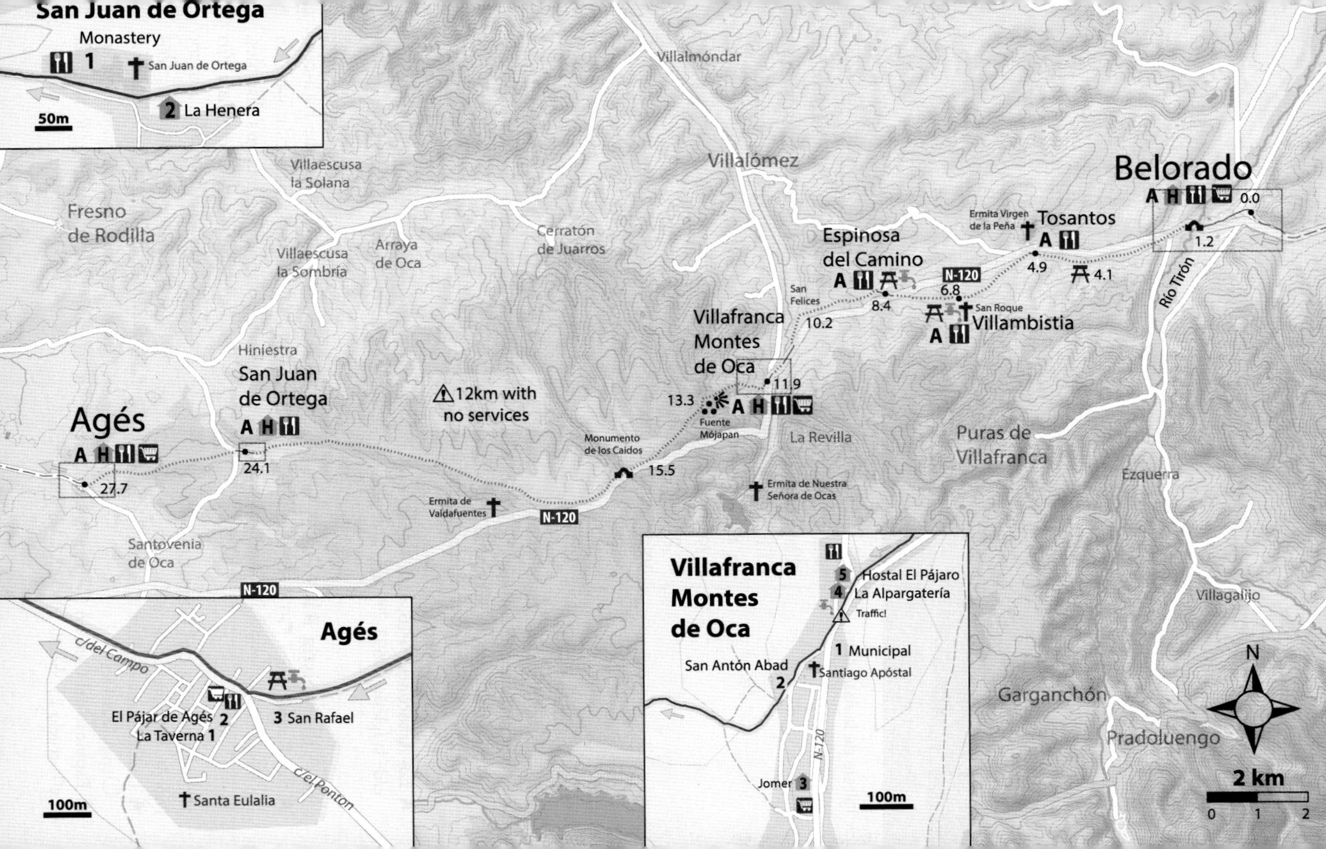

San Juan de Ortega
Monastery
1
San Juan de Ortega
2 La Henera
50m
Villalmóndar
Villalómez
Belorado
A H
0.0
1.2
Río Tirón
Ermita Virgen de la Peña
Tosantos
A
4.9
4.1
Espinosa del Camino
A
N-120
6.8
8.4
San Roque
Villambistia
A
San Felices
10.2
Villafranca Montes de Oca
11.9
13.3
A H
Fuente Mójapan
La Revilla
Puras de Villafranca
Ezquerra
Villagalijo
Garganchón
Pradoluengo
N
2 km
0 1 2
Villaescusa la Solana
Fresno de Rodilla
Villaescusa la Sombría
Arraya de Oca
Cerratón de Juarros
Hiniestra
San Juan de Ortega
A H
12km with no services
Monumento de los Caidos
15.5
Ermita de Nuestra Señora de Ocas
Ermita de Valdafuentes
N-120
Agés
A H
24.1
27.7
Santovenia de Oca
N-120
Agés
c/del Campo
El Pájar de Agés 2
La Taverna 1
3 San Rafael
c/el Ponton
Santa Eulalia
100m
Villafranca Montes de Oca
5 Hostal El Pájaro
4 La Alpargatería
Traffic!
1 Municipal
San Antón Abad
2
Santiago Apóstal
N-120
Jomer 3
100m

Iglesia de la Asunción in Espinosa

0.0 *Leave Belorado by crossing the Plaza Mayor and exiting on the far side via c/Hipolito Lopez Bernal. Turn R on N-120 (1.2km) and pass a small picnic area to cross the river on a wooden bridge near a stone bridge attributed to San Juan de Ortega. Continue on a dirt path parallel to the highway. Pass a picnic area (4.1km) and join the road to Tosantos.*

4.9 **Tosantos** contains the 17th-century Iglesia de San Esteban. Leaving Tosantos look to the R at the cliff north of the village to see the **Ermita Virgen de la Peña** ("Our Lady of the Cliff"), built into the rock face above the town. Legend has it an 8th-century statue of the child Jesus was hidden in this cave under a bell to protect it from invading Muslims. It may be possible to visit the hermitage by asking for the key at the house across from #18, or those staying at the parochial albergue can visit with a local guide. *Leave Tosantos on a dirt path, which brings you to Villambistia.*

4.9 Tosantos A

Pop. 53, Spanish: *todos los santos* "all the saints."

- **A** ☆ **San Francisco de Asis** (par, 30, don): , c/Santa Marina, 947-580371, Mar-Oct, communal meals, prayer service with ritual of reading notes by past pilgrims
- **A** **Los Arancones** (16, €10): W D, c/de la Iglesia, 693-299063, all year

6.8 **Villambistia** has a local tradition which says that immersing your head in the fountain will cure you of tiredness, worth a try! *Follow the dirt path out of Villambistia, cross highway N-120 into Espinosa.*

6.8 Villambistia A Pop. 47

- **A** **San Roque** (muni, 14, €6): W D @, Plaza Mayor 1, 680-501887, all year

8.4 **Espinosa** has the 16th-century Iglesia de la Asunción with an image of one of Santiago's disciples, San Indalecio. *Leave town via a dirt road through vast wheat fields. Pass the ruins of* ***San Felices de Oca (10.2km),*** *a 9th-century Mozárabic monastery, and the path joins highway N-120 (10.9km). Turn R to walk*

8.4 Espinosa del Camino A

Pop. 36, Spanish: "thorny"

- **A** **La Campaña** (10, €17 w/): 678-479361, 1pm Mar-Oct
- **A** **Espinoso del Camino** (10, €5): W D, c/Barruelo 23, 630-104922, all year

carefully along the road or on the faint footpath on the shoulder to Villafranca Montes de Oca. ⚠ *Be extremely careful entering town via the busy highway N-120, which has little to no shoulder.*

11.9 **Villafranca Montes de Oca**

Pop. 147, Latin: "French town of the hills"

1. **A Municipal** (60, €5 summer, €7 winter): , c/Mayor 17, 691-801211, all year
2. **A H San Antón Abad** (26, €5-10/-/30-45): , c/Hospital 4, 947-582149, Mar-Nov 15, restored historic pilgrim hospital
3. **H Pensión Jomer** (-/€55): , c/Mayor 52, 947-582146
4. **H La Alpargatería** (€20/36): , c/Mayor 2, 686-040884
5. **H El Pájaro** (€20/36): c/La Plaza, 947-582029

11.9 Villafranca Montes de Oca was once a Roman city named *Auca* (from which *Oca* comes), home to the 18th-century **Iglesia de Santiago** with a statue of Santiago Peregrino and baptismal font constructed of a huge shell. The historic Hospital de la Reina hosted up to 18,000 pilgrims per year in the 17th century and has been converted into a boutique hotel and albergue. *From the main street, turn R uphill to the church and continue past the San Antón hotel. Leave town on a dirt track, which is pleasantly shaded. These are the mountains of Oca that so terrified medieval pilgrims! On the steep way up you will pass the* ***Sierra del San Millán lookout (13.2km)*** *over the forest.*

The supermarket of Villafranca is on the main road 350m past the church turnoff—make sure you are stocked to Agés! **Fill water; there is none for 12km until San Juan de Ortega.**

13.3 **Fuente Mójapan** is found at the top, (the "bread-moistening spring") used by medieval pilgrims to gussy up their stale bread (today the spring is marked "*no potable*"). In fall, look for mushrooms, which Domenico Laffi wrote in the 1600s were "as big as a straw hat." *Continue on a wide dirt path (fire protection swathe) through thick forest with brilliant heather.*

Steep ascent in the Oca mountains

15.5 **El Monumento de los Caídos** ("Monument to the Fallen") stands at the top, which remembers victims of the Spanish Civil War from the Burgos area. *Continue steeply downhill, cross a small stream by a bridge (15.9km), and rise steeply back up. The flat path continues for a while before descending gradually and leaving the forest behind. As you emerge from the pine forest, a dirt path will guide you to the hamlet of San Juan de Ortega.*

24.1 San Juan de Ortega A H Pop. 23, Spanish: "St. John of the nettles," internet kiosk

1. A **Monastery** (par, 70, €7): , ©947-560438, ©Mar-Oct, historic building, garlic soup served
2. H **La Henera** (€45/55): , c/La Iglesia 4, ©606-198734, ©Apr-Oct

24.1 San Juan de Ortega, or Juan Velásquez, was a young priest and disciple of Santo Domingo (p. 96) who was born near Burgos. San Juan helped Santo Domingo in the construction of bridges in Logroño, Santo Domingo and Nájera. After Domingo's death, Juan went on pilgrimage to Jerusalem. On the journey, he was caught up in a shipwreck and prayed to San Nicolás de Bari to save him. When he survived, he returned to the Burgos area determined to serve pilgrims in the notoriously dangerous and difficult Oca mountains. He is attributed with developing the road from Villafranca to Burgos (from which he took his name *de Ortega,* "of the nettles") as well as a hospice and monastery in the wilderness.

San Juan de Ortega June 2: San Juan de Ortega festival and local pilgrimage

Iglesia de San Juan de Ortega and monastery

Along with being considered the patron saint of innkeepers, San Juan also became known as the saint of fertility. Legend says that when his tomb was opened, the air was fragrant and a swarm of white bees flew out. Queen Isabel la Católica was perhaps the most famous barren woman to pray at his tomb. She visited twice and conceived two children, named Juan and Juana.

The **Iglesia de San Juan de Ortega** includes the saint's tomb with scenes from the legends of his life, including his shipwreck and the white bees. One capital is said to serve a calendar function and is illuminated by sunlight on certain days of the year. Another capital depicts the battle between Roland and Ferragut. An evening pilgrim mass is offered daily and one bar offers hearty *platos combinados*.

Leave San Juan de Ortega by the only road, and turn R on a dirt path (24.4km). Follow this path until a paved road brings you to the pleasant village of Agés.

27.7 **Agés**: The sweet 16th-century Iglesia de Santa Eulalia is said to have once housed the body of King García de Nájera before it was moved to the royal pantheon in Nájera. A short detour to the south from the church will take you to a small bridge attributed to San Juan de Ortega along the Río Vena.

Entering Agés

Church in Agés

27.7 **Agés** A H Pop. 65

1. A **La Taverna** (muni, 36, €8-10): , c/Del Medio 21, 947-400697, 11am all year, operated by La Taverna bar
2. A **El Pájar de Agés** (34, €10): , c/Medio Paralela 12, 947-400629, Mar-Oct, ask about "la casa roja" with beds for €5
3. A H **San Rafael** (10, €10/-/45): , c/Adobera 18, 947-430392, Mar-Oct, vegetarian and Celiac (gluten free) meals

12 AGÉS TO BURGOS

22.3km
(13.9mi)

5-6 Hours
Difficulty:
P 79%, 17.7km
U 21%, 4.6 km

A Albergues:
Atapuerca 2.5km
Cardeñuela 8.8km
Orbaneja 10.9km
Burgos 22.3km
Tardajos 33.3km

Alt. Routes:
Three options to enter Burgos (p. 113):
1) Villafría, 23.3km
2a) Castañares, 22.6km
2b) River, 23.1km

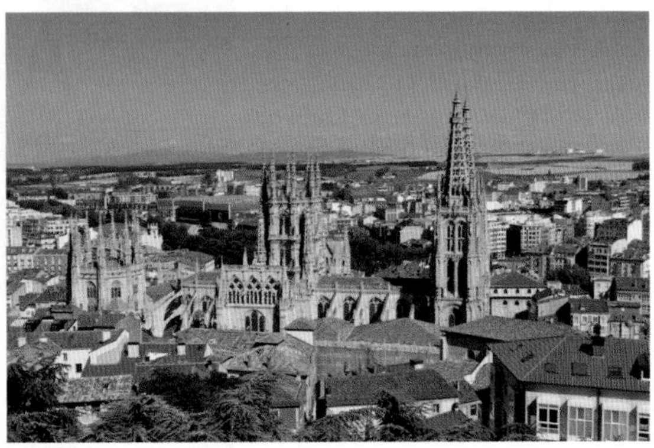

Gothic cathedral of Burgos

Climb the Sierra Atapuerca near prehistoric ruins. Stroll along Río Arlanzón and wander the mind-boggling Burgos Cathedral.

The first half of this day consists of quiet roads between quaint villages and peaceful dirt paths through pine forests. Prepare for the second half of the day entering Burgos, which can be a long tiring walk through urban industrial zones. There are three possible approaches to Burgos; one is not completely marked. We recommend that you take the road less traveled and leave the markings behind at the town of Castañares to cross over the Río Arlanzón and walk along the river

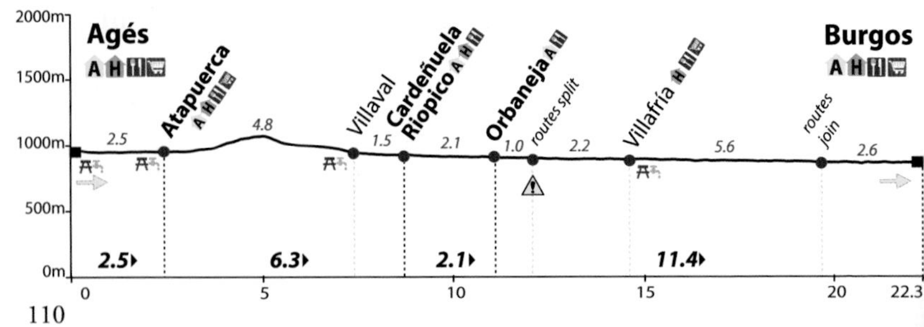

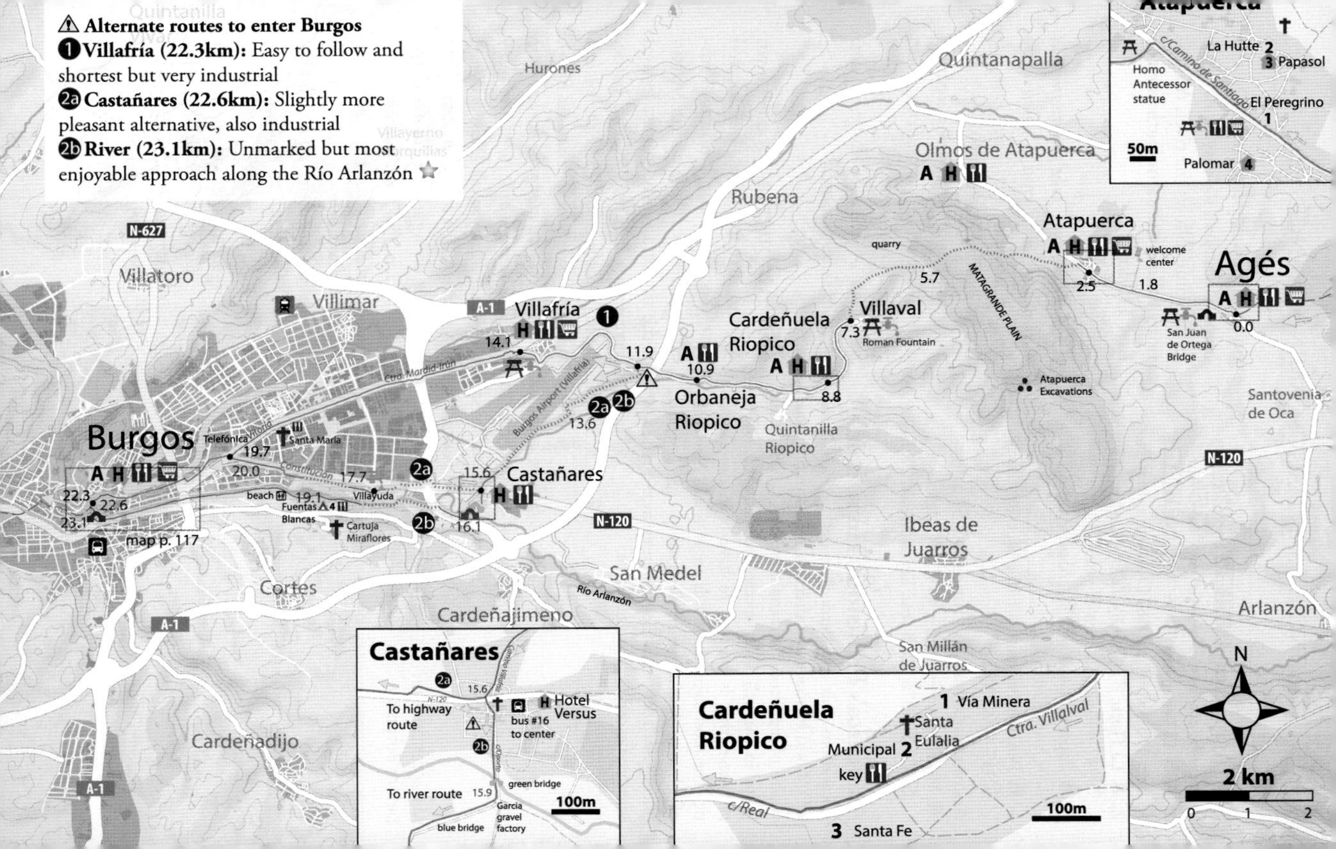
⚠ Alternate routes to enter Burgos
1 Villafría (22.3km): Easy to follow and shortest but very industrial
2a Castañares (22.6km): Slightly more pleasant alternative, also industrial
2b River (23.1km): Unmarked but most enjoyable approach along the Río Arlanzón
Hurones
Quintanapalla
Olmos de Atapuerca
Rubena
Atapuerca
welcome center
Agés
quarry
5.7
2.5
1.8
0.0
MATAGRANDE PLAIN
San Juan de Ortega Bridge
Villaval
7.3
Roman Fountain
Cardeñuela Riopico
8.8
10.9
11.9
Orbaneja Riopico
Quintanilla Riopico
Atapuerca Excavations
Santovenia de Oca
N-120
N-627
Villatoro
Villimar
A-1
Villafría
14.1
Ctra. Madrid-Irún
Burgos Airport (Villafría)
13.6
Burgos
Telefónica
Vitoria
19.7
Santa María
20.0
Constitución
17.7
Castañares
15.6
16.1
beach
19.1
Villayuda
Fuentas Blancas
Cartuja Miraflores
22.3
22.6
23.1
map p. 117
Ibeas de Juarros
San Medel
Cortes
Río Arlanzón
Cardeñajimeno
Arlanzón
San Millán de Juarros
Cardeñadijo
N
2 km
0
1
2
Atapuerca
La Hutte 2
3 Papasol
Homo Antecessor statue
c/Camino de Santiago
El Peregrino 1
50m
Palomar 4
Castañares
15.6
N-120
Camino Villafría
To highway route
Hotel Versus
bus #16 to center
c/Oporto
green bridge
To river route
15.9
Garcia gravel factory
blue bridge
100m
Cardeñuela Riopico
1 Vía Minera
Santa Eulalia
Municipal 2
key
Ctra. Villalval
c/Real
100m
3 Santa Fe

2.5 **Atapuerca** Pop. 206
Spanish: *ata* "to tie," *puerca* "pig," Apr-Sept,
1. **El Peregrino** (36, €8/-/35): , Crta 105, 661-580882, 1pm, Mar-Nov
2. **La Hutte** (18, €6): , c/de Enmedio 38, 947-430320, 1pm all year
3. **Papasol** (-/€58): , c/de Enmedio 36, 947-430320
4. **Pensión Palomar** (-/€40): , c/Revilla 22, 947-400675

Accommodations in Olmos (+2.5km)
A **Municipal** (24, €7): , c/La Iglesia, 633-586876, all year, key at Mesón Hidalgo

Atapuerca's Prehistoric Humanoids

Excavations near Atapuerca were declared a UNESCO World Heritage Site after revealing a tremendous wealth of prehistoric humanoid artifacts (>90% of all found in Europe!) A new species was identified, *Homo antecessor*, that is believed to have been cannibalistic. The most significant finds are in the **Museum of Human Evolution in Burgos** (p. 116), which offers guided daily excursions to the excavation site and interpretive center near Atapuerca.

on peaceful shady dirt paths. Despite being unmarked, it's easy to navigate as the route follows the river. **All options follow the same path for the first 11.9km.**

0.0 *From Agés, take the main road out of town and cross a small stone bridge attributed to San Juan de Ortego over the Río Vena (0.6km). Pass a turnoff for the Atapuerca welcome center (1.8km, +800m), offering tours in Spanish of the archaeological park, a recreation of early dwellings. Follow the road into Atapuerca.*

2.5 **Atapuerca** is best known for the archaeological site located near the town. The looming 15th-century Gothic Iglesia de San Martín is the site of a yearly August festival recreating a famous medieval battle. *Leave via the main road to reach a statue of homo antecessor (2.8km). Turn L here on a dirt path and walk uphill along the barbed wire fence of an army base to the L. Pass through pine forest and spiny shrubs. At the hill crest cross the wide Matagrande Plain to a high point with a bench to enjoy the view down to Burgos and a first glimpse of the flat meseta (5km). At the sign for* ***Valle del Riopico (5.7km)****, either follow the slightly shorter local path down into the village of Villalval (water and a Roman fountain) or head R along the waymarked path, which goes another way on the west side of* ***Villalval (7.3km)*** *with a depressing view of an open strip quarry. Take the paved road to Cardeñuela.*

Matagrande Plain before Burgos

8.8 Cardeñuela de Riopico is a quiet little town with an albergue. *Continue along the quiet paved road through* ***Orbaneja (10.9km).*** *⚠ 1km past Orbaneja arrive at a split near a housing development with two options (1 and 2a/2b). All options to Burgos are within 1km of each other in length.*

8.8 Cardeñuela de Riopico A H

1. **A Via Minera** (26, €8): c/La Iglesia 1, 652-941647, Mar-Oct, rooms with 2, 4 or 6 beds
2. **A Municipal** (16, €5): c/Santa Eulalia next to church, 646-249597
3. **A H Santa Fe** (14, €8-10/25/35): c/Los Huertos 2, 626-352269

10.9 Orbaneja A

A El Peregrino (18, €5): c/Principal 1, 648-604577, all year

11.9 ⚠ Alternate Routes:

❶ Villafría Option

This option follows the historical route, and most people walk this way. In the present day this means walking along the airport fence, through the town of Villafría and almost 7km of unpleasant walking along the A-1 highway by industrial factories. Bus #8 from Villafría skips this part (every 30 min. on weekdays).

14.1 Villafría H Pop. 926

H Hotel Buenos Aires (€25/37): c/Vitoria 349, km 245, 947-483740

H Hostal Iruñako (€30/45): Ctra N-1, km 245.5, 947-484126

H Las Vegas (€30/50): c/Vitoria 319, 947-484453

Follow the arrows through fields and over train tracks into ***Villafría (14.1km)****. From Villafría, follow N-1 all of the way into town to where it meets N-120/Av. de la Constitution, where the Castañares option joins from the L (19.7km). Turn R past the Vía de la Plata mall and onto c/de las Calzadas, crossing a bridge to enter the Old City on c/San Juan. Stay straight following signs to reach the main albergue (23.3km).*

Castañares Option

is route provides a slightly more attrac- e way to enter the city. *At the junction, n L on a dirt road to the corner of the field (13.6km) to pass through fields to* ***stañares (15.6km).*** *Turn R on N-120 the fountain. [River Route option splits into 2a/2b here, 2b instructions in the following section.] llow alongside busy N-120 until signs direct you L into the suburb of Villayuda (17.7km). Fol- a derelict c/de Villafranca to cross railroad tracks (18.8km), turning R then L to take Av. de la nstitución (19.1km) to join the Villafria option (20.0km) for the remaining 2.6km to the main ergue (22.6km), option 1, description above.*

15.6 Castañares H Pop. 305

H Hotel Versus (-/€50): Crta de Logroño, 947-474977

Cartuja de Miraflores monastery

Cartuja de Miraflores Monastery
A Carthusian monastery from the 15th century housing the exquisite alabaster tombs of Queen Isabel's parents, King Juan II and Isabel de Portugal. The golden retablo by Gil de Siloé was crafted with gold brought back from the new world by Christopher Columbus himself, and features luminescent imagery including Santiago and Spanish monarchs. A Carthusian community still lives here, known for their white robes and vow of silence.

Free, M-Sa 10:15am-3pm, 4-6pm, Su 11am-3pm, 4-6pm 947-252586

Recommended detour: *At the Fuente de Prio beach, turn L at the brick electric pole uphill to the paved road. Follow a sign up a dirt road to the entrance of the monastery. Bus #17 from the Plaza de España in Burgos passes the monastery.*

2b River Option

This is by far the most pleasant way to enter Burgos (some waymarking past Castañares, but fairly simple to navigate along the river). *From Castañares (15.6km, 2a option), cross over the N-120 highway to the south of town. Walk past a paved playground on the L and leave town on a small paved road passing over a small green bridge (15.9km), just before a T by a gravel factory "Garcia." Turn R on the gravel path, which veers L and passes over a bright blue footbridge (16.1km). After the bridge, turn R on paved path that goes through a forest and underpass (16.9km). Continue along a dirt path on the south side of the river.*

Fuentes Blancas camping area A **(19.1km)** and **Fuente de Prio beach** provide a outdoor recreation area in summer. *For the detour to Cartujas Miraflores Monastery, turn L here (+0.8km). From Fuente de Prio beach, continue along the river on this pedestrian path all the way to the* ***Santa María bridge (22.6km)****, which leads through the Santa María arch into the plaza just in front of the spectacular Cathedral! The main albergue (23.1km) is on c/Fernán Gonzáles, accessible by stairs just behind the cathedral.*

Blue footbridge on the river option entrance to Burgos (above)

Gothic cathedral of Burgos (opposite)

Alabaster tomb carving in Cartuja de Miraflores

Along the Arlanzón River in Burgos

22.3 **Burgos** is a magnificent city with immeasurable wealth of historic art and architecture. A rest day to visit the sites is well worth your time.

† Catedral de Burgos

(€7, €3.50 with credential, ⏲daily 10am-6pm, free Tues after 4:30pm, includes audio guide)

A UNESCO World Heritage site, the entrance fee includes a detailed brochure of the many naves, chapels and pieces of art. Don't miss the *Capilla del Condestable*, which contains a staggering Mudéjar-Gothic dome, unbelievably realistic 16th-century tombs, the *Retablo de Santa Ana*, created by the famous Gil de Siloé and his son, and the main retablo, also created by Siloé's son. The holiest object for local believers is

Burgos
Mar 17: San Antón, including a ceremony of blessing for pets
Spring: La Noche Blanca large cultural event
June: San Pedro y San Pablo festival

Queso de Burgos is a local specialty, a fresh cheese often eaten with honey, quince or walnuts.

Santo Cristo de Burgos, a sculpture of Jesus on the cross said to be made with real skin and hair (and legend has it, needs to be shaved!) His chapel must be entered from a separate outdoor entrance, as a place of worship as opposed to the rest of the cathedral, which serves more as a museum. Worship areas open 8:30am-1:30pm, 4:30pm-8pm and are to be visited only for prayer (no photos).

Castillo de Burgos (€3.70, 11am-1:30pm, 5-8pm 947-203857, Cerro de San Miguel) The park around the castle provides a beautiful vantage point over the city; one of the few places you can take in the whole of the cathedral.

Museum of Human Evolution (€6 adults/€4 pilgrims, Tu-F 10am-2:30pm, 4:30-8pm, weekends, holidays, July-Sept 10am-8pm, closed Mon, free Wed afternoon 902-024246, Paseo de la Sierra de Atapuerca) New well-organized museum of the most important artifacts from the Atapuerca excavations. For €9, pilgrims can visit the museum and be transported to the excavation site for a tour in Spanish; €13 all-day ticket includes the museum, excavations and tour of a recreation of a prehistoric village.

Sacristy ceilng in the Burgos Cathedral

Museo de Burgos (€1.20, Tu-Sa 10am-2pm, 5-8pm, Su 10am-2pm, 947-265875, c/Marianda 13)

Centro de Arte Caja de Burgos (free modern art museum, c/Saldaña, 947-256550)

Arco Santa María (free, M-Sa 11am-2pm, 5-9pm, Su 11am-2pm, 947-288868), near Puente de Santa María

On the way out of town, you may wish to visit the **Monasterio de las Huelgas** and **Hospital del Rey** (p. 122).

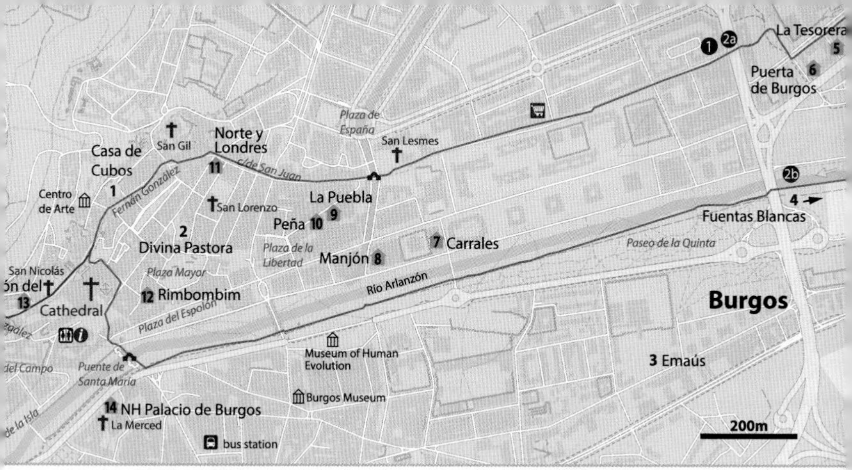

22.3 Burgos A H Pop. 178,574, Gothic: *Baurgs* "fortified city"

1. A **Casa de Cubos** (assoc, 150, €5): c/Fernán González 28, 947-460922, 12pm summer, 2pm winter, all year, lockers
2. A **Divina Pastora** (assoc, 16, €5): c/Lain Calvo 10, 947-207952, 12pm, Apr-Oct
3. A **Emaús** (par, 20, €5): c/San Pedro de Cardeña 31, 12pm, Apr-Oct, communal meals by donation, evening pilgrim blessing
4. A **Fuentes Blancas** (camping, dm €8): 947-486016, see map p. 111
5. H **La Tesorera** (-/€35): c/Vitoria 79, 947-223592
6. H **Puerta de Burgos** (-/€45): c/Vitoria 69, 947-241000
7. H **Carrales** (€20-33/35-55): c/Puente Gasset 4, 947-263547
8. H **Manjón** (€25-35/35-45): Gran Teatro 1, 947-208689
9. H **La Puebla** (€45/55): c/La Puebla 20, 948-200011
10. H **Pensión Peña** (-/€30 shared bath): c/Pueblo 18, 947-206323
11. H **Norte y Londres** (-/€45): Plaza Alonso Martínez 10, 947-264125
12. H **Rimbombim** (-/€50): c/Sombrerería 6, 947-261200
13. H **Mesón del Cid** (-/€60): Plaza Santa María 8, 947-208715, cathedral views
14. H **NH Palacio de Burgos** (-/€85): c/de la Merced 13, 947-479900, historic building

pilgrim never goes without sleep

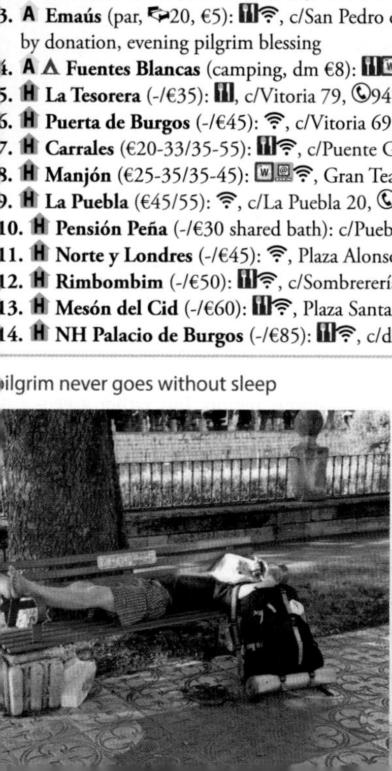

Display in the Museum of Human Evolution

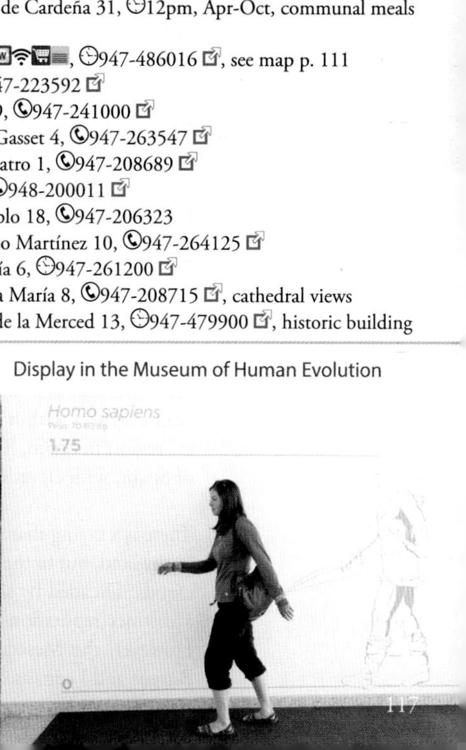

Homo sapiens

1.75

13-21

MESETA

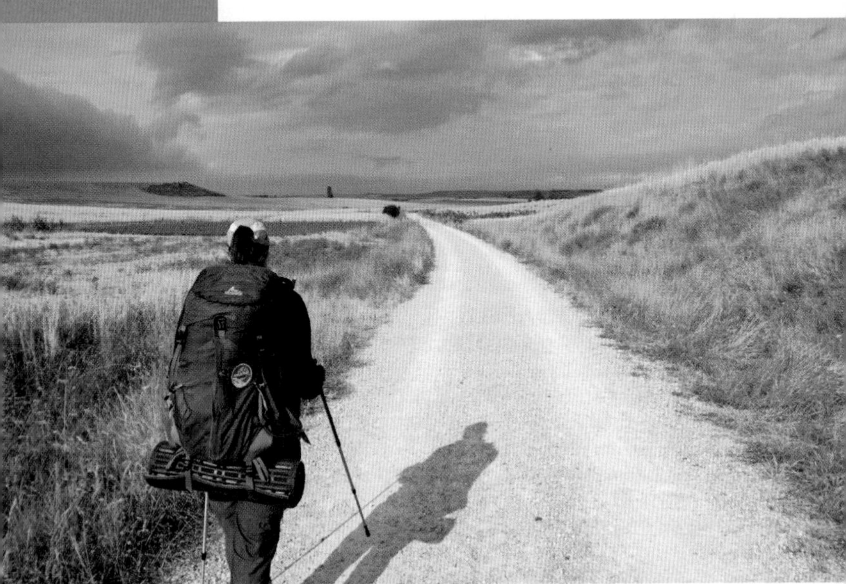

Meseta scenery of wheat fields and big skies

Highlights include long views of big skies, vibrant cities with awe-inspiring cathedrals, massive flocks of sheep and rolling fields of grain.

The Meseta is not an autonomous region, but rather a geographical area within the region of Castilla y León—the largest region in Spain. This central high plateau makes up 40% of Spain, with elevation ranging from 400-1000m.

There is a saying that the landscape of the Meseta is not found in the land, but in the sky with its diverse colors and expansive clouds. Dreaded by some, relished by others, the Meseta has a distinct reputation for being boring, repetitive and bleak. However, the Meseta is also home to such vibrant cities as Burgos and León, and there is a certain beauty and awe in the endless horizon and wide open space. To the north you will glimpse the jutting mountains of the Cordillera Cantábrica. Towns are often set down in shallow river valleys, practically invisible along the horizon until the entrance.

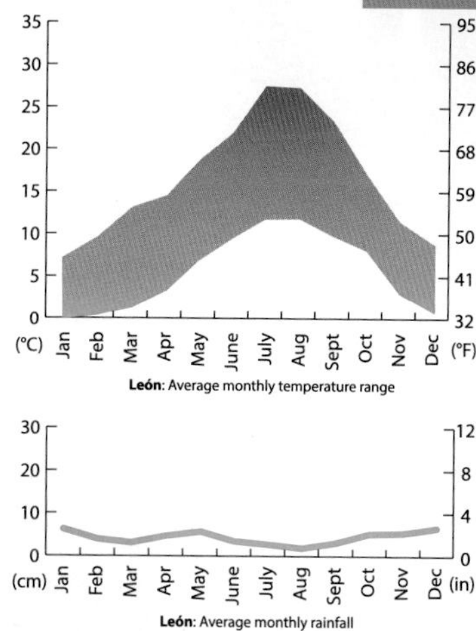

The lack of trees means little to no shade, so be sure to wear sufficient sun protection. Medieval pilgrim records often complain of becoming hopelessly disoriented and lost in the Meseta, though recent tree planting along the trail helps to keep pilgrims heading the right direction. The Meseta can be blistering hot in summer and quite cold in winter. The flat landscape glimmers with golden wheat and flocks of sheep ramble the area along ancient sheep paths known as *cañadas*.

This landscape inspired such notable characters as Don Quixote de la Mancha (in the southern Meseta), and the spiritual and mystical St. Teresa of Avila and St. John of the Cross. In spite of the monotony, perhaps the Meseta can serve as a memorable wilderness experience.

With the lack of stone in this area, you may notice more buildings made of brick or adobe. Many towns feature *bodegas*, wine cellars dug into the earth that resemble hobbit homes, as well as mudbrick dovecotes. Some of the traditional foods include suckling pigs, snails and *morcilla*—a blood sausage stuffed with rice, onions and spices.

Bodega on the meseta

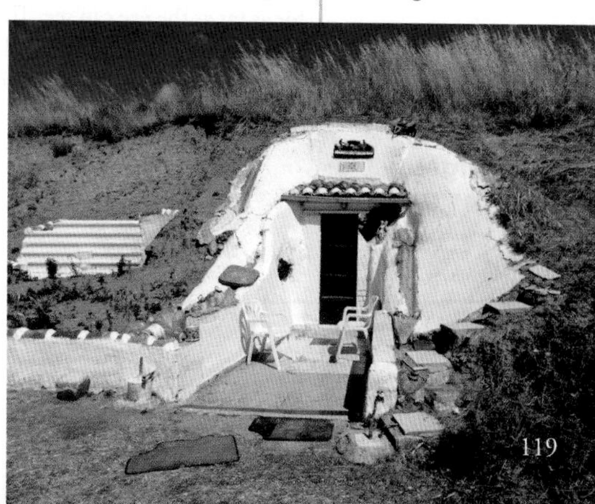

13

BURGOS TO HONTANAS

31.4km
(19.5mi)

7-9 Hours
Difficulty:
P 25%, 8.0km
U 75%, 23.4km

A Albergues:
Tardajos 11.0km
Rabé 13.0km
Hornillos 20.9km
San Bol 26.5km
Hontanas 31.4km
San Antón 37.0km

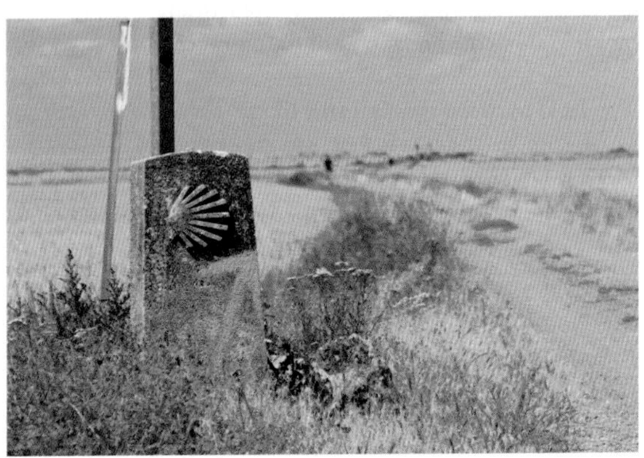

Meseta wheat fields before Hontanas

Trade the urban landscape of Burgos for the peaceful Meseta, walking through field after field of wheat, past the healing San Bol stream.

This day leaves behind the frantic city pace of Burgos with its whizzing cars and factories and enters the peaceful and at times monotonous landscape of the Meseta, characterized by long flat sections of wheat fields, with nothing but more fields for as far as the eye can see. This is a long stage but has enough intermediary stops with good services to take a few relaxing breaks. Be prepared for little to no shade.

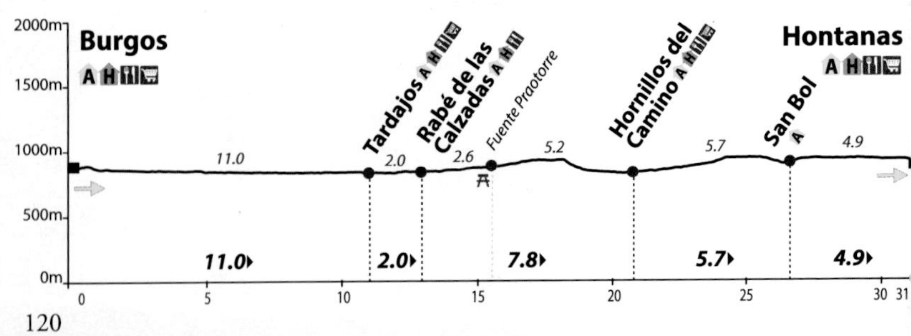

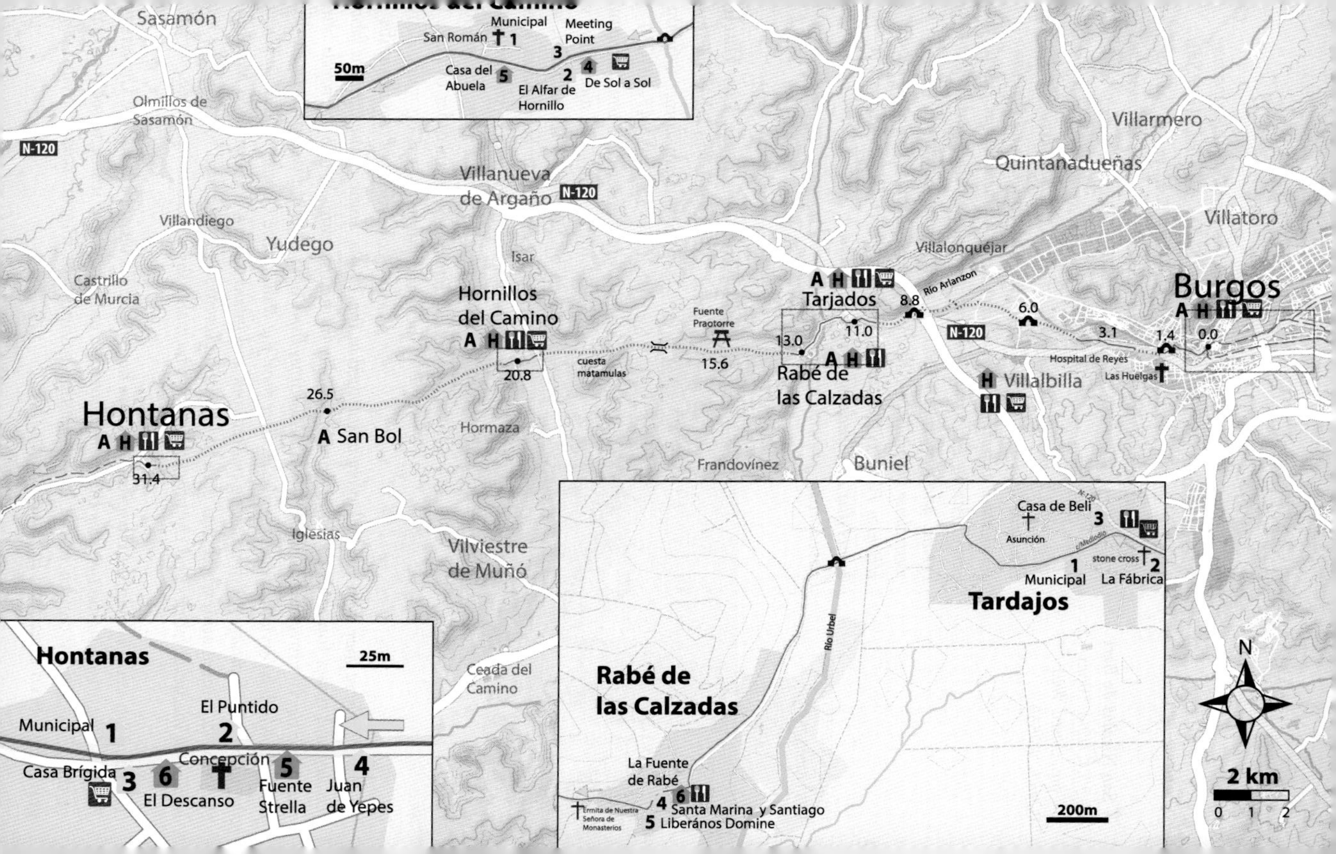

Hornillos del Camino
San Román
Municipal 1
Meeting Point 3
50m
Casa del Abuela 5
2 El Alfar de Hornillo
4 De Sol a Sol
Sasamón
Olmillos de Sasamón
N-120
Villanueva de Argaño
Villandiego
Yudego
Castrillo de Murcia
Isar
Hornillos del Camino
A H
20.8
cuesta matamulas
Fuente Praotorre
15.6
13.0
11.0
Tarjados
A H
8.8
Río Arlanzon
6.0
3.1
1.4
0.0
Burgos
A H
Villarmero
Quintanadueñas
Villatoro
Villalonquéjar
Hospital de Reyes
Las Huelgas
Villalbilla
H
Rabé de las Calzadas
A H
26.5
A San Bol
Hontanas
A H
31.4
Hormaza
Frandovínez
Buniel
Iglesias
Vilviestre de Muñó
Ceada del Camino
Hontanas
25m
El Puntido
Municipal 1
2
Concepción
Casa Brígida 3
6 El Descanso
5 Fuente Strella
4 Juan de Yepes
Casa de Beli
3
Asunción
stone cross 2
1 Municipal
La Fábrica
Tardajos
Río Urbel
Rabé de las Calzadas
La Fuente de Rabé
6
Ermita de Nuestra Señora de Monasterios
4 Santa Marina y Santiago
5 Liberános Domine
200m
N
2 km
0 1 2

0.0 *Leave Burgos (map p. 117) via c/Fernan Gonzalez, passing* ***Iglesia de San Nicolas de Bari****, the* ***Solar del Cid, Arco San Martín*** *and* ***Puente Malatos (1.4km)*** *"bridge of the sick" through a green shady park. Pass two supermarkets on route. After the bridge, cross highway N-120. Continue on the main route, turn through the stone door to the R and follow markings through El Parral park. [To visit* ***Real Monasterio de Las Huelgas*** *and/or* ***Hospital de Reyes****, continue straight to leave the marked Camino route on Paseo de los Comendadores.] At the end of Parque El Parral, pass the Ermita de Santo Amaro el Peregrino, and turn R through the Puerta Romeros. Turn L to walk west along highway N-120. Pass under a railroad and turn R on c/Benito Pérez Galdós out of town (3.1km). The road soon becomes dirt and leads to a small park and bridge (6.0km) with a paved road toward Villalbilla. At the roundabout after the*

† **San Nicolás de Bari**
€1.50, 12-1:30pm, 5-7pm, closed Wed
947-260539

Real Monasterio de Las Huelgas

Real Monasterio de Las Huelg
"Royal Monastery of the Pleasure (€6, Tu-Sa 10am-2pm, 4-6:30p Su 10:30am-3pm 947-201630 visitors must enter on a tour in Spani offered on the hour) The monastery w created by Alfonso VIII in 1175, w transformed one of his palaces into luxurious convent where widow nob women could retreat from the world decadence. Today an order of nuns li here and guide visitors on tours. A ma nificent collection of royal tombs a displayed, where they were found largely untouched in the 1940s. Some of the opulent fabri jewelry and riches found in the tombs are on display in the museum. While the royals buri here were heavily involved in warfare with Muslims, their final resting place draws beautifu from the Mudéjar style, particularly the cloister roof, the walls of the *Capilla de la Asunción*, a the *Capilla de Santiago*, with amazing plasterwork and inlaid ceiling. The Santiago Matamo statue has a jointed arm, which was used in knighting ceremonies. The final room houses a co lection of medieval fabrics and clothing, many of which also show Islamic influence.

The late 12th-century pilgrim **Hospital de Reyes** houses the Faculty of Law at the University Burgos. A Santiago statue oversees the niche above the entrance. Step inside to see the remai of the 13th-century church to the L with Gothic paintings of pilgrim scenes. Many pilgr graves have been unearthed in the cemetery.

bridge, turn R on the paved road, then a quick L onto a dirt footpath. This footpath leads out toward the train tracks, passing under the tracks (6.8km) and across an overpass (7.6km) to turn L and continue along highway N-120 on dirt paths.

Pass under the highway near the Río Arlanzón through a green park area (8.8km, with an apology from the construction workers on a plaque) and cross the paved road by the grain tower (9.1km). Turn R on the road and pass over the Río Arlanzón for the last time (9.3km). Continue on the paved road into Tardajos, where the trail turns L on c/Mediodia (10.4km) to zigzag through town and leaves via a 1-lane asphalt road.

Stone crucero outside of Tardajos

11.0 **Tardajos** was once the Roman city of *Augustóbriga*, at the junction of the *Vía Trajana* and a north-south road. Note the 18th-century **stone cross** before town. During medieval times, three churches were here, one said to house St. Francis on his pilgrimage to Santiago. The **Iglesia de Nuestra Señora de la Asunción** remains, where Teresa of Ávila was said to have taken communion. *After 1km cross Río Urbel (11.9km, popular for fishing and crabbing) and veer L to Rabé de las Calzadas.*

11.0 **Tardajos** A H Pop. 856

1. A **Municipal** (18, don): c/Asunción, 947-451189, Mar 19-Nov 1, simple and basic, clean with friendly volunteers
2. A H **La Fábrica** (14, €12-15/-/35): c/de Fábrica 27, 646-000908
3. A H **Casa de Beli** (26, €10/-/45): General Yagüe 16, 947-451234, all year

13.0 **Rabé de las Calzadas** A H

Pop. 221, May come from "rabbi" or "riverbank"

4. A **Hospital Santa Marina y Santiago** (8, €8): Francisco Ribera 6, 670-971919, Apr-Oct, some negative reports
5. A **Liberános Domine** (24, €8): Francisco Ribera 10, 695-116901, all year
6. H **La Fuente de Rabé** (€30/40): c/Santa Marina 17, 947-451191, vegetarian dinner otion

13.0 Rabé de las Calzadas

The section of medieval path to Rabé was swampy and treacherous, featured in a popular pilgrim song:

De Tardajos a Rabé	*From Tardajos to Rabé*
no te faltarán trabajos.	*you will not lack for troubles.*
Y de Rabé a Tardajos,	*And from Rabé to Tardajos,*
liberanos Domine!	*Deliver us, oh Lord!*

Leave Rabé on a dirt road, passing the sweet Ermita de Nuestra Señora de Monasterios (13.4km). Begin the steady climb up onto the meseta, gaining about 125m of elevation.

20.9 **Hornillos del Camino** A H Pop. 61, Spanish: "little ovens [or kilns] of the Camino"

1. A **Municipal** (32+, €6): , Plaza de la Iglesia, 689-784681, all year, basic
2. A **El Alfar de Hornillo** (20, €9): , c/Cantarranas 8, 654-263857, Apr-Oct
3. A H **Meeting Point** (36, €8/-/30): , c/Cantarranas 3, 608-113599, Mar-Oct
4. H **De Sol a Sol** (€35/45): , c/de Los Cantarranas 7, 649-876091
5. H **Casa del Abuelo** (€40/45 w/): , c/Real 44, 661-869618

La Fuente Praotorre (15.6km) provides shade on the way up, though the water pump was broken at time of research. *From the high point (18.1km), experience the vast emptiness of the meseta, punctuated only by bird calls and the wailing wind. Descend again via a steep path known as the cuesta matamulas ("mule-killing incline"). At the bottom, cross a road and head into Hornillos. On the way into town pass a well-equipped shop.*

Hornillos
Late July: Celebration of the rooster story

For a summer cool-off, walk just past town to the **Hontanas unicipal pool** (€2, 12-8pm)

20.8 Hornillos del Camino

was quite possibly an ancient city, but few remains have been excavated from its earliest days. Just before town, ruins of the San Lázaro hospice for lepers can be seen to the south. Ruins of a medieval pilgrim hospital have also been found. The town fountain (*fuente de gallo*) features a rooster on top because of a story that says that Napolean's troops stole all the chickens in Hornillos while the townspeople were at Mass. The soldiers killed the chickens and snuck them out of town in their drums. When confronted by the townspeople, the soldiers denied everything, but one rooster miraculously came back to life and gave a mighty crow from within the drum, proving the soldiers' guilt.

The path to Hornillos

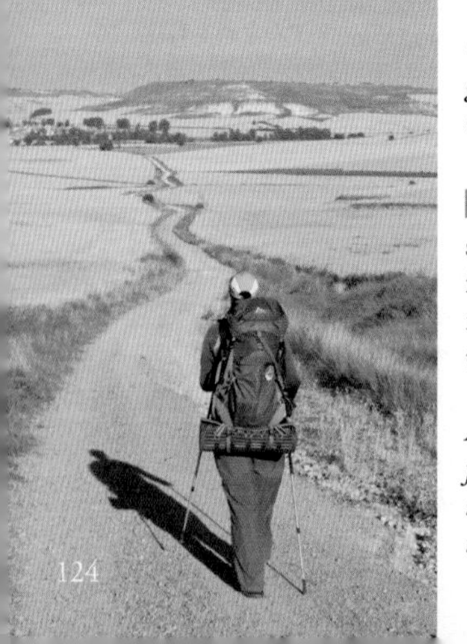

Continue straight out of town on a dirt road, which gradually ascends and descends through shadeless wheat fields to the clearly marked turnoff to San Bol.

26.5 **San Bol's** legend has it that pilgrims who soak there feet in the fountain will be cured of all foot pain. The luscious green yard is a great place to relax. Ruins scattered nearby are from the monastery of San Boadilla from the 11th century.

After the San Bol turnoff, the trail rises and continues for 5km of classic meseta Camino. Just when you think it can't possibly be any further, rapidly descend and the tower of the church of Hontanas will burst into view.

31.4 **Hontanas** is named for the numerous springs and abundant water in the area. The 14th-century **Iglesia de la Inmaculada Concepción** can be found along the main road. Italian pilgrim Domenico Laffi in the 1670s complained bitterly about the dangers of packs of wolves prior to Hontanas and the inhospitable welcome he received:

"With God's help we crossed this deserted waste land and reached the village of Hontanas. It lies hidden in the valley of a little river, so that you scarcely see it until you have reached it... They have a strong palisade round the huts to guard against wolves which come at night to attack them... There are so many of them that you see them in packs, like flocks of sheep... So whenever you want to cross this desert you must do it in the middle of the day when the shepherds are out with their huge dogs... Having reached this wretched place by evening, we ate a little bread with garlic... Then we went to bed on the ground because there was nowhere else."

Today you'd be hard-pressed to find a wolf, and good food and beds are in abundance. Several modern pilgrim narratives mention Victorino, a Camino character (now retired) who used to entertain pilgrims by drinking an entire liter of wine from a *porrón* jar in one draw. According to comedian Hape Kerkeling, "He pours a liter of red wine over his hair, inhales it through his nose, and blows it into his mouth while warbling a tune."

26.5 **San Bol** A (also called Sambol)
San Boadilla, a local saint
A **Arroyo de San Bol** (muni, 12, €5): 628-927317, Apr-Oct, dinner €6, Rustic and simple, communal dinner

31.4 **Hontanas** A H
Pop. 70, Italian: "fountains"
1. A **Municipal** (20, 35+ overflow, €5): c/Real 26, 628-927317, all year
2. A H **El Puntido** (46, €5/-/25): c/Iglesia 6, 947-378597, all year, call in winter
3. A **Casa Brígida** (14, €7): c/Real 15, 628-927317, mid Mar - mid Oct, beautiful historic house
4. A H **Juan de Yepes** (54, €7/-/35): c/Real 1, 638-938546, Mar-Oct
5. H **Fuente Strella** (€25-35/35-45): c/Iglesia 6, 947-377261
6. H **El Descanso** (-/€35): c/Real 16 947-377035

Entering Hontanas

14

HONTANAS TO BOADILLA DEL CAMINO

28.5km
(17.7mi)

6-8 Hours
Difficulty:
P 32%, 9.0km
U 68%, 19.5km

A Albergues:
San Antón 5.6km
Castrojeriz 9.4km
San Nicolás 18.3km
Itero 20.3km
Boadilla 28.5km
Frómista 34.3km

Approaching Castrojeriz

Visit the enigmatic ruins of San Antón and the medieval castle of Castrojeriz, sleep in a church in San Nicolás or go for a swim in Boadilla.

Most of this day is on pleasant dirt tracks with two towns offering pilgrim services. The hill after Castrojeriz is especially steep (both up and down) so be sure to reserve energy and take plenty of water for this shadeless section. After San Nicolás, the path crosses from Burgos province into Palencia. Note that Boadilla does not have a shop, so bring any supplies you may need for an overnight there.

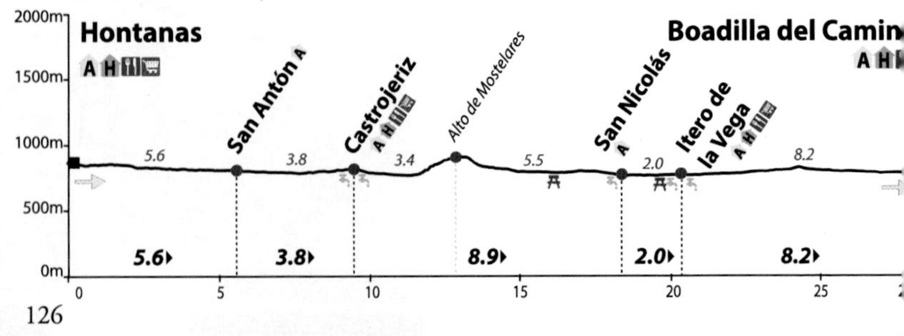

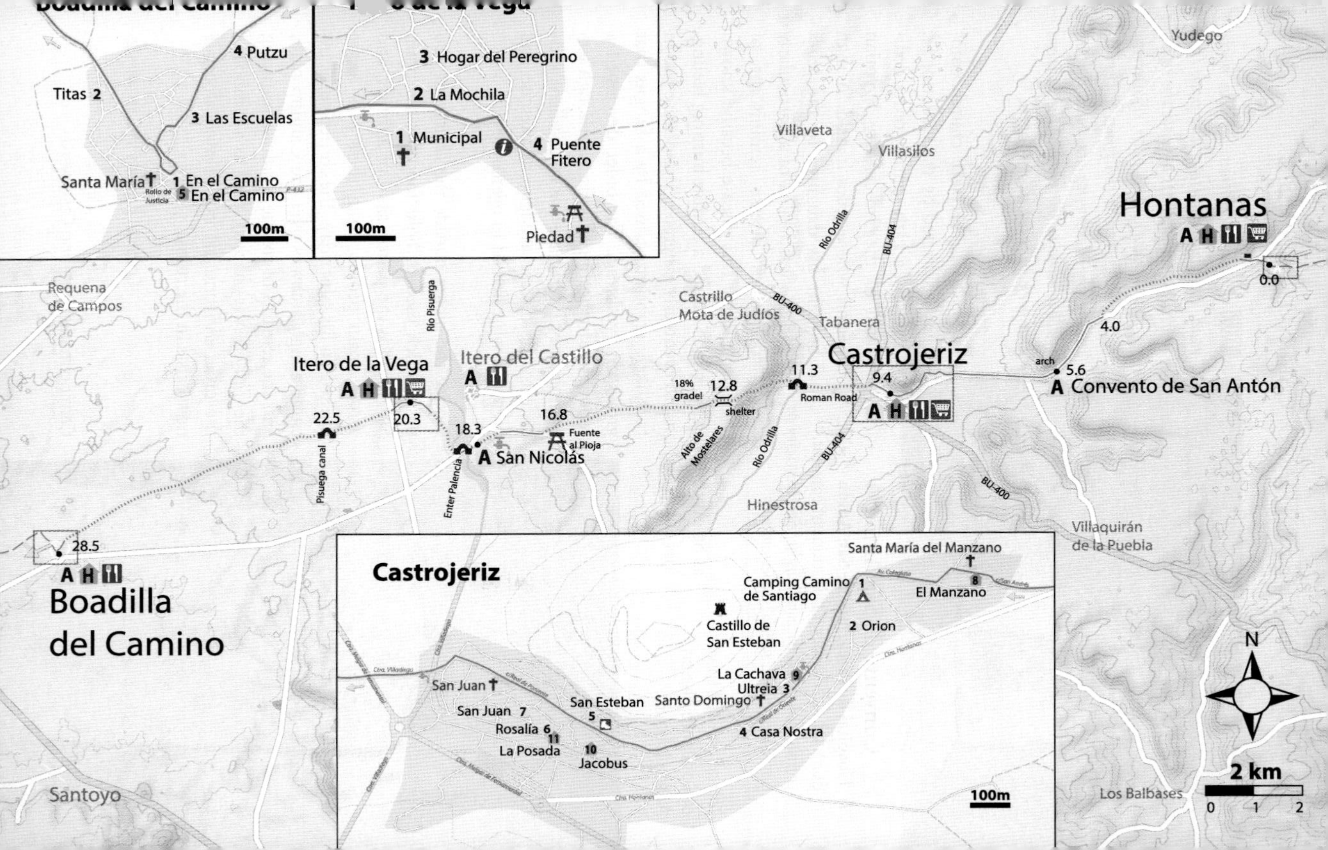

Hontanas
A H
0.0
4.0
arch
5.6
A Convento de San Antón
Castrojeriz
9.4
A H
11.3
Roman Road
18%
grade!
12.8
shelter
Alto de Mostelares
16.8
Fuente al Pioja
18.3
A San Nicolás
Enter Palencia
Itero del Castillo
A
Itero de la Vega
A H
20.3
22.5
Pisuega canal
Río Pisuerga
28.5
A H
Boadilla del Camino
Yudego
Villaveta
Villasilos
Río Odrilla
BU-404
BU-400
Castrillo Mota de Judíos
Tabanera
Hinestrosa
Villaquirán de la Puebla
Requena de Campos
Santoyo
Los Balbases
N
2 km
0
1
2
Titas 2
4 Putzu
3 Las Escuelas
Santa María
Rollo de Justicia
1 En el Camino
5 En el Camino
100m
3 Hogar del Peregrino
2 La Mochila
1 Municipal
4 Puente Fitero
Piedad
100m
Castrojeriz
Santa María del Manzano
Camping Camino de Santiago 1
8 El Manzano
2 Orion
Castillo de San Esteban
La Cachava 9
Ultreia 3
Santo Domingo
4 Casa Nostra
San Esteban 5
San Juan
San Juan 7
Rosalía 6
11 La Posada
10 Jacobus
100m

5.6 Convento de San Antón A

A Hospital de Peregrinos de San Antón (12, don): , May-Sep , in ruins of convent, communal meals by candlelight, no electricity or hot water, basic, special experience

Tau on the bell tower of Convento de San Antón (above)

0.0 Leave Hontanas on the main road, continuing onto a dirt path (hot weather alternative is to walk the shaded paved road). The path rejoins the road (4.0km), and continues to the ruins of the Convento de San Antón. Walk around to the back of the convent and peek in if the door is open.

5.6 **San Antón** church complex was started by the Order of St. Anthony, a 11th-century order dedicated to the 3rd-century Egyptian hermit whose relics it held. A man brought his daughter to the relics and she was healed of a particularly pernicious disease reminiscent of leprosy. This disease became known as St. Anthony's Fire, which caused a terrible burning feeling, loss of circulation and eventually gangrene. This disease was in fact likely ergotism, caused by a fungus that grows on rye bread. The order developed a reputation for healing this disease, though serendipitously, pilgrimage was an excellent antidote to the disease as vigorous exercise and plenty of wine helped to overcome it.

Notice the niches outside the church as you pass, which used to hold food for the poor. St. Antón is the patron saint of animals, and across Spain people bring their pets to be blessed on his saint's day. The church ruins include a high archway over the Camino path, and the remains of rosette windows featuring the *Tau* cross (t-shaped), used as a symbol of the order. An unusual but beloved albergue now exists in the ruins.

Colorful flowers in Castrojeriz

Camino marker entering Castrojeriz

The trail continues on the paved road right through the Arch of San Antón and follows a pleasant quiet shaded road to Castrojeriz (9.4km), easily identifiable with its imposing castle ruins on the hill above. The trail winds through this classic medieval city, which seems to be perpetually on siesta with hardly a soul out on the street.

9.4 **Castrojeriz** occupies a perfect position for defense along the steep mesa topped by the **Castillo de San Esteban**. The Romans used the castle, said to be founded by Julius Caesar, to protect the roads to Galicia's lucrative gold mines. The city changed hands frequently until coming under Christian rule in the 10th century. The charter for the city was progressive for its day—the punishment for killing a Jew was the same as for killing a Christian.

9.4 Castrojeriz A H

Pop. 873, Latin: *Castrum Sigerici* "Castle of (King) Sigerici," Plaza Mayor, 3, 947-377001

1. A H **Camping Camino de Santiago** (35, €6/25/32): W D, c/Virgen del Manzano, 947-377255, Mar-Oct
2. A H **Orion** (22, €11/30/40): W D, Av. de la Colegiata 28, 649-481609, Jan 15-Dec 15, serve Korean dinner vegan option
3. A H **Ultreia** (28, €9/-/45): W D, c/Real de Oriente 77, 947-378640, Apr-Oct
4. A **Casa Nostra** (26, €6.50): W D, c/Real Oriente 52, 947-377493, Feb-Nov
5. A **San Esteban** (assoc, 30, €5): , Plaza Mayor, 947-377001, all year, historic
6. A **Rosalía** (32, €10): W D, c/Cordón 2, 947-373714, Mar-Oct
7. A **San Juan** (muni, 28, don): c/Cordón 7, 947-377400, Apr-Oct, basic facilities
8. H **El Manzano** (€25/35): W D, c/Colegiata 5, 620-782768
9. H **La Cachava** (€37/55): W D, c/Real de Oriente 83, 947-378547
10. H **Jacobus** (€39/59): , Plaza Puerta del Monte, 947-378647
11. H **La Posada/Mesón de Castrojeriz** (-/€64): , c/Cordón 1, 947-377400

Iglesia de Santa María del Manzano just before Castrojeriz

Franks and Jews settled in the town, which became a way station on the pilgrimage road with five churches and seven pilgrim hospitals along the "long road" through the city. Don't miss the impressive 13th-century Gothic **Iglesia de Santa María del Manzano**. Legend has it that Mary appeared to St. James from an apple tree and he was so startled that his horse reared up and came down heavily, leaving hoofprints in the stone outside the entrance.

On the way through town, pass the 16th-century **Iglesia de Santo Domingo**—note the ominous carved skulls along the wall with the message *O Mors* (Latin: Oh death). The 13th-century **Iglesia de San Juan de los Caballeros** features an ornate Mudéjar ceiling. The castle looming above Castrojeriz goes back to pre-Roman times, used and built upon by the Romans, Visigoths, Moors and Christians. The view is well worth the climb, but probably only practical if you are staying the night in town.

✝ **Iglesia de Santa María del Manzano** (€2, ⌚Jun-Sep 10am-2pm, 5-7pm, ✆947-377036)

Leaving Castrojeriz, cross highways BU-404 and BU-400 and continue straight on a gravel path that joins a restored Roman road before passing over a marshy area on a wooden bridge over the ***Río Odrilla (11.3km)****. Thousands of tons of stone were brought here to create a Roman causeway through the swampy Odrilla Valley for transporting gold and other minerals. The remains of Roman mines are still visible to the R, as well as a seam of mica running up the hill. The path climbs steeply up to the* ***Alto de Mostelares (12.8km)****. At the top is a small shelter for shade. ⚠ The downhill has been paved in cement and reaches a grade of 18%; proceed with caution. The path continues as gravel through more shadeless wheat fields.*

Castrojeriz
Late May: Garlic festival

16.8 Fuente al Pioja

Relief comes at Fuente al Pioja (the "Flea's fountain") where local fellows regularly offer coffee, fruit and other snacks along a shady picnic area. A natural spring offers untreated water, though locals say it is safe to drink. *Follow a paved road and turn L onto a dirt path, with Itero del Castillo visible amongst the trees in the valley off route.*

+1.1 **Itero del Castillo** A Pop. 105

A **Municipal** (1.0km off-route, 12, €10 with dinner): , c/Sol, 642-213560, Apr-Nov, ask for key in Bar El Castillo

18.3 San Nicolás Chapel

Pass the friendly San Nicolás chapel and albergue, who practice foot washing for pilgrims that stay overnight. Clean restrooms are located behind the chapel in the yellow modern building.

18.3 **San Nicolás Chapel** A

A **San Nicolás** (assoc, 12, don): , Jun-Sep, to the L before the bridge, communal meals, 13th-c. church restored and run by an Italian Confraternity, no electricity [except in WC/shower house in back], ritual of foot washing

Dawn view near Castrojeriz

A cyclist passes through wheat fields before Boadilla

*After San Nicolás cross over the **Río Pisuerga (18.5km)** on a paved bridge, turning R past a picnic area and welcome sign to **Palencia** (river is the border between Burgos and Palencia provinces). A pilgrim bridge was first commissioned here in the 11th century by Alfonso VI to unify the territories of Castile and León.*

The *Codex Calixtinus* provided ambiguous information about *Tierra de Campos*, the territory you are entering. It is "full of royal treasure, of gold and silver, fabrics and the strongest horses, and flush with bread, wine, fish, milk and honey. It is however lacking in firewood and the people are evil and vicious."

Itero de Vega
Aug: Itero Rock heavy metal festival

20.3 **Itero de Vega** A H
Pop. 177, Spanish: "boundary of the meadow"

1. A **Municipal** (12, €5): ,
   Plaza de la Iglesia, 605-034347, all year
2. A **La Mochila** (28, €6-8): ,
   c/Santa Ana 3, 979-151781, all year
3. A **Hogar del Peregrino** (8, €12): ,
   c/Santa María 17, 979-151866, all year
4. A H **Puente Fitero** (22, €7/28/38): ,
   c/Santa María 3, 979-151822

20.3 **Itero de Vega**: Reaching the outskirts of town, the road becomes paved. To the L is a the 13th-century Ermita de la Piedad, with a picnic area and water. *Continue through town and leave via a wide dirt road. Cross the **Pisuega canal (22.5km)** on a small bridge. Arrive to Boadilla del Camino after a long desolate road over a gentle hill on a mesa.*

28.5 Boadilla del Camino

is built in a circular plan, suggesting that it was fortified in medieval times. The Gothic **Rollo de la Justicia** outside of the **Iglesia de Santa María de la Asunción** symbolizes the independence granted to Boadilla in the 15th century, as they were then permitted to publicly torture and hang their own criminals. At its largest, the town supported a monastery and four churches. The **Canal de Castilla** begins here, which the camino follows to Frómista.

The Canal de Castilla was built from 1753-1859, covering 207km. The canal was used for ships that were pulled by mules on tow paths. Today the canals are used to irrigate agricultural fields.

28.5 Boadilla del Camino A H

Pop. 124, Latin: *boava* "ox."

1. **A ☆ En el Camino** (48, €7/-/26-31): , Plaza el Rollo, 979-810284, Mar-Nov, large garden & pool, pilgrim menu
2. **A Titas** (12, €10): , c/Mayor 7, 979-810776, all year
3. **A Las Escuelas** (muni, 12, €5): , c/Escuelas, 625-026677, all year
4. **A Putzu** (16, €7): , c/las Bodegas 9, 677-225993, all year, mixed reports
5. **H Hotel En el Camino** (€35/45): , Plaza el Rollo, 979-810999

Rollo de la Justicia in Boadilla del Camino

15 BOADILLA TO CARRIÓN DE LOS CONDES

24.5km
(15.2mi)

6-7 Hours
Difficulty:
P 16%, 4.0km
U 84%, 20.5km

A Albergues:
Frómista 5.8km
Población 9.1km
Villarmentero 14.8km
Villalcázar 19.0km
Carrión 24.5km
Calzadilla 41.5km

Alt. Route:
Río Ucieza Route, +1.5km (p. 136)

Almost halfway to Santiago!

Meander along canals, gaze at stunning column capitals, see the miraculous Virgen Blanca and sing with nuns in Carrión.

This day begins along the Canal de Castilla to Frómista, then along the road to Población. Then choose between two alternates, the more obvious and better-marked path along a gravel path parallel to the highway or a river route that follows the small Río Ucieza and provides more shade and peace and quiet, but is not as well marked. The routes meet in Villalcázar for the last slog to Carrión parallel to the road.

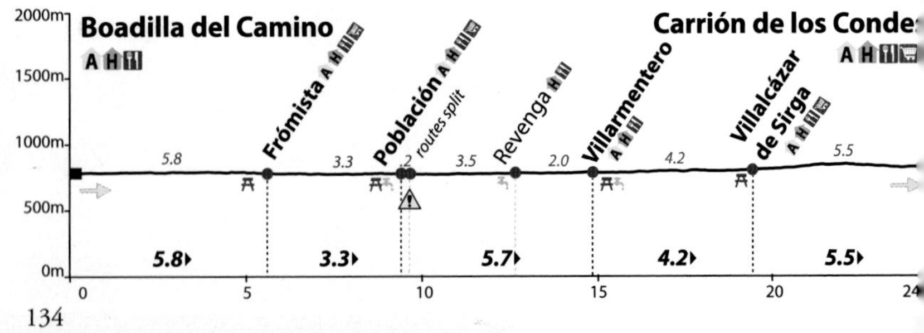

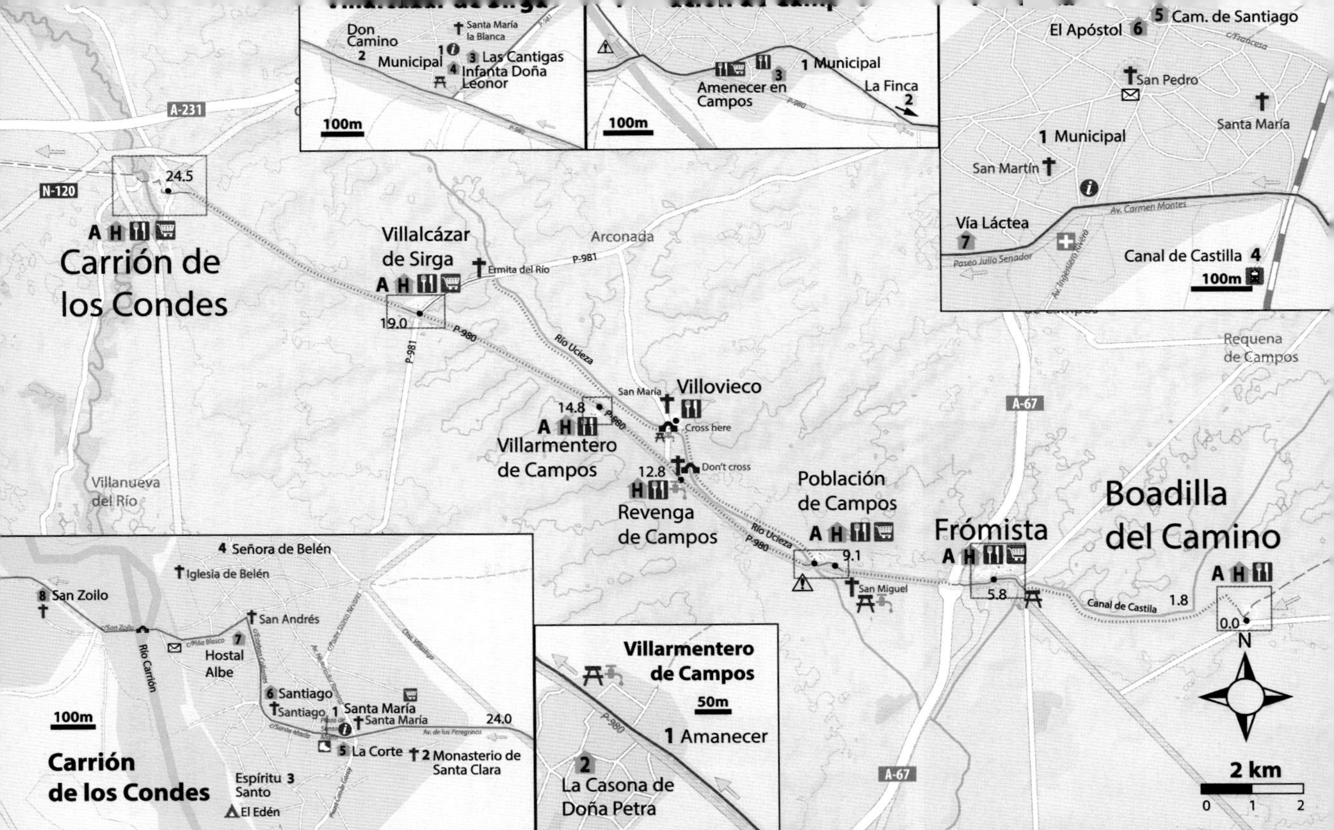
Carrión de los Condes
A H
24.5
N-120
A-231
Villalcázar de Sirga
A H
19.0
P-981
P-980
Ermita del Río
Arconada
Río Ucieza
Villanueva del Río
14.8
A H
Villarmentero de Campos
San María
Villovieco
Cross here
Don't cross
12.8
H
Revenga de Campos
Población de Campos
A H
9.1
San Miguel
A-67
Frómista
A H
5.8
Boadilla del Camino
A H
Canal de Castila
1.8
0.0
Requena de Campos
N
2 km
0
1
2
Don Camino
2 Municipal
Santa María la Blanca
1
3 Las Cantigas
4 Infanta Doña Leonor
100m
1 Municipal
3 Amenecer en Campos
La Finca 2
100m
5 Cam. de Santiago
El Apóstol 6
c/Francesa
San Pedro
Santa María
1 Municipal
San Martín
Av. Carmen Montes
Vía Láctea
7
Paseo Julio Senador
Av. Ingeniero Rivera
Canal de Castilla 4
100m
4 Señora de Belén
Iglesia de Belén
8 San Zoilo
San Andrés
c/San Zoilo
Río Carrión
c/Piña Blasco
7 Hostal Albe
6 Santiago
Santiago
1 Santa María
Santa María
24.0
5 La Corte
2 Monasterio de Santa Clara
Espíritu Santo 3
El Edén
100m
Carrión de los Condes
Villarmentero de Campos
50m
P-980
1 Amanecer
2 La Casona de Doña Petra

Sunrise over Canal de Castilla (upper)

Iglesia de San Martín in Frómista (lower)

0.0 *From Boadilla, follow the trail out of town via a dirt road that veers L by a fence and barn. The trail joins the* ***Canal de Castilla (1.8km)*** *and follows the flow all the way to Frómista. Entering Frómista, the trail passes over a dam complex and under the railroad tracks into town. The trail passes Av. Ingeniero Rivera, which has a variety of services.*

5.8 **Frómista** has been a breadbasket farming area since Celtic times until being destroyed by the Moors and later rebuilt in the 12th century. When the Jews of Castilla y León were systematically attacked in 1391, Frómista absorbed some of the Jewish refugees, though the Jewish population was exiled in 1492. In spite of being a successful market town in the 15th century, the town declined until a revival in 1773 when the canal brought water and enabled agriculture to again thrive. Visit the Romanesque **Iglesia de San Martín** (€1.50, pilgrims free Wed, 10am-2pm, 4:30-8pm) for its amazing capitals and corbels, with the overall construction based on the cathedral of Jaca.

⚠ Alternate: Río Ucieza Route, +1.5km

This route is not well marked but is easy to navigate because it closely follows the river. The scenery is more natural than the primary route along the road. Turn R immediately before the bridge after Población and follow the faint 4X4 track closest to the river. This track is often overgrown with flowers, grass and thistles so be sure to wear long pants. Don't cross the first bridge unless to visit the town of Revenga and/or cross over to the primary path. Continue to the town of ***Villovieco****, which has a fountain and church. Turn L and cross over the bridge. There is a picnic area, small snack stand and water. The trail continues to the R directly after the bridge (before picnic area) on a well-marked dirt road. Follow this road until you meet a paved road with the* ***Ermita de Nuestra Señora del Río*** *to the L, which houses a Mary statue said to have swum upstream to the spot during a flood! Turn L and follow the paved road (P-981) to rejoin the main trail in* ***Villalcázar de Sirga.***

Frómista Cheese Museum: free, 979-810012, 10am-2pm, 5-8pm weekdays

Friday is Frómista's market day.

The trail leaves Frómista on the sidewalk over a bridge, which becomes a dirt track parallel to the highway for 3.3km to Población de Campos, with 13th-century Ermita de San Miguel off to the L when the trail turns R into town.

9.1 Población de Campos

has existed since the 11th-century and housed two pilgrim hospitals. Just after Población, the alternate route splits to the R at the small bridge. *See sidebar opposite for alternate river route. For the standard route, continue straight on a gravel track next to the highway, with the river on the R. Pass through* ***Revenga de Campos*** ***(12.8km)****. Continue straight to Villarmentero.*

14.8 Villarmentero

has a Mudéjar-style ceiling in the 16th-century Iglesia de San Martín de Tours. *Follow the same path along the road to Villalcázar de Sirga.*

19.0 Villalcázar

: Turn R if you wish to enter Villalcázar and visit the church (retablo of St. James and an image of Mary said to perform miracles) or continue straight to bypass the town on dirt road parallel to highway.

5.8 Frómista A H

Pop. 846, Possibly from Latin *frumentum* "grain"

1. A **Municipal** (56, €8): Plaza de San Martín, 979-811089, Feb-Nov
2. A **Estrella del Camino** (32, €9): Ejército Español, 979-810399, Mar-Oct
3. A **Betania** (5, don): Av. Ejército Español 26, 638-846043, Dec-Feb only, call ahead
4. A H **Canal de Castilla** (40, €18/20/30 w/): c/La Estación 2, 979-810193, Apr-Oct
5. H **Camino de Santiago** (€28/48): c/Francesa 26, 979-810282
6. H **Hostal El Apóstol** (€37/48): Av Ejército Español 5, 979-810255
7. H **Pensión Vía Láctea** (€37/43): Julio Senador 1, 696-009803

9.1 Población de Campos A H

Pop. 140, Spanish: "town of the fields"

1. A **Municipal** (18, €4): Paseo del Cementerio, all year, very basic, key at hotel
2. A **La Finca** (20, €9): Crta 980 km 16, 979-067028, all year
3. H **Amanecer en Campos** (€30/45): c/Fuente Nueva, 979-811099

14.8 Villarmentero A H Pop. 11

1. A H **Amanecer** (36, dm €6, dbl cabin €18, teepee €6, hammock €3): c/José Antonio 2, 662-279102, Mar-Oct
2. H **Casona Doña Petra** (€40/50): c/Ramon y Cajal 14, 979-065978

19.0 Villalcázar de Sirga A H Pop. 174

Latin: *villa* (town), Arabic *cazar* (castle), *sirga* (road)

1. A **Municipal** (20, don): Plaza de Peregrino, 979-888041, Apr-Oct
2. A **Don Camino** (20, €7): c/Real 23, 979-888163, Apr-Oct
3. H **Hostal Las Cantigas** (€30/40): c/Durango 2, 979-888027
4. H **Infanta Doña Leonor** (€32/40): Av. de Condes Toreno, 979-888118

Evening singing with the nuns of Santa María in Carrión

According to tradition, Villalcázar was under the protection of the Knights Templar (p. 143). The Camino did not originally pass through this town, but later detoured when the fame of the **Virgen Blanca** ("white virgin") and her many miracles spread. She is on display in the 13th-century **Iglesia de Santa María la Blanca** (€1, ⏲10:30am-2pm, 4-6pm). A 1530 retablo has scenes from the life of Saint James, including his legendary run-in with the magician Hermogenes, who later converted to Christianity and burned his magic books.

Carrión
Aug 22: San Zoilo patron saint day
Thursday is market day, faithfully held since 1618.

Continue on the path along the road, and when Carrión de los Condes comes into view, cross the highway to the L and enter the city on Av. de los Peregrinos (24.0km). The trail is marked through the old town just past ⓘ *Tourist Information. Santa María albergue is in the center, just off the Plaza de Santa María.*

24.5 Carrión de los Condes

was a wealthy and important Camino town, with as many as 10,000 citizens in the Middle Ages and no less than 14 pilgrim hospitals. According to legend, Charlemagne camped here in his campaign against the Moors, who had succeeded in building a castle in Carrión in the 8th century (now **Iglesia de Belén**). It was also home to famous medieval poet Sem Tob, a Jewish rabbi known for his epic poem *Proverbios Morales*.

The **Iglesia de Santiago** was reconstructed in 1845 after the original 12th-century structure was lost in a fire. The original façade remains and the building houses a small art museum. **Iglesia de Santa María del Camino** commemorates the legend of the 100 virgins, in which the Moor rulers demanded 100 Christian virgins each year from the Christian ruler Mauregato. The Christians prayed that this travesty would end, and the Moors were chased away by a herd of bulls. Look for two bulls on each of the jambs. Evening pilgrim Mass is offered.

The 13th-century **Monasterio de Santa Clara**, which now offers an albergue, was said to house Saint Francis on his pilgrimage.

The town is named for a legend that the Cid's daughters married counts in this area, whom the Cid had killed after they tried to rob him (hence *Los Condes*, "the counts"). See El Cid (p. 86).

Be sure to procure enough supplies for the 18km stretch without services on the trail tomorrow.

Crosses in Carrión de los Condes

24.5 Carrión de los Condes

Pop. 2,221, nearby Carrión river

1. A **Santa María** (par, 52, €5): ©979-880768, Mar-Oct, Plaza Santa María, nuns offer an evening session of folk singing
2. A H **Monasterio de Santa Clara** (par, 31, €5/22/44): c/Santa Clara 1, ©979-880837, Mar-Nov
3. A **Espíritu Santo** (par, 90, €5): c/San Juan 4, ©979-880052, all year
4. A **Señora de Belén** (par, 92, €22): c/Leopoldo 4, ©979-880031, all year
5. H **La Corte** (€35/45): c/Santa María 36, ©979-880138
6. H **Santiago** (-/€40): Plaza de los Regentes 8, ©979-881052
7. H **Hostal Albe** (-/€28, €34 w/kitchenette): c/Esteban Collantes 21, ©979-880-913
8. H **Real Monasterio San Zoilo** (€55/80): Obispo Souto, ©979-880049, 1km after town on way

Camping El Edén (tent €20, cabins €80): c/Tenerías 11, ©979-880714, Apr-Oct

16

CARRIÓN DE LOS CONDES TO TERRADILLOS DE LOS TEMPLARIOS

26.6km
(16.5mi)

6-7 HOURS
DIFFICULTY:
P 28%, 7.6km
U 72%, 19.0km

A ALBERGUES:
Calzadilla 17.0km
Ledigos 23.3km
Terradillos 26.6km
Moratinos 29.8km
San Nicolás 32.4km

ALT. ROUTE:
Small detour after Calzadilla de la Cueza (p. 142)

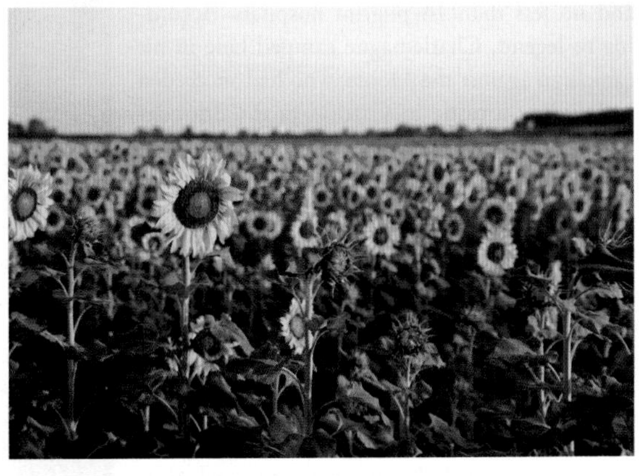

Fields of sunflowers after Carrión

Pass fields of blooming sunflowers, trace ancient Roman roads, step back into Templar history.

This day begins with a long, straight slog on the *Via Aquitana*, an ancient Roman route that has been restored. This is one of the longest stretches between towns on the Camino Francés: 17km to Calzadilla de la Cueza, no water sources and very minimal coverage for any bathroom breaks. The only respite is a seasonal snack stand offering drinks and sandwiches at about the halfway point to Calzadilla.

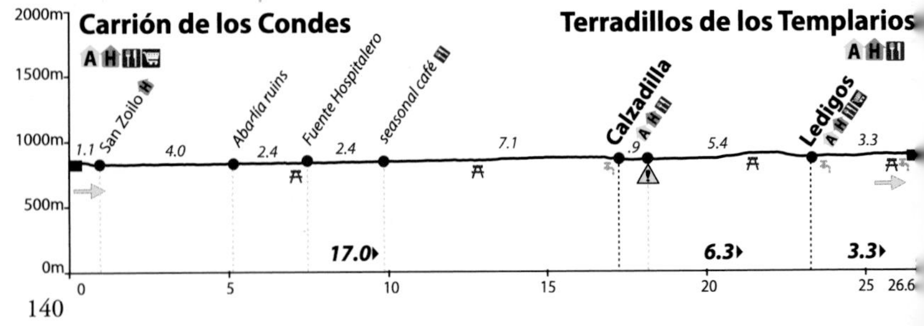

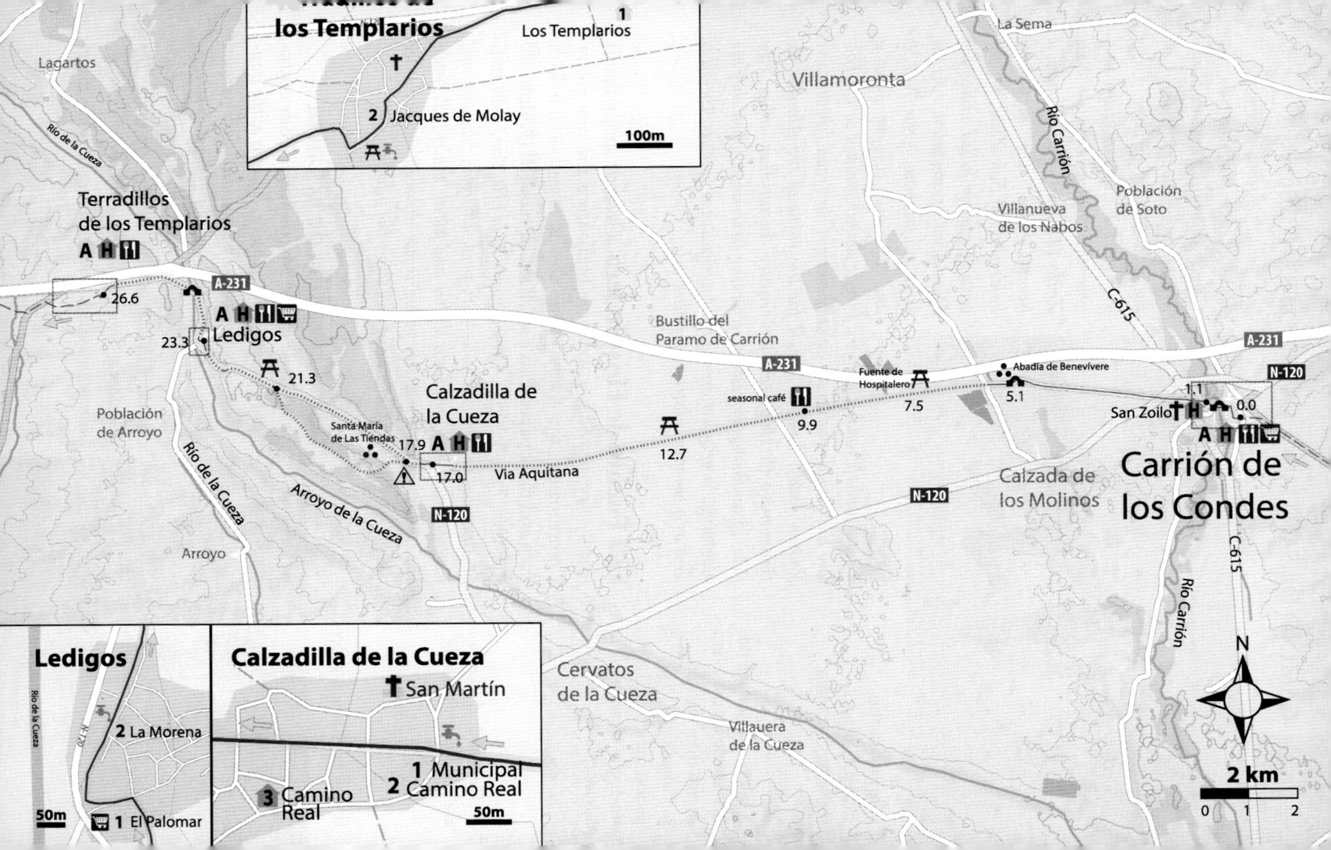
los Templarios
1 Los Templarios
2 Jacques de Molay
100m
Lagartos
Río de la Cueza
Terradillos
de los Templarios
A H
A-231
26.6
A H
Ledigos
23.3
21.3
Población
de Arroyo
Río de la Cueza
Arroyo
Arroyo de la Cueza
Santa María
de Las Tiendas
17.9
Calzadilla de
la Cueza
A H
17.0
N-120
Via Aquitana
12.7
Bustillo del
Paramo de Carrión
A-231
seasonal café
9.9
Fuente de
Hospitalero
7.5
Abadía de Benevívere
5.1
Villamoronta
Río Carrión
Villanueva
de los Nabos
Población
de Soto
La Sema
C-615
A-231
N-120
1.1
0.0
San Zoilo
A H
Carrión de
los Condes
Calzada de
los Molinos
N-120
C-615
Río Carrión
Cervatos
de la Cueza
Villauera
de la Cueza
N
2 km
0 1 2
Ledigos
Río de la Cueza
N-120
2 La Morena
1 El Palomar
50m
Calzadilla de la Cueza
San Martín
1 Municipal
2 Camino Real
3 Camino
Real
50m

Pilgrims on the straight Roman route to Calzadilla

0.0 *Leave Carrión de los Condes from the Plaza de Santa María and follow the shells in the sidewalk out of town. Cross over the Río Carrión bridge and note the* ***Monasterio de San Zoilo (1.1km)*** *to the L, now a luxury hotel. The monastery holds relics of San Zoilo, a 4th-century martyr killed under the Diocletian persecution. At a large roundabout, cross N-120 and continue straight onto a 1-lane asphalt road (there is a bicycle detour marked to L). Follow this paved road to an equally straight dirt road (the historic Roman road). Look to the R for the ruins of the* ***Abadía de Benevívere (5.1km)****, a 11th-century Augustinian abbey. Pass fields of sunflowers (girasoles), stunning in summer when they are blooming. Sunflowers are a prime agricultural product; the oil is used as a cheaper substitute for olive oil.*

A horse and carriage ride is available for the 17km stretch from Carrión to Calzadilla, €15 per person (min 5 pax), leaving at 10am, book in advance: ✆867-885147.

7.5 **Fuente de Hospitalero**, a historic spring that is usually dry, provides a welcome break from the monotony. Unfortunately, the shady picnic area is often overrun with trash and toilet paper. Pass a small **snack stand (9.9km),** ⏲ Apr-Oct, 7am-3:30pm. *Cross a paved road (10.2km) with graffiti intended to motivate you—bar, pool, albergue, 9km, ánimo! Continue to a rest area with shelter and picnic tables (12.7km), but unfortunately the water pump is not drinkable. Finally see the church tower of Calzadilla and enter the hamlet.*

Do a little dance, you are halfway to Santiago!

A welcome snack shop

17.0 Calzadilla de la Cueza

has Iglesia de San Martin with a 16th-century Renaissance altarpiece. *The rest of the standard way to Ledigos is on a dirt path parallel to N-120. [⚠ There is also an option to turn off to the L for short alternate routes, which are slightly longer than the primary route. The "Palomar route" passes an adobe dovecote, common in this area as the doves were useful for pest control, fertilization and for food. This one was particularly ornate but is largely eroded away.] The main route passes the ruins of Santa María de las Tiendas, a former monastery and pilgrim hospital. Cross the highway one more time and arrive to Ledigos.*

17.0 **Calzadilla de la Cueza**
Pop. 54, Spanish: "little road on the Cueza river"
1. **Municipal** (34, €5): , c/Mayor 1, 670-558954, all year
2. **Camino Real** (80, €7): , c/Travesía Mayor 8, 979-883187, all year
3. **Camino Real** (-/€40): , c/Travesía Mayor 5, 979-883187

23.3 **Ledigos** contains Iglesia de Santiago with a lovely image of the saint, but the church is rarely open. *From Ledigos, the path passes back over the highway and onto another dirt path parallel to the highway, across the* ***Río de la Cueza (24.5km)*** *and into Terradillos.*

23.3 **Ledigos** Pop. 74
1. **El Palomar** (52, €6-8/11/18): , c/Ronda de Abajo, 979-883605, Mar-Nov, bar/shop in albergue
2. **La Morena** (37, €8/-/34): , c/Carretera 3, 626-972118

26.6 **Terradillos de los Templarios** was once home to a 13th-century church belonging to the **Knights Templar**, but is one of the few pilgrimage towns that never had a pilgrim refuge until modern times. Iglesia de San Pedro contains a Gothic crucifix but is rarely open. The church is built of brick rather than stone, as this area has very little local stone. Set aside from the N-120 highway, Terradillos has a peaceful sleepy town feel.

26.6 **Terradillos de los Templarios**
Pop. 78, Spanish: "small Templar terraces"
1. **Los Templarios** (52, €8-10/28/38): , 667-252279, late Mar-Oct
2. **Jacques de Molay** (49, €8-10): , c/Iglesia, 979-883679, Feb-Nov

The Knights Templar were a medieval military order responsible for protecting pilgrims. While the order was popular and successful for almost 200 years, grand master Jacques de Molay was arrested in 1307 (on Friday the 13th, possibly the origin of this superstitious date) and burned at the stake for heresy and a variety of trumped-up charges. The order was disbanded in disgrace, though many think the charges had more to do with politics than any actual wrongdoing.

17

TERRADILLOS TO CALZADILLA DE LOS HERMANILLOS

26.4km
(16.4mi)

5.5-7 Hours
Difficulty:
P 17%, 4.6km
U 83%, 21.8km

A Albergues:
Moratinos 3.2km
San Nicolás 5.8km
Sahagún 12.8km
Calzada 18.0km
Calzadilla 26.4km
Reliegos 44.0km

Alt. Stage 17A:
Terradillos to Burgo Mansilla, 30.9km
(p. 150 PU)

A Alt. Albergues:
Same to Calzada
Bercianos 23.3km
Burgo Ranero 30.9km
Reliegos 44.1km

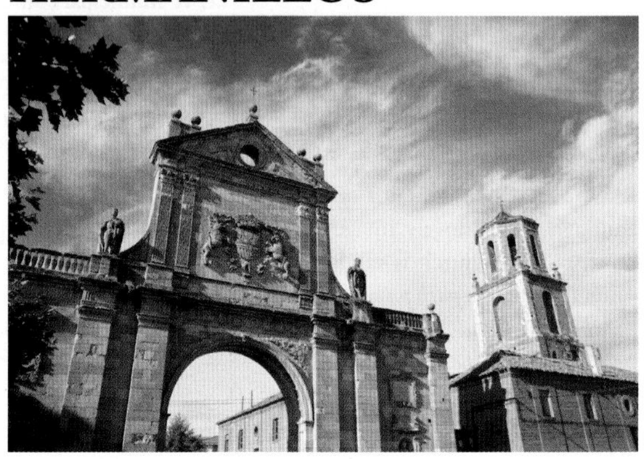

The regal arch of San Benito in Sahagún

See small-town Meseta life with mudbrick buildings, view impressive ruins in Sahagún, enjoy big sky scenery.

From Terradillos to Sahagún, the trail largely parallels the N-120 road through Meseta scenery and small towns with mudbrick houses. Sahagún has a wealth of historic buildings. At the split in Calzada de Coto, choose between the more remote northern route along the Roman *Via Trajana* to Calzadilla (recommended) or stay on the southern *Real Francesa* route, which parallels the paved road on a gravel track.

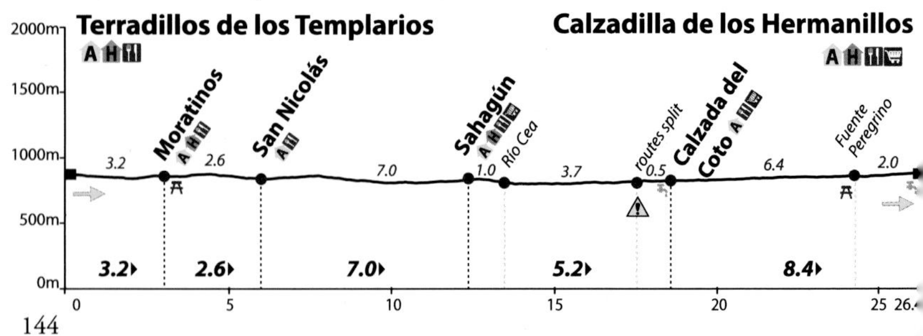

Calzadilla de los Hermanillos
El Burgo Ranero
Villamuñio
Las Grañeras
Real Francesa
A-231
26.4
24.4
30.9
Fuente del Peregrino (shelter)
Via Trajana
Calzada de Coto
18.0
17.5
23.3
21.7
Nuesta Señora de Perales
Bercianos del Real Camino
N-120
Codornillos
Villalmán
Joara
Villalebrín
Riosequillo
Río Valderaduey
Lagartos
Terradillos de los Templarios
Moratinos
San Nicolás del Real Camino
Sahagún
13.8
12.8
10.4
Virgen del Puente
5.8
3.2
0.0
San Pedro de las Dueñas
Galleguillos de Campos
Villemar
N
2 km
0 1 2
Casa el Cura 3
Via Trajana 2
Municipal 1
San Bartolomé
c/Mayor
100m
Sahagún
Viatoris 2
Los Balcones del Camino 7
El Ruedo 5
Escarcha 6
San Tirso
San Juan
Trinidad
1
La Codorniz 11
El Labriego 4
Madres Benedictinas 3
Alfonso VI 8
Cluny, Municipal
La Bastide du Chemin 9
Don Pacho 10
Puerta de Sahagún 12
Pedro Ponce
Roman Bridge Puente Canto
Río Cea
Santuario de la Peregrina
200m
El Burgo Ranero
La Laguna 3
1 Domenico Laffi
Piedras Blancas 4
El Peregrino 5
2 El Nogal
c/Fray Pedro
c/Real
100m
Calzada de Coto
A San Roque
c/San Roque
c/Real
Ermita de San Roque
17.5
100m
Bercianos
2 Santa Clara
Rivero 3
San Roque
c/Mayor
1 Bercianos
100m
San Nicolás
Nicolás de Bari
Laganares
50m
Moratinos
1 San Bruno
San Tomás
2 Moratinos
50m

3.2 Moratinos A H Pop. 68

1. A H **San Bruno** (assoc, 32, €9/25/32): , c/Ontanón 9, 979-061465, Apr-Jan, run by Italian Association
2. A H **Moratinos** (10, €10/35/45): c/Real 12, 979-061466, all year

5.8 San Nicolás del Real Camino A

Pop. 48, Spanish: "St. Nicolás of Royal Camino"

A **Laganares** (20, €9): (free), Plaza de la Iglesia, 979-188142, Mar 15-Oct

0.0 *Leave Terradillos by a dirt track lined with poplar trees south of highway N-120 and continue to the village of Moratinos.*

3.2 **Moratinos**: The name suggests that this village may have once been Muslim or had a significant Muslim population. Many *moriscos* (Muslims who converted to Catholicism) settled as farmers in the flat areas of Castilla, only to be removed in 1609. There's not much to see in the 16th-century Iglesia Parroquial de San Tomás, but the roofed porch provides a shady spot for a break. *After town, rejoin the dirt track south of the highway to San Nicolás del Real Camino.*

5.8 **San Nicolás del Real Camino** was also under Templar control until the late 12th century. The mudbrick Iglesia de San Nicolás de Bari was rebuilt in the 18th century but has a Baroque retablo inside. *Continue to the dirt track parallel to the highway. At the* ***Río Valderaduey (10.0km)****, cross and leave the highway to the R and continue perpendicular away from the highway to* ***Ermita Virgen del Puente (10.4km)****, built in Sahagún Mudéjar style. From here, the route approaches Sahagún by dirt path. The trail is waymarked through Sahagún in a way that avoids the most interesting churches and monuments, so be sure to check the city map* *(p. 145)* *to detour to points of interest.*

Bridge leading to Ermita Virgen del Puente before Sahagún

12.8 Sahagún

Looking at Sahagún today you would never guess its great significant in medieval times, second in the kingdom of León only to León city. King Alfonso VI was educated in Sahagún and sought refuge there while warring with his brother and richly rewarded the city when he emerged victoriously. He invited the Benedictines of Cluny to run the monastery, and the city became a center of Cluniac development (hence the name of the municipal albergue, Cluny). The city thrived with a diverse populace including Muslims and Jews. Sahagún's historic architecture illustrates the Romanesque-Mudéjar style, which incorporated Islamic decorative motifs and was built primarily out of brick rather than stone.

12.8 Sahagún

Pop. 2,820, *San Facundo*, a martyr killed nearby

1. **Cluny** (muni, 64, €5): , c/Arco 78, 987-782117, all year, smaller facility in winter
2. **Viatoris** (50, €5-8/18/25): Travesía El Arco 25, 987-780975, Mar-Oct, bike rental
3. **Madres Benedictinas** (par, 12, €8/25/36): (free), c/Antonio Nicolas 40, 987-781139
4. **El Labriego** (19, €8): , Av. Bermejo y Calderón 9, 722-115161, all year
5. **El Ruedo** (€35/55): , Plaza Mayor 1, 987-781834
6. **Escarcha** (€20/30): c/Regina Franco 12, 987-781856
7. **Los Balcones del Camino** (€35/45): , Av Constitución 53, 676-838242
8. **Alfonso VI** (€30/40): , c/Antonio Nicolás 4, 987-781144
9. **La Bastide du Chemin** (€28/40): , c/del Arco 66, 987-781183
10. **Don Pacho** (-/€35): Constitución 84, 987-780775
11. **La Codorniz** (€40/50): , c/Av. Constitución 97, 987-780276
12. **Puerta de Sahagún** (€60/90): , c/Burgos, 987-781880

Camping Pedro Ponce (tent €8): , Av. Tineo 1, 987-780415

After crossing the railroad tracks into town, the first churches on the way are the modern **Iglesia de la Trinidad**, an imposing mudbrick building housing the municipal albergue and Tourist Information, and next to it the bright **Iglesia de San Juan de Sahagún**, a Neoclassic structure that holds the remains of the martyred saints Facundo and Primitivo. From the albergue turnoff, the Camino is marked through Sahagún in a way that misses most of the architectural treasures, staying straight on *c/Arco*, then R on *c/Antonio Nicolás* through the city.

To detour to the historic sites, turn R past the albergue and take *c/El Arco* out to visit **Iglesia de San Lorenzo**, a 13th-century Romanesque-Mudéjar church with horseshoe arches and an interesting 1730 retablo. Turn L and head down through the *Plaza Mayor* to *c/Constitución* and *Plaza San Tirso,* which features numerous historical monuments.

Sahagún
July 2: Festival de Peregrina
Late Oct: Leek festival (*feria de puerro*)
Saturday is market day.

Iglesia San Tirso in Sahagún

Little remains of the once-great Clunian Monasterio de San Facundo, which in its heyday controlled over 100 monasteries throughout Tierra de Campos. Most of the remains were destroyed in the 19th century, first by the Peninsular War, then by fire. An 1835 clock tower looms above the ruins and the 1662 **Arco de San Benito** looks particularly regal with its lions and massive coat of arms.

At the Monastario de la Virgin Peregrina in Sahagun you can get a pilgrim certificate for €3 that declares you have passed the halfway point of the Camino.

On the other side of the ruins is **Iglesia de San Tirso**, another early 12th-century Mudéjar style church, whose impressive tower was rebuilt after a 1945 collapse. The nearby **Convento de las Madres Benedictinas** contains a 🏛 small museum featuring the Virgen de la Peregrina, patroness of Sahagún, brought to the museum from the Santuario de la Peregrina, a 13th-century church once part of a Franciscan monastery. This pilgrim virgin motif comes from a legend that lost pilgrims were guided here by a woman with a lighted staff.

⚠ Stage Options: 17 and 17A

☆ Via Trajana (via Calzadilla), 26.6km (17)
Recommended as the route is farther from the highway, more remote and follows a Roman road. Shorter distance than alternate, but **4.4km farther** to Mansilla in the next stage.

Real Francesa (via Burgo Ranero), 30.9km (17A)
Alternate route that shadows the highway but has more intermediary services (description p. 148). Allows shorter next stage.

Routes reconvene in Reliegos on stage 18 (p. 154).

Leave Sahagún via the marked route on c/Antonio Nicolás and cross the ***Río Cea (13.8km)*** *on the Puente Canto ("the singing bridge"), first built by Alfonso VI. Look for a grove of poplars to the R near the campground of Pedro Ponce; these are said to correspond to the Legend of the Flowering Lances, in which Charlemagne's troops stuck their lances in the ground while they slept. By morning they found that the lances had become trees and sprouted leaves and bark, which was considered an inauspicious sign. Many were lost in the battle after they had to hew down their own lances.*

Continue parallel to the highway on a dirt track. ⚠ At the junction of N-120 and N-601 (17.5km), two route options diverge and reconvene in Reliegos in stage 18. The recommended route description is below, and the alternate is on p. 148.

17.5 Via Trajana Route via Calzada de los Hermanillos

(alternative via el Burgo Ranero, p. 148)

The northern route follows the original Roman route, the *Via Trajana.* While today the straight path and planted shade trees make navigation easy, in medieval times this desolate area of the Camino was a notorious place to get lost as one could lose all sense of direction in the monotonous, featureless landscape. *At the split, take the R option and cross over A-231 on an overpass and enter Calzada de Coto.*

Stone crucero in Calzadilla

18.0 Calzada de Coto was one of many villages under the control of the monastery in Sahagún. Today it contains a church dedicated to Saint Stephen. *Pick up a dirt path on the outskirts of town, and continue straight to cross train tracks (20.3km) and on to the* ***Fuente del Peregrino (24.4km)****, with a shady rest area and playground. Keep straight to enter Calzadilla de los Hermanillos.*

18.0 Calzada de Coto A Pop. 259
Spanish: "boundary road"
A **San Roque** (muni, 36, don): c/Real, 987-781233, all year, basic, ask for key in bar

26.4 Calzadilla de los Hermanillos was named for the Benedictine monks sent from Sahagún who built the Ermita de la Virgen de los Dolores with Mozárabic brick details. Iglesia de San Bartolomé was built in the 16th-17th centuries, and features a statue of Saint Bartholomew wrestling with a demon.

26.4 Calzadilla de los Hermanillos A H
Pop. 146, Spanish: "little road of the little brothers"

1. A **Municipal** (22, don): c/Mayor 1, 987-330023, all year
2. A H **Via Trajana** (10, €15/-/35): c/Mayor 55, 987-337610, Apr-Nov
3. H **Casa el Cura** (€35/45): c/la Carretera 13, 987-337647

Walking parallel to the road on the alternate route

⚠ Alternate Stages 17A-18A: Real Francesa

17A: Terradillos to Burgo Ranero, 30.9km
18A: Burgo Ranero to Mansilla (via Reliegos), 19.2km
*distances measured from Terradillos

Stage 17A
P 13%, 4.0km
U 87%, 26.9km

17.5 *From the split, follow arrows L at the roundabout after crossing N-120. Pass a sign showing the route and a small monument before continuing on a dirt track parallel to a small quiet road. Pass the* ***Ermita de Nuestra Señora de Perales (21.7km)*** *"Our Lady of the Pear Trees," site of a former pilgrim hospital just east of Bercianos del Camino.*

23.3 Bercianos del Real Camino

Pop. 195, *Bercianos* likely refers to people from Bierzo region settled here after the Reconquista

1. **A ☆ Bercianos** (+500m, par, 46, don): c/Santa Rita 11, 987-784008, Apr-Oct, communal meals and singing
2. **A H Santa Clara** (8, €8/-/25-30): c/Iglesia 3, 605-839993, July-May
3. **H Rivero** (€35/40): c/Mayor 12, 987-784287

23.3 Bercianos del Camino

was also administrated by the monastery of Sahagún. The town has one small chapel of San Roque since the main Iglesia de San Salvador collapsed in 1998. The tower has been reconstructed in metal and can be seen off to the R on the way into town. *Leaving Bercianos, continue on the now-familiar parallel dirt track to Burgo Ranero.*

30.9 **El Burgo Ranero** was a wool-producing town, the biggest business of Castilla during the Middle Ages. Huge flocks of sheep (up to 40,000) were tended. They grazed in the mountains in summer while the Meseta fields were occupied with wheat, and returned in winter via specially developed sheep roads known as *cañadas*. Even today you may have the privilege of witnessing a flock of sheep blocking your path as they cross the Camino on an ancient *cañada*. If coming from Terradillos, El Burgo Ranero is the most logical town for overnight. Below is the route description for the following stage, which reconnects with the main route in Reliegos, corresponding to the map on p. 153.

30.9 **El Burgo Ranero** A H

Pop. 826, Spanish: "town of frogs," or perhaps a distortion of *burgo granero*, or "town of wheat"

1. A **Domenico Laffi** (muni, 28, don): Plaza Mayor, ✆987-330023, all year
2. A **El Nogal** (assoc, 30, €7-10): c/Fray Pedro 42, ✆627-229331, Easter-Oct
3. A H **La Laguna** (18, €8/30/40): c/La Laguna 12, ✆987-330094, Mar-Nov
4. H **Piedras Blancas** (€30/45): c/Fray Pedro 32, ✆987-330094
5. H **El Peregrino** (€30/45): c/Fray Pedro 36, ✆987-330069

Stage 18A
P 6%, 1.2km
U 94%, 18.0km

To continue on alternate stage 18A to rejoin the main route, follow the gravel path next to a quiet paved road. Be prepared for few services and little shade to ***Reliegos (13.0km)****. A few picnic areas are present, but no water sources. At Reliegos, this alternate route joins with the recommended route coming from Calzada de los Hermanillos (p. 154). The distance from El Burgo Ranero to* ***Mansilla de las Mulas*** *is 19.2km.*

Mudbrick albergue Domenico Laffi in Burgo Ranero

18

CALZADILLA DE LOS HERMANILLOS TO MANSILLA DE LAS MULAS

23.6km
(14.7mi)

6-7 Hours
Difficulty:
P 22%, 5.4km
U 78%, 18.2km

A Albergues:
Reliegos 17.6km
Mansilla 23.6km
Villarente 29.6km
Arcahueja 33.9km

Alt. Stage 18A:
Burgo Ranero to Reliegos, 19.2km
(p. 151 P U)

A Alt. Albergues:
(from Burgo Ranero)
Reliegos 13.2km
Mansilla 19.2km
Villarente 25.2km
Arcahueja 29.5km

Priests along the Roman road to Reliegos

Tread remote Roman paths and climb medieval walls in Mansilla de las Mulas, enjoy the freedom of the open road.

This is an isolated day, far from towns and paved roads, along one of the best sections of Roman road in all of Spain. Be sure to bring sufficient water and food for the 17.6km without services until Reliegos, where this route joins the southern route from El Burgo Ranero (details in stage 17, p. 151) and continues into Mansilla parallel to a paved road.

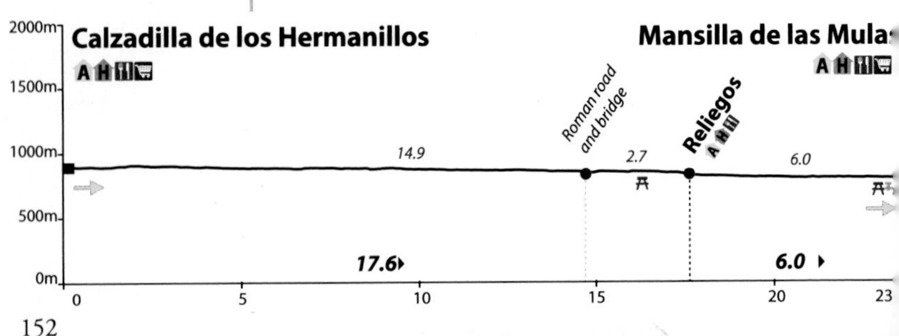

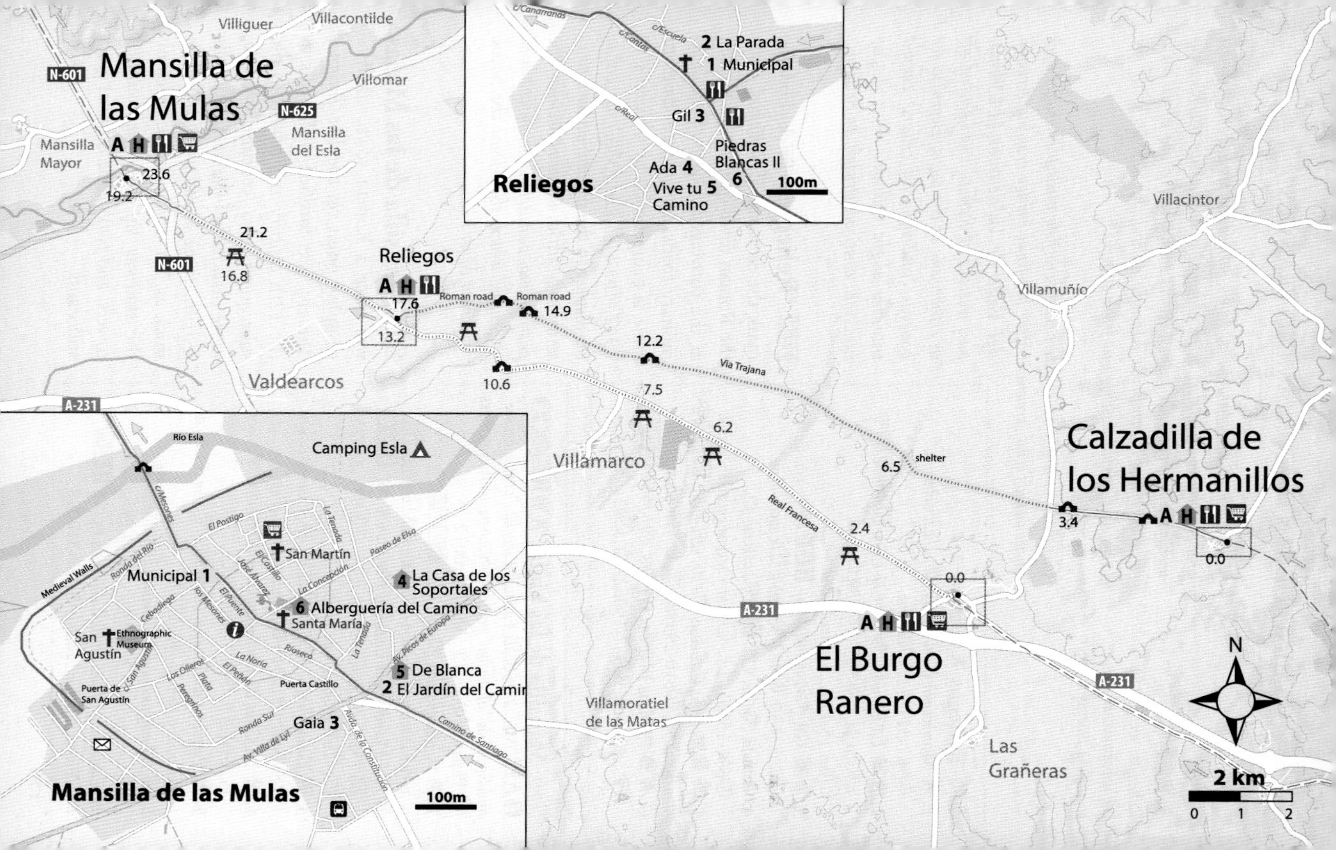

Mansilla de las Mulas
Villiguer
Villacontilde
Villomar
N-601
N-625
Mansilla Mayor
Mansilla del Esla
23.6
19.2
21.2
16.8
Reliegos
17.6
13.2
Roman road
Roman road
14.9
12.2
Via Trajana
10.6
Valdearcos
7.5
6.2
Villamarco
6.5
shelter
Real Francesa
2.4
0.0
A-231
El Burgo Ranero
Villamoratiel de las Matas
Las Grañeras
Villacintor
Villamuñío
Calzadilla de los Hermanillos
3.4
0.0
N
2 km
0
1
2
Reliegos
2 La Parada
1 Municipal
Gil 3
Piedras Blancas II
6
Ada 4
Vive tu 5 Camino
c/Canarranas
c/Escuela
c/Cantas
c/Real
100m
Mansilla de las Mulas
Río Esla
Camping Esla
c/Mesones
El Postigo
San Martín
La Tenada
Paseo de Elsa
El Castillo
José Álvarez
La Concepción
4 La Casa de los Soportales
6 Alberguería del Camino
Santa María
Medieval Walls
Ronda del Río
Municipal 1
Cebadiega
los Mesones
El Puente
San Agustín
Ethnographic Museum
La Noria
Rioseco
Av. Picos de Europa
5 De Blanca
2 El Jardín del Camin
Los Olleros
El Peñón
Plata
Peregrinos
Puerta Castillo
Puerta de San Agustín
Ronda Sur
Gaia 3
Avda. de la Constitución
Av. Villa de Lyl
Camino de Santiago
100m

⚠ Routes join in Reliegos; see p. 151 for information on route via Burgo Ranero

0.0 *Leave Calzadilla on c/Mayor, where the path leaves asphalt and continues on a dirt path along the same route the Romans used to transport gold from Galicia to Rome. To the north on a clear day the Cantábrica Mountains will be visible, with the Picos de Europa peeking out from behind.*

Continue straight on the dirt path, crossing multiple bridges over small canals and streams. After the final bridge crossing ***Arroyo del Valle de Valdearcos (14.9km)****, pass sections of Roman road fenced off to either side of the path. Begin to see bodegas (underground cellars) carved into the slight hillside. At a 4-way junction, continue straight to Reliegos.*

17.6 **Reliegos** A H Pop. 237

1. **A Municipal** (45, €5): c/Escuela, 987-317801, all year
2. **A H La Parada** (36, €7/-/30): c/Escuela 7, 987-317880, Jan 15-Dec 20, small
3. **A H Gil** (14, €8/-/30): c/Cantas 30, 987-317804, Easter-Nov
4. **A Ada** (20, €7): c/Real 42, 691-153010, Mar-Oct, vegetarian meals
5. **A H Vive tu Camino** (20, €9/-/35): c/Real 56, 610-293986, Mar-Oct
6. **A H Piedras Blancas II** (8, €9/-/45): c/Cantas, 987-190627, Mar-Oct

17.6 **Reliegos**: Brick bodegas mark the entrance of Reliegos, once the Roman town of *Palantia* located at the convergence of three Roman military roads. Its modern claim to fame is being struck by a meteor in 1947. The 17.3 kilo (38lb) meteor is on display in the natural science museum in Madrid. *Leaving Reliegos, the path follows parallel to the quiet paved c/Cantas, which then joins the paved road into Mansilla.*

23.6 **Mansilla de las Mulas** A H

Pop. 1,950, Latin: *mansella* "small estate" and Spanish "of mules" refers to historic mule markets

Plaza del Pozo 12, 987-310012

1. **A Municipal** (76, €5): c/del Puente 5, 661-977305, Mar-mid Dec
2. **A El Jardín del Camino** (32, €8-10): c/Camino de Santiago 1, 987-310232, all year, call in winter
3. **A Gaia** (18, €8): Av. Constitución 28, 699-911311, all year ex. Feb
4. **H La Casa de los Soportales** (€36/48): Pl Arrabal 9, 987-310232
5. **H Pensión de Blanca** (€25/40): Av. Picos de Europa 4, 626-003177
6. **H Alberguería del Camino** (€38/56): c/Concepción 12, 987-311193

Camping Municipal Esla (tent €6.8): c/Fuente de los Prados, 987-310089

23.6 **Mansilla de las Mulas** was once a Roman town, likely a stopping point on the *Via Trajana.* The city was fortified with walls in the 12th century and rebuilt in the subsequent two centuries. Today, more than half of the medieval walls remain, some as tall as 14m and as thick as 3m. It is possible to climb the stairway up into the rounded towers, and two of the original gates still stand.

Mansilla with grazing sheep near the historic city walls

Iglesia de Santa María was the only church in Mansilla until 1220 when five churches were added, and Santa María has outlasted them all (though it was rebuilt in the 18th century). The church contains a Baroque retablo and a Gothic Virgin Mary. Ruins of the 14th-century **Iglesia de San Martín** have been incorporated into a government building, the **Casa de Cultura**. The former 🏛 **Convent of San Agustín** has been converted into an attractive ethnographic museum beautifully displaying over 3,500 local artifacts, such as farming implements, textiles and traditional costumes (€5, 🕒10am-2pm, 5-8pm summer, closed Mon ✆987-311923, c/San Agustín 1).

Mansilla is also the backdrop of the famous 1605 novel *La Pícara Justina*. The Río Esla provides a shaded pleasant area for a walk or wade in the evening.

🎂 **Mansilla de las Mulas**
November 11: San Martín patron saint day
Early September: Pilgrimage from León
Bacallao mansillés, cod in a special garlic sauce, is a local specialty.

19

MANSILLA DE LAS MULAS TO LEÓN

17.9km
(11.1mi)

4-5 Hours
Difficulty:
P 42%, 7.6km
U 58%, 10.3km

A Albergues:
Villarente 6.0km
Arcahueja 10.3km
León 17.9km
Virgen 25.6km

Luminous stained glass in the León Cathedral

Stand in awe of León's luminous Gothic cathedral and Romanesque Real Colegiata de San Isidoro, splurge on a night at San Marcos Parador.

If you were going to skip one day of the Camino, this would be it. Much has been done to improve the safety of the pilgrim approach to León, with pedestrian bridges and overpasses, but the route still involves a lot of industrial walking. Be on alert for trail markers, detours and traffic! The effort is well-rewarded with the fascinating sites and history of the vibrant city of León.

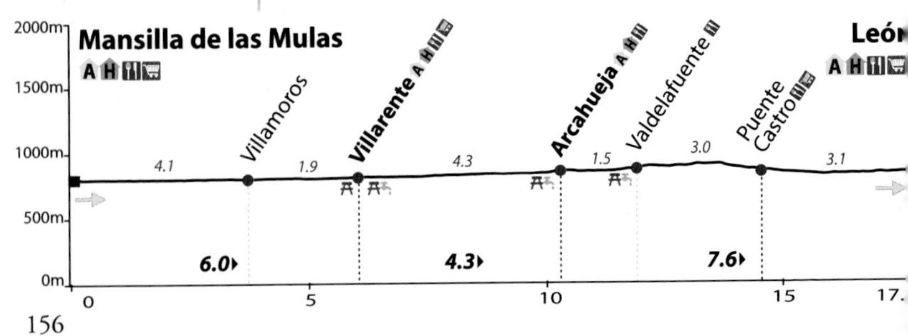

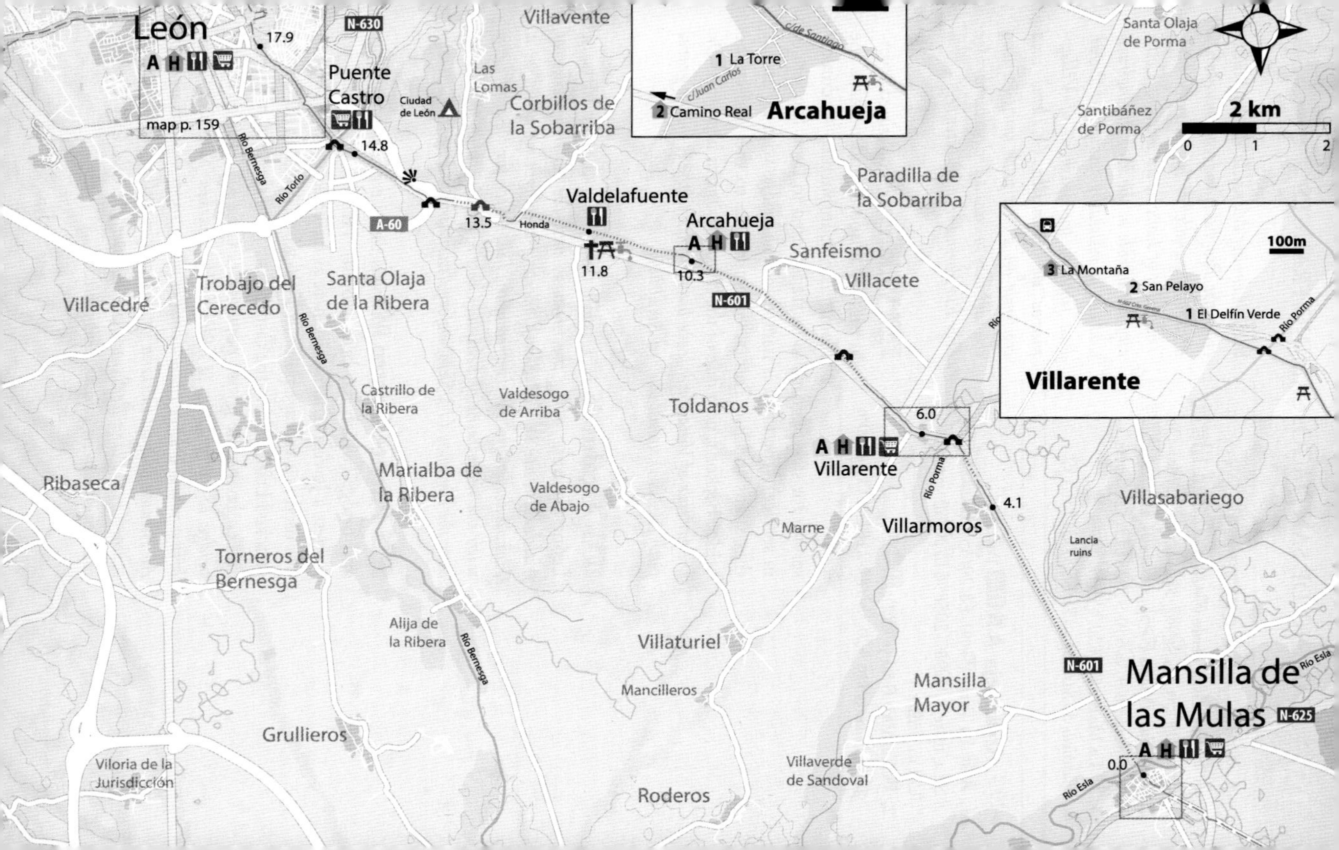
León
17.9
map p. 159
N-630
Puente
Castro
Ciudad
de León
14.8
Río Torío
Río Bernesga
A-60
13.5
Honda
Villavente
Las
Lomas
Corbillos de
la Sobarriba
Valdelafuente
11.8
Arcahueja
10.3
N-601
1 La Torre
c/Juan Carlos
c/de Santiago
2 Camino Real
Arcahueja
Santa Olaja
de Porma
Santibáñez
de Porma
2 km
0
1
2
Paradilla de
la Sobarriba
Sanfeismo
Villacete
3 La Montaña
2 San Pelayo
1 El Delfín Verde
Río Porma
100m
Villarente
Villacedré
Trobajo del
Cerecedo
Santa Olaja
de la Ribera
Castrillo de
la Ribera
Valdesogo
de Arriba
Toldanos
6.0
Villarente
Ribaseca
Marialba de
la Ribera
Valdesogo
de Abajo
Villasabariego
4.1
Villarmoros
Marne
Lancia
ruins
Torneros del
Bernesga
Alija de
la Ribera
Villaturiel
Mancilleros
Mansilla
Mayor
N-601
Mansilla de
las Mulas
N-625
Río Esla
0.0
Grullieros
Viloria de la
Jurisdicción
Villaverde
de Sandoval
Roderos

6.0 Villarente Pop. 342
1. **El Delfín Verde** (20, €6/25/40): , Crta 601 km 15, 987-312065, Mar-Oct
2. **San Pelayo** (56, €8/-/40): , c/El Romero 9, 650-918281, all year
3. **La Montaña** (€30/45): , Camino de Santiago 17, 987-312161

10.3 Arcahueja Pop. 194
1. **La Torre** (30, €8/20/35): , c/La Torre 1, 987-205896, all year, call in winter
2. **Camino Real** (-/€72): , Ctra N-601, km 320, 987-218134, +400m

0.0 *Leaving Mansilla de las Mulas, cross the Río Esla and continue on a dirt path parallel to highway N-601. The ruins of Lancía, an ancient Celtic city, are visible to the R of the highway and can be visited by detour [+1.2km]. Pass through the outskirts of* ***Villarmoros de Mansilla (4.1km)*** *and continue on a dirt path until joining the highway to cross a pedestrian bridge over Río Porma into Villarente.*

6.0 **Villarente** contained several pilgrim hospitals and perhaps the Camino's first ambulance—a donkey service for sick pilgrims to be transported to León (no longer in service). The town is named for the bridge with 20 arches that spans the Río Porma. A picnic area to the L after the bridge beckons, near one of the historic pilgrim hospitals. *On the far side of Villarente, leave busy N-601 to the R onto a gravel path (7.2km) uphill toward Arcahueja.*

10.3 **Arcahueja** is a small town near the outskirts of León. *Continue along the highway past the northern edge of* ***Valdelafuente (11.8km)****, meeting the highway again at a Honda dealership. At the crest of the hill, watch for views of León with the mountains of behind. Cross a massive blue footbridge over the highway (13.5km) before descending to Puente Castro.*

14.8 **Puente Castro** was the site of a Roman fort and bridge (which has been rebuilt). Hebrew grave markers suggest a Jewish community here as far back as 905. The hill was used as a vantage point in 1196 when Aragón and Castile attacked León, taking the castle, destroying the Jewish quarter and enslaving the Jewish population. *Cross Río Torío on a footbridge to enter León (15.9km). The marked path into León brings you to a large roundabout of major roads. Stay straight on Av. Alcalde Miguel Castaño for the parochial albergue and downtown. Cross Plaza de Santa Ana to enter the Old City with its cobblestone streets and ancient walls.*

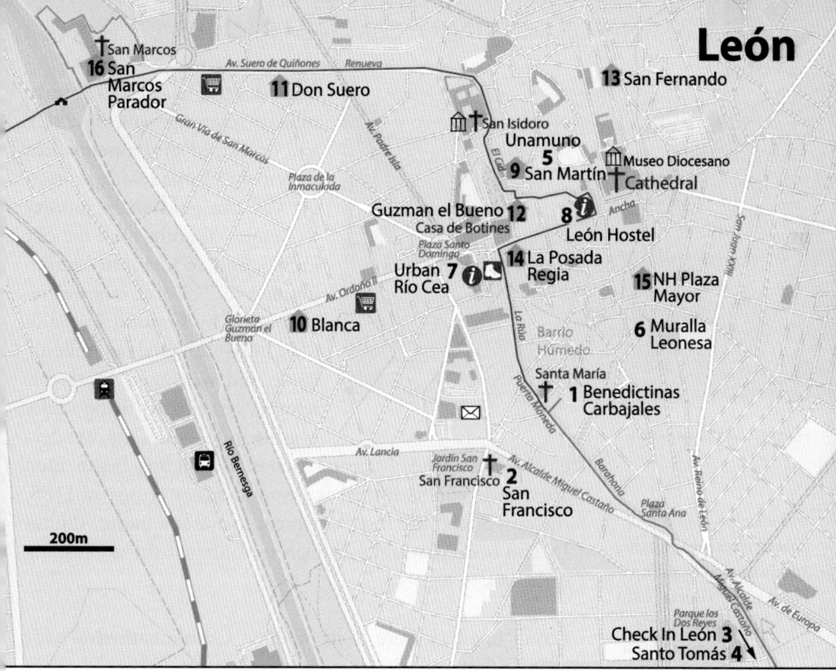

León A H

4,305, In Spanish, *León* means "lion," but the name comes from the Latin military term for legion.

enedictinas Carbajales (par, 132, €5 w/): , Plaza Santa María del Camino, 87-252866, all year, evening Mass and pilgrim blessing, stuffy dorms

an Francisco de Asis (par, 100+, €10/-/30): , Av. Alcalde Miguel Castaños 4, 7-215060, all year, laundry and internet are free

heck In León (40, €10): , c/Alcalde Miguel Castaño 88, 987-498793, all year

anto Tomás de Canterbury (54, €8): , Av. Lastra 53, 987-392626, Feb-Nov

Unamuno (86, €10/20/30): , c/San Pelayo 15, 987-233010

Muralla Leonesa (65, €10/-/40): , c/Tarifa 5, 987-177873, Mar-Oct

Hostel Urban Río Cea (8, €18/-/€45 w/) , c/Legión VII 2, 639-179386, a. y.

León Hostel (14, €12-13/-/30): , c/Ancha 8, 987-079907, all year

ostal San Martín (€25/35): , Plaza de Torres de Omaña 1, 987-875187

Pensión Blanca (€30/43): , c/Villafranca 2, 987-251991

Hostal Don Suero (€24/40): , c/Suero de Quiñones 15, 987-230600

Guzmán el Bueno (€33/50): , c/Lopez Castrillón 6, 987-236412

Hospederia San Fernando I (€35/40): , Av. de los Cubos 32, 987-220731

Hotel La Posada Regia (€50/60): , c/Regidores 9, 987-213173

NH Plaza Mayor (-/€120): , Plaza Mayor 15-17, 987-344357

Parador de San Marcos (-/€130-200): , Plaza de San Marcos 7, 987-237300

dad de León (tent €10, cabin €45): , 987-269086, 3km out of city

Historic walls of León

179.9 León began as a Roman military encampment in 29CE and developed into a permanent settlement charged with protecting Galician gold on its journey to Rome. Visigoths took the city in 585, only to lose it to Muslim invaders in 712. The city was reconquered by Ordoño I around 850, who initiated a building boom and welcomed Mozárabic refugees (Christians living under Muslim rule). The city was leveled in 988 by Al-Mansur's troops. Rebuilding began soon after, and León flourished as a wool industry center. In 1188, the city hosted the first Parliament in Europe under Alfonso IX and became wealthy enough to construct the astonishing cathedral.

León has a wealth of dozens of other churches and historical buildings. Head to **Tourist Info** for additional information (opposite cathedral on Plaza de Reglas, 987-237082).

León's finest treasure is its sublime Gothic **cathedral** (€5, M-Sa 9:30am-1:30pm, 4-8pm Su 8:30am-2:40pm, 5-8pm/ winter closed 1hr earlier 987-875770) featuring 1,800m² of magnificent stained glass windows from the 13th-15th centuries. Without a flashy central retablo, the cathedral lets the streaming light steal the show. This is the fourth church on this spot, began in 1205 and completed in record time (about 100 years). From across the square, the whole of the west façade can be taken in. The serene *Virgen Blanca* welcomes from below the central tympanum. Choir stalls are intricately carved with biblical characters along with some humorous depictions of creative vices. The seven chapels contain Gothic tombs such as that of Ordoño II, with a scene of the crucifixion. El Cid (p. 86), an epic knight born in Burgos in 1040, is buried in the center of the cathedral.

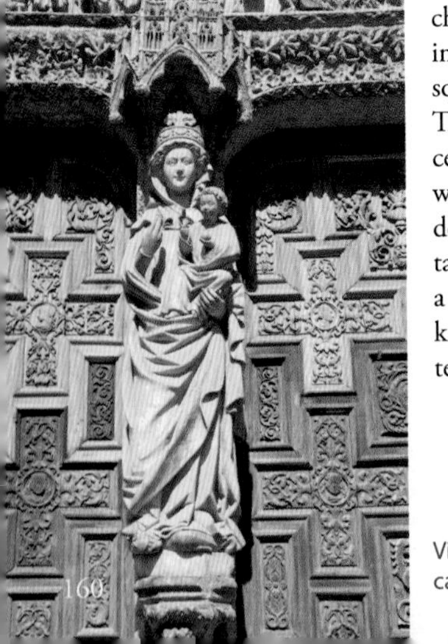

Virgen Blanca (left) at the west entrance of the León cathedral (right)

León
Late June: Trout festival
October 5: Patron saint day, Sunday before celebrates the medieval Christians being freed from giving 100 virgins to their Muslim overlords (p. 139)
Wed and **Sat** are market days in the Plaza Mayor, 9am-2pm

The **Museo Diocesano** (€5, M-F 9:30-2pm, 4-7:30pm Sa 9:30-2pm, 4-7pm, Su closed, reduced hours in winter) houses almost 1,500 pieces of sacred art, including Hispano-Islamic textiles, Hebrew funerary stones and a 1576 sculpture, *Christ on the Cross*.

The impressive **Real Colegiata de San Isidoro** (987-876161) is one of the premier Romanesque structures, setting the standard for all of northern Spain. The 11th-century complex was commissioned by the pious Fernando I to house relics returned by Muslims after their defeat in the Reconquista. The relics of San Isidoro of Seville (ca. 560-636) are housed in the basilica.

The **Panteón de los Reyes** and **Museo de San Isidoro**, across the plaza from the basilica, can be visited on a guided tour in Spanish (€5, summer: M-Sa 9am-8pm, Su 9am-2pm). The 12th-century fresco paintings in the pantheon are a highlight, with remarkable representations of the 12 months on its arches. There are 44 tombs, including 23 kings, demonstrating the site's importance. Doña Urraca's jeweled chalice

A pilgrim statue rests outside off Hostal San Marcos Parador

Nightlife in the historic *Barrio Húmedo*

is another must-see of the museum. The impressive library contains texts from as far back as the 10th century and a particularly lovely illuminated Bible. The basilica also features a *Puerta del Perdón,* which pilgrims who were unable to continue to Santiago could walk through to receive substitute indulgences.

For evening entertainment, check out León's **Barrio Húmedo** (literally "wet neighborhood") in the Old City, known for its high concentration of bars and tradition of free tapas with drinks.

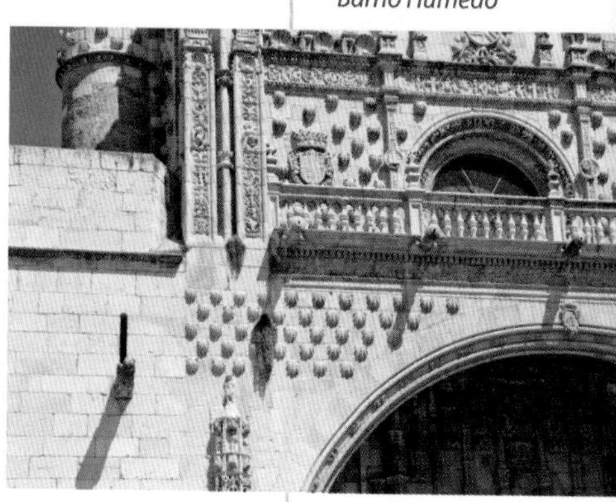

Shell motif on Hostal San Marcos

Antonio Gaudí's modernist **Casa de Botines** (1893) incorporates Gothic elements but retains Gaudí's unique whimsical style. The building originally housed a department store and is now a bank.

On the way out of town, pass **Hostal San Marcos**, a sumptuous 15th-century pilgrim hospital now restored as a modern Parador hotel, which was featured in the film *The Way* as the place where Martin Sheen's character treats his friends to a night of luxury. A dozing pilgrim statue rests barefoot in the plaza facing San Marcos.

Wedding in the León Cathedral

20

LEÓN TO VILLAR DE MAZARIFE

21.5km
(13.4mi)

5-6 HOURS
DIFFICULTY:
P 73%, 15.6km
U 27%, 5.9km

A ALBERGUES:
Trobajo 4.5km
Virgen 7.7km
Mazarife 21.5km
Villavante 31.1km
Hospital 36.7km

ALT. STAGE 20A:
León to Villadangos, 20.8km (p. 168 P U)

A ALT. ALBERGUES:
Trobajo 4.5km
Virgen 7.7km
Valverde 11.5km
Villadangos 20.8km
San Martín 25.4km
Hospital 32.8km

Colorful house in Villar de Mazarife

Visit the legendary church of Virgen del Camino, abandon pavement for earthen paths, visit mudbrick churches.

The exit from León is no more glamorous than the entrance with about 8km of city walking including some highly industrialized area. These can be skipped with bus A1 to Virgen de Camino, where the path leaves the León metro area. The path splits again, with the recommended route to the south and a northern route (p. 168) parallel to the N-120 road. The recommended route is longer but much more scenic. The routes converge in Hospital and again before Astorga.

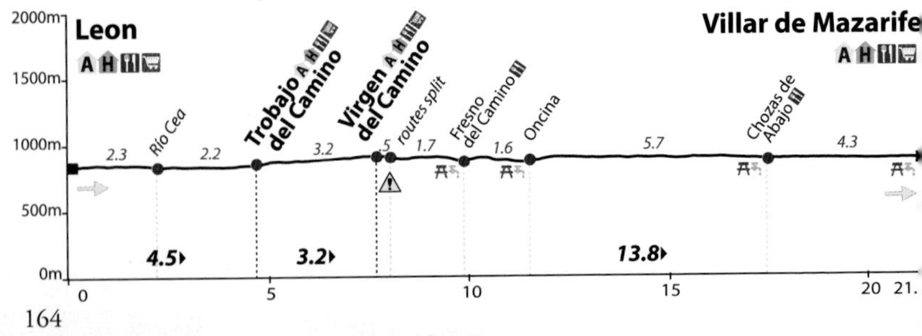

León
0.0
Puente
Castro
La Virgen
del Camino
León Airport
7.7
8.2
N-120
A-66
A-71
Montejos
del Camino
Valverde
11.5
San Miguel
13.5
9.9
Fresno
del Camino
11.5
Oncina
Quintana
de Raneros
Santovenia de
la Valdoncina
Robledo de
la Valdoncina
Villanueva
del Carnero
Onzonilla
Chozas
de Arriba
Chozas
de Abajo
17.2
shade
20.8
Villadangos
del Páramo
Fojedo
Villar de Mazarife
21.5
Viloria de la
Jurisdicción
Cembranos
N
2 km
0
1
2
Municipal 1
4 Libertad
Alto 3
Páramo
Santiago
100m
Camino de Santiago
La Virgen del Camino
San Froilán
and Plaza 2
Virgen del
Camino
3
Villapaloma
1
Don Antonino
y Doña Cinia
to Villadangos
8.2
to Villar de Mazarife
100m
Villar de Mazarife
San Antonio de Pádua 1
2 Casa de Jesús
3 Tío Pepe
Santiago
Camino León
100m

4.5 Trobajo del Camino
Pop. 21,378
A **Casa Simón** (26, €16.50 w/): , c/Guzmán el Bueno 52, 987-807552, a. y.
H **El Abuelo** (€35/50): , c/Los Mesones 6, 987-801044

7.7 Virgen del Camino
Pop. 4,820
1. A **Don Antonino y Doña Cinia** (muni, 40, €6): , Av. Padre Eustoquio 16, 987-302800, Apr-Oct
2. H **Hostales San Froilán and Plaza** (€31/45): , c/Peregrinos 1, 987-302019, side by side
3. H **Villapaloma** (€34/46): , Av. Astorga 47, 987-300990

0.0 *From the parochial albergue, take c/Ancho and walk to the cathedral (map p. 159). Turn back to wind your way west to reach c/Renueva. Follow this road to San Marcos and continue across **Río Bernesga (2.3km)** on a 16th-century stone bridge to head straight through the suburb of **Trobajo del Camino (4.5km)** and onward to Virgen del Camino.*

7.7 Virgen del Camino

The **Basílica de la Virgen del Camino** is a modern church (1961) of artistic significance, unique along the Camino. The location stems from a legend that in 1505 the Virgin appeared to a shepherd here. The shepherd went to the bishop to build a hermitage on the spot, but the bishop was not convinced. The Virgin Mary told the shepherd to use a slingshot to throw a stone and build the shrine wherever the stone landed. The shepherd obeyed, and the small stone became a boulder, a miracle that convinced the bishop to build the church.

One legend says that a Christian was being held captive inside a strong box in North Africa in 1522. The Virgin Mary knew of this man's plight and his desire to visit her church, so she miraculously transported him here, box, chains and all. The sacristy of the current church houses the box and chains. The church became a local pilgrimage site and was recently elevated to the rank of a minor basilica. The modern façade features the 12 disciples, and the interior includes the Baroque retablo from the former church.

Basílica de la Virgen del Camino

⚠ Just past Virgen del Camino near a small park with a Santiago statue, the trail splits into two options (8.2km). The recommended route via Villar de Mazarife to the far L on gravel, and the alternate route via Villadangos along the N-120 road (p. 168).

Villar de Mazarife Route

The recommended route to Villar de Mazarife crosses over highways A-66 and A-71 and onto a quiet country road to ***Fresno del Camino*** *(9.9km) and follows the same road over the railroad tracks and Río Oncina to* ***Oncina de la Valdoncina (11.5km)****. Leave town on a small paved road that becomes a pleasant dirt path through fields, with some slight incline to a flat plateau into* ***Chozas de Abajo*** ***(17.2km)****, known for its fall potato festival. The path becomes paved again through town and follows a paved road to the outskirts of Villar de Mazarife past a pilgrim mosaic into the town.*

21.5 Villar de Mazarife A H

Pop. 391, Mozarabic surname

1. **A H San Antonio de Pádua** (50, €8/-/30-50): W D @, c/Leon 33, 987-390192, a. y.
2. **A Casa de Jesús** (60, €5): K W @, c/Corujo 11, 987-390697, all year
3. **A H Tío Pepe** (26, €9/30/40-50): W @, c/El Teso 2, 987-390517, Mar-Nov

21.5 Villar de Mazarife

is a friendly pilgrim town with the mudbrick **Iglesia de Santiago** featuring several images of the saint. There's even an eclectic museum of art and local artifacts called **Casa Museo Antolin** (free entrance). A medieval-style mosaic greets visitors at the entrance.

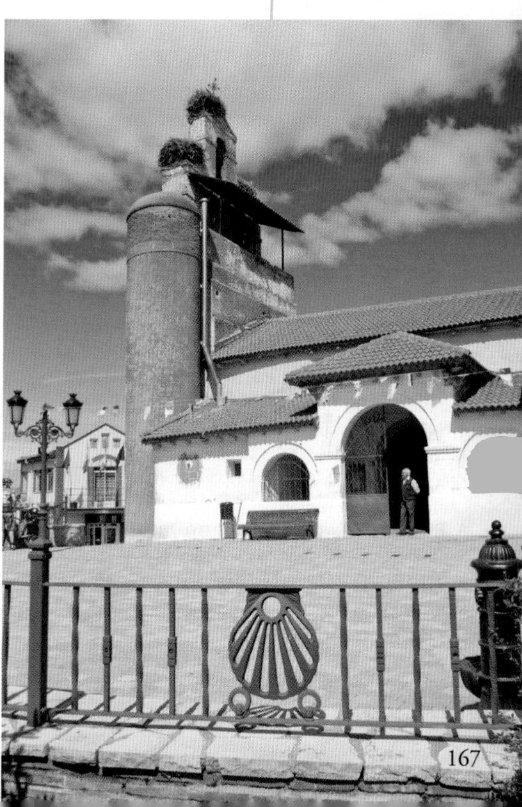

Iglesia de Santiago in Villar de Mazarife

Pilgrim statue in Villar de Mazarife

⚠ Alternate Stages: Villadangos Route

20A: León to Villadangos, 20.8km
P 55%, 11.4km
U 45%, 9.4km

While this route was the historic Camino Francés, today it follows a monotonous path next to highway N-120 with whizzing traffic and industrial stretches. The route is about 5km shorter over the course of two stages and has slightly less pavement, but is much less scenic than the recommended route. *From the split after Virgen del Camino, stay R uphill past a cemetery and straight through the highway junction and along the N-120 road.*

11.5 **Valverde de la Virgen** is the first town with services. Soon afterwards the path passes through **San Miguel del Camino** (**13.5km**), which had a 12th-century pilgrim hospital. Today a local man offers candy and nuts to passing pilgrims. *The track parallel to the highway continues all the way to Villadangos del Páramo through industrial areas.*

11.5 **Valverde de la Virgen** A Pop. 213
A **La Casa del Camino** (32, €8): Camino El Jano 2A, 669-874750, all year

20.8 **Villadangos del Páramo** A H Pop. 1,140 Spanish: "town of Angos [a French surname] of Páramo [this region]."

1. A **Municipal** (54, €5): Crta a Villadangos del Páramo, 671-010786, all year, call in winter
2. A H **San Pancracio** (17, €10/10/20): Crta km 18, 987-390230, 1.6km before town
3. H **Alto Páramo** (€21/31): N-120 km 18, 987-390425
4. H **Libertad** (€35/45): c/Padre Ángel Martínez 25, 987-390123

Camping Camino de Santiago: N-120 km 324, 987-680253, Apr 15-Sept 25

20.8 **Villadangos del Páramo** is the site of an 1111 battle between Queen Urraca of León and Alfonso I of Aragón (who were married at the time). Their marriage was meant to unite the kingdoms but instead resulted in civil war. The modern **Iglesia de Santiago** has a chancel depicting the Battle of Clavijo and a Santiago Matamoros image appears to leap out from the altar. The town straddles the highway and provides good pilgrim services and is the logical overnight stop if starting in León.

21A: Villadangos to Astorga, 27.1km

P 49%, 13.5km

U 51%, 13.6km

From ***Villadangos (map p. 171)****, follow the main street and leave town via a dirt path that crosses a small footbridge past the ruins of a former pilgrim hospital. This shady dirt path goes out to highway N-120 and across onto a path on the L side of the highway next to a canal. Note camping area to L. Enter San Martín del Camino (4.6km). Be careful crossing the busy N-120 highway.*

4.6 San Martín del Camino

is a village from the 13th century, which housed a pilgrim hospital in the 17th century. *Continue on the dirt path parallel to highway. Rejoin the recommended route in* ***Hospital de Órbigo (12.0km, p. 173)****.*

⚠ *From Hospital, follow the recommended route (p. 173) or turn L at the outskirts of Hospital to follow a marked track along highway N-120.*

The routes rejoin in 10.3km at the ***Crucero de Santo Toribio (22.3km, p. 174)*** *outside of Astorga, saving 1.2km, but sacrificing scenery. The shortest distance from Villadangos to Astorga is 27.1km, using this road route.*

4.6 San Martín del Camino A H

Pop. 517

1. A **Municipal** (68, €5): , 676-020388, all year, under the water tower
2. A **La Casa Verde** (8 beds, €10 w/): , Travesía Estación 8, 646-879437, all year
3. A H **Santa Ana** (96, €6/20/30): , 987-378653, all year
4. A H **Vieira** (40, €7/-/25): , Av. Peregrinos, 987-378565, all year, vegetarian and gluten free meals

A stone arrow marks the way to Villar de Mazarife

21

VILLAR DE MAZARIFE TO ASTORGA

31.5km
(19.6mi)

7-9 Hours
Difficulty: ▬■□
P 48%, 15.0km
U 52%, 16.5km

A Albergues:
Villavante 9.6km
Hospital 15.2km
Villares 17.6km
Santibañez 20.2km
San Justo 28.1km
Astorga 31.5km
Valdeviejas 34.3km

Alt. Stage 21A:
Villadangos to Hospital to Astorga (p. 169 P U)

A Alt. Albergues:
(from Villadangos)
Hospital 12.0km
San Justo, 23.7km
Astorga 27.1km
Valdeviejas 29.9km

Pilgrim statue in Astorga

Imagine the excitement of a medieval joust in Hospital de Órbigo. Visit Roman ruins and a chocolate factory in Astorga.

The first half of this stage offers the last of flat Meseta scenery before the path becomes more rolling and green in preparation for the Cantabrian Mountains in the next stage. Hospital de Órbigo is a pleasant halfway point to enjoy medieval ambiance. The alternate routes meet in Hospital, but split again at the far end of town, with the slightly longer recommended route to the north. The two reconvene just before Astorga at a marvelous viewpoint into the city.

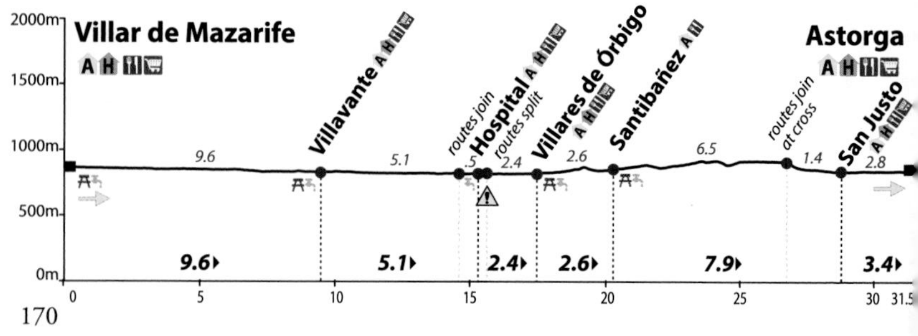

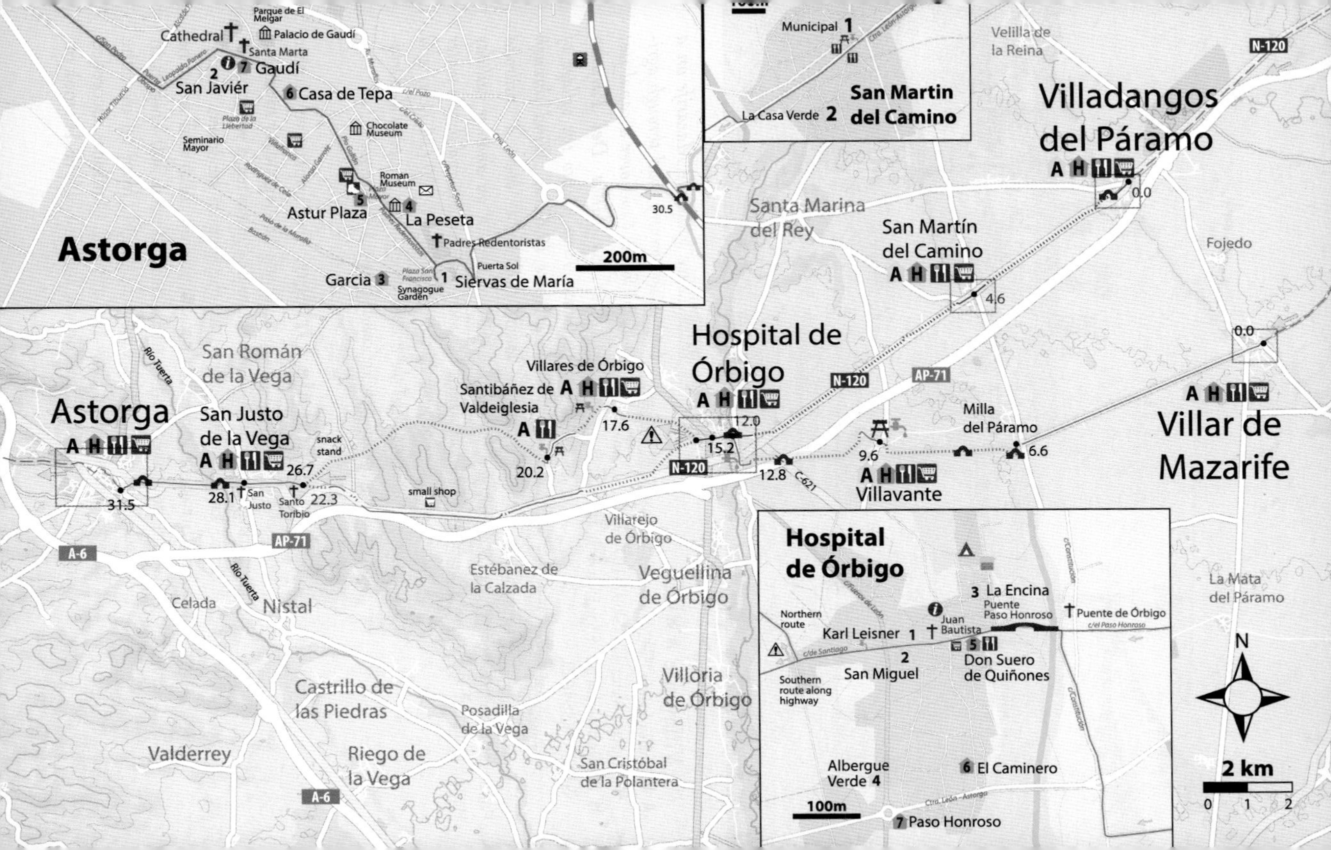
Astorga
Cathedral
Parque de El Melgar
Palacio de Gaudí
Santa Marta
2 San Javiér
7 Gaudí
6 Casa de Tepa
Seminario Mayor
Chocolate Museum
Roman Museum
5 Astur Plaza
4 La Peseta
Padres Redentoristas
Puerta Sol
Garcia 3
1 Siervas de María
Synagogue Garden
200m
30.5
San Martin del Camino
Municipal 1
La Casa Verde 2
Villadangos del Páramo
0.0
Velilla de la Reina
Santa Marina del Rey
San Martín del Camino
4.6
Fojedo
N-120
Hospital de Órbigo
12.0
15.2
12.8
C-621
AP-71
Villares de Órbigo
Santibáñez de Valdeiglesia
17.6
20.2
Milla del Páramo
9.6
6.6
Villavante
Villar de Mazarife
San Román de la Vega
Astorga
31.5
San Justo de la Vega
28.1
San Justo
snack stand
26.7
Santo Toribio
22.3
small shop
Río Tuerta
A-6
Celada
Nistal
Villarejo de Órbigo
Estébanez de la Calzada
Veguellina de Órbigo
Villoria de Órbigo
Castrillo de las Piedras
Posadilla de la Vega
Valderrey
Riego de la Vega
San Cristóbal de la Polantera
La Mata del Páramo
Hospital de Órbigo
Northern route
Southern route along highway
Karl Leisner 1
Juan Bautista
2 San Miguel
3 La Encina
Puente Paso Honroso
Puente de Órbigo
5 Don Suero de Quiñones
6 El Caminero
Albergue Verde 4
7 Paso Honroso
100m
N
2 km
0 1 2

Paso Honroso bridge in Hospital de Órbigo

9.6 Villavante A H

A H **Santa Lucía** (24, €8.5/-/24-40): , Doctor Vélez 17, 692-107693, Apr-Oct

H **Molino Galocha** (€35/55 w/): , 987-388546

0.0 *Leave Villar de Mazarife on a long quiet country road through agricultural fields. Cross over a canal just south of* ***La Milla Del Páramo (6.6km)****. Turn R into the village of* ***Villavante (9.6km)****. Wind through town and cross over a railroad (10.4km), joining road C-621 to turn R on another railway overpass (12.8km). Turn L almost immediately and skirt a water treatment plant to turn R. Cross the busy N-120 (14.1km) and continue straight until the historic bridge into Hospital de Órbigo, meeting the other route coming from Villadangos.*

15.2 **Hospital de Órbigo**: The impressive Gothic bridge over the Río Órbigo is the site of a legendary medieval jousting competition. Don Suero de Quiñones, a wealthy Leonese knight, was rejected by the woman he loved. In his heartbreak, he locked his neck in an iron collar and swore he would not take it off until he had defeated 300 knights in jousting. The call went out, and knights from all over the kingdom came in the Holy Year of 1434. Quiñones succeeded in his quest, freeing him from the torment of love. He took off the collar and made a pilgrimage to Santiago where he left a bejeweled bracelet, which can still be seen in the cathedral museum. The bridge became known as **El Paso Honroso** "the Honorable Pass." Looking south from the bridge into a grove of poplars, one can imagine the brilliant flags, trumpets blowing and excitement of a medieval joust. *Follow the main road through Hospital, and at the edge of town, ⚠ turn R at the option to continue on the recommended route to Villares de Órbigo or stay straight to take the* ***alternate route (description p. 169)****. The recommended route is 0.8km longer, but has nicer scenery.*

17.6 Villares de Órbigo is a friendly town with a church featuring a Santiago Matamoros. *After Villares, you'll see rolling hills again! Pass over a small hill into* ***Santibañez de Valdeiglesias (20.2km)****, where Iglesia de la Trinidad has a Santiago Matamoros. From Santibañez, continue on a lovely dirt path through oak groves and orchards. Pass a seasonal snack stand (25.1km). Climb up to the magnificent view of Astorga at a large stone cross.*

15.2 Hospital de Órbigo A H

Pop. 1,031

1. **A Karl Leisner** (par, 90, €5): c/Álvarez Vega 32, 987-388444, all year
2. **A San Miguel** (36, €7): c/Álvarez Vega 35, 987-388285, Apr-Nov
3. **A H La Encina** (16, €9.50/-/40): Suero de Quiñones, 987-361087, all year
4. **A ☆ Albergue Verde** (26, €9): Av. Fueros de León 76, 689-927926, 12pm Easter-Oct, vegetarian meals, yoga
5. **H Don Suero de Quiñones** (€50/70): c/Álvarez Vega 1, 987-388238
6. **H El Caminero** (€35/50): c/Sierra Pambley 56, 987-389020
7. **H Paso Honroso** (€35/50): N-120 km 335, 987-361010

Δ Municipal Camping (tent €6.50): N-120 km 31, 987-361018

17.6 Villares de Órbigo A H

A H Villares de Órbigo (22, €7/-/20): c/Arnal 21, 987-132935, Feb-mid Dec

20.2 Santibañez de Valdeiglesias A

A Parroquial (par, 20, €6): Caromonte 3, 626-362159, Mar-Oct

A Camino Francés (14, €7): c/Real 68, 987-361014, Apr-Oct

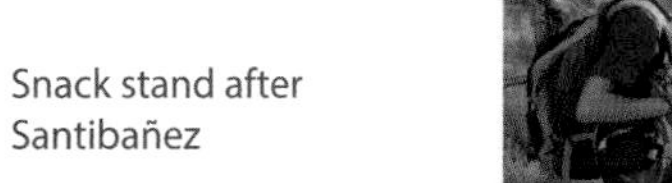

Snack stand after Santibañez

Crucero de Santo Toribio above Astorga

26.7 Crucero de Santo Toribio is named for the 5th-century bishop of Astorga who was said to have fallen to his knees at this spot when he was banished from his beloved city. Look for the spires of the cathedral and beyond the city to the Cantabrian Mountains on the Camino ahead.

28.1 San Justo de la Vega

A Refugio Amanecer (11, don): , c/Real 61, 622-566468

H Hostal Juli (€30/45): , c/Real 56, 987-617632

Continue on a paved road down to ***San Justo (28.1km)****, where the Iglesia de San Justo contains a 17th-century retablo. From San Justo, continue on the sidewalk next to the highway, crossing over the* ***Río Tuerta (28.7km)*** *and then over the train tracks on an elaborate maze of a footbridge (30.5km). Continue uphill to enter Astorga Old City through the Puerta Sol into the Plaza de San Francisco.*

Pilgrims crossing the train tracks to enter Astorga

Inside Astorga's awe-inspiring cathedral

31.5 **Astorga** is a pleasant city with interesting and varied historical buildings, just the right size to not be too overwhelming with main sites confined to the small Old City. First a Celtic settlement, Astorga developed into an important Roman city at the crossroads of the *Vía Trajana* and the *Vía de la Plata*, as well as an important center for Christianity. According to legend, both St. James and St. Paul preached here. The bishopric of Astorga was one of the earliest Christian titles. The city passed to the Visigoths in the 5th century and was destroyed by the Muslims in 714, then reconquered by Ordoño I in the mid-9th century. After León was destroyed by Al-Mansur's army, Astorga acted as the capital of the kingdom. The city flourished with the pilgrim trade and housed 21 pilgrim hospitals, the second most on the Camino Francés (after Burgos). One of these hosted Saint Francis of Assisi on his pilgrimage in 1214.

The 15th-century **Astorga Cathedral** (free, winter 9:30-1pm, 4:30-6pm; summer 9-12pm, 5-6:30pm, 987-615429) features an impressive Baroque façade and one of the best Renaissance retablos on the route, completed by a disciple of Michelangelo and Raphael (Gaspar Becerra).

31.5 **Astorga** A H

Pop. 12,078, Latin: *Asturicus* regional name of the ancient Astur tribe, c/Eduardo de Castro 5 across from Gaudí building, 987-618222, free

1. A **Siervas de María** (assoc, 250, €5): , Plaza San Francisco 3, 987-616034, all year
2. A **San Javier** (95, €8): , c/Portería 6, 987-618532, Apr-Nov
3. H **Pensión Garcia** (€20/30 shared bath): , c/Postigo 3, 987-616046
4. H **La Peseta** (€48/60): , Plaza de San Bartolomé 3, 987-617275
5. H **Astur Plaza** (-/€80): , Plaza de España 2, 987-618900
6. H **Casa de Tepa** (€72/82): , c/Santiago 2, 987-603299
7. H **Hotel Gaudí** (€50/65): , Eduardo Castro 6, 987-615654

Next to the cathedral is **Iglesia de Santa Marta**, connected by a plain 14th-century cell historically used to imprison prostitutes. Passing pilgrims would share food through the bars as an act of charity. The inscription above the window still reads, "*Acuérdate de mi juicio, porque así será el tuyo. A mí ayer, a ti hoy.*" ("Remember how I was judged, for your judgement will be the same. Yesterday to me, today to you.")

In the same plaza stands the **Palacio de Gaudí**, which was a palace for Archbishop Juan Bautista Grau Villespinós until his death, when it sat empty until serving as a military headquarters for the Falange movement. In 1963, the current 🏛 **Museo de los Caminos** (€3, 🕘Tu-Sa 10am-2pm, 4-8pm, Su 10am-2pm, ✆987-616882) was installed inside with an impressive collection of religious art associated with the Camino. Walk around behind the museum to see a nice section of the defensive walls, originally Roman but reconstructed in the 9th century.

Astorga Cathedral interior

🏛 **Museo Romano** (€3, 🕘10:30am-2pm, 5-7:30pm, closed Sun afternoon and Mon ✆987-616937) features artifacts from the Roman period, including an interesting gravestone that is explained in a short film displayed in a Roman tunnel known as an *Ergástula*. The ℹ Tourist Information offers a guided tour of the Roman ruins called the *Ruta Romana* (€4, ✆ 987-618222, 2 hours, Spanish language). Mosaics and ruins are displayed in the Plaza San Francisco.

Gaudí's Bishop's Palace now houses the Museo de los Caminos.

Chocolate lovers should visit the **Museo del Chocolate** (€2, Tu-Sa 10:30am-2pm, 4-6pm, Su 11am-2pm, closed Mon, 987-618222), which documents the chocolate industry that flourished in Astorga in the 18th-19th century. The museum features a modest collection of antique machinery and wrappers, an interesting film (in Spanish) on chocolate making and (the best part) a tasting session with a variety of chocolate, including one made with the local *cecina* sausage.

Before leaving, make sure you have enough cash to get you to Ponferrada as there are no ATMs in between. Astorga is also the last place to get any warmer clothing you may need for the colder mountains ahead tomorrow.

Astorga
Late July: Fiesta de Ástures y Romanos, celebrating Asturian and Roman culture
Aug 22: Santa Marta patron saint day with gladiator fights and chariot races
Tuesday is market day.

Roman mosaics in Astorga

22-25 CANTABRIAN MTNS & EL BIEZO

A view of Villafranca del Bierzo from the *Camino Duro* to Pradela

Highlights include magnificent mountain scenery, enigmatic Maragato culture, quaint stone villages and the towering cross at Cruz Ferro.

This section is characterized by the wild and rocky Cantabrian Mountains and the sheltered microclimate in the valley of El Bierzo.

The trail passes through a region of the *Maragato* culture, centralized in about 40 villages around Astorga. This mysterious group is rumored to be descended from the Berbers of North Africa, who arrived with the Muslim conquest in the 8th century and later converted to Christianity. Maragato men traditionally worked as muleteers, mule drivers who transported goods (especially fish and gold) around the peninsula.

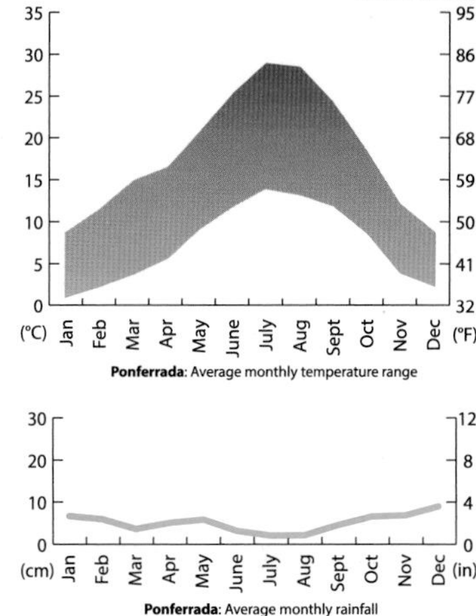

Ponferrada: Average monthly temperature range

Ponferrada: Average monthly rainfall

Restaurants in the area offer *Cocido Maragato*, an extremely filling meal that is served in a kind of "reverse order," beginning with a hearty meat dish (incorporating a dizzying array of meats: blood sausage, chicken, pork, pig's ear, pig's snout, bacon, chorizo), followed by the vegetables (usually chickpeas and cabbage) and finished off with a thick noodle soup and dessert.

The Bierzo region has come into its own as a wine region and in 1989 became its own DOC (*Denominacion de Origen*). The low altitude makes it possible to harvest the grapes up to one month earlier than other regions. You can ignore the advice given by 15th-century German pilgrim Hermann Künig con Vach regarding El Bierzo: "When you get there, drink wine sparingly as it burns like a candle and can scorch your very soul."

Local architecture becomes quite interesting as the trail enters regions with Celtic influence. Look for circular thatched stone buildings, called *pallozas*. You will also see plenty of *hórreos*, rectangular stone corncribs that are elevated off the ground to protect the corn from vermin. Common trees include holly, birch and maple, and fauna includes wild boar, roe deer, badgers and wolves.

Passing over the Cantabrian Mountains

22 ASTORGA TO FONCEBADÓN

25.9km
(16.1mi)

6.5-8 Hours
Difficulty:
P 26%, 6.8km
U 74%, 19.1km

A Albergues:
Valdeviejas 2.8km
Murias 5.1km
Santa Catalina 9.4km
El Ganso 13.7km
Rabanal 20.5km
Foncebadón 25.9km
Manjarín 30.3km

The ruins of Guacelmo's pilgrim hospital near Foncebadón

Explore the mysterious Maragato culture and experience the ambiance of tiny stone villages nestled in the mountains.

Today begins the slow steady climb toward the high point of the Camino Francés, reached in the following stage. The landscape and buildings change as the Camino draws nearer to the wild hills of Galicia. Vegetation becomes more scrubby, typical houses are low stone structures with thatch or slate roofs, and the weather becomes more dreary and overcast.

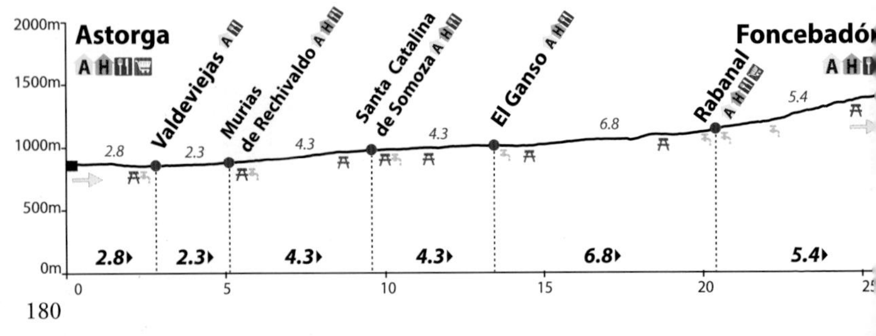

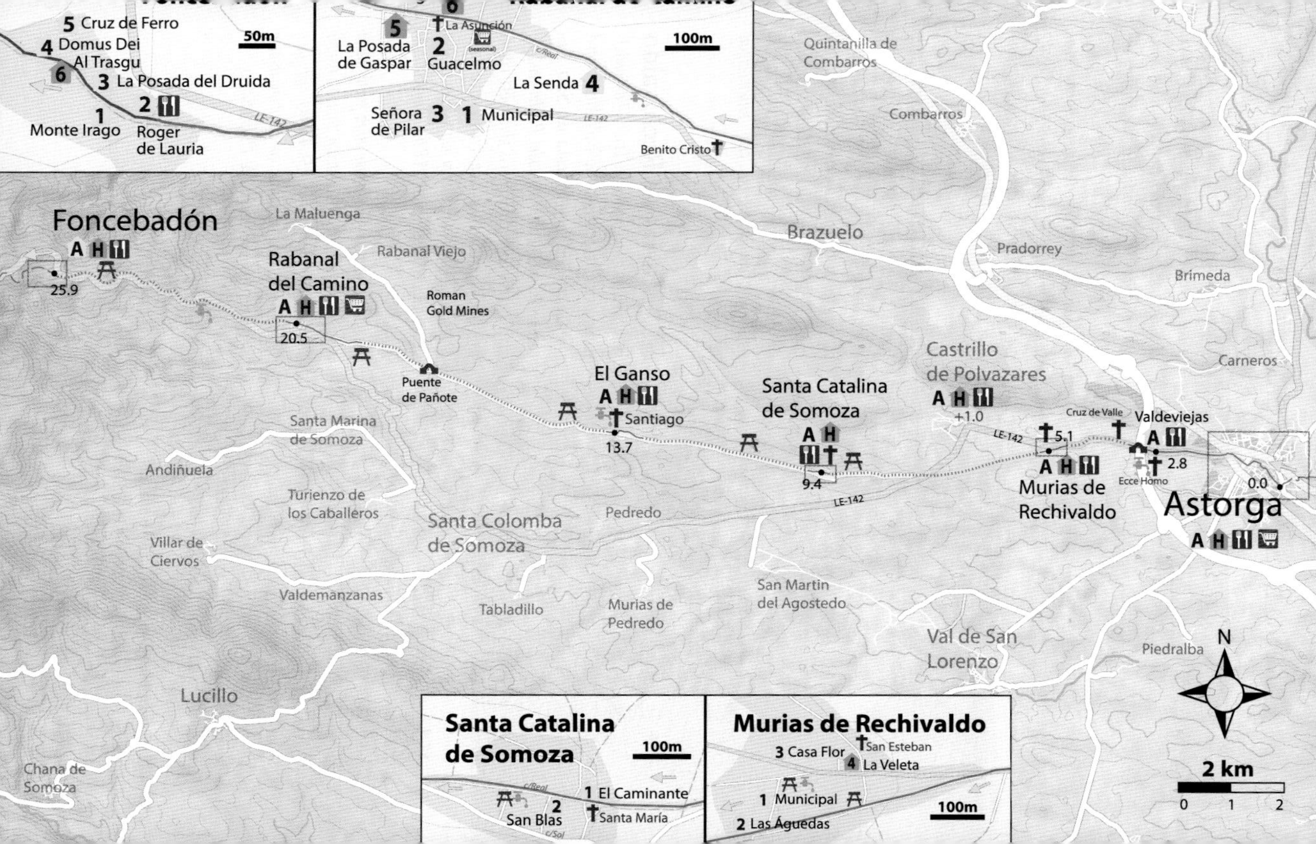

5 Cruz de Ferro
4 Domus Dei
Al Trasgu
6
3 La Posada del Druida
2
1
Monte Irago
Roger
de Lauria
LE-142
50m
5
La Posada
de Gaspar
La Asunción
(seasonal)
2
Guacelmo
c/Real
La Senda 4
Señora
de Pilar
3
1 Municipal
LE-142
Benito Cristo
100m
Quintanilla de
Combarros
Combarros
Foncebadón
A H
25.9
La Maluenga
Rabanal Viejo
Rabanal
del Camino
A H
20.5
Roman
Gold Mines
Puente
de Pañote
Brazuelo
Pradorrey
Brimeda
Carneros
El Ganso
A H
Santiago
13.7
Santa Catalina
de Somoza
A H
9.4
Castrillo
de Polvazares
A H
+1.0
Cruz de Valle
Valdeviejas
A
5.1
2.8
LE-142
A H
Murias de
Rechivaldo
Ecce Homo
0.0
Astorga
A H
Santa Marina
de Somoza
Andiñuela
Turienzo de
los Caballeros
Santa Colomba
de Somoza
Pedredo
LE-142
Villar de
Ciervos
Valdemanzanas
Tabladillo
Murias de
Pedredo
San Martin
del Agostedo
Val de San
Lorenzo
Piedralba
Lucillo
Chana de
Somoza
N
2 km
0
1
2
Santa Catalina
de Somoza
100m
c/Real
1 El Caminante
2
San Blas
Santa María
c/Sol
Murias de Rechivaldo
3 Casa Flor
San Esteban
4 La Veleta
1 Municipal
2 Las Águedas
100m

0.0 *Leave Astorga by following arrows through town (map p. 171) past the cathedral and turning L onto c/Leopaldo Panero and leaving on c/Puerta Obispo. Turn R on c/San Pedro past a church with interesting mosaics. Arrive to minor highway LE-142 on the northwest edge of town. Follow this road, passing through Valdeviejas.*

2.8 **Valdeviejas** houses the Ermita del Ecce Homo, a former pilgrim hospital. To access the simple albergue and Iglesia de San Verésimo, turn R at the Ermita. *Follow the road to Murcias de Rechivaldo, veering L (4.7km) to pass by the municipal albergue.*

5.1 **Murias de Rechivaldo** is a Maragato village (p. 178) with many traditional stone buildings and the 18th-century **Iglesia de San Esteban** with a *Virgen de Pilár* image and outside staircase to the bell tower. Most building are from the late 19th century as many constructions were destroyed in an 1846 flood.

Follow the marked wide dirt path past the albergue and fountain out of town to ***Santa Catalina (9.4km)****, or detour 1km on the road to first visit the picturesque Castrillo de Polvazares.*

Stone arrow on the path after Santa Catalina

2.8 **Valdeviejas** A Pop. 156

A **Ecce Homo** (muni, 10, €5): 620-960060, Mar-Oct, all beds-not bunks

5.1 **Murias de Rechivaldo** A H P. 108

1. A **Municipal** (14, €5): W, Crta Santa Colomba, 669-067433, Mar-Oct
2. A H **Las Águedas** (30, €9/-/50): W D, c/Camino de Santiago 52, 636-067840, Mar-Nov
3. A H **Casa Flor** (15, €10/-/60): Crta Santa Colomba 54, 609-478323
4. H **La Veleta** (€41/55 w/): W, Plaza Mayor 1, 616-598133

+1.0 **Castrillo de Polvazares** is a traditional Maragato village whose stone buildings have been sensitively restored as a tourist attraction. Author Concha Espina used the location as the backdrop to her novel *La Esfinge Maragata.*

+1.0 Castrillo de Polvazares A H
Pop. 70, Off route +1.0km
A **Municipal** (8, €5): , c/Jardín, 655-803706, Apr-Oct
H **Cuca la Vaina** (€40/60): , c/Jardín, 987-691034
H **Casa Coscolo** (€40/50): , c/La Magdalena 1, 987-691984

9.4 **Santa Catalina de Somoza** is another traditional village, all but deserted, with a modern Iglesia de Santa María. *Walk down the central c/ Real and continue on a dirt path along the road to el Ganso.*

9.4 Santa Catalina A H Pop. 60
1. A H **El Caminante** (22, €5-7/20/35): , c/Real 2, 987-691098 , all year
2. A H **San Blas** (20, €5/-/35): , c/Real 11, 987-691411 , all year

13.7 **El Ganso**: The tiny crumbling hamlet of El Ganso once held the Hospital de San Justo, a 12th-century Benedictine pilgrim shelter as well as a 13th-century monastery, but nothing remains of either. The architecture today is very traditional with some now rare thatched roofs. Iglesia de Santiago has a 16th-century statue of the saint. The ghost-town feel today is somewhat enlivened by Mesón Cowboy, a Tex-Mex bar, as well as an albergue that at maximum capacity basically doubles the town's population.

13.7 El Ganso A H P. 30, Spanish: "goose"
A **Gabino** (18, €8 w/): , c/Real 9, 660-912823 , Easter-Oct
H **Apartamentos Gabino** -/€60): , c/Real, 625-318585

Continue parallel to the road, passing a venerable old tree with a bench under its branches, affectionately called el Roble del Peregrino "the pilgrim's oak," said to watch over weary pilgrims. Pass the remains of a Roman gold mine known as La Fucarona and the 18th-century Ermita del Bendito Cristo de la Vera Cruz at the entry to Rabanal.

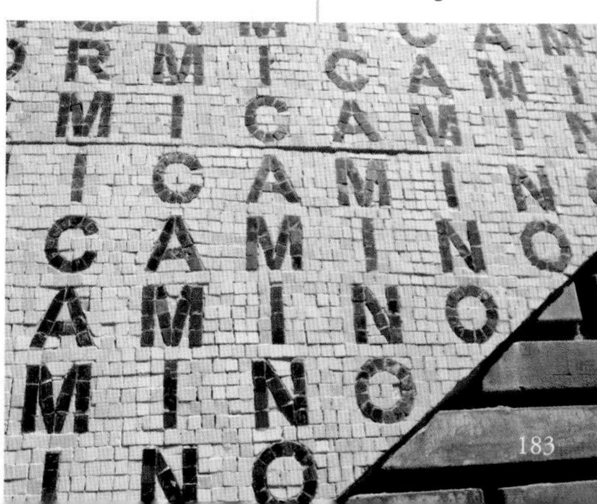

Camino mosaics on a church on the way out of Astorga

20.5 Rabanal del Camino A H

Pop. 73, Small shop (closed in winter)

1. **A Municipal** (32, €5): W D, Plaza de Jerónimo, 678-568795, Apr-Oct
2. **A Guacelmo** (assoc, 46, don w/): D, c/Calvario 4, 987-691901, Apr-Oct, friendly UK volunteers prepare English tea
3. **A H Nuestra Señora de Pilar** (68, €5/35/-): W, Plaza de Jerónimo, 987-631621, all year
4. **A La Senda** (34, €5-7): W D, c/Real, 696-819060, Apr-Oct 20, formerly "el Tesín"
5. **H La Posada de Gaspar** (€41/54): W, c/Real 27, 987-631629
6. **H Hostería el Refugio** (€35/50): W D, c/Real 74, 987-631592

The monks at Santa María de la Asunción also offer accommodations for 2-10 nights; arrange by calling 987-631528 between 10am and 1pm or emailing monteirago@gmail.com.

20.5 Rabanal del Camino

is another beautiful and isolated Maragato village brought back to life by modern pilgrim passage. This was the end of the 9th stage of the *Codex Calixtinus,* and many pilgrims stopped to rest from the ascent and find refuge from the wolves and bandits that plagued the León mountains. The Knights Templar ran a fort here to protect passing pilgrims. A legend says that one of Charlemagne's knights married a Muslim woman in Rabanal.

The heavily reconstructed **Iglesia de Santa María de la Asunción** contains a 12th-century image of San Roque. The church is currently operated by the Benedictine Abbey of San Salvador del Monte Irago and offers a moving Vespers service with Gregorian chant and an evening pilgrim blessing. The 12th-century Hospital de San Gregorio has been converted into a modern albergue by the British Confraternity, named Guacelmo after the 10th-century monk who founded a hermitage in nearby Foncebadón. *Follow c/Real out of Rabanal onto a dirt track coming alongside the paved road. The entrance to Foncebadón is marked with a wooden cross.*

Rabanal makes a nice overnight stop, but pushing on to Foncebadón will shorten the already-long day tomorrow. Be forewarned that it is all uphill!

Pilgrims socialize at Guacelmo albergue in Rabanal

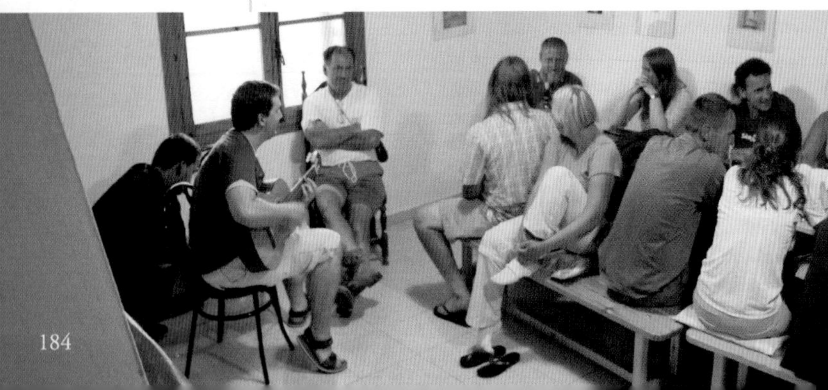

Monte Irago albergue in Foncebadón

25.9 **Foncebadón**: Practically deserted in the 1980s, Foncebadón has made a comeback as a stopping point for modern pilgrims. Amidst crumbling stone buildings and cold weather even in summer, some of the wildness of the Irago Mountains of old can be felt. The traditional stone houses with slate roofs or thatched with local broom provide a timeless ambiance. The Roman road went through this pass, and its protected location below Cruz Ferro made Foncebadón a logical pilgrim stop.

Paolo Coelho's *The Pilgrimage* describes his mystical experience in Foncebadón in which he wrestles with a large black dog. In Shirley Maclaines' *The Camino*, she also encounters vicious dogs in Foncebadón. Today the village offers several albergues and cafés and a rustic, timeless atmosphere.

25.9 **Foncebadón** A H Pop. 13

1. A **Monte Irago** (35, €8): , 695-452950, all year, vegetarian options, fireplace, moderate hippie vibe, yoga
2. A **Roger de Lauria** (20, €7): , c/Real, 625-313425, formerly Convento de Foncebadón, all year
3. A **La Posada del Druida** (20, €7): , c/Real, 696-820136, Mar-Oct
4. A **Domus Dei** (par, 18, don): , c/Real, , Apr-Oct, communal meals, simple facility, vespers
5. A **La Cruz de Fierro** (34, €10): , 699-752144
6. H **Al Trasgu** (€24/36): , c/Real, 987-053877

23 FONCEBADÓN TO PONFERRADA

27.1km
(16.8mi)

6-8 Hours
Difficulty:
P 32%, 8.6km
U 68%, 18.5km

A Albergues:
Manjarín 4.4km
El Acebo 11.5km
Riego 14.7km
Molinaseca 19.5km
Ponferrada 27.1km
Cacabelos 43.6km

⚠ Alt. Route:
Shortcut to Ponferrada albergue, saves 1.4km (p. 190)

Enjoy mountain scenery in the Irago Mountains

Place a stone at Cruz Ferro, have coffee with modern-day Knights Templar at Manjarín, visit a Templar castle in Ponferrada.

This stage begins with more climbing to Cruz Ferro and the high point of the Irago Mountains before the steep descent down to Ponferrada. Typical Maragato mountain villages with slate-roofed houses like El Acebo offer services. On a clear day, the mountain views are superb. Be prepared for the possibility of cold, rain and wind.

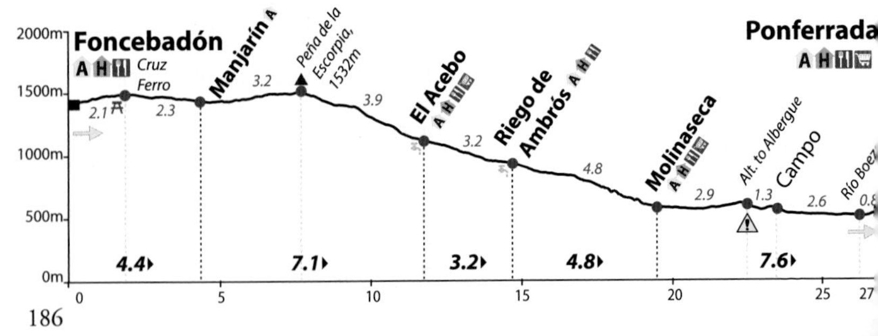

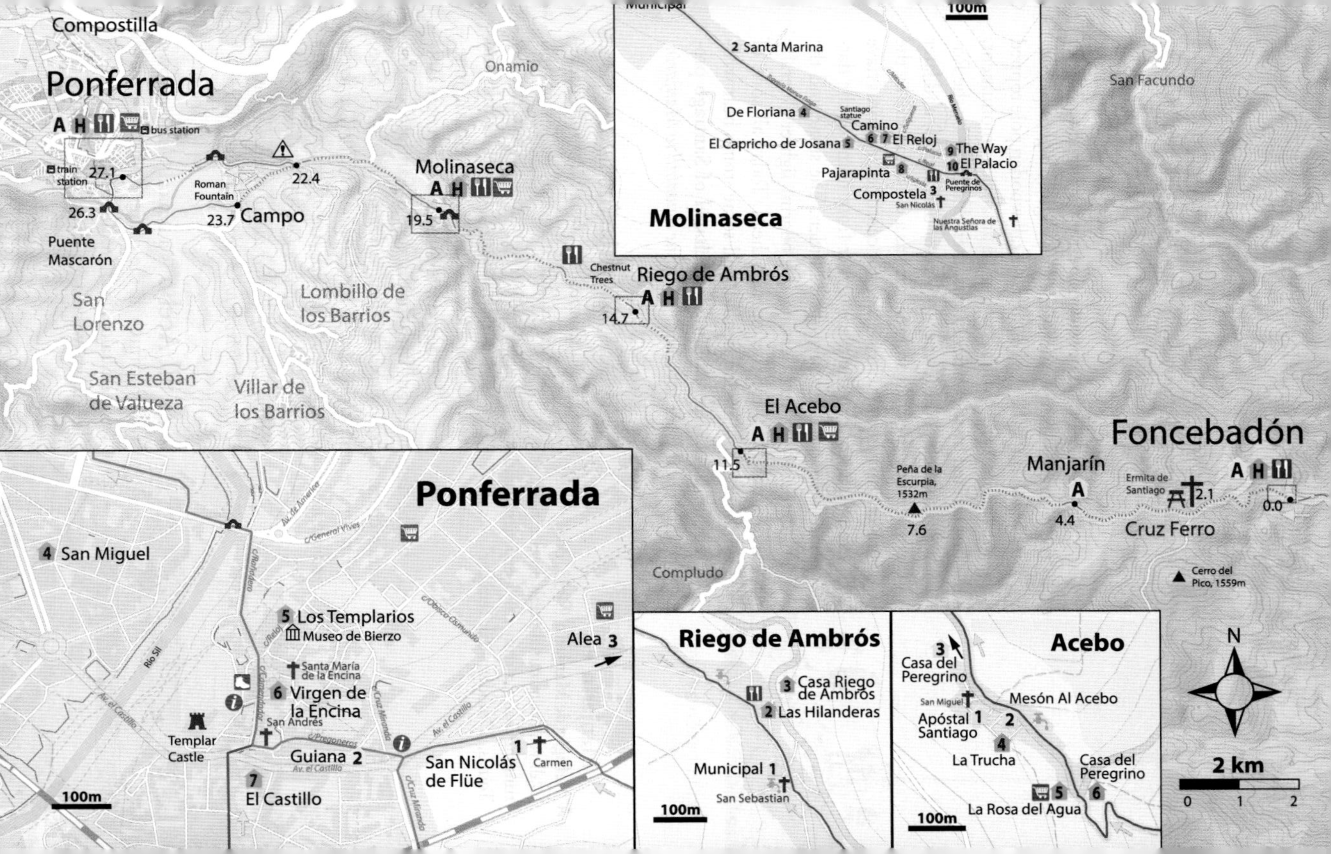

Compostilla
Ponferrada
A H
bus station
train station
27.1
26.3
Puente Mascarón
Roman Fountain
22.4
23.7
Campo
Onamio
Molinaseca
A H
19.5
San Lorenzo
Lombillo de los Barrios
San Esteban de Valueza
Villar de los Barrios
Chestnut Trees
Riego de Ambrós
A H
14.7
El Acebo
A H
11.5
Compludo
Peña de la Escurpia, 1532m
7.6
Manjarín
A
4.4
Ermita de Santiago
2.1
Cruz Ferro
Foncebadón
A H
0.0
Cerro del Pico, 1559m
San Facundo
N
2 km
0
1
2
Molinaseca
100m
Municipal
2 Santa Marina
De Floriana 4
Santiago statue
Camino
El Capricho de Josana 5
6 7 El Reloj
9 The Way
10 El Palacio
Pajarapinta 8
Puente de Peregrinos
Compostela 3
San Nicolás
Nuestra Señora de las Angustias
Ponferrada
4 San Miguel
5 Los Templarios
Museo de Bierzo
Santa María de la Encina
6 Virgen de la Encina
San Andrés
Templar Castle
Guiana 2
7 El Castillo
San Nicolás de Flüe
1 Carmen
Alea 3
Av. de America
c/General Vives
c/Obispo Osmundo
c/Rañadero
c/Reloj
c/Comendador
c/Cruz Miranda
c/Pregoneros
Av. el Castillo
Río Sil
100m
Riego de Ambrós
3 Casa Riego de Ambrós
2 Las Hilanderas
Municipal 1
San Sebastian
100m
Acebo
3 Casa del Peregrino
San Miguel
Apóstal 1 Santiago
2 Mesón Al Acebo
4 La Trucha
Casa del Peregrino 6
5 La Rosa del Agua
100m

Pilgrims at Cruz Ferro

0.0 *Leave Foncebadón on the main dirt road, passing horse pastures and the ruins of Guacelmo's medieval pilgrim hospital. Ascend through scrubby heather and gorse, cross the road and arrive at a Camino highlight, the Cruz Ferro.*

2.1 **Cruz Ferro** occupies nearly the highest point of the entire Camino Francés (there's a slightly higher pass after Manjarín). The site consists of a tall wooden pole topped with an iron cross. This is said to be an ancient monument, first erected by the ancient Celts, then dedicated by the Romans to their god Mercury (protector of travelers) and later crowned by the cross and renamed as a Christian site by the 9th-century hermit Guacelmo. For centuries, pilgrims have brought a stone to the place (either from home or the flatlands below) to represent their burden. The stone and the burden are left here, leaving the pilgrim lighter (literally and figuratively) for the journey ahead. Today all sorts of symbolic items are left behind, and some stones bear written messages. The small modern **chapel of Santiago** provides a good place for a rest. *Continue downhill to Manjarín.*

4.4 **Manjarín** A

A **Refugio de Manjarín** (35, don): all year, communal meal, no electricity or running water, a truly rustic experience with Tomás, a "modern-day Templar"

4.4 **Manjarín**: This enigmatic little spot features a most unusual albergue, administrated by Tomás who considers himself a modern-day Templar, last of his order. Drinks and snacks are available as well as a none-too-private outhouse. Recognizable by bright flags and signs with the distance to Santiago, among other cities. *After continuing through beautiful heather fields, arrive at the true high point of the Camino (1520m) where a radio tower is visible to the R (7.6km). [Go off route here on the wide dirt path up to a large cairn for a breathtaking view of Ponferrada in the valley below.] Descend sharply for 3.9km to El Acebo.*

Signs at Manjarín

11.5 **El Acebo** is a typical Camino town with a church at the center and houses with wooden balconies flanking the pilgrim route. The town was larger in medieval times and received a tax break for maintaining the pilgrim road markers over the Foncebadón pass. The 15th-century **Iglesia de San Miguel** contains an image of John the Baptist. On the way out of town is a statue in remembrance of 70-year-old German cyclist Heinrich Krause who died of a bicycle accident there in 1987. *Follow the road until a dirt path to the L (13.6km) leads into Riego de Ambrós.*

14.7 Riego de Ambrós'

16th-century Iglesia de San Sebastián features a Baroque retablo. After Riego you will pass a spectacular grove of massive chestnut trees (15.6km), which practically beg you to take a rest stop under their wise branches. *A picturesque dirt footpath leads down to Molinaseca.*

19.5 Molinaseca:

On the way into Molinaseca pass the **Santuario de Nuestra Señora de las Angustias**, built into the rock to the R with a 18th-century Baroque retablo. Medieval pilgrims carved off slivers of the wooden door for good luck, though today the doors are iron plated. Turn L to cross the medieval **Puente del Peregrino** over the Río Meruela. The water to the R of the bridge is dammed up for refreshing summer swimming. Pass the **Iglesia de San Nicolás**, which contains a 17th-century retablo. Molinaseca is a pretty, quiet town with good pilgrim facilities and makes a great overnight spot if you prefer to avoid the larger city of Ponferrada.

Approaching the slate roofs of El Acebo

11.5 El Acebo A H

Pop. 37, Spanish: "holly"

1. A **Apóstal Santiago** (par, 23, don): , Pl. de la Iglesia Apr-Oct, shared meals, vespers
2. A H **Mesón El Acebo** (18, €7/-/24): , Real 16, 987-695074, mid Jan-mid Dec
3. A **La Casa del Peregrino** (96, €10/35/50): , Crta Compludo, 987-057793, Jan 10 - Dec 20, end of town

These 2 albergues only open if the others are full:

A **La Taberna de José** (14, €6): 987-695074

A **Elisardo Panizo** (muni, 10, €6): basic

4. H **La Trucha** (€35/45 w/): , c/La Cruz 10, 987-695548, great vegetarian meals
5. H **La Rosa del Agua** (€35/50 w/): , c/Real 52, 616-849738
6. H **Casa del Peregrino** (€40/50 w/): , c/Real 67, 987-057875

14.7 Riego de Ambrós A H

Pop. 42, Spanish: "irrigation of Ambros," likely a family name

1. A **Municipal** (30, €5): , c/Real, 987-695190, Mar-Oct
2. H **Las Hilanderas** (€35/55 w/): , c/Real 44, 658-031095
3. H **Casa Riego de Ambrós** (-/€40): , c/Astorga 3, 616-123557

19.5 **Molinaseca**

Pop. 854, Spanish: "dry mill"

1. **A Municipal** (26+, €5): , Av. Fraga Iribarne, 987-453077, all year
2. **A Santa Marina** (56, €7): , Av. Fraga Iribarne, 987-453077, Mar-Nov
3. **A Compostela** (30, €9-11): , c/Iglesia 39, 987-453057, Apr-Nov
4. **H De Floriana** (€55/65): 987-453146
5. **H El Capricho de Josana** (€43/61): , Plaza del Santo Cristo, 987-453167
6. **H Camino** (-/€50): c/Real 5, 653-504330
7. **H El Reloj** (-/€40 w/): , 987-453124
8. **H Pajarapinta** (€35/50 w/): , c/Real 30, 987-453040
9. **H The Way Hostel** (€45/55): , c/El Palacio 10, 637-941017
10. **H El Palacio** (-/€50): , c/El Palacio 19, 987-453094

Molinaseca

Aug: Virgen de las Angustias procession

Aug 17: Fiesta del Agua—huge city-wide water fight

Leave Molinaseca on the paved road. After the albergues at the far side of town, turn R at the tennis courts (scarcely marked) and a quick L on a gravel path to avoid the road. Rejoin and cross the paved road (22.2km).

*[⚠ For a shortcut directly to the Ponferrada albergue saving 1.4km, continue on the main road following arrows (22.4km, map p. 187).] Otherwise follow markers downhill to the L on a dirt road turning paved into **Campo (23.7km)**, with its Roman fountain and parish church next to a massive oak tree. Continue on the road to cross **Puente Mascarón (26.3km)**. Continue straight on c/Cruz Miranda to the albergue, or follow markings to access the downtown area and castle, and/or continue along the Camino.*

27.1 **Ponferrada** started off as a Celtic settlement, followed by a Roman mining town. The city was destroyed first by the Visigoths and then Muslim invaders. After the Reconquista, Bishop Osmundo of Astorga commissioned a pilgrim bridge here, which was unusually constructed with steel beams, giving the city its modern name. Ponferrada was a booming pilgrimage town, with diverse merchants including Franks and Jews, who were protected during a 15th-century restriction that called for segregating communities. The railroad came to the city in 1882 and in the 1940s the town grew with the coal industry.

While the historic center retains its charm, much of the new city is modern and industrial. The most impressive site is the **Templar castle** (€6, Tu-Sa 11am-2pm, 4-6pm, Su 11am-2pm), built in the 13th century over a destroyed Visigoth fort, which was built over a Roman fort, which was built over a pre-Roman castro. Soon after its completion, the Templars were banished. The entrance is impressive with a coat of arms over the door. According to legend, the castle holds all kinds of secret Templar symbolism, such as the 12 towers representing the 12 months or the 12 disciples.

✝ Iglesia de Santa María de la Encina (9am-2pm, 4:30-8:30pm), on the Plaza Encinas, houses an image of Mary said to be originally in the Astorga cathedral, but it was hidden in the 9th century for protection from invading Muslims. Years later, the image was miraculously found in an oak tree, hence the name "Our Lady of the Oak." There is a statue in the plaza depicting the miracle.

Museo de Bierzo
(Tu-Sa 11am-2pm, Oct-Apr 4-7p, 5-8:30pm May-Sept, Su 11am-2pm, 987-414141, *c/del Reloj 5*), housed in the former jail, displays artifacts ranging from pre-Roman to ethnographic, featuring an in-depth display of the archaeological theory of how the castle was built.

Ponferrada
Summer: Noche Templario medieval festival with costumed knights
September: Virgen de la Encina patron saint day
Wednesday & Saturday: market days

Iglesia San Nicolás in Molinaseca (left)
Templar Castle in Ponferrada (right)

27.1 **Ponferrada** A H
Pop. 68,508 Latin: *pons ferrata* "iron bridge"
c/Gil y Carrasco 4, 987-424236, M-Sa 10am-2pm, 4-8:30pm, Su 10am-2pm

1. **A San Nicolás de Flüe** (par, 175+ , don): , c/de la Loma, 987-413381, all year, can get very crowded, evening Mass
2. **A H Guiana** (90, €12/-/50): , Av. del Castillo 112, 987-409327, Mar-Oct, bicycle repair shop, sauna
3. **A Alea** (18, €10): , c/Teleno 33, 987-404133, Mar 15-Nov 30
4. **H Hostal San Miguel** (€25/36): , c/Juan de Lama 14, 987-426700
5. **H Hotel Los Templarios** (€35/50): , c/Florez Osorio 3, 987-411484
6. **H Virgen de la Encina** (€40/63): , c/Comendador 4, 987-409632
7. **H El Castillo** (€45/55): , Av. el Castillo 115, 987-456227

24

PONFERRADA TO VILLAFRANCA DEL BIERZO

24.2km
(15.0mi)

6-7 Hours
Difficulty:
P 69%, 16.8km
U 31%, 7.4km

A Albergues:
Columbrianos 5.6km
Camponaraya 10km
Cacabelos 16.5km
Pieros 18.0km
Villafranca 24.2km
Pereje 29.8km
Trabadelo 34.2km

Villafrana del Bierzo on the Río Burbia

Stroll through vineyards and fruit orchards, experience Medieval and Rennaisance history in Villafranca del Bierzo and dip your feet in the Río Burbia.

After leaving Ponferrada's urban area, the trail soon enters the Bierzo region with its temperate microclimate, ideal for viticulture. The scenery is green with vineyards, cherry orchards, wildflowers and trees. The mountains of Galicia loom ahead, and beautiful Villafranca lies nestled among the foothills along the Río Burbia.

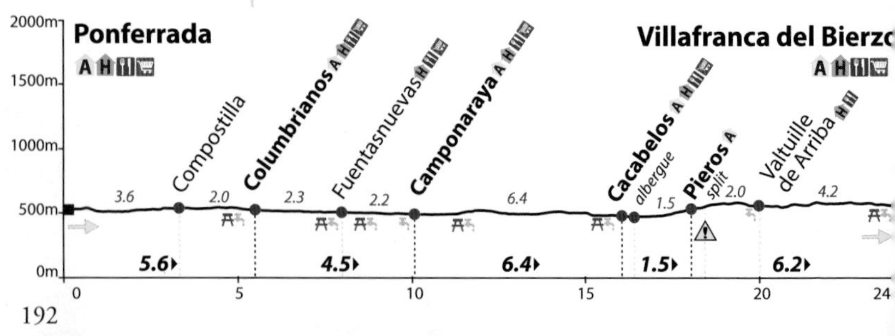

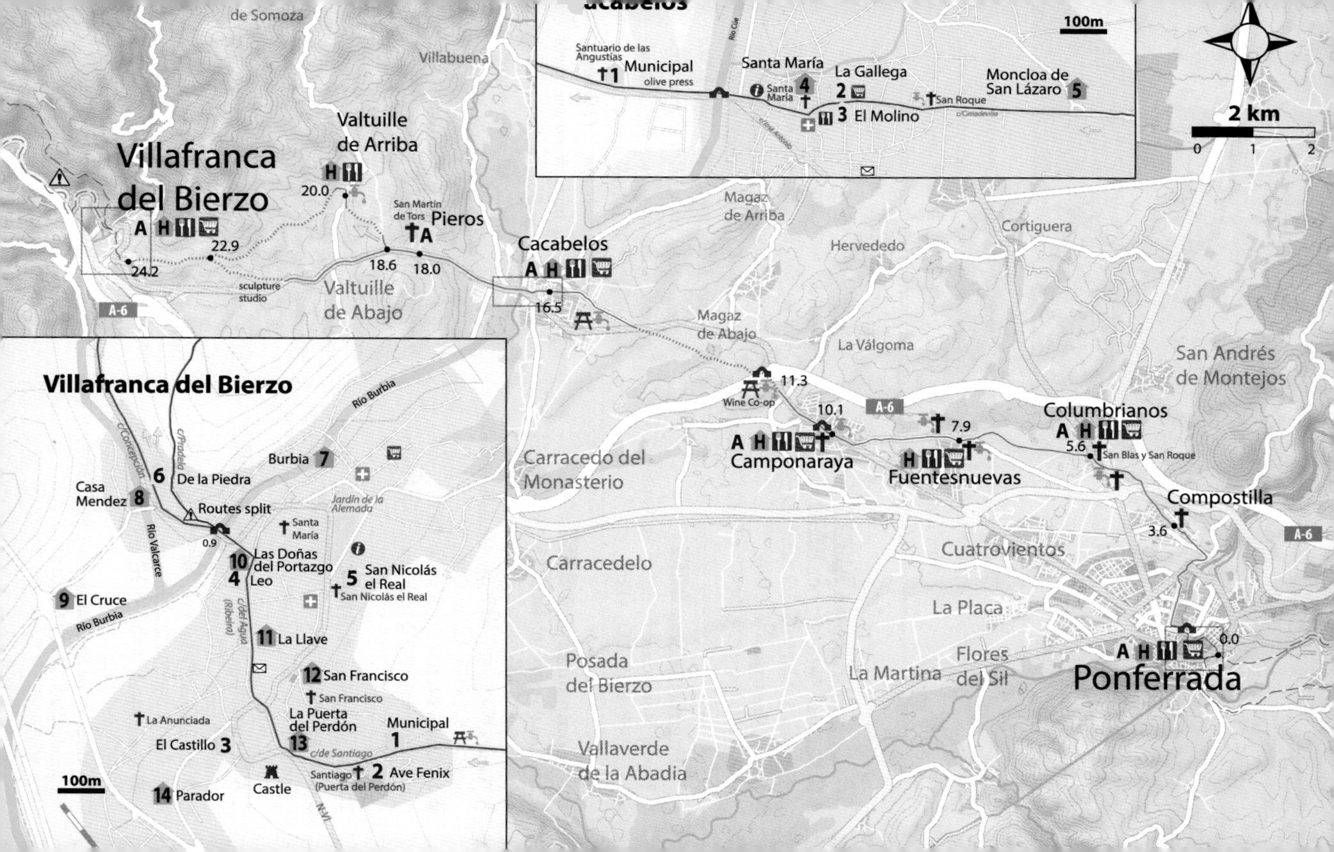

Villafranca del Bierzo
A H
22.9
24.2
de Somoza
Villabuena
Valtuille de Arriba
H
20.0
San Martín de Tors
Pieros
A
18.6
18.0
sculpture studio
Valtuille de Abajo
A-6
Cacabelos
A H
16.5
Magaz de Arriba
Magaz de Abajo
Hervededo
Cortiguera
La Válgoma
11.3
Wine Co-op
10.1
A H
Camponaraya
A-6
7.9
H
Fuentesnuevas
Carracedo del Monasterio
Carracedelo
Columbrianos
A H
5.6
San Blas y San Roque
San Andrés de Montejos
Compostilla
3.6
A-6
Cuatrovientos
La Placa
Flores del Sil
La Martina
Posada del Bierzo
Vallaverde de la Abadia
A H
0.0
Ponferrada
2 km
0
1
2
Santuario de las Angustias
1 Municipal
olive press
Río Cúe
Santa María
4
Santa María
c/José Antonio
La Gallega
2
3 El Molino
San Roque
c/Cimadevilla
Moncloa de San Lázaro
5
100m
Villafranca del Bierzo
c/Concepción
c/Pradela
Río Burbia
Burbia 7
6 De la Piedra
Casa Mendez 8
Routes split
0.9
Río Valcarce
Jardín de la Alemada
Santa María
10 Las Doñas del Portazgo
4 Leo
5 San Nicolás el Real
San Nicolás el Real
9 El Cruce
Río Burbia
c/del Agua (Ribeira)
11 La Llave
12 San Francisco
San Francisco
La Anunciada
La Puerta del Perdón
13
c/de Santiago
Municipal
1
El Castillo 3
Santiago
(Puerta del Perdón)
2 Ave Fenix
Castle
N-VI
100m
14 Parador

0.0 *From the Ponferrada Albergue, make your way to the castle (map p. 187) and turn R to walk through the downtown area. Turn L over the Río Sil on a bridge, then turn R on c/Río Ardieles. Turn R at a park, then R again at a plaza with a statue of a large drop of blood honoring blood donors. Pass through a roundabout, then L at signs for Compostilla and walk through the suburb of* ***Compostilla (3.6km)****. Stay straight through an underpass to* ***Columbrianos (5.6km)****, then stay L at Ermita San Blas y San Roche leaving town. Pass a cross and drinking fountain entering* ***Fuentesnuevas (7.9km)****, then stay straight until* ***Companaraya (10.1km)****, where the trail turns R on the main road passing vending machines with free wifi, cafés and a mini market. On the edge of Companaraya, after the Wine Co-op (11.3km, offering a glass of wine and pincho for €1), take the gravel path by the picnic area through expansive vineyards to cross the highway and a picnic area to the outskirts of Cacabelos.*

5.6 Columbrianos A H

A H San Blas (18, €11/30): wifi, c/San Blas 5, ☎675-651241, all year

H Hostal Monteclaro (€23/40): Av. Antonio Cortés 24, ☎987-455982, +1km

7.9 Fuentasnuevas H

H Hostal Monteclaro (€23/40): Av. Antonio Cortés 24, ☎987-455982, +1km

10.1 Companaraya A H

A Medina (20, €10): wifi, Av. Camino de Santiago 87, ☎987-463962, all year

A Naraya (26, €8): wifi, Av. De Galicia 506, ☎987-459159, Apr-Oct

H La Casita B&B (€27/38 w/): wifi, Pl Constitución 35, ☎653-736228, all year

16.5 Cacabelos A H Pop. 5,495

1. **A H Municipal** (70, €5): wifi, Plaza del Santuario, ☎987-547167, Apr-Oct, all rooms with 2 beds
2. **A H La Gallega** (30, €10/25/40): wifi, c/Santa Maria 23, ☎987-549476
3. **A El Molino** (14, €10): wifi, c/Santa María 10, ☎676-690900, all year, closed Tues
4. **H Santa María** (€30/45): c/Santa María 20, ☎987-549588
5. **H Moncloa de San Lázaro** (-/€75): wifi, Cimadevilla 97, ☎987-546101

16.5 Cacabelos: A long typical Camino town, Cacabelos once supported six pilgrim hospitals as a booming commercial center. In Roman times, it served as an administration center for gold mining. Today pilgrims can visit Iglesia de Santa María, with its 13th-century Virgen Mary on the concrete tympanum. At the bridge on the far side of town, an old mill and wooden olive press are displayed to the R. The town's unusual pilgrim albergue is located on the far side of the bridge alongside the Santuario de las Angustias, a hermitage with a most curious retablo featuring a young Jesus playing cards with San Antonio de Padua. *After Cacabelos, the route follows near the highway into the hamlet of Pieros.*

18.0 **Pieros** A Pop. 35
A **El Serbal y la Luna** (18, €5): c/El Pozo 15, 639-888924 Mar-Nov, vegetarian meals

20.0 **Valtuille de Arriba** H Pop. 139
H **La Osa Mayor** (€25/40 w/, pilgrim price): , 654-152305

Cacabelos
Apr/May: Wine festival

18.0 **Pieros**: La Iglesia de San Martín de Tours was commissioned in 1086 by Osmundo, the same bishop of Astorga who built the bridge of Ponferrada. The Templars ran a pilgrim hospital here as well as a leper hospice. *Walk on the edge of the highway out of Pieros to turn R off of the road (18.6km). Continue to* ***Valtuille de Arriba (20.0km)*** *through beautiful cherry orchards and fields mostly on a dirt path. [The road option is half highway and half dirt path. The two options come together just outside of Villafranca del Bierzo (22.9km).] The two most popular albergues are on the near side of town near the Iglesia de Santiago, farther from restaurants and stores. If you stay here, be sure to walk into the main part of town to see the wealth of historical buildings.*

Walking through vineyards before Villafranca (left)

Pilgrim statue in Villafranca (below)

24.2 **Villafranca del Bierzo** is one of the most beautiful towns on the Camino, retaining much of its medieval and Renaissance character in spite of an increase of modern hotels and buildings. Several Roman *castrum* have been found in the area, with the strategic location at the confluence of the rivers Burbio and Valcarce and just below the mountain pass. This location later drew merchants

24.2 Villafranca del Bierzo

Pop. 3,505, ©987-540028, Av. Diez Ovelar 10, 10am-2pm, 4-7pm

1. **A Municipal** (62, €6): , ©987-542356, Mar-Nov, overflow of 100+ in summer
2. **A Ave Fenix** (assoc, 80, €6): , c/Santiago 10, ©987-540229, all year, communal meals, run by Jesús Jato, a classic Camino character, sometimes offer a *queimada* and healing rituals
3. **A El Castillo** (24, €10): , c/Castillo 8, ©987-540344, Apr-Nov
4. **A Leo** (24, €10): , c/Ribadeo 10, ©987-542658, Mar-Nov
5. **A H San Nicolás el Real** (75, €5-8/30/45) , San Nicolás 4, ©696-978653, all
6. **A H De la Piedra** (32, €8/-/24): (free), c/Espíritu Santo 14, ©987-540260, 12:30, Mar-Nov, run by a delightful couple from Madrid
7. **H Hostal Burbia** (€36/46): , c/Fuente Cubero, ©987-542667
8. **H Casa Mendez** (€34/44): , c/Espíritu Santo 1, ©987-540055
9. **H Hostal El Cruce** (€18/25, quad €40): , c/El Salvador 41, ©987-540185
10. **H Las Doñas del Portazgo** (€57/65): , c/Ribadeo 2, ©987-542742
11. **H La Llave** (€44/56): , c/del Agua 7, ©648-030888
12. **H San Francisco** (€39/49): , Plaza Mayor 6, ©987-540465
13. **H La Puerta del Perdón** (€42/55 w/): , Plaza de Prim 4, ©987-540614
14. **H Parador** (-/€75+): , Av. Calvo Sotelo 28, ©987-540175, pool and sauna, one of the least expensive Paradors

from all over, giving the city its names (literally "city of the Franks" but more accurately, of the "foreigners.") Villafranca marks the end of the 10th stage in the *Codex Calixtinus* and was home to numerous pilgrim hospitals.

Puerta del Perdón of Iglesia de Santiago in Villafranca

Life wasn't all that easy for the people of Villafranca, who suffered an outbreak of plague in 1589 and destruction by flood in 1715. In the Peninsular Wars of the early 19th century, French soldiers overtook the city only to be driven back by British soldiers who ravaged Villafranca, destroying the castle and stealing from churches.

Today Villafranca is a great place to rest up for the ascent toward O Cebreiro the following day and to wander the picturesque streets. On the way into town, pass the **Iglesia de Santiago** to the L, with its **Puerta del Perdón**, a doorway for pilgrims who were too sick to continue to Santiago. They could walk through the door in lieu of completing the pilgrimage and receive

Villafranca's lush botanical garden

the same indulgences. **Iglesia de San Francisco**, according to legend, was founded by Saint Francis of Assisi himself on his pilgrimage to Santiago. Don't miss the Mudéjar ceiling and excellent Renaissance *Retablo de la Inmaculada* in the chapel to the R of the entrance. The church has been restored after being used as a military barracks. The 17th-century **Iglesia de San Nicolás el Real** has an interesting Baroque façade; Domenico Laffi mentions receiving Mass here in 1673. The **Convento de la Anunciada** features one of the oldest cypress trees in Europe at over 400 years of age.

Villafranca
May 1: Spring festival
June: Poetry festival
Sept 14: Patron saint day

Be sure to stroll down *Calle del Agua* to see the 19th-century mansions replete with original coats of arms. The castle destroyed by the French has been restored, but is privately owned and cannot be entered. One of the modern albergues, the Ave Fenix, is run by the Jesús Jato, somewhat of a Camino legend. The original albergue burnt to the ground and was replaced by an intermediate tent city until the current building was completed. The albergue sometimes puts on a *queimada* (see p. 205) and offers healing rituals to pilgrims.

Queimada celebration in Villafranca

25 VILLAFRANCA TO LA FABA

23.7km
(14.7mi)

6-8 Hours
Difficulty: ▬■□
P 95%, 22.4km
U 5%, 1.3km

A Albergues:
Pereje 5.6km
Trabadelo 10.0km
La Portela 14.1km
Ambasmestas 15.4km
Vega 16.9km
Ruitelán 19.1km
Herrerías 20.5km
La Faba 23.7km
Laguna 26.4km
O Cebreiro 28.7km

Alt. Route:
Camino Duro,
+1.6km (p. 203)

Camino Duro Alt.
Triacastela to La Faba
P 57%, 14.3km
U 43%, 11.0km

Pradela 8.9km

Drink in captivating mountain and valley scenery on heather-lined earthen tracks, savor the shade of chestnut trees.

While the trail doesn't officially enter Galicia until just before O Cebreiro, the culture, landscape and architecture today all reflect Galician characteristics. Leaving Villafranca, the routes split with the more challenging but beautiful route turning to the R just before the bridge. While the flyover highway traffic can be distracting, the numerous Valcarce Valley villages provide quaint respite. Save energy for the final uphill to La Faba along sometimes muddy or slippery trails.

Mountain views from the Camino Duro

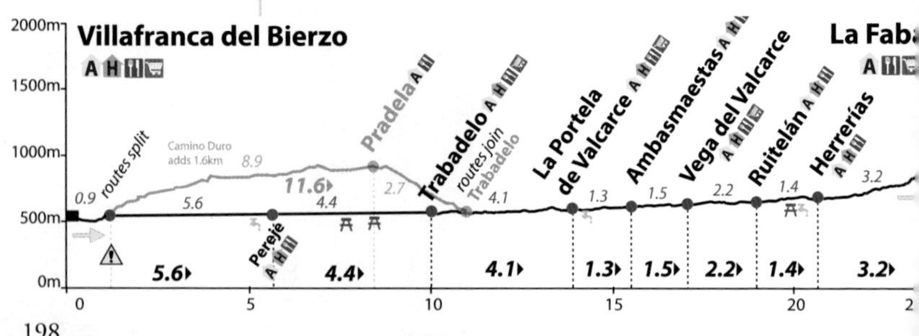

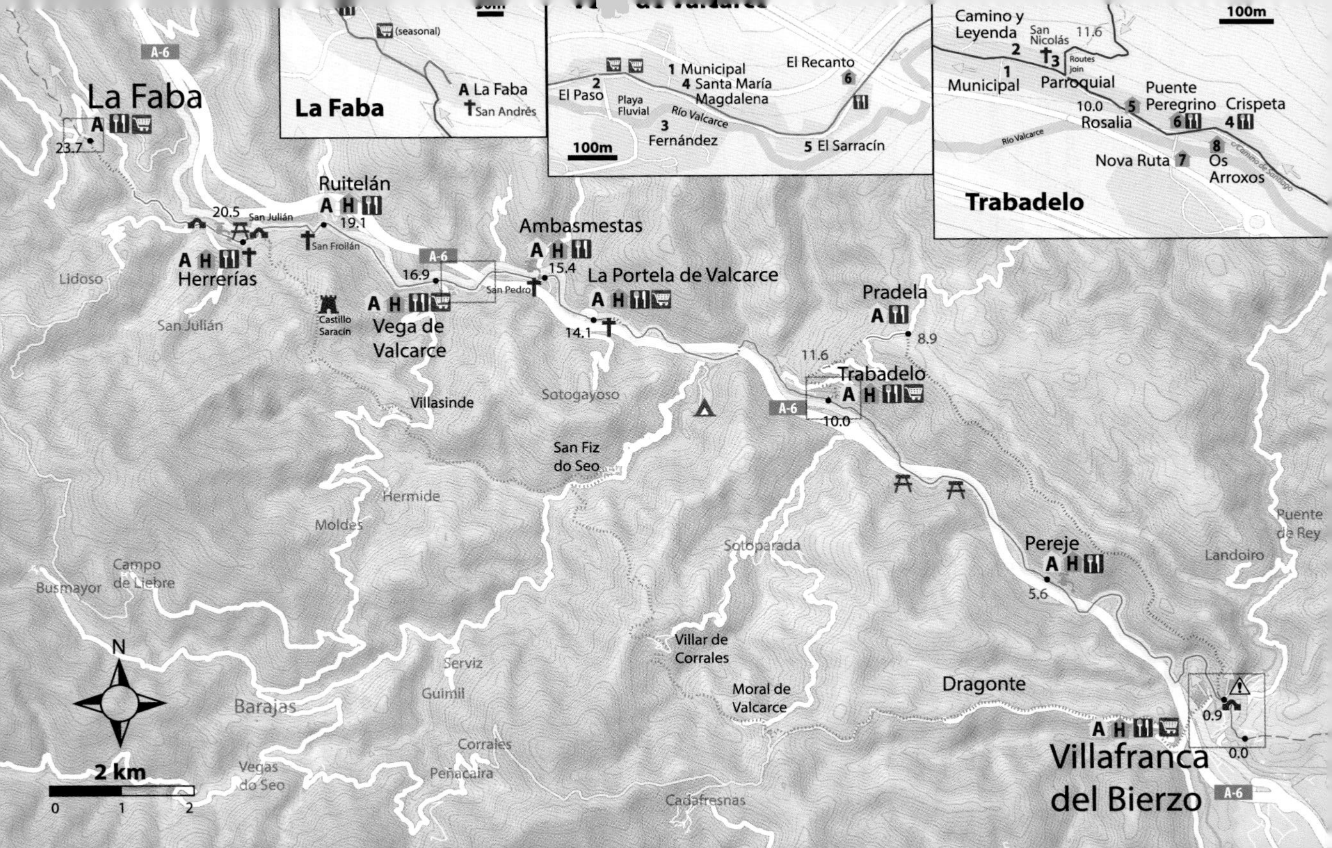

La Faba
A-6
23.7
Ruitelán
20.5
San Julián
19.1
San Froilán
Herrerías
Lidoso
San Julián
Castillo Saracín
16.9
Vega de Valcarce
San Pedro
Ambasmestas
15.4
La Portela de Valcarce
14.1
Villasinde
Sotogayoso
San Fiz do Seo
Hermide
Moldes
Campo de Liebre
Busmayor
Serviz
Guímil
Barajas
Corrales
Vegas do Seo
Peñacaira
Cadafresnas
Pradela
8.9
11.6
Trabadelo
10.0
Sotoparada
Villar de Corrales
Moral de Valcarce
Pereje
5.6
Puente de Rey
Landoiro
Dragonte
0.9
0.0
Villafranca del Bierzo
N
2 km
0
1
2
(seasonal)
La Faba
San Andrés
La Faba
2 El Paso
Playa Fluvial
Río Valcarce
3 Fernández
1 Municipal
4 Santa María Magdalena
El Recanto 6
5 El Sarracín
100m
Camino y Leyenda 2
San Nicolás 3
11.6
Routes join
1 Municipal
Parroquial
10.0
Rosalia 5
Puente Peregrino 6
Crispeta 4
Nova Ruta 7
8 Os Arroxos
Río Valcarce
Camino de Santiago
Trabadelo
100m

⚠ Route Options:

Primary highway route, 23.7km; This shorter and more popula route is entirely paved and on the shoulder of a highway next to a crash barrier all the way to Trabadelo.

Alternate high route "Camino Duro," 25.3km (p. 203); While this route is 1.6km longer and climbs much more in elevat than the highway route, the effort is rewarded with stunning view and earthen paths. Rejoins alternate route in 10.7km.

Route Options: Stay L for primary route, R for high route

The Camino Duro route option reduces the Triacastela to La Faba stage from 95% paved to 57%.

0.0 *Follow trail markings through Villafranca and across the river. ⚠ The split for route options (0.9km) is directly after the bridge and has a blue sign indicating straight for the Camino and R for the "path through the mountains, high difficulty."*

For the lower route, keep straight at the bridge leaving Villafranca. Much of the day's walking will be on a track parallel to the highway, with crash barriers providing protection from traffic. Because of the superhighway flyover passing above, the traffic on the old highway is fairly light. This primary route passes through Pereje, with its excellent municipal albergue, and rejoins the alternate route in Trabadelo.

5.6 **Pereje** A H Pop. 39

A **Municipal** (55, €6): , c/Camino de Santiago, 987-540138, all year, no bunk beds, beautiful facility, green yard

H **Las Coronas** (€36/46): c/Camino de Santiago, 987-540138

10.0 **Trabadelo** A H Pop. 456

1. A **Municipal** (36, €5): , c/Camino de Santiago, 687-827987, Apr-Oct
2. A H **Camino y Leyenda** (8, €8-12/-/28): , 628-921776, Apr-Oct
3. A **Parroquial** (22, €5): , c/Iglesia, 630-628130, all year
4. A H **Crispeta** (20, €6-8/25/44): , c/Camino de Santiago, 620-329386, all year, call in winter
5. H **Rosalia** (-/€45): , c/Camino de Santiago, 696-978652
6. H **El Puente Peregrino** (€30/38): , c/Camino de Santiago 153, 987-566500
7. H **Nova Ruta** (-/€60): , 987-566431
8. H **Os Arroxos** (€40/50): , c/Camino de Santiago, 987-566529, jacuzzi

5.6 **Pereje** was the site of a pilgrim hospital, donated by Doña Urraca to the O Cebreiro monastery in 1118. The hospital was in commission until land reforms in 1835. *Continue along the road to Trabadelo.*

10.0 **Trabadelo**: Little remains of the historic buildings of Trabadelo, which included two chapels, a pilgrim hospital and castle, whose owners exacted pilgrims tolls until banned by the king. Iglesia de San Nicolás survives with its Romanesque virgin. The entrance to town features immense chestnut trees, and the modern lumber industry is evident with piles of fresh-cut logs. *The route continues on the main road out of Trabadelo to La Portela.*

14.1 Portela de Valcarce

After passing through a parking lot across from the Hotel Valcarce complex, (local products and fruit shop), the path enters this wayside village. *Continue along the road to Ambasmestas.*

15.4 Ambasmestas

The name comes from the confluence here of the Balboa and Valcarce rivers. There is an 18th-century stone church. *Continue on the same road to Vega de Valcarce.*

16.9 Vega de Valcarce

The largest town of the day, Vega de Valcarce is located on a wider section of the valley well-suited to agriculture, with many gardens. Emperor Carlos V is said to have spent a night in Vega in 1520 and records indicate the presence of a Jewish quarter. From here, **Castillo de Sarracín**, a 9th-century castle reconstructed in the 14th-15th centuries, is visible below the village to the L. If you stay in Vega, save energy for a hike up to the ruins (30 min. each way). *Continue on the same road as it goes up to Ruitelán.* Vega de Valcarce is the last "full-service" town until Triacastela, so consider if you need to top off on cash, pharmacy items or snacks.

14.1 Portela de Valcarce A H

Pop. 37, Spanish: "gate of the Valcarce [river]"

- A H **El Peregrino** (28, €9/25/35): Cam. Santiago 5, 987-543197, Mar-Oct
- H **Hotel Valcarce** (€30/56): , Autovia A-6, 987-543180

15.4 Ambasmestas A H

Pop. 46, Spanish: "waters mixing"

- A **Camynos** (10, €10/35/45): , Antigua VI 43, 609-381412, Apr-Nov
- A H **Casa del Pescador** (34, €10-12/-/30-45): , Crta N-VI, 603-515868, mid Mar-mid Nov, vegetarian meals
- A **Das Animas** (18, €5): , c/Campo Bajo 3, 619-048626, Apr-Oct, across creek in bright green building
- A H **El Rincón Apóstol** (16, €17/-/40 w/): , N-VI 1, 987-543099, Mar-Oct
- H **CTR Ambasmestas** (€30/45): , Antigua VI 19, 987-543247, all year

16.9 Vega de Valcarce A H

Pop. 703, Spanish: "meadow on the Valcarce [river]," in bakery/café

1. A **Municipal** (72, €5): , c/Pandelo, 606-792791, basic
2. A **El Paso** (28, €10): , Crta N-VI 6, 628-104309, all year, call in winter
3. A H **Fernández** (30, €8/15/30): , Pl Ayuntamiento 3, 987-543027, all year
4. A **Santa María Magdalena** (16, €9/18/26): , N-VI 57, 987-543230, Mar-Nov
5. A **Sarracín** (18, €10): , Crta N-VI 32, 696-982672, Feb-Nov
6. H **Recanto** (€42/56): N-VI 83, 987-543202

19.1 Ruitelán A H Pop. 23

- A H **Pequeño Potala** (34, €5/-/30): , Crta A Coruña 22, 987-561322, all year, Buddhist vibe, massage, veg. dinner

Pilgrim shells for sale in Vega del Valcarce

19.1 Ruitelán is home to the Iglesia de San Juan Bautista, which belongs to the far-off diocese of León. On the L at the end of town is the chapel of San Froilán, who lived as a cave hermit here before becoming bishop of León. *The trail finally leaves the highway on a side road to the L through the hamlet of San Julián. Cross a 15th-century bridge to enter Herrerías. This is the last you'll see of highway walking until Palas de Rei—enjoy!*

20.5 Herrerías was an iron-working town with the iron forge visible across the river. Domenico Laffi described the town in the 17th century as "on the riverbank. Here they excavate iron from the hills and bring it to the village, where there is a furnace for smelting it. They have a large iron hammer driven by waterpower, as well as forging tongs and bellows. All these tools are of immense size. The village is small and its huts are roofed with straw." Today a picnic area along the creek welcomes visitors. The fountain in town is known anecdotally as *La Fuente de Don Quiñones*, of jousting fame in Hospital de Órbigo. A 12th-century English pilgrim hospital was once located on the far side of town.

Guided horse rides are available for the uphill from Herrerías to O Cebreiro, 2 hours, €34.50 638-041823, Apr-Oct

20.5 Herrerías A H
Pop. 44, Spanish: "the blacksmiths"
- A **Albergue Herrerías** (17, €5): W D, 654-353940, mid Apr-Oct, vegetarian
- A H **Casa Lixa** (30, €11/42-55): W D, c/Camino de Santiago 35, 608-528715
- H **Paraíso Bierzo** (-/€59): 987-684138
- H **Capricho de Josana** (€43/61 w/): c/Camino de Santiago, 987-119300
- H **Casa Polín** (-/€30): c/Camino de Santiago 6, 987-543039

23.7 La Faba A
Pop. 27, Spanish: "the bean"
- A **Albergue de la Faba** (assoc, 66, €5 w/): W D, 630-836865, 2pm, mid Mar-Oct, evening ecumenical service, German Association

The trail begins climbing a quiet paved road, but splits to the L soon onto a steep rocky path through a lush chestnut forest on a delightful dirt path. The trail emerges into the tiny village of La Faba, a good place to rest and fortify for more uphill hiking tomorrow.

23.7 La Faba's church, **Iglesia de San Andrés**, is the last of the diocese of Astorga, offering an evening pilgrim mass. A German confraternity operates the albergue next door. The Refugio Vegetariano, a decidedly eastern establishment, offers vegetarian meals, massage and some mattresses on the floor. A small, adequate shop could provide dinner fare, and the town bar offers a *menú*.

Pilgrim statue outside of La Faba albergue

Alternate: Camino Duro, +1.6km

e alternate Camino Duro route turns to the R uphill before the bridge leaving Villafranca (see oto on p. 200) and climbs a mountain, while the primary route stays in the valley.

From the split, the path becomes a dirt path, which is initially very steep with nice views back to Villafranca. The track flattens out with lovely views and joins a paved road to the edge of ***Pradela (8.9km)****. At the T turn L to continue on the trail or R to enter the Pradela. The path descends steeply on and off the paved road to* ***Trabadelo (11.6km)*** *(walk the road for a more gradual but longer descent), where the two routes join.*

8.9 **Pradela** A

A **Albergue Lamas** (10, €5): , c/Calella, 677-569764, Mar-Nov

Mountain scenery and earthen paths on the alternate route via Pradela

26-31 GALICIA

A typical green Galician forest scene

In Galicia, **Xunta albergues** (municipal) have a standard fee (€6) that includes disposable sheet and pillow case. Available year-round, you may need to call for the key in winter. Xunta albergues tend to have two small oddities: 1) kitchens without cookware; 2) bathroom facilities that are not very private (such as showers without curtains or doors).

Highlights include flowing rivers, glorious mountain views, Celtic architecture and culture, timeless rural villages, and arriving to the grand cathedral!

Galicia is the last of the autonomous regions on the Camino and home to the much-anticipated Santiago de Compostela. The official languages of Galicia are Spanish and Galician *(Galego)*, spoken by a whopping 90% of inhabitants (compared to only about 30% of Basques who speak Euskara).

Excavations have shown evidence of megalithic prehistoric cultures in Galicia, including a proliferation of dolmens, or megalithic burial chambers. Later the area was settled by a Celtic tribe who became known as Galicians, and many symbols of Celtic culture remain right down to the traditional bagpipe music. These inhabitants built fortified villages, or *castrum*, some of which were inhabited until the 8th century, and some ruins can still be seen today.

Galicians, as the Celts they are, were known for being fiercely independent (think Braveheart) and resistant to foreign rule. Foreign occupations of the Iberian peninsula tended to peter out before conquering Galicia, as the Roman, Suevi and Muslim conquests all fell short of overcoming them. The region had a reputation for witchcraft and pagan beliefs. Even today, pilgrims can sometimes participate in the *queimada* tradition of preparing a drink from alcohol and setting it on fire to ward off evil spirits.

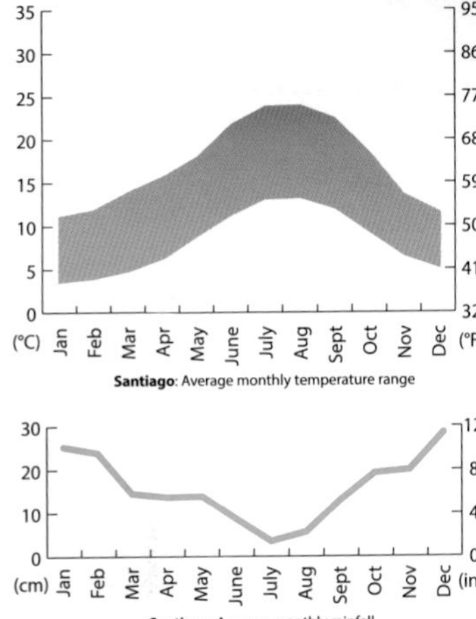

Santiago: Average monthly temperature range

Santiago: Average monthly rainfall

Galicia is known as *o país dos mil ríos*, "the country of a thousand rivers" for its free-flowing water, including the largest river, the Miño, which the Camino crosses over at Portomarín. Its wet reputation extends to the weather, with high average rainfall, so be sure to have your rain jackets and pack covers handy! The forested and rainy ecology is quite a far cry from what is usually thought of as Spanish climate, and you may feel like you have stepped into Ireland!

For local cuisine, seafood rules the roost, including the superlative *Pulpo á la Gallega* (boiled octopus) as well as squid, razor clams and goose barnacles. Fishing is the largest industry in the region, which depends on its Atlantic coastline and the many rivers and fjords. *Caldo Gallego* (Galician stew) is also frequently on offer, a mixture of white beans, potatoes, turnips, ham, pork, chorizo and collard greens.

Many forests have been planted with invasive eucalyptus trees, used for papermaking, which is edging out the traditional rural occupation of raising cattle. Some original oak and chestnut forests remain, including ancient beauties before Ponferrada. Native species include the hearty Galician Pony, and woodlands provide an ideal habitat for rabbits, wild boar and deer.

The Galician language is very similar to Portuguese and has much in common with Spanish. The letter X is much more prominent, pronounced as a "sh" sound. For example *Igrexa* instead of *Iglesia* (church). Vowel sounds are often drawn out and dipthongized (*cruceiro* instead of the Spanish *crucero*, or wayside cross). Galician also drops the "l" from definite articles *(la, los/las)* so "the house" would be *a casa* rather than the Spanish *la casa* (*el* becomes *o*).

26 LA FABA TO TRIACASTELA

25.7km
(16.0mi)

6-8 Hours
Difficulty:
P 16%, 4.1km
U 84%, 21.6km

A Albergues:
Laguna 2.7km
O Cebreiro 5.0km
Liñares 8.0km
Hospital 10.5km
Alto do Poio 13.4km
Fonfría 16.8km
Fillobal 22.2km
Triacastela 25.7km
A Balsa 28.3km
Calvor 39.3km

Mountain views on the way to O Cebreiro

Enter the misty mountains of Galicia and enjoy stunning views. Observe traditional rural architecture as you pass through villages to the historic town of Triacastela.

The challenging climb to O Cebreiro is well rewarded with breathtaking mountain views. Traditional Galician villages provide frequent amenities and whimsical country scenery. Be prepared for cold, wet or foggy weather. The descent to Triacastela is quite steep and can be muddy and slippery.

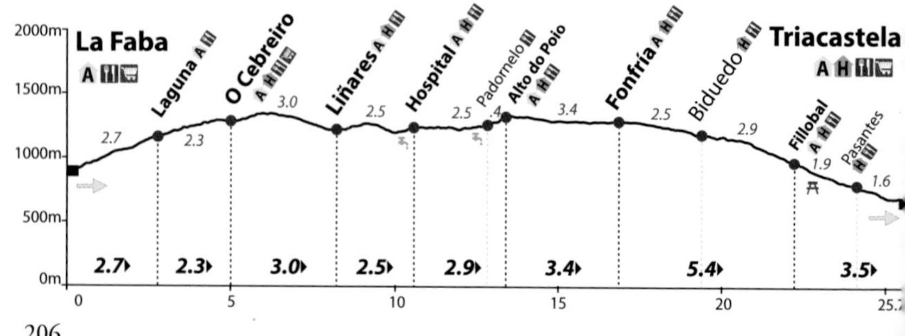

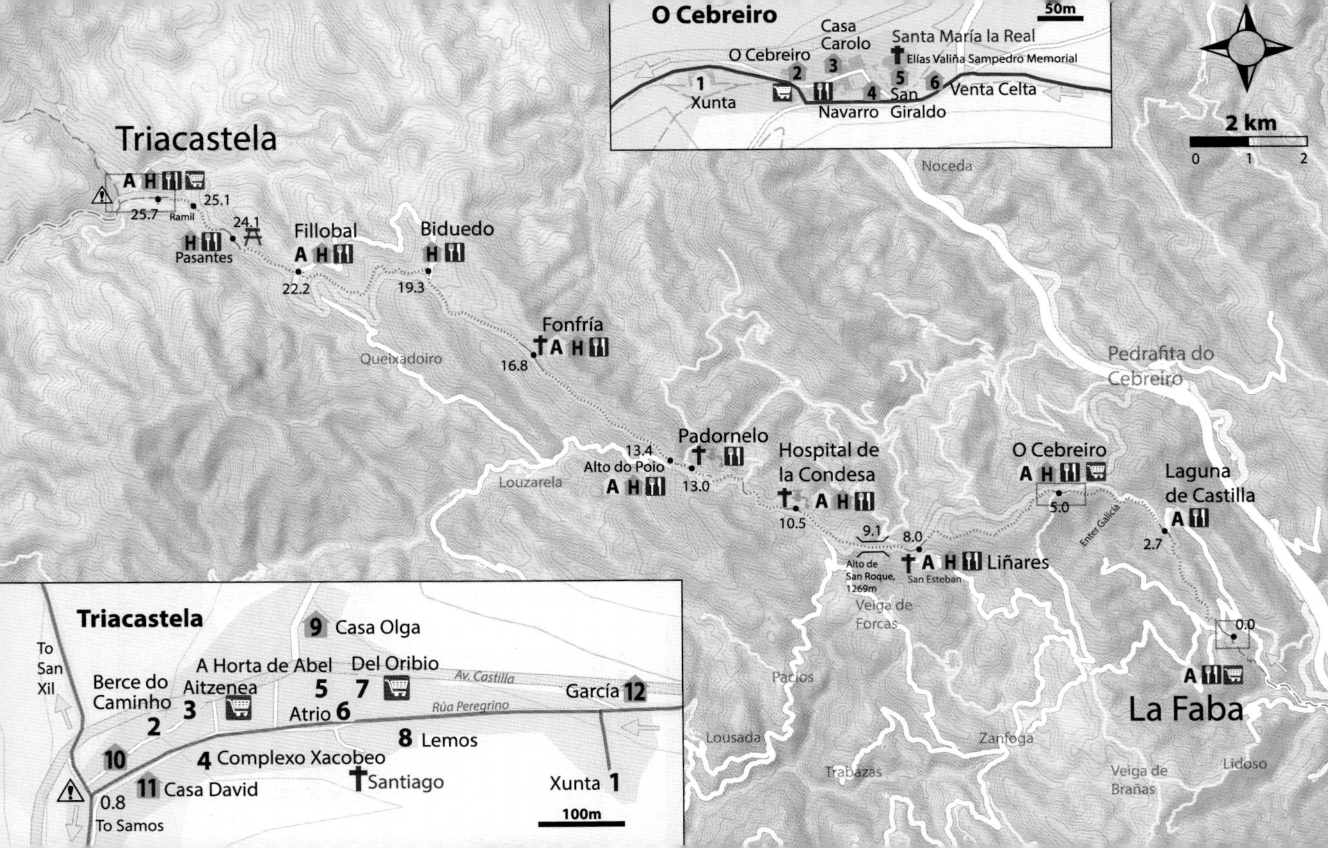
O Cebreiro
50m
Casa Carolo
Santa María la Real
Elías Valiña Sampedro Memorial
O Cebreiro
2
3
5
6
1
Xunta
4
San Giraldo
Navarro
Venta Celta
2 km
0
1
2
Triacastela
A H
25.1
25.7
Ramil
24.1
H
Pasantes
Fillobal
A H
22.2
Biduedo
H
19.3
Noceda
Fonfría
A H
16.8
Queixadoiro
Pedrafita do Cebreiro
Padornelo
13.4
Alto do Poio
A H
13.0
Louzarela
Hospital de la Condesa
A H
10.5
9.1
Alto de San Roque, 1269m
8.0
A H
Liñares
San Esteban
O Cebreiro
A H
5.0
Enter Galicia
Laguna de Castilla
A
2.7
0.0
A
La Faba
Veiga de Forcas
Pacios
Lousada
Trabazas
Zanfoga
Veiga de Brañas
Lidoso
Triacastela
9 Casa Olga
To San Xil
Berce do Caminho
2
A Horta de Abel
Aitzenea
3
5
Del Oribio
7
Av. Castilla
García 12
Rúa Peregrino
Atrio 6
8 Lemos
10
4 Complexo Xacobeo
Santiago
11 Casa David
0.8
To Samos
Xunta 1
100m

2.7 **Laguna de Castilla** A
Pop. 27, Spanish: "Lagoon of Castile"
A H **Albergue a Escuela** (30, €9/25/40): , c/Camino de Santiago, 987-684786, 12pm Mar-Oct

0.0 *Leave La Faba along a pleasant tree-lined lane. Stay to the R upon emerging from the trees to walk uphill with beautiful views to reach Laguna.*

A stone stele marks the entrance into Galicia.

2.7 Laguna de Castilla

is officially the last town in Castilla, modeling many typical Galician features such as *pallozas* (p. 209) and *hórreos* (one of the largest on the route, p. 179). About 1km after Laguna, a colorful cement *stele* will mark your official **entrance into Galicia**, the final region on the Camino, where Santiago de Compostela is located. Cement markers count down the kilometers to Santiago through Galicia. The Xunta Galicia began the process of replacing the markers with brand new ones in 2016. The old markers, in spite of inaccurate distances and being covered with graffiti, were so loved that a petition was started to reinstate the original markers. *Continue straight through the scrubby gorse and heather to meet the road into O Cebreiro.*

5.0 **O Cebreiro** is the Camino's first official Galician town**,** a welcoming mountaintop village that retains its historic character. The albergue is the first of many run by the **Xunta**, the governing body of Galicia. They are mostly purpose-built modern buildings or renovated schoolhouses with good facilities but a somewhat sterile atmosphere (p. 205). O Cebreiro bears evidence of occupation since ancient times, including a Roman way station that guarded the road to the Galician mines. The town grew to greater prominence with the pilgrim road.

The **Iglesia de Santa María la Real** is a reconstruction of the medieval church that was destroyed in the early 19th century. In the reconstruction, traces of a pre-Romanesque church were found. The baptismal font, virgin and chalice reliquary are from the medieval church.

5.0 **O Cebreiro** A H Pop. 1,228
1. A **Albergue do Cebreiro** (Xunta, 104, €6): , 660-396809, 1pm, a.y., no cookware
2. H **Hotel O Cebreiro** (€40/50): , c/Cebreiro 10, 982-367182
3. H **Casa Carolo** (-/€35-48): c/Cebreiro 20, 982-367168
4. H **Navarro** (-/€49): , c/Cebreiro, 982-367007
5. H **San Giraldo de Aurillac** (€45/60): c/Cebreiro, 982-367125, next to church
6. H **Venta Celta** (-/€40): c/Cebreiro 19, 982-367137

Local tradition says that the **Holy Grail** (the chalice from which Jesus drank wine at the Last Supper) was hidden away in O Cebreiro. In the year 1300, a faithful parishioner trudged through a snowstorm to receive communion at the O Cebreiro church. The priest mocked the man for going to such trouble for just a bit of bread and wine. At that moment, the elements miraculously transformed into real flesh and blood. The virgin, still on display in the church, was said to have moved her head to have a better look. The event was later declared an official miracle by Pope Innocent VIII. When Queen Isabel passed through 200 years later she donated an ornate reliquary for the remains. The Galician coat of arms incorporates the chalice and host as central symbols. The church offers daily Mass at 🕒7pm.

Iglesia de Santa María in O Cebreiro

Visit a 🏛 museum of local artifacts housed in a **palloza**, (free, 🕒11am-12pm, 3-7pm) a traditional building type found all over the Celtic world. Pallozas are oval stone buildings with thatched roofs, well suited for the tough environment of Galicia, often divided with space for animals and for humans, as well as a lofted sleeping area. They have no chimneys, and smoke escapes through the thatch. These structures are visible in various stages of construction or decay along the pilgrimage road in Galicia. Pallozas were inhabited into the 1960s.

Elías Valiña Sampedro bust in O Cebreiro

O Cebreiro is known for being the birthplace of **Father Elías Valiña Sampedro**, a local priest who was instrumental in the 20th-century revival of the Camino de Santiago. He is said to have initiated the yellow arrow symbol and is also responsible for the cement markers in Galicia. A bust of his head to the R of the church commemorates his life and contributions.

After the Xunta albergue, either follow the arrows down to the paved road or the dirt path from behind the albergue; both lead to Liñares.

O Cebreiro
Sept 8-9: Santa María and Santo Milagro
March: Cheese festival
Late Sept: Cattle fair

8.0 Liñares A H Pop. 69, Spanish: "linens"
A **Linar do Rei** (20, €10/-/40): , 616-464831, Mar-Nov
H **Casa Jaime** (-/€40): , c/Liñares 2, 982-367166, all of hamlet's services here

10.5 Hospital de la Condesa A H
Pop. 17, Spanish: "the Countess' Hospital"
A **Xunta** (20, €6): , 660-396810, 1pm, all year, no cookware
H **Mesón O Tear** (-/€25-36): , Hospital da Condesa 14, 982-367183

13.4 Alto do Poio A H
A **Albergue del Puerto** (16, €6): , 982-367172, poor reports
H **Santa María do Poio** (€30/40): Alto do Poio, 982-367096

8.0 Liñares grew flax to make linen garments. The town is referenced in documents as far back as the 8th century and mentioned in the *Codex Calixtinus*. The stone Iglesia de San Esteban is originally from 1120 but has been restored. *After Liñares, the trail continues to the R on a smaller paved road, then a L onto a dirt path. Follow an incline up the Alto de San Roque.*

9.1 Alto de San Roque features a modern bronze statue of a windswept pilgrim. In spring and summer, the area is alive with wildflowers in every hue and is a good place to look for birds of prey circling above. *Continue on the dirt path across the street from the statue, joining a paved road into Hospital de la Condesa.*

10.5 Hospital de la Condesa: The name suggests there was once a pilgrim hospice here, but any sign of it has been lost. The rustic stone church at the far side of town was built in 1963. *Leave Hospital on the paved road and soon turn R onto a smaller paved road signposted Saburgos. In 300m, turn off L onto a dirt path and pass through* ***Padornelo*** ***(13.0km),*** *which once housed the priory of the Hospitalers of San Juan de Jerusalén and now has a late 19th-century church also dedicated to St. John. From here the trail climbs steeply up to Alto do Poio.*

Pilgrim statue at Alto San Roque

13.4 **Alto do Poio** once housed a medieval hermitage and a church belonging to the Order of Saint John. Today it has a bit of a truck stop feel as the trail reconnects with the main road. *Continue to the R on a dirt track parallel to the paved road into Fonfría.*

16.8 **Fonfría** once housed the hospice of Santa Catalina, built in 1535, which was reported in 1789 to be in quite bad shape with the roof caving in. The lodging is recorded as providing heat, salt, water and a bed with two blankets to healthy pilgrims, and for ill pilgrims an extra 1/4lb of bread, eggs and butter. *Leave town on the dirt path parallel to the main road into the hamlet of Biduedo.*

19.3 **Biduedo** once had a pilgrim hospice and hermitage, but nothing remains. The modern stone church is said to be the smallest on the entire Camino. *The trail continues on a wide rocky dirt path, descending steeply to cross the paved road into several small hamlets on the way into Triacastela:* ***Fillobal (22.2km)****,* ***As Pasantes (24.1km)*** *and* ***Ramil (25.1km)****, which contains several truly massive chestnut trees. The road is paved into town, with the Triacastela Xunta albergue on the L.*

16.8 **Fonfría** A H
Pop. 41 Spanish: "cold fountain"
A H **A Reboleira** (64, €8/-/26): c/Camino de Santiago 15, 982-181271, Mar-Nov
A H **Linar do Rei** (20, €10/-/40): 616-464831, Mar-Nov
H **Casa de Lucas** (-/€36): c/Fonfría 25, 690-346740
H **Galego** (€25/37): c/Fonfría 9, 982-161461
H **Núñez** (-/€40): 982-161335

19.3 **Biduedo** H Pop. 31
H **Casa Quiroga** (-/€35): 982-187299
H **Casa Xato**: (€25/30), 982-187301

22.2 **Fillobal** A
A **Fillobal** (18, €9/-/30): c/Fillobal 2, 666-826414, all year

Massive tree at the entrance to Triacastela

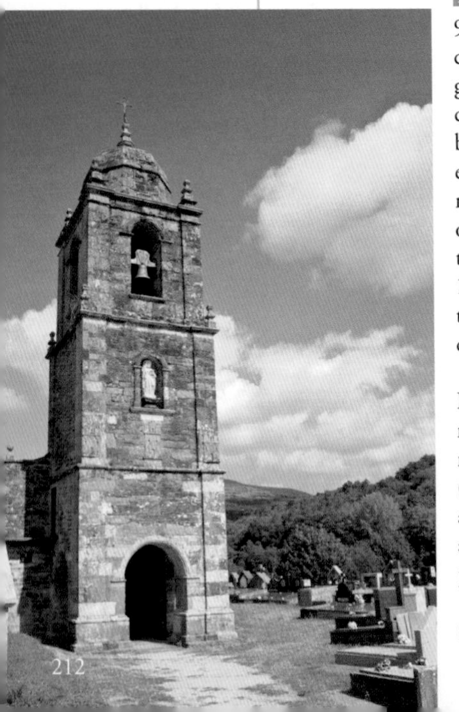

25.7 **Triacastela** was founded in the 9th centtury by Count Gatón, who was charged with repopulating the Bierzo region after the Reconquista. The three castles for which the town is named were built in the early 10th century and apparently destroyed in the same century with nothing remaining today, save the image on the coat of arms of Triacastela. The town held some political clout in the 13th century when Alfonxo IX spent time there and raised money for his successful bid to reconquer Sevilla.

In the *Codex Calixtinus,* Triacastela marked the end of stage 11 and signaled the end of the Galician mountains (though there are still a few smaller ups and downs to go before Santiago). The area is rich in limestone, and medieval pilgrims would often carry a large stone 100km to the limekiln in Castañeda near Santiago to be used in the making of the

cathedral. Imagine the many hands that helped to build! (And be grateful you don't need to add any rocks to your pack in this day and age.)

The **Iglesia de Santiago** is mostly from the 18th century—note the three castles on the coat of arms on the tower. Evening pilgrim Mass is offered here by a particularly passionate priest. Several cafés along the main street have pilgrim *menús*.

Triacastela
July 16: Virxe de Carme
Aug 17: San Mamede

Rounding the bend to Triacastela (above left)

Enjoying the rainbow at the Xunta albergue in Triacastela (above right)

Iglesia Santiago in Triacastela (left)

25.7 **Triacastela** A H

Pop. 772, Latin: "three castles"

1. A **Albergue de Triacastela** (Xunta, 56, €6): 982-548087, 1pm all year, one of the nicer Xunta albergues (rooms of 4 and green lawn)
2. A **Berce do Caminho** (27, €8): c/Camilo José Cela 11, 982-548127, all year
3. A **Aitzenea** (44, €8): Plaza Vista Alegre 1, 982-548076, Apr-Oct
4. A H **Complexo Xacobeo** (36, €9/35/40): c/Leoncio Cadórnigo 12, 982-548037, all year
5. A H **A Horta de Abel** (14, €9/-/40): Peregrino 5, 608-080556, Apr-Oct
6. A H **Atrio** (20, €9/-/40): c/Peregrino 1, 982-548488, Feb-Nov
7. A **Del Oribio** (27, €9): c/Castilla 20, 982-548085, all year
8. A **Lemos** (12, €9/35/40): Av. Castilla 24, 677-117-238, all year
9. H **Casa Olga** (from €16 per person): Rúa do Castro, 982-548134
10. H **Vilasante** (€30/40): Camilo José Cela 7, 982-548116
11. H **Casa David** (€30/40): Av. Camilo José Cela 8, 982-548144
12. H **García** (-/€30-40): Peregrino 8, 982548024

27 TRIACASTELA TO BARBADELO

23.0km
(14.3mi)

5-6 Hours
Difficulty:
San Xil Route:
P 42%, 9.8km
U 58%, 13.2km

A Albergues:
A Balsa 2.6km
Calvor 13.6km
San Mamede 14.9km
Sarria 18.7km
Vilei 22.3km
Barbadelo 23.0km
Serra 24.7km
Morgade 30.7km
Ferreiros 32.0km

Alt. Stage 27A:
Samos Route,
29.5km (p. 220 A)

Samos Route:
P 39%, 11.4km
U 61%, 18.1km

Picturesque chapel in Calvor

Visit the Benedictine monastery of Samos. Feel the excitement of new pilgrims joining the path in Sarria.

Two options lead to Sarria/Barbadelo; both follow a mix of paved and unpaved path and have pleasing rural scenery. The most direct primary route via San Xil is 6.5km shorter (23.0km), passing through small hamlets. The longer route (29.5km) passes the Samos monastery, a fascinating historical site that includes a pilgrim albergue. The Samos route includes some beautiful countryside, but the overall route has slightly more distance on pavement than the San Xil route (though a lower overall %). Both routes are lovely!

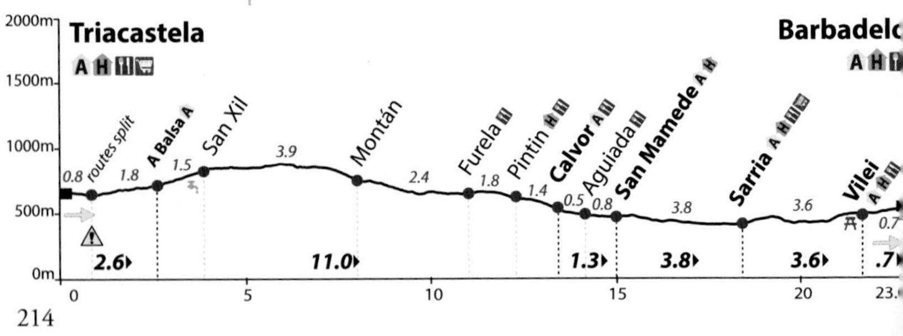

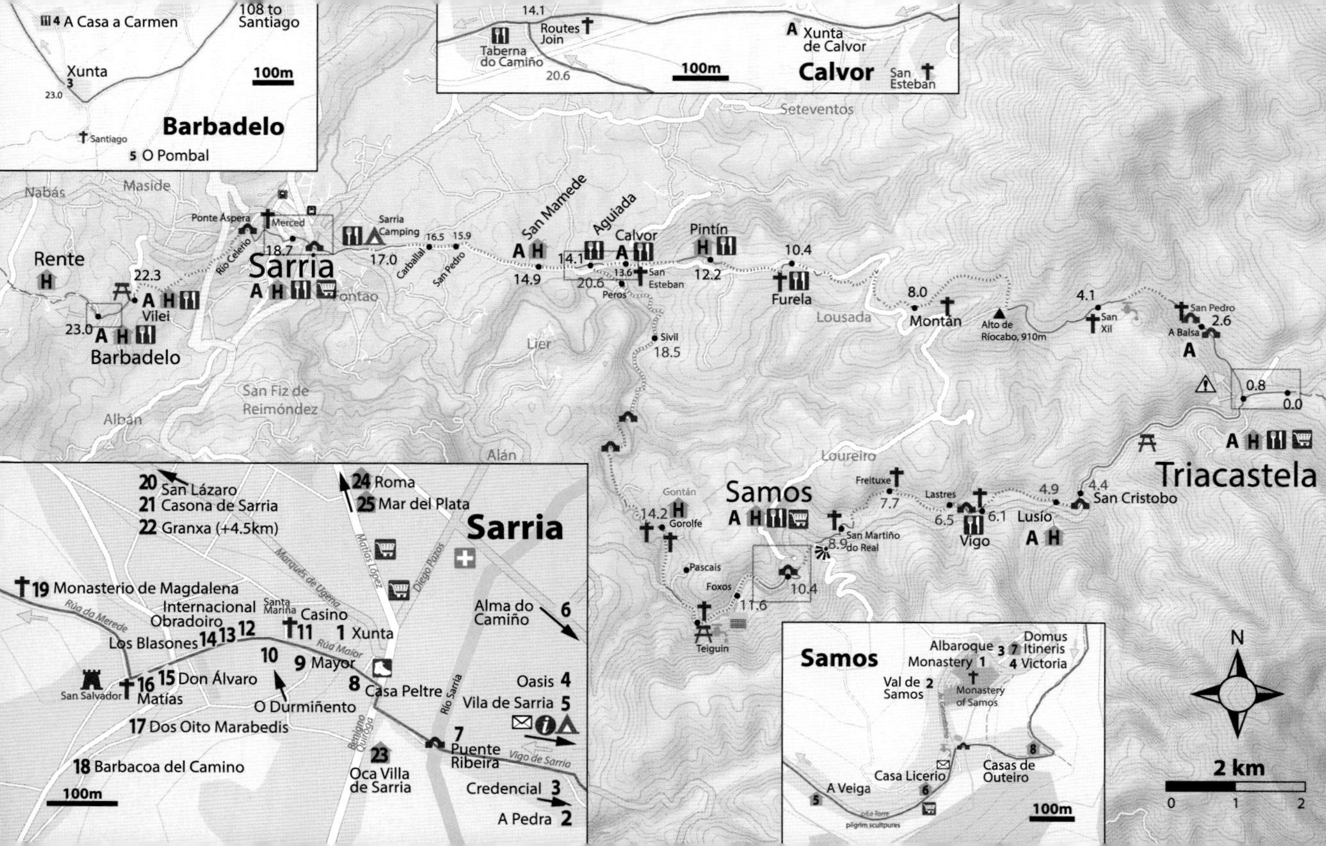

4 A Casa a Carmen
108 to Santiago
Xunta
3
23.0
100m
Barbadelo
Santiago
5 O Pombal
14.1
Routes Join
Taberna do Camiño
20.6
A Xunta de Calvor
100m
Calvor
San Esteban
Seteventos
Nabás
Maside
Ponte Áspera
Merced
Río Celeiro
18.7
Sarria
Sarria Camping
16.5
15.9
17.0
Carballal
San Pedro
San Mamede
Aguiada
Calvor
Pintín
14.1
14.9
20.6
13.6
San Esteban
Peros
12.2
10.4
Furela
Rente
22.3
Vilei
23.0
Barbadelo
Fontao
Lier
Sivil
18.5
Lousada
8.0
Montán
Alto de Ríocabo, 910m
4.1
San Xil
San Pedro
2.6
A Balsa
0.8
0.0
San Fiz de Reimóndez
Albán
Alán
Loureiro
Triacastela
Freituxe
7.7
Lastres
6.5
6.1
Vigo
4.9
4.4
San Cristobo
Lusío
Gontán
14.2
Gorolfe
Samos
San Martiño do Real
8.9
Pascais
Foxos
11.6
10.4
Teiguín
20 San Lázaro
21 Casona de Sarria
22 Granxa (+4.5km)
24 Roma
25 Mar del Plata
Sarria
Matías López
Diego Pazos
Marqués de Ugena
19 Monasterio de Magdalena
Rúa da Merede
Internacional
Obradoiro
Santa Mariña
Casino
Los Blasones 14 13 12
11
1 Xunta
Rúa Maior
10
9 Mayor
San Salvador
16 Matías
15 Don Álvaro
O Durmiñento
8 Casa Peltre
17 Dos Oito Marabedis
18 Barbacoa del Camino
Benigno Quiroga
23 Oca Villa de Sarria
Río Sarria
7 Puente Ribeira
Vigo de Sarria
Alma do Camiño 6
Oasis 4
Vila de Sarria 5
Credencial 3
A Pedra 2
100m
Samos
Albaroque 3
Monastery 1
Val de Samos 2
7 Domus Itineris
4 Victoria
Monastery of Samos
Casa Licerio
6
Casas de Outeiro
8
A Veiga
5
pilgrim sculptures
100m
N
2 km
0
1
2

2.6 **A Balsa** A

A **El Beso** (12, €9): , 633-550558, all year, communal dinner by donation with vegetables from the garden

0.0 *Leave Triacastela via the main road. ⚠ At the far edge of town, the trail splits (0.8km), with the primary San Xil route to the R, and the alternate Samos route (p. 220) to the L. For the **San Xil Route**, turn R and cross the main road (0.8km). Continue straight at the sign for San Xil on a minor paved roads through delightful forest. Turn off to the R and walk over a bridge over a creek. Walk through the hamlet of **A Balsa (2.6km)** and pass a small ermita, then pass over another small bridge. Pass a large pool of water with a huge seashell. Continue steeply uphill through oak and chestnut forest to the hamlet of San Xil.*

4.1 **San Xil** has a church that features a 15th-century chalice. Continue uphill to Alto de Riocabo and turn R on dirt footpath with nice views. *Keep walking to **Montán (8.0km)**, whose Iglesia de Santa María has a Romanesque nave. The trail continues through hamlets including **Furela (10.4km)**, with its Capilla de San Roque featuring a retablo. Continue through the hamlet of **Pintín** **(12.2km)**,* [H **Casa Cines**: -/€36, Lugar Pintín 5, 982-167939]; *turn off the road to the R to follow a dirt path to Calvor.*

Shell fountain before San Xil

13.6 **Calvor** was once the site of a pre-Roman castro known as Astorica. While its Iglesia de San Esteban was founded in the 8th century, most of what remains today is from the 19th century.

14.1 **Aguiada**: The trail reconnects with the alternate route at a convenient café for an afternoon pick-me-up. *Follow the paved road on a parallel dirt track past Albergue Paloma y Leña in **San Mamede del Camino (14.9km)** and*

Green forest path near San Xil

then ***Sarria camping (17.0km)****, both to the R. Enter Sarria's outskirts and pass* 🛈 ***Tourist Information (17.6km)****, continuing uphill and crossing a bridge into the heart of Sarria.*

Sarria is a major starting point for those wishing to do the minimum 100km to receive a Compostela. During the busy season, this can drastically change the character of your experience as beds become scarce and groups enter the Camino who may be less familiar with pilgrim etiquette. The Xunta albergue often fills up with newcomers as soon as it opens, but private albergues abound. While Sarria is a convenient and well-equipped pilgrim town, take a look at the churches, grab supplies from the readily available stores, and continue on to Barbadelo for a more rural and relaxed setting.

13.6 Calvor A Pop. 80

A **Xunta** (22, €6): W D, 660-396812, 1pm, all year, basic, free transport to/from restaurant (685-140635), no cookware

14.9 San Mamede del Camino A H

A H **Paloma y Leña** (20, €10/25/40): W D, San Mamede del Camino 4, 982-533248, Mar-mid Nov, vegetarian options

18.7 **Sarria** A H

Pop. 13,590, c/Vigo 15 982-530099, Peregrino Teca, c/Benigno Quiroga 16, 982-530190

1. A **Xunta** (40, €6): W D, Rúa Maior 79, 660-396813, 1pm, all year, fills up early with grou starting the Camino, no cookware, credenciales available
2. A H **A Pedra** (15, €10/30/35): W D, Vigo de Sarria 19, 982-530130, Mar-Oct
3. A **Credencial** (28, €9): W D, c/Peregrino 50, 982-876455, all year
4. A **Oasis** (27, €10): W D, Camino a Triacastela 12, 982-535516, Mar-Oct
5. A **Vila de Sarria** (€7, cabin €25): W, 982-535467, Apr-Oct, 1km before town
6. A **Alma do Camiño** (100, €9): W D, Calvo Sotelo 199, 982-876768, mid Feb-mid D
7. A H **Puente Ribeira** (28, €9-10/25/40) W D, r/do Peregrino 23, 982-876789, Mar-
8. A **Casa Peltre** (22, €10): W D, Escalinata Maior 10, 606-226067, Mar-Oct
9. A **Mayor** (16, €10): W D, Rúa Maior 64, 685-148474, Apr-Nov
10. A **O Durmiñento** (40, €10): W D, Rúa Maior 44, 600-862508, Mar-Dec
11. A **Casino** (28, €10): W D, Rúa Maior 65, 982-886785
12. A H **Internacional** (44, €10/-/45): W D, Rúa Maior 57, 982-535109, all year
13. A **Obradoiro** (38, €8): W D, Rúa Maior 49, 982-532442, Apr-Oct
14. A **Los Blasones** (42, €9): W D, Rúa Maior 31, 600-512565, Mar-Nov
15. A **Don Álvaro** (40, €9): W D, Rúa Maior 10, 982-531592, all year
16. A H **Matías** (30, €9/15/30-40): W D, Rúa Maior 4, 982-534285, mid Mar-mid Nov
17. A **Dos Oito Marabedis** (22, €10): W D, c/Conde Lemos 23, 629-461770, May-Oct
18. A H **Barbacoa de Camino** (18, €10/-/29): W D, Esqueiredos 1, 619-879476, Mar-
19. A **Monasterio de Magdalena** (par, 100, €10): W D, Av. de la Merced 60, 982-533568, mid Mar-Oct, historical building
20. A H **San Lázaro** (28, €10/-/35): W D, c/S. Lázaro 7, 659-185482, Apr-Oct
21. A H **Casona de Sarria** (26, €10/-/35): W D, San Lázaro 24, 982-535556, all year
22. A H **Granxa de Barreiros** (46, €10/18/34): W D, Crta LU-633 km 54, 982-533656, Mar-Nov, free pickup from Sarria (4.5km)
23. H **Oca Villa de Sarria** (-/€60): , c/Benigno Quiroga 49, 982-533873
24. H **Roma** (€39/50): , Calvo Sotelo 2, 982-532211
25. H **Mar del Plata** (€48/58): , c/Formigueiros 5, 982-530724

18.7 **Sarria** was likely a pre-Roman settlement, first documented in the 6th century, which became an important pilgrim stopping point. King Alphonse IX, who sponsored some building projects in the city, died in Sarria in 1230 on his pilgrimage to Santiago. Of the remains of the medieval castle, only one reconstructed tower remains. The town is known for antiques fairs held at the ruins site several times per month.

Follow *Rúa Maior* past a number of private albergues as well as the modern **Iglesia de Santa Mariña** to the R, then the Romanesque **Iglesia de San Salvador** to the L and the 12th-century **Monasterio de la Magdalena** on the way out

Sarria hosts a cattle market on the 6th, 20th and 27th of each month. A popular local cow is the *Rubia Gallega* (Galician Blond) characterized by a russet red color.

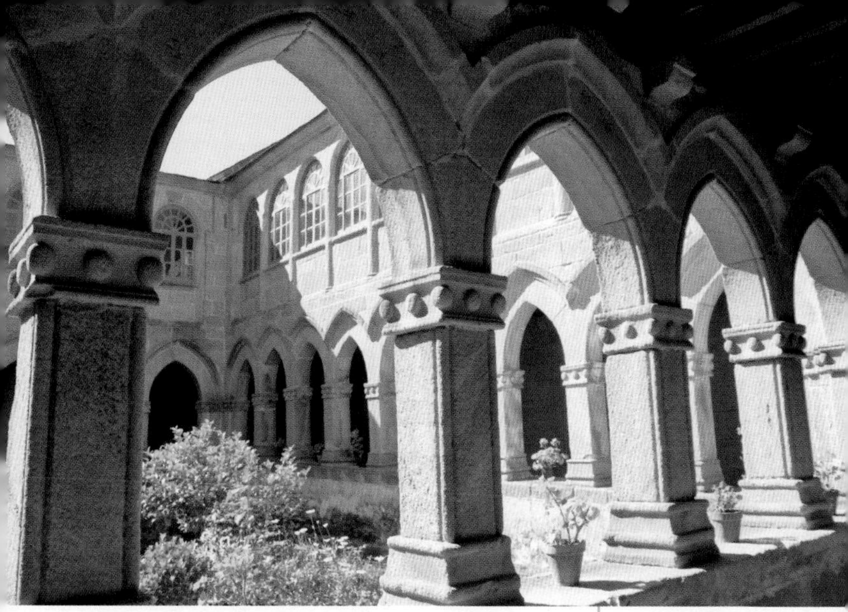

of town, which sometimes features art exhibits in the cloister and has a new albergue. *Leave Sarria via the medieval **Ponte Áspera bridge (19.8km)** over the Río Celerio and continue on a dirt path through a marvelous oak forest, crossing under the railroad and rejoining the paved road through the hamlet of **Vilei (22.3km)**. A rest area to the L offers a wide array of vending machines. A few hundred meters ahead, enter Barbadelo.*

Cloister of Monasterio de la Magdalena in Sarria

✝ Iglesia de Santa Mariña offers daily pilgrim Mass 7:30pm, credenciales are also available.

23.0 **Barbadelo** is mentioned in the *Codex Calixtinus* in which the author denounces the commercialism of the pilgrimage road. There's not too much commercialism to be found here currently other than a small snack stand in summer. The monastery was founded in 874 and came under the control of Samos Monastery. By the 12th century it supported a pilgrim hospital. The current Iglesia de Santiago features some interesting sculptures and offers a pilgrim Mass.

23.0 **Barbadelo/Vilei** A H Pop. 232

1. A H **Casa Barbadelo** (48, €9-12/-/40): W D @, km 108, 982-531934, Apr-Oct, good reports
2. A H **108 to Santiago** (14, €8/29/35): W D, 634-894524, Mar-Nov
3. A **Xunta** (18, €6): W D, 660-396814, no cookware, mixed gender shower, all year
4. A H **Casa Carmen** (28, €10/-/35): @, Barbadelo 3, 982-532294, Apr-Oct, free
5. A **O Pombal** (12, €10): W D, 686-718732, Apr-Oct

Samos monastery

⚠ Alternate Stage 27A: Samos Route

Triacastela to Barbadelo (via Samos), 29.5km

A SAMOS ROUTE:
Lusío 4.9km
Samos 10.4km
San Mamed 21.5km
Sarria 25.2km
Vilei 28.8km
Barbadelo 29.5km
Morgade 36.9km

For the Samos option, follow signs to the L on the edge of Triacastela. Follow the paved road for 3.4km until crossing over the Río Oribio with a L turn into the hamlet of ***San Cristobo (4.4km).*** *Cross back over the river on a cement bridge and continue on a dirt path through forest. A sign will indicate the* ***turnoff (4.9km) for the Lusío albergue*** (+400m). *Continue through* ***Vigo*** 🍴 ***(6.1km)*** *with a church containing a statue of Santiago Peregrino. Turn R out of the hamlet, following a sign to the R toward Lastres over a small bridge and through the tiny hamlet of* ***Lastres (6.5km).*** *Pass by* ***Capela Freituxe (7.7km),*** *a white chapel in a small hamlet. Continue straight through* ***San Martiño do Real (8.9km),*** *turning R at the T after the village. Pass through a cement tunnel, then continue straight on a dirt path to a nice Samos viewpoint. Wind down to Samos, crossing over the Río Sarria. After the bridge, turn R to visit the monastery or L to continue on the Camino.*

4.9 Lusío A H

A Xunta (60, €6): , 659-721324, all year, bring food or be prepared to walk 1km to Renche restaurant, beautiful restored monastery, +400m

10.4 Samos Monastery

(€3, M-Sa 10am-12:30pm, 4:30-6:30pm; Su 12:45-1:30pm, 4:30-6:30pm) held regional importance since it was founded the 6th century and has included a pilgrim hospital since the 11th century, which is still in commission! In spite of its wealth and prestige (controlling over 300 other monasteries), Samos fell victim to theft and, more recently, fire, which destroyed the majority of the abbey in 1537 and again in 1951, causing significant damage. Samos was the seat of the Benedictine order in the early 19th century and produced seven bishops.

10.4 Samos A H Pop. 1,614

1. **A Monastery** (par, 70, don): 982-546046, basic, 3:30pm, all year, entrance behind by gas station, vespers at 7:30
2. **A Val de Samos** (48, €9): K W D @, Av. Compostela 16, 982-546163, mid Apr-mid Oct
3. **A H Albaroque** (6, €9/-/30): W D, c/Salvador 1, 982-546087, Feb-Nov
4. **A H Victoria** (€9/25/35): W, c/Salvador 4, 982-546022
5. **H Hotel A Veiga** (€35/46): W, Av. Compostela 61, 982-546052
6. **H Casa Licerio** (€35/46): W, Av. Compostela 44, 653-593814, run by an American pilgrim
7. **H Domus Itineris** (€18/30): W D, c/Salvador 3, 982-546088
8. **H Casas de Outeiro** (-/€80): K, c/Fontao 13, 680-379969, spa

The monastery's exterior features a 9th or 10th-century Mozarabic chapel 200m from the main building. The monastery's imposing façade dates from the 18th century in the Baroque style. The monastery is still in use, and monks provide guided tours of the interior for €3. The cloisters are particularly nice, including the *Claustro de las Nereidas*, centered around a fountain, and the *Claustro de Feijóo* said to be the largest in Spain. The library bears the Latin maxim, "A cloister without a library is like a fort with an armory" and is "armed" with over 30,000 volumes.

Follow the paved road out of town, past a plaza with pilgrim sculptures along a park and recreation area to the L in the hamlet of ***Foxos (11.6km)****. A well-marked* ***R turn (12.7km)*** *on a narrow paved lane takes you off the main road. The path alternates between paved, cobblestone and dirt and winds through agricultural fields, cow pastures and the picturesque rural hamlets of* ***Pascais, Gorolfe*** [**H Casa de Díaz** (-/€44): W, Vilachá 4, 982-547070] ***(14.2km), Sivil (18.5km)*** *and* ***Perros (20.1km)****. This alternate route reconnects with the main route in* ***Aguiada (20.6km)****.*

Picnic area on Samos Route

28

BARBADELO TO HOSPITAL ALTA DA CRUZ

29.5km
(18.3mi)

6-7.5 HOURS
DIFFICULTY:
P 41%, 12.0km
U 59%, 17.5km

A ALBERGUES:
Serra 1.7km
Morgade 7.7km
Ferreiros 9.0km
Mirallos 9.3km
Pena 9.9km
Mercadoiro 12.7km
Vilachá 15.6km
Portomarín 17.7km
Gonzar 25.7km
Castromaior 27.0km
Hospital 29.5km
Ventas 31.2km
Ligonde 34.7km

Early morning light leaving Barbadelo

Break the 100km to Santiago mark! Cross the long bridge to Portomarín, visit a fortress-church, traverse small villages.

Today's route climbs to the Alto de Páramo, dips down to the riverside town of Portomarín and ascends again toward the Sierra Ligonde. The path passes almost constantly through small nearly-abandoned hamlets. Many villages and towns offer intermediate accommodations, including Portomarín with many albergues and the last grocery shop until Palas de Rei in the next stage.

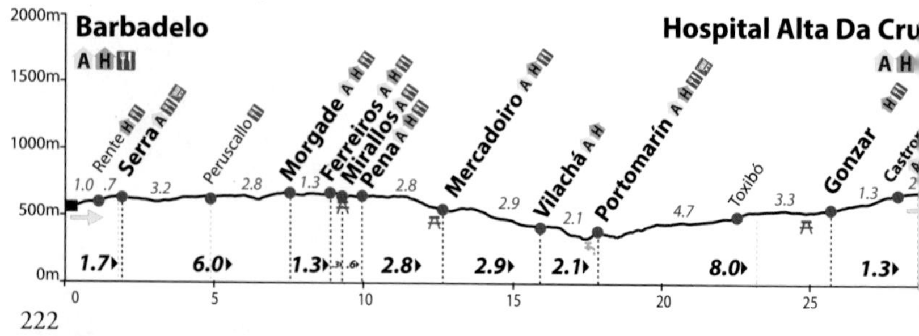

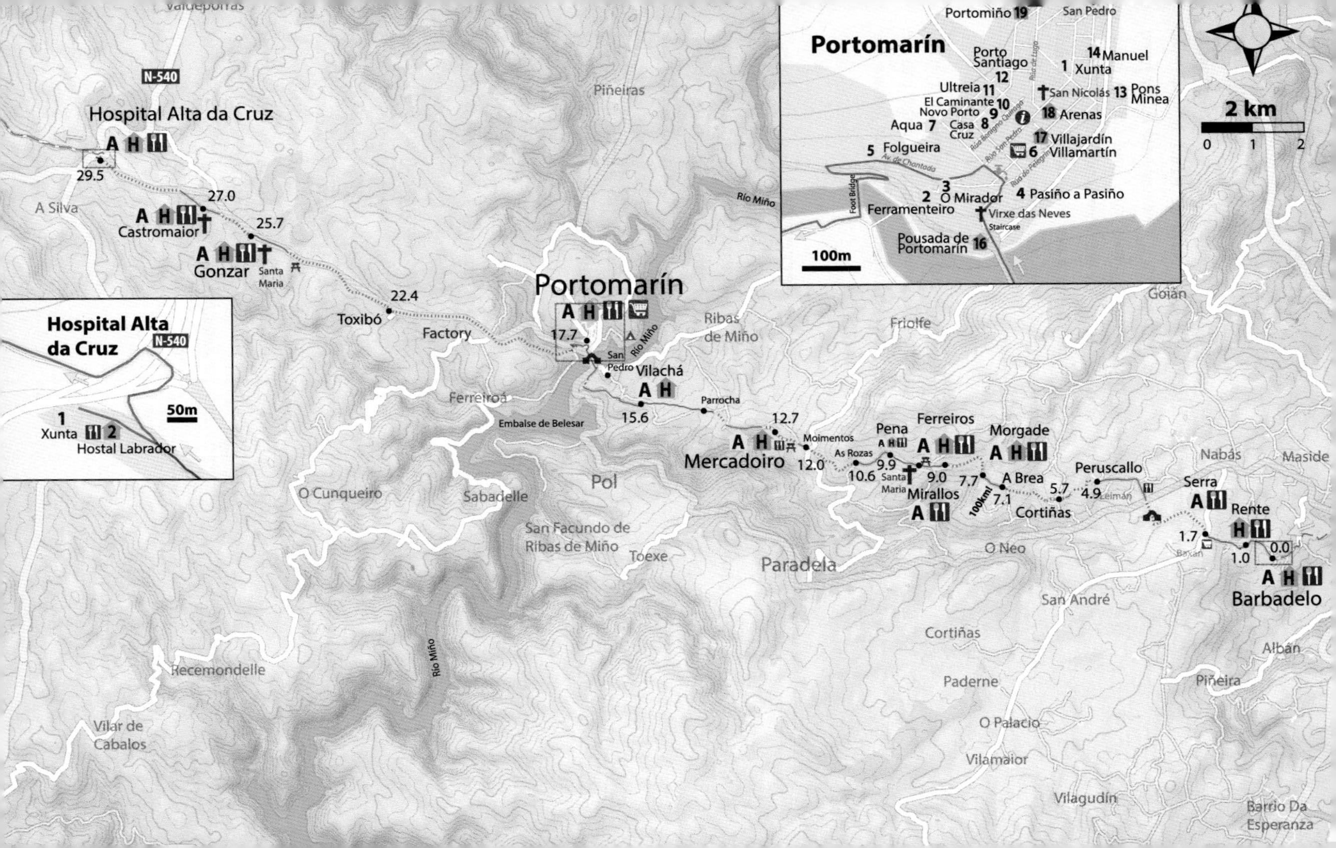

Portomarín
Portomiño 19
San Pedro
Porto Santiago 12
14 Manuel
1 Xunta
Ultreia 11
San Nicolás
13 Pons Minea
El Caminante 10
Novo Porto 9
Casa Cruz 8
18 Arenas
Aqua 7
17 Villajardín
6 Villamartín
5 Folgueira
3
2 O Mirador
4 Pasiño a Pasiño
Ferramenteiro
Virxe das Neves
Staircase
Foot Bridge
Pousada de Portomarín 16
100m
2 km
0
1
2
Hospital Alta da Cruz
N-540
29.5
A Silva
27.0
Castromaior
25.7
Gonzar
Santa Maria
22.4
Toxibó
Factory
Piñeiras
Río Miño
Portomarín
17.7
San Pedro
Vilachá
15.6
Parrocha
Ribas de Miño
Ferreiroá
Embalse de Belesar
12.7
Mercadoiro
Moimentos
12.0
As Rozas
10.6
Pena
9.9
Santa Maria
9.0
Ferreiros
Mirallos
7.7
100km!
Morgade
A Brea
7.1
5.7
Cortiñas
4.9
Leimán
Peruscallo
Serra
Rente
1.7
Baxán
1.0
0.0
Barbadelo
Friolfe
Goián
Nabás
Maside
O Neo
San André
Paradela
Pol
Toexe
San Facundo de Ribas de Miño
Sabadelle
O Cunqueiro
Recemondelle
Vilar de Cabalos
Cortiñas
Paderne
O Palacio
Vilamaior
Vilagudín
Albán
Piñeira
Barrio Da Esperanza
Hospital Alta da Cruz
N-540
50m
1 Xunta
2 Hostal Labrador

0.0 *Leave Barbadelo via the small paved road behind the Xunta albergue and turn off to the L at the Rente signpost. Pass* ***Rente (1.0km)*** [H **Casa Nova de Rente** (€30/40): 982-187854], *and continue on a pleasant path in the forest past* ***Serra (1.7km)****, across a paved road and later a highway past the hamlet of Pena to enter* ***Peruscallo (4.9km)****. The forest path continues along a dry stone wall through numerous tiny hamlets including* ***Cortiñas (5.7km)****,* ***Brea (7.1km)****, and Morgade.*

7.7 **Morgade**: Look for the nice wooden hórreo near the only building. A small stone hermitage can be seen to the R just after Morgade. *The path follows the paved road through Ferreiros.*

9.0 **Ferreiros** houses the Iglesia de Santa María de Ferreiros, which once sponsored a pilgrim hospital of which nothing remains. The church retains a few traces of its Romanesque history and has a stone baptismal font in front. There are grapevines in the vicinity, the first on the path since El Bierzo. *Turn R at the sign for the Igrexa Romana in* ***Mirallos (9.3km)****, which once manufactured nails for shoe making and repair. The trail continues along the paved road through another series of tiny hamlets, more populated with farm implements than people:* ***Pena (9.9km)****,* ***As Rozas (10.6km)*** *and* ***Momientos (12.0km)*** *up to the high point Alto de Páramo, which affords nice views, before the trail winds downhill into the hamlet of Mercadoiro.*

1.7 **Serra** A
A **Molino Marzán** (16, €10): W D, 679-438077, Mar-Oct, 1km past Mercado da Serra

7.7 **Morgade** A H Pop. 4
A H **Casa Morgade** (6, €10/-/30): W D, 982-531250, Easter-Oct

9.0 **Ferreiros** A H Pop. 106
Spanish: "blacksmiths"
A **Xunta** (22, €6): W D, 660-396815, 1pm, all year, no cookware
A H **Casa Cruceiro** (16, €10/-/40): W D, 982-541240, Apr-Nov

9.3 **Mirallos** A
A **Mirallos** (20, don): 982-157162

9.9 **Pena** A H
A H **Casa do Rego** (6, €10/-/40): W D, c/A Pena 4, 982-167812, Easter-Oct

12.7 **Mercadoiro** A H
A H **Albergue de Mercadoiro** (32, €10/-/40): W D, Aldea Mercadoiro 2, 982-545359, Mar-Nov 15

12.7 **Mercadoiro** is basically made up of a restaurant and albergue housed in a restored 18th-century structure. *Continue steeply down through* ***Parrocha (14.3km)*** *and Vilachá.*

15.6 **Vilachá** A H

A H **Casa Banderas** (8, €10/-/40): W D, 982-545391, Apr-Oct, nicely-restored historic stone house

15.6 **Vilachá** offers one albergue in a restored historic stone building draped in flags. *Soon Portomarín comes into view across the river. Pass through* ***San Pedro (16.9km)*** *hamlet directly before the long and rebuilt bridge over the* ***Río Miño (17.3km)****. Cross the bridge and either turn L at the base of the staircase to bypass Portomarín, or walk up the stairs to enter the city. It is worth detouring into town for supplies, to visit the church or for an overnight stop.*

The much-celebrated 100km marker (left)

Portomarín is famous for its *Orujo*, a liquor made from the grape remains left over after making wine.

17.7 **Portomarín** has been around for a while with a bridge from at least the late 10th century, but the current city is a relocation of the historic city including buildings transferred stone by stone. This was all due to a dam constructed in 1956, which flooded the former city that was located on both sides of the river. Today the water is normally low enough to see the remnants of the former city including the Roman bridge. Many bridges have spanned the river at this strategic point. Al-Mansur destroyed an early bridge in his campaign of devastation in 997. After being rebuilt, the bridge was taken out again by the 1112 war between Queen Urraca and her husband. Later, Urraca had the bridge rebuilt along with a pilgrim hospital. The strategic town needed to be protected, and this role fell first to the Order of Santiago, then to the Order of San Juan de Jerusalén.

Iglesia de San Juan/ Nicolás in Portomarín

Portomarín is the last place to get groceries or pharmacy supplies until Palas de Rei (stage 29), so stock up as needed.

Remains of the former Portomarín now flooded by the Río Miño

The town became an important pilgrim stopping point, including for royal pilgrims such as King Ferdinand and Queen Isabella. Domenico Laffi described it as, "an excellent place that has plenty of everything." The city declined in the 19th century as the nearby city of Lugo rose to prominence.

At the top of the staircase entering town is the relocated **Capela da Virxe das Neves**, a chapel with an image of the virgin traditionally thought to protect from drowning. The main church in town is the **Iglesia de San Nicolás** with its fortress-like appearance and prominent rose window. The portal was crafted by Master Mateo, a famous architect who also built the *Pórtico de Gloria* in the Santiago Cathedral. The church was transported brick by brick from its old location.

Leave Portomarín via a rickety metal footbridge to a pleasant forest path uphill, out of the Río Miño basin. Cross the paved road past a foul-smelling factory along the road, and cross back over to skirt the town of ***Toxibó (22.4km)***. *After a few kilometers of dirt path, rejoin the road past café Descanso de Rey into Gonzar.*

17.7 **Portomarín** A H Pop. 1,737, Spanish: "bridge over the Miño River"

1. A **Xunta** (110, €6): c/Fraga Iribarne, 982-545143, no cookware, 1pm, all year, crowded in summer, credenciales available
2. A **Ferramenteiro** (130, €10): c/Chantada 3, 982-545362, Mar-Oct
3. A **O Mirador** (27, €10): c/Peregrino 27, 982-545323, all year
4. A **Pasiño a Pasiño** (30, €10): Rúa Compostela 25, 665-667243, all year
5. A **Folgueira** (32, €10): Av. Chantada 18, 982-545166, all year
6. A **Villamartín** (22, €10): Rúa do Peregrino 11, 982-545054, Apr-Oct
7. A **Aqua** (10, €10): c/Barreiros 2, 608-921372, Mar-Nov
8. A **Casa Cruz** (16, €10): c/Benigno Quiroga 16, 982-545140, all year
9. A **Novo Porto** (22, €10): c/Benigno Quiroga 12, 982-545277, Apr-Oct
10. A H **El Caminante** (12, €10/30/42): Sánchez Carro 7, 982-545176, Apr-O
11. A H **Ultreia** (15, €10/-/40): c/Diputación 9, 982-545067, all year
12. A H **Porto Santiago** (14, €10/20/30): c/Diputación 8, 618-826515, all ye
13. A H **Pons Minea** (24, €10/40/50): Av. Sarria 11, 610-737995, Apr-Oct
14. A H **Manuel** (16, €10/-/25): Rúa do Miño 1, 982-545385, Apr-Oct
15. A H **Casa Marabillas** (16, €15/-/35 w/): c/Monte 3, 744-450425, Mar-C
16. H **Pousada de Portomarín** (-/€75-95): Av. Sarria, 982-545200
17. H **Villajardín** (€40/60): Rúa Miño 14, 982-545054
18. H **Pensión Arenas** (€38/50): Plaza Conde de Fenosa 5, 982-545386
19. H **Portomiño** (-/€45): Av. de Sarria 2, 982-547575

25.7 **Gonzar** is a tiny hamlet with some impressive oak trees near the entrance to town. With two albergues, it is a peaceful spot to overnight, with traditional rural agricultural buildings and a simple Iglesia de Santa María. *Continue on a dirt path to Castromaior.*

25.7 Gonzar A H Pop. 43

A **Xunta** (28, €6): , on the highway, 982-157840, 1pm, all year

A H **Casa García** (26, €10/-/35): , Gonzar 3, 982-157842, Mar-Oct, good reports

27.0 **Castromaior**: Traces of a Roman encampment were found in the area of Castromaior. The Romanesque church has a Baroque retablo and a wooden virgin statue. A traditional legend recounts that Moors were living in the area of Castromaior. A girl who worked as a swineherd left a sacrifice of a basket of pig snouts. When she returned the next day, the snouts had turned to lumps of coal. She pocketed one of the lumps and later found that it had turned to gold. She hurried back to the basket but found the other lumps had disappeared. We're not sure what lesson is to be learned from this tale! *A dirt parallel track along the paved road will take you to Hospital Alta de Cruz.*

27.0 Castromaior H Pop. 30

A **Ortiz** (18, €10): , c/Castromaior 2, 982-099416, all year

H **Casa Maruja** (€15/20): , c/Castromaior 8, 982-189054

According to the *Codex Calixtinus*, the Camino between Portomarín and Palas de Rei was infamous for prostitutes who would lurk in the woods and tempt individual travelers. Those who were caught had their noses cut off as punishment.

29.5 **Hospital Alta da Cruz** is another tiny hamlet located along the highway. There's not much to it other than a fairly new albergue and a hotel/restaurant.

29.5 Hospital Alta da Cruz A H

1. A **Xunta** (32, €6): , along highway, 982-545232, 1pm all year, no cookware
2. H **Hostal Labrador** (-/€30): , Alto Hospital 2, 982-545303

Two roads diverging after Barbadelo

29 HOSPITAL ALTA DA CRUZ TO MELIDE

28.4km
(17.6mi)

7-8 Hours
Difficulty: ▬□□
P 41%, 11.7km
U 59%, 16.7km

A Albergues:
Ventas 1.7km
Ligonde 5.2km
Eirexe 5.9km
Portos 8.0km
Os Chacotes 12.4km
Palas de Rei 13.4km
San Xulián 16.9km
Pontecampaña 17.9km
Casanova 19.2km
Melide 28.4km
Boente: 33.9km

Green shaded forest after Palas de Rei

Roam earthen paths through lush forest. Sample Melide's celebrated boiled octopus with a cool glass of Ribeiro white wine.

This stage traverses rolling hills, alternating between dirt tracks and quiet country lanes. Small villages offer frequent services with many intermediate accommodations options. Leave Lugo province behind and enter **A Coruña**, now firmly in the seafood zone where octopus is the claim to fame.

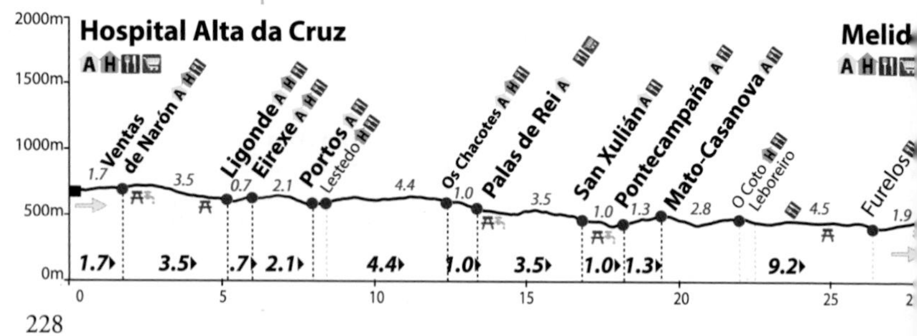

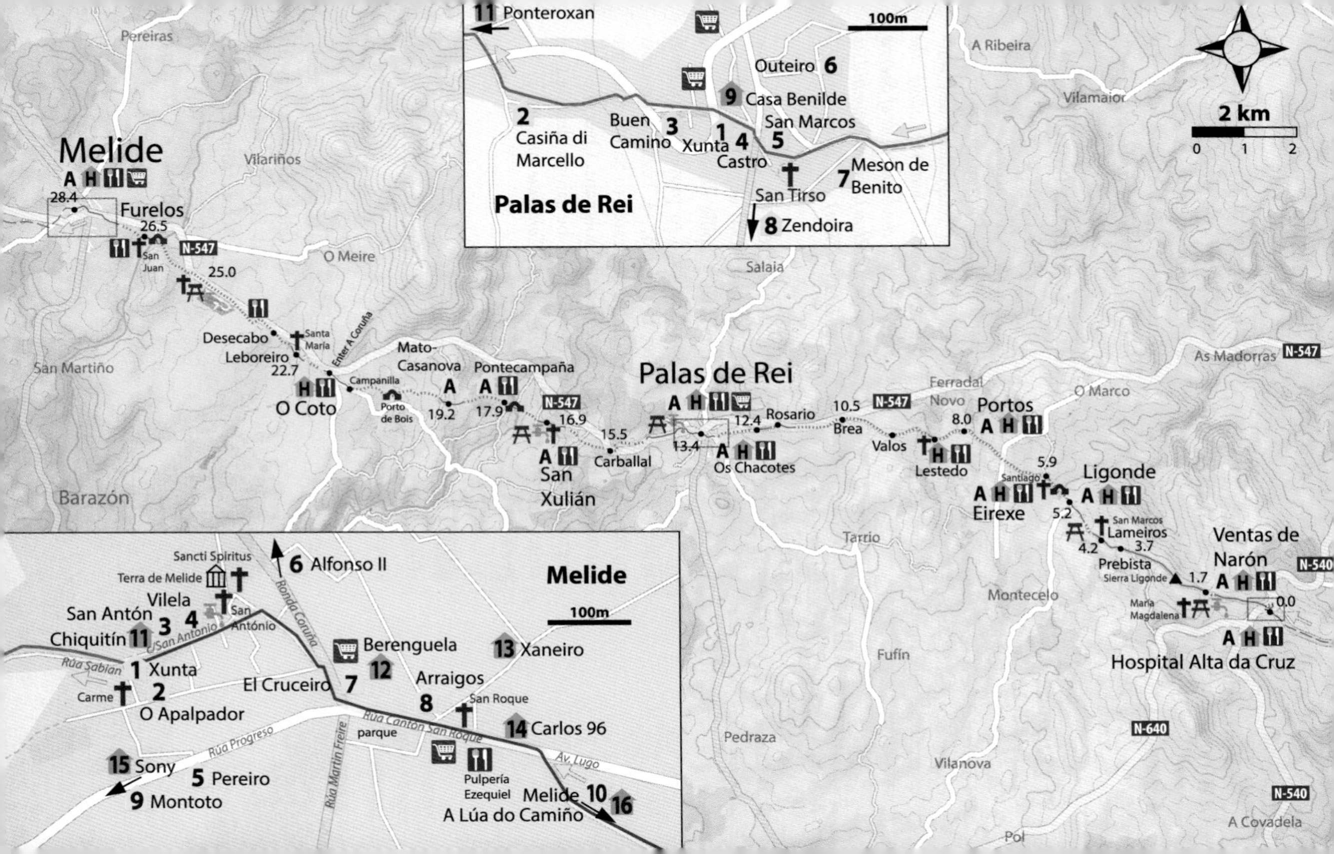
2 km
0 1 2
Melide
Furelos
28.4
26.5
San Juan
25.0
N-547
Pereiras
Vilariños
O Meire
San Martiño
Barazón
Desecabo
Santa María
Leboreiro
22.7
Enter A Coruña
O Coto
Campanilla
Porto de Bois
Mato-Casanova
19.2
Pontecampaña
17.9
16.9
San Xulián
15.5
Carballal
Palas de Rei
13.4
12.4
Os Chacotes
Rosario
10.5
Brea
Valos
Lestedo
Ferradal
Novo
8.0
Portos
O Marco
As Madorras
5.9
Santiago
Eirexe
Ligonde
5.2
San Marcos
Lameiros
4.2
3.7
Prebista
Sierra Ligonde
1.7
Ventas de Narón
María Magdalena
0.0
Hospital Alta da Cruz
N-540
N-640
A Ribeira
Vilamaior
Salaia
Tarrio
Montecelo
Fufín
Pedraza
Vilanova
Pol
A Covadela
11 Ponteroxan
100m
Outeiro 6
9 Casa Benilde
San Marcos
2 Casiña di Marcello
Buen Camino 3
1 Xunta
4 Castro
5
San Tirso
7 Meson de Benito
8 Zendoira
Palas de Rei
Melide
100m
Sancti Spiritus
Terra de Melide
6 Alfonso II
Ronda Coruña
Vilela
San Antón
3 4
San António
Chiquitín 11
C/San Antonio
Rúa Sabian
1 Xunta
Carme
2
O Apalpador
El Cruceiro
7
Berenguela
12
13 Xaneiro
Arraigos
8
San Roque
14 Carlos 96
Rúa Cantón San Roque
parque
Rúa Martín Freire
Rúa Progreso
15 Sony
5 Pereiro
9 Montoto
Pulpería Ezequiel
Melide 10
16
A Lúa do Camiño
Av. Lugo

1.7 Ventas de Narón A H Pop. 120
A H **O Cruceiro** (22, €10/-/30-35): Ventas 6, 658-064917, Mar-Oct
A H **Casa Molar** (18, €10/-/30): Ventas 4, 696-794507, Mar-Oct

5.2 Ligonde A H Pop. 64
A **Escuela de Ligonde** (muni, 20, €8): 679-816061, Apr-Oct
A **Fuente del Peregrino** (par, 20, don): c/Ligonde 4, 687-550527, May-Oct, communal meals, run by Christian association

5.9 Eirexe A H Pop. 23, Galego: "church"
A **Xunta** (20, €6): c/Airexe 17, 982-153483, 1pm all year, no cookware
A H **Eirexe** (6, €10,/-/30-35): c/Airexe 14, 982-153475, Easter-Oct

0.0 *Leave Hospital and double back to cross over Highway N-540. Follow the path parallel to the paved road to Ventas de Narón, a good place for breakfast if you slept in Hospital.*

1.7 **Ventas de Narón** was the site of an 820 battle between Christian and Muslim armies. A pilgrim hospital was located next to the Capilla María Magdalena just outside of town. *Continue along the paved* road *to the high point of* ***Sierra Ligonde (2.2km)****, then downhill to* ***Prebista (3.7km)*** *and Lameiros.*

4.2 **Lameiros** consists of one house (with two coats of arms) and the small Capilla de San Marcos, a saint believed to protect crops from foul weather. Shortly after the "town," a 1672 stone cross marks the site of a former chapel dedicated to San Lázaro; the carved virgin and child are especially poignant. Over the next stretch, ruins of ancient castrum can be faintly detected on either side of the pilgrimage road. *Continue onward to Ligonde.*

5.2 **Ligonde**: Coats of arm from local historic families still grace the walls of older houses. *Cross the small Río Ligonde to reach Eirexe.*

Wooden *hórreos*, used for grain storage in Galicia

5.9 **Eirexe** houses a 13th-century Iglesia de Santiago with engraved capitals with images of birds. Across from the church is a former pilgrim hospital in use up to the 18th century. *Continue downhill; soon after town, the Camino passes its first of many eucalyptus trees.*

Wise old trees in the Galician forest

8.0 **Portos** houses one small albergue. *The trail continues uphill along the paved road through the hamlet of **Lestedo (8.5km)**,* [H **Rectoral de Lestedo** (-/€70): 🍴, ✆982-153435, on R before town]. *Continue on the dirt path parallel to the road through **Valos (9.3km)**, **Brea (10.5km)** and Rosario.*

> **8.0 Portos** A 🍴 Pop. 2
> A H **A Paso de Formiga** (8, €10/-/40): 🍴 W D wifi, c/Portos 4, ✆618-984605

11.8 **Rosario** was a traditional site for pilgrims to recite the rosary, and on a clear day the mountain of *Pica Sacra* can be seen near Santiago de Compostela in the distance.

12.4 **Os Chacotes**: About 1km before Palas de Rei, the Camino passes through the park and recreation area of Os Chacotes, featuring an albergue, a municipal swimming pool and lots of peaceful green space. *Follow an unpaved path into Palas de Rei, past the church and into the center of town to the Xunta albergue.*

> **12.4 Os Chacotes** A H 🍴 🛒
> (recreation area 1km before Palas de Rei)
> A **Os Chacotes** (Xunta , 112, €6): W D, c/As Lagartas, ✆607-481536, all year, no cookware
> H **Complejo La Cabaña** (€55/75): 🍴 W D wifi, c/Doctor Pardo Ouro, ✆982-380750

13.4 Palas de Rei A H

Pop. 3,743, Spanish: "Palace of the King"

1. A **Xunta** (60, €6): Av. Compostela 19, 660-396820, 1pm all year, downtown, no cookware, mixed gender showers without doors
2. A **Casiña di Marcello** (17, €10): Aldeia de Abaixo 13, 640-723903, Apr-mid Nov, communal dinner
3. A **Buen Camino** (42, €10): Rúa del Peregrino 3, 982-380233, Mar 15 - Oct 15
4. A **Castro** (56, €10): Av. de Ourense 24, 609-080655, all year
5. A H **San Marcos** (72, €10/-/50): Travesía Iglesia, 982-380711, Mar-Oct
6. A **Outeiro** (50, €10): Pl Galicia 25, 982-380242, Mar-Oct
7. A **Mesón de Benito** (100, €10): Rúa da Paz, 636-834065, Apr-Oct
8. A H **Zendoira** (28, €10/25/35): c/Amado Losada 10, 608-490075, Mar-Oct, bed pods w/curtain, bike workshop
9. H **Hotel Casa Benilde** (€41/67): c/Mercado, 982-380717
10. H **Pensión Palas** (€40/45): c/San Tirso, 982-380065
11. H **Hostal Ponteroxan** (-/€33): Compostela 109, 982-380132, 1.6km after town

16.9 San Xulián A Pop. 46

A **O Abrigadoiro** (18, €12): 676-596975, Easter-Oct

The path from Palas de Rei to Melide crosses through several eucalyptus forests. The trees are planted for papermaking and lumber because of their relatively fast growth time.

13.4 Palas de Rei: The name comes from a legend that purports that the Visigoth King Witiza, an Arian heretic, constructed a palace here. The town is mentioned in the *Codex Calixtinus* as the endpoint for the 12th stage. Few historical buildings remain, save the **Iglesia de San Tirso**, which retains a few traces of its earlier Romanesque incarnation. *The route leaves Palas de Rei and criss-crosses the main highway mostly on dirt paths to* ***Carballal (15.5km)*** *where it leaves the road to San Xulián.*

16.9 San Xulián: The church retains Romanesque elements in its capitals and corbels and has a Neoclassic retablo. Houses here have a different architectural style, with tile roofs rather than slate or thatch.

The legend of St. Julian (Xulián in Galician) is particularly sad. On the night he was born, his father witnessed witches cursing the baby to one day murder his parents. As a youth, Julian was hunting when he came across a stag who warned him of his fate. To avoid completing this destiny, Julian left home and traveled to Galicia to be as far from his parents as possible. Years later, Julian's parents went on pilgrimage to Santiago and while on the road by chance they were offered hospitality by Julian's wife. Julian was out hunting at the time and returned to see two bodies in his bed. He assumed they were his wife and a lover, and so he became enraged and stabbed them both to death with his sword, only to discover he had unwittingly fulfilled his murderous destiny. In penance, he dedicated himself fully to the pilgrimage road and built seven pilgrim hospitals.

*Continue over the Río Pambre to **Pontecampaña (17.9km)**. The same track meets a paved road to Mato-Casanova.*

17.9 **Pontecampaña** A

A **Casa Domingo** (18, €10): , ☏630-728864, Easter-Oct, communal dinner

19.2 **Mato-Casanova** has one albergue and one off route that will come pick up pilgrims for meals or overnight. *Leave the hamlet along the paved road, which splits R onto a dirt path. Pass over a small cement bridge, the **Porto de Bois,** where a major battle was fought in the 14th century. The stream below the bridge was said to have run red with blood. Continue along the road through the hamlets of **Campanilla (21.3km)** and **A Coto**. Cross from the region of Lugo to A Coruña just before A Coto. Continue on a dirt path through the forest to the paved road into Leboreiro.*

19.2 **Mato-Casanova** A Pop. 8

A **Xunta** (20, €6): , ☏982-173483, 1pm, all year, no cookware

A H **(A Bolboreta)** 1.5k off route (8, €13/27/37 w/): (free), c/Vilar de Remonde, ☏609-124717, all year

22.0 **O Coto** H

H **Los Dos Alemanes** (€30/40): , ☏630-910803

H **Casa de los Somoza** (€46/54): ☏605-883268

22.7 **Leboreiro** was a booming pilgrim stopover in the 11-13th century. The **Iglesia de Santa María** contains an image of the virgin that legend says was found in the nearby fountain when light and a pleasant fragrance emitted. Villagers took the image to the church, but that night the virgin went right back to the fountain. After a few days of back and forth, the locals made the tympanum and dedicated the church to her and the image finally deemed to stay put in the church. The church features interesting wall paintings from the 15th century. A traditional *palloza* can be seen outside of the church, and a former pilgrim hospital is located across the street.

15th-century wall paintings in Iglesia de Santa María in Leboreiro

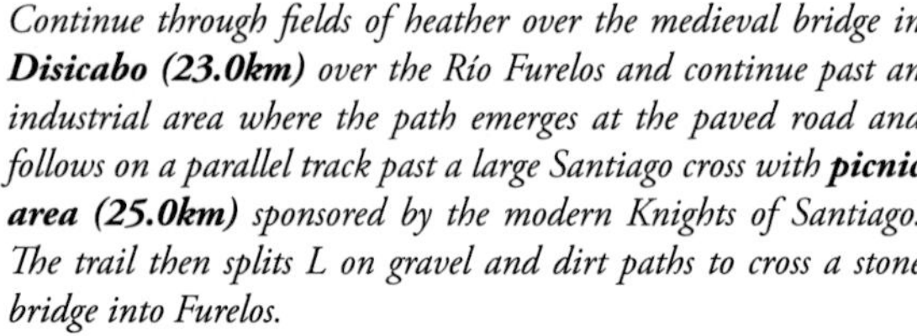
Continue through fields of heather over the medieval bridge in ***Disicabo (23.0km)*** *over the Río Furelos and continue past an industrial area where the path emerges at the paved road and follows on a parallel track past a large Santiago cross with* ***picnic area (25.0km)*** *sponsored by the modern Knights of Santiago. The trail then splits L on gravel and dirt paths to cross a stone bridge into Furelos.*

Melide
May: *Melindres* festival (little honey cakes)
Aug 15-21: Fiesta de San Roque
July 21: Fiesta de Carme

The 15th of each month and last Sunday of the month host large outdoor markets.

26.5 **Furelos**: (Pop. 135) The Hospitalers of San Juan de Jerusalén once controlled Furelos. The arched bridge into town is medieval. The town hosted at least one pilgrim hospital, still visible after the bridge on the L. The Iglesia de San Juan is mostly reconstructed with a few original elements.

Continue parallel to the paved road to the outskirts of Melide where a cobblestone path leads via Av. de Lugo into the heart of the city past several good octopus restaurants. Continue past the park in the center of Melide and turn R toward the churches, then turn L again to the Xunta Albergue.

Stone crucero in Melide

28.4 **Melide**

The area around Melide contains Neolithic dolmens and prehistoric castrum, suggesting that the area was well settled in prehistoric times. The town became a transportation and commerce hub in the Middle Ages, with four large pilgrim hospitals. **Museo da Terra de Melide** (free, 10:30am-1:30pm, 5-8pm, Su 11am-2pm) highlights regional history and local artifacts. Like many Camino towns, Melide's churches and monuments are spread along the path. **Iglesia de San Roque** features 14th-century tombs with local coats of arms, and the stone cross outside depicts the crucifixion.

Octopus,
a Melide specialty,
at Pulpería Ezequiel

Iglesia de Sancti Spiritus was constructed in the late 15th century using stones from the former castle and contains a Baroque retablo. On the way out of Melide is the simple **Capela de Carme**, built in 1755. Today Melide is well known for its *Pulpo á la Gallega*, boiled octopus served with olive oil, paprika, a hunk of bread and a ceramic bowl of cold, refreshing Ribeiro wine. **Pulpería Ezequiel** is a good local place to experience this Galician delicacy, though on Sundays it may even be available on the street dished up from a huge copper pot. The northern Camino Primativo joins the Francés route in Melide.

4 **Melide** A H Pop. 7,824

A **Xunta** (156, €5): , c/San Antonio, 660-396822, 1pm all year, no cookware
A **O Apalpador** (30, €10): , c/San Antonio 23, 679-837969, all year
A **San Antón** (36, €10): , c/San Antonio 6, 981-506427, Mar-Oct
A H **Vilela** (24, €10/-/28): , c/San Antonio 2, 616-011375, all year
A H **Pereiro** (45, €10/40/45): , c/Progreso 43, 981-506314, all year
A **Alfonso II El Casto** (35, €10): , Ac. Toques e Friol 52, 981-506454
A **O Cruceiro** (72, €10): Ronda Coruña 2, 616-764896, Mar-Oct
A **Arraigos** (20, €10): , Cantón S. Roque 9, 646-343370, all year
A **Montoto** (40, €10): , Rúa Codeseira 31, 646-941887
A **Melide** (42, €10): , Av. de Lugo 92, 627-901552, Easter-Oct, lockers
H **Chiquitin** (€35/50): , c/San Antonio 18, 981-815333
H **Pensión Berenguela** (€30/40): , c/San Roque 2, 981-505417
H **Hotel Xaneiro** (€35/45): , Av. Habana 43, 981-506140
H **Hotel Carlos 96**: (-/€50): , Av. Lugo 119, 981-507633
H **Hospedaje Bar Sony** (€20/30): , Rúa Cedeseira, 981-506473
H **A Lúa do Camiño** (€25/35): , c/Circunvalación, 620-958331

30

MELIDE TO ARCA

33.0km
(20.5mi)

8-10 HOURS
DIFFICULTY:
P 30%, 10.0km
U 70%, 23.0km

A ALBERGUES:
Boente 5.5km
Castañeda 7.8km
Ribadiso 10.8km
Arzúa 13.9km
A Peroxa 17.3km
Salceda 24.7km
Brea 27.6km
Santa Irene 30.4km
Arca 33.0km

A pair of boots retired at kilometer 25

Walk peaceful forest paths, sample creamy Arzúa cheese, excitement builds as you near your goal!

A long stage with constant ups and downs through small villages and the larger pilgrim town of Arzúa. Frequent services, but be ready for 7.4km without accommodations between A Peroxa and Salceda. Fragrant eucalyptus groves provide plenty of shade.

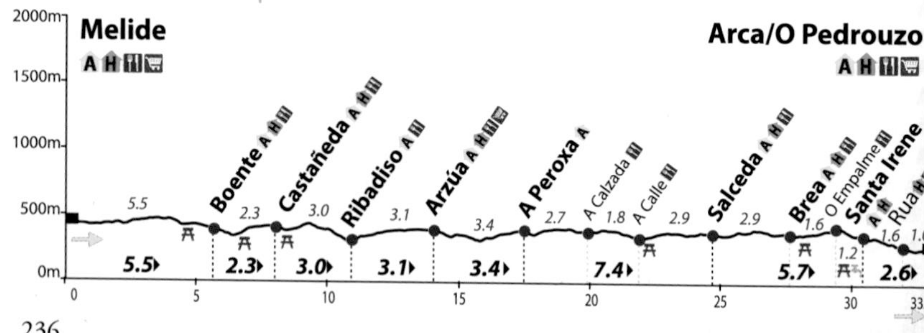

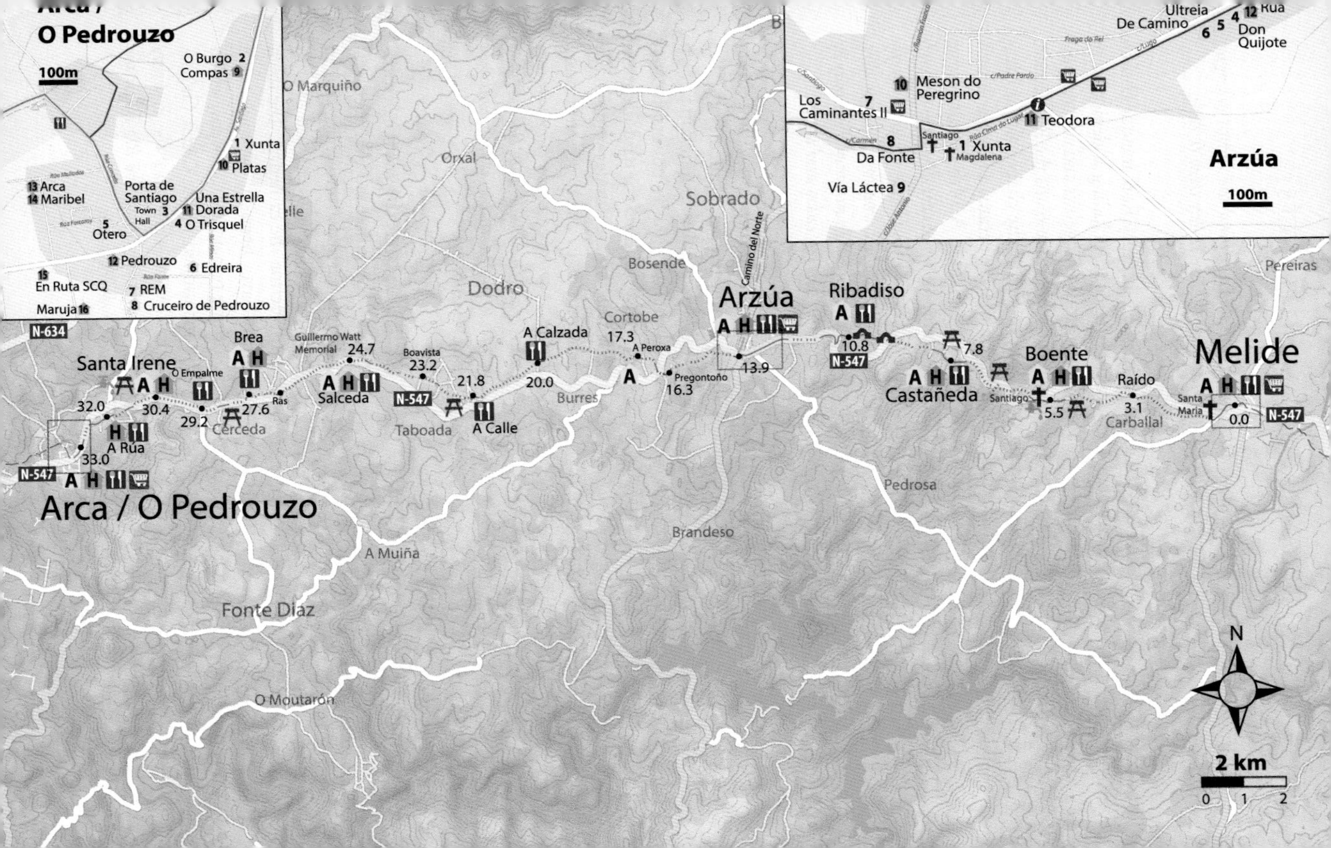
Arca / O Pedrouzo
100m
O Burgo 2
Compas 9
1 Xunta
10 Platas
13 Arca
14 Maribel
Porta de Santiago
Town Hall 3
Una Estrella
11 Dorada
4 O Trisquel
5 Otero
12 Pedrouzo
6 Edreira
15 En Ruta SCQ
7 REM
Maruja 16
8 Cruceiro de Pedrouzo
Arzúa
100m
Ultreia
De Camino
12 Rua
4 5 6
Don Quijote
10 Meson do Peregrino
Los Caminantes II 7
11 Teodora
8 Da Fonte
Santiago
1 Xunta
Magdalena
Vía Láctea 9
O Marquiño
Orxal
Sobrado
Camino del Norte
Bosende
Dodro
Cortobe
N-634
Santa Irene
O Empalme
Brea
Guillermo Watt Memorial
24.7
Boavista
23.2
21.8
A Calzada
20.0
17.3
A Peroxa
Pregontoño
16.3
Arzúa
13.9
Ribadiso
10.8
N-547
7.8
Boente
Castañeda
Santiago
5.5
Raído
3.1
Carballal
Melide
Santa María
0.0
32.0
30.4
29.2
27.6
Ras
Salceda
Taboada
A Calle
Burres
Cerceda
A Rúa
33.0
Arca / O Pedrouzo
A Muiña
Pedrosa
Brandeso
Fonte Díaz
O Moutarón
Pereiras
N
2 km
0 1 2

0.0 *Leave Melide on Rúa Sabían behind the Xunta albergue. Pass Iglesia de Santa María de Melide in less than 0.7km.*

0.7 **Santa María** is a 12th-century Romanesque church with notable 15th-century frescoes including a depiction of the trinity surrounded by the four evangelists and twelve apostles. Just after the church, a small bridge spans the Río Lázaro. There is a small house here, originally the chapel of San Lázaro, where the Iglesia de Santa María operated a leprosarium. A tomb in front now serves as a planter. A 14th-century stone roadside cross follows. *Continue on a pleasant dirt path through several tiny hamlets, including* ***Raído (3.1km)****. The trail briefly comes along the highway, but splits to the L and continues on dirt. Continue through pleasant shaded forest. In summer there may be a wayside fruit stand offering raspberries, cakes and water.*

5.5 **Boente**: This small town features the 20th-century Iglesia de Santiago incorporating earlier elements and has both a Santiago Peregrino and Matamoros. A fountain known as the *Fonte da Saleta* is said to have curative powers, located next to a stone *rollo* or roadside cross. Boente's streets underwent major renovations in 2011, now in tip-top shape. *Continue under the highway and cross the small Río Boente to a wide unpaved track, which will just skirt Castañeda.*

7.8 **Castañeda** was the destination of the limestone that medieval pilgrims carried from Triacastela to be finished in the ovens and used in constructing the cathedral. The town must have been a welcome site! Nothing remains of the ovens, which are mentioned in the *Codex Calixtinus*. *Cross a bridge over the highway one more time before the Río Iso at the Puente de Ribadiso.*

5.5 Boente A H Pop.137

A H **Albergue Boente** (54, €11/-/35): W D @, 981-501974, Mar-Nov

A **Os Albergues** (30, €11): W D @, 981-501853, Mar-Oct

7.8 Castañeda A H Pop. 159

A H **Santiago** (4, €11/-/30-35): W D, 981-501711, call in winter

H **Casa Rural Milia** (€36/45): Lugar Portela, 981-501625

10.8 Ribadiso da Baixo A H

A **Xunta** (70, €6): W D, 981-501185, 1pm, all year, no cookware, restored historic buildings along the river

A H **Los Caminantes** (56, €10/-/35): W D @, 647-020600, Apr-Oct

A **Milpés** (24, €10): W D, c/Ribadiso 7, 981-500425

10.8 Ribadiso da Baixo

The location of the bridge dates back to the 6th century. The pilgrim hospital of San Antón in Ribadiso served pilgrims in the 16th century and was restored in 1993 to return to use as a Xunta albergue. *The path leaves Ribadiso along the paved road, crossing under the highway once more and into Arzúa.*

Arzúa street café

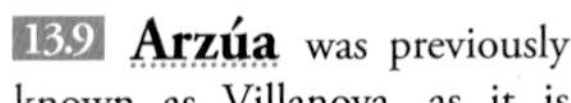

13.9 Arzúa was previously known as Villanova, as it is called in the *Codex Calixtinus*. Ample evidence exists of both pre-Roman and Roman settlement nearby. When the area was reconquered, Arzúa was repopulated with Basque people. Two pilgrim hospices were located here. The **Iglesia de Santiago** is a 20th-century structure with a 19th-century retablo depicting the battle of Clavijo and Santiago Matamoros' appearance.

The town is firmly in dairy country and known for its delicious creamy cheese. The central plaza features a statue of a cheesemaker, and an annual March cheese festival sells over 100,000 cheeses each year. This was the traditional stopping point before Santiago for medieval pilgrims. *Leaving Arzúa, turn L after the park in the center of town, then a R turn onto a smaller road to exit the town via a dirt track.*

From Arzúa to Arca the trail passes through numerous hamlets with few services other than water and cafés. There's just a bit of undulation with several shallow river valleys. Most of

13.9 Arzúa A H Pop 6,328

1. **A Xunta** (48, €6): K W D, Cima de Lugar 6, 660-396824, 1pm, all year, no cookware
2. **A De Selmo** (50, €10): K W D, c/Lugo 133, 981-939018
3. **A Santiago Apóstol** (72, €12): K W D, c/Lugo 107, 981-508132, all year
4. **A Don Quijote** (50, €10): K W D, c/Lugo 130, 981-500139, all year
5. **A Ultreia** (39, €10): K W D, c/Lugo 126, 981-500471, all year
6. **A De Camino** (46, €10): W D, c/Lugo 118, 981-500415, Mar-Nov
7. **A Los Caminantes II** (28, €10): K W D, c/Santiago 14, 647-020600, Apr-Oct
8. **A Da Fonte** (20, €12): K W D, c/do Carmen 18, 604-002380, Mar-Oct
9. **A Vía Láctea** (60, €10): K W D, c/José Neira Vilas 26, 981-500581, all year
10. **H Meson do Peregrino** (€36/50): c/Ramón Franco 7, 981-500145
11. **H Hostal Teodora** (€38/48): c/Lugo 38, 981-500083
12. **H Pensión Rúa** (€35/45): W D, c/Lugo 130, 981-500139

Colored doors along the path in Boente

the trail is off road with shade from the prolific eucalyptus trees. Pass by the blink-and-you'll-miss-them tiny hamlets of ***Preguntoño (16.3km)****,* ***A Peroxa (17.3km)****,* ***A Calzada*** *(****20.0km****) and* ***A Calle*** *(****21.8km****), where the path takes you directly under an hórreo straddling the trail. After* ***Boavista (23.2km)****, continue along the N-547 in* ***Salceda*** *(****24.7km****).*

17.3 A Peroxa A

A Camiño das Ocas (30, €10): , 648-404780, all year, +400m

24.7 Salceda A H

A Boni (20, €12): , 618-965907, Mar-Oct

A H Alborada (10, €12/-/50): , 981-502956, Apr-Oct

A H Pousada de Salceda (8, €12/-/47): , N-547 km 75, 981-502767, all year, +400m to the left

27.6 Brea A H

A El Chalet (12, €10/-/35): , c/A Brea 5, 659-380723, Apr-Oct

H O Mesón (€32/44): , c/A Brea 16, 981-511040

H The Way (€42/42): , c/A Brea 36, 628-120202, +150m

30.4 Santa Irene A H

A Xunta (36, €6): , 660-396825, 1pm, all year, no cookware, restaurant +1.5 km

A Santa Irene (15, €13): , 981-511000, Apr-Oct, charming

A Astrar (24, €10-12): , c/Astrar 18, 608-092820, Mar-Nov, +700m

32.0 A Rúa H

H Casa O Acivro (€36/46): , A Rúa 28, 981-511316

H Hotel O Pino (€38/50): , A Rúa 9, 981-511035, +200m

The Camino crosses back and forth over the highway several times en route to Arca. Soon after Salceda, note the ***memorial to Guillermo Watt (25.6km)****, a pilgrim who died here in 1993 one day shy of Santiago. Pass through the hamlet of* ***Ras (27.0km)*** *and back across the highway after* ***Brea (27.6km)****. Pass a picnic area at Alto de Santa Irene followed by* ***O Empalme*** *(****29.2km****), returning along the highway to Santa Irene.*

30.4 **Santa Irene** has a small 18th-century chapel dedicated to Saint Irene, which has a Baroque retablo, as well as a covered fountain with a 1692 image of the saint. Saint Irene was a Portuguese martyr from the 7th century. If staying in the Xunta albergue, remember the closest restaurant is 1.5km away.

Pass back under the highway and continue through the village of ***A Rúa (32.0km)****, with its impressively large eucalyptus trees. Reach Arca and turn L to enter town for accommodations or services, or continue straight to bypass Arca, passing one café on the far side of town (saves 0.6km).*

Popular lunch spot in Arca

33.0 **Arca (O Pedrouzo)** once housed the Hospital de Santa Eulalia de Arca and the Capilla de San Antón de Arca, though nothing remains of them today. There is a modern Iglesia de Santa Eulalia de Arca and impressive oak trees near town hall. Today the town is bisected by the highway but provides ample accommodations and services.

.0 **Arca** A H Pop. 5,050 (also O Pino or O Pedrouzo), 638-612496, 12-6pm daily in summer, Deportes Remanso, c/Pedrouzo 11, 981-511380

A **Xunta** (120, €6): Av. Lugo 30, 660-396826, 1pm, all year, behind post office

A H **O Burgo** (10, €10/-/40): Lugo 47, 630-404138, Apr-Oct

A **Porta de Santiago** (54, €10): Av. Lugo 11, 981-511103, Mar-Nov

A **O Trisquel** (68, €10): Rúa do Picón 1, 616-644740

A **Otero** (36, €10): c/Forcarei 2, 671-663374, Apr-Oct

A **Edreira** (56, €10): c/da Fonte 19, 981-511365, Mar-Oct

A **REM** (50, €10): Av. de la Iglesia 7, 981-510407, all year

A **Cruceiro de Pedrouzo** (94, €10): Av. la Iglesia 7, 981-511371, Mar-Oct

H **Pensión Compas** (€25/35): Av. Lugo 47, 981-511309

H **Pensión Platas** (€40/55): Av. Lugo 26, 981-511378

H **Una Estrella Dorada** (€25/35 w/): Av. Lugo 10, 630-018363

H **Pensión Pedrouzo** (€25/35): Av. de Santiago 13, 671-663375

H **Pensión Arca** (€30/50): c/Mollados 25, 657-888594

H **Pensión Maribel** (€35/45): c/Mollados 23, 981-511404

H **En Ruta SCQ** (€25/30): Av. Santiago 23, 981-511471

H **Pensión Maruja** (€15/25): Rúa Nova 9, 981-511406

31 ARCA TO SANTIAGO DE COMPOSTELA

20.0km
(12.4mi)

4-5.5 Hours
Difficulty: ▬□□
P 66%, 13.1km
U 34%, 6.9km

A Albergues:
Lavacolla 10.0km
Monte Gozo 15.1km
San Lázaro 17.4km
Santiago 20.0km
Castelo 30.4km

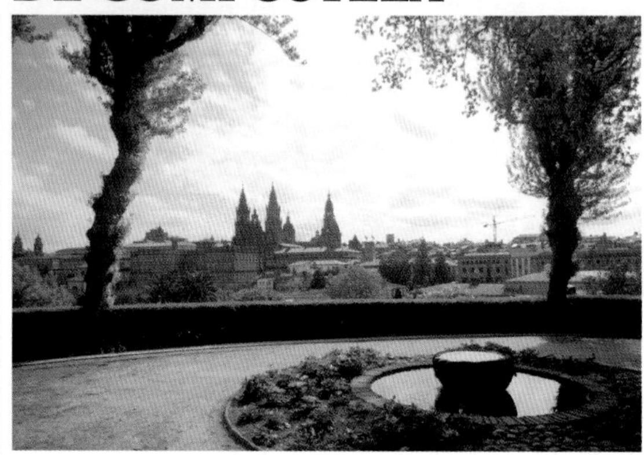

View of Santiago Cathedral from Alameda Park

Traverse eucalyptus forests, glimpse the first view of Santiago from Monte de Gozo, head to the cathedral and receive your well-deserved Compostela!

The path today passes through more eucalyptus forests and several small villages to arrive at Monte de Gozo, within sight (on a clear day) of Santiago's cathedral spires. The last 5km are city walking. The atmosphere entering Santiago is often jubilant, with singing, shouting and congratulations, no matter how dreary the weather. Leave early to arrive in time for the noon pilgrim mass.

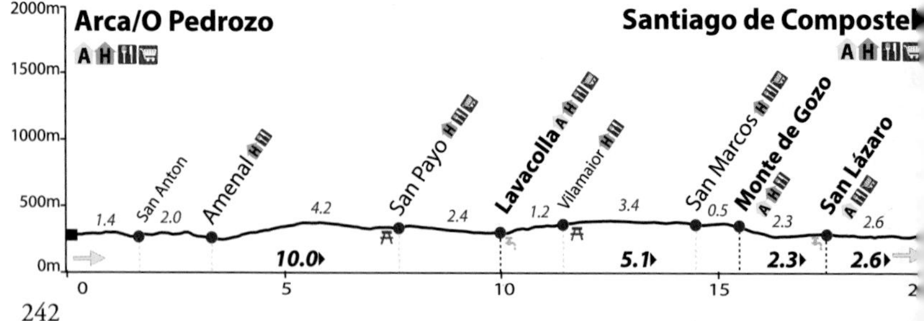

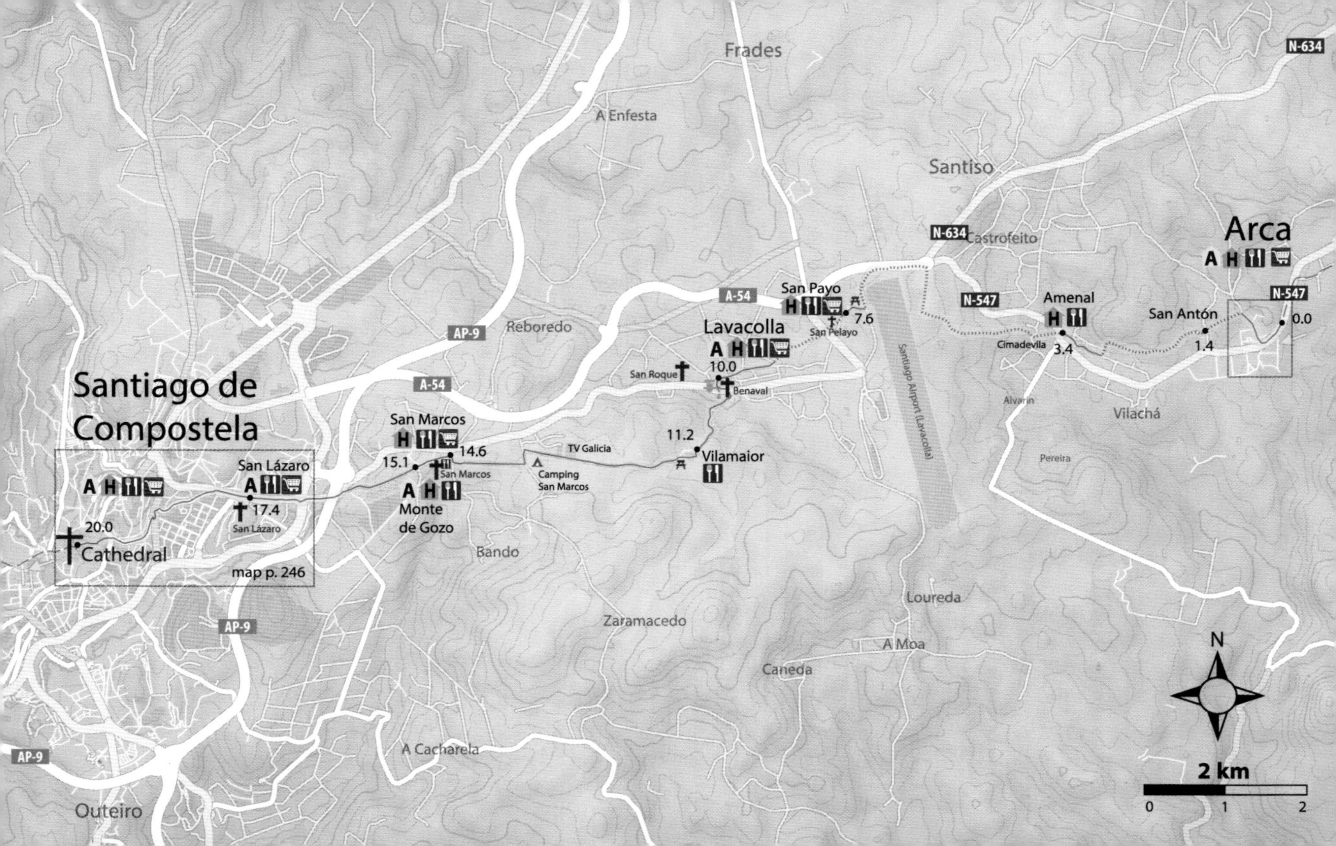

Arca
A H
N-634
N-547
0.0
San Antón
1.4
Amenal
H
3.4
Cimadevila
Alvarin
Vilachá
Pereira
Castrofeito
Santiso
Frades
Santiago Airport (Lavacolla)
San Payo
H
7.6
San Pelayo
A-54
Lavacolla
A H
10.0
San Roque
Benaval
11.2
Vilamaior
A Enfesta
Reboredo
AP-9
TV Galicia
Camping
San Marcos
San Marcos
H
14.6
15.1
San Marcos
A H
Monte
de Gozo
Bando
Loureda
A Moa
Caneda
Zaramacedo
A Cacharela
Santiago de
Compostela
San Lázaro
A
17.4
San Lázaro
A H
20.0
Cathedral
map p. 246
Outeiro
N
2 km
0
1
2

7.6 San Payo Pop. 25
Porta da Santiago, Lugar San Paio, 981-908536

10.0 Lavacolla
Pop. 171 "place of washing"
- A **Lavacolla** (34, €12): c/Lavacolla 35, 981-897274
- H **Casa Lavacolla** (-/€42): c/Lavacolla 20, 659-881868
- H **San Paio** (€38/49): 981-888205
- H **Garcas** (€35/50): c/Naval 2, 981-888225
- H **Ruta Jacobea** (-/€69): c/Lavacolla 41, 981-888211
- H **Pazo Xan Xordo** (-/€60): Xan Xordo 6, 981-888259, +900m

14.6 San Marcos Pop. 828
H **Hotel Akelarre** (€35/45): Av. de San Marcos 37, 981-552689

0.0 *Walk on the main road of Arca; turn R at the Town Hall and continue past a café. Turn L on a dirt footpath through a eucalyptus forest. Pass* ***San Antón (1.4km)*** *and continue on a paved road to pass under the highway into* ***Amenal (3.4km)***, [H **Hotel Amenal** (€50/60 w/): 981-510431]. *Leave Amenal on a path that skirts the airport and passes through San Payo on a paved road.*

7.6 San Payo is named for a Christian child who was martyred for refusing to convert to Islam. *Leave town on the paved road, then turn off onto a dirt path to the R. Go through an underpass and continue straight to the outskirts of Lavacolla.*

10.0 Lavacolla (Latin: "*Lavamentula*") literally means "wash private parts." Medieval pilgrims seldom if ever bathed (and "ridiculed Muslim and Jewish enthusiasms for personal hygiene," [Gitlitz and Davidson, 341]), so apparently took advantage of the small stream to cleanse themselves for arrival in Santiago. The **Iglesia de Benaval/San Pelayo** is named for a miracle in which accused revolutionary Juan Pourón cried out *Ven e valme* "Come and save me," when he was to be hung. He died instantaneously and was spared the hanging. The 1840 church stands on the earlier location of a 12th-century monastery. At the far end of town, Ermita de San Roque is now used as a barn.

Laffi recorded: "There is a river in a wooded place two miles from Santiago called Lavacolla, in which French pilgrims, out of respect for the Apostle, wash not only their private parts but, stripping off their clothes, clean all the dirt from their bodies."

Leave Lavacolla by a dirt path with a small bridge over the stream—convenient if you want to repeat medieval ablutions! Pass through ***Vilamaior (11.2km)***, [H **De Amancio** (-/€50): Vilamaior 9, 981-897086] *and continue on the paved road. Turn L at the sign for* ***Camping San Marcos (13.4km)***, *then R and follow the road into* ***San Marcos (14.6km)*** and along the road to Monte de Gozo.

15.1 Monte de Gozo: This last hill before Santiago is the first place where pilgrims see the cathedral spires. Medieval pilgrims fell to their knees, shouting in joy and breaking out into song. There was a tradition that pilgrims would race here from Lavacolla, with the first to arrive crowned "king." Today the site has been so modernized that some find it a disappointment rather than a joy. A massive vacation city was built in 1993 with a capacity of thousands. Rows of low buildings resemble army barracks, but on the bright side, there is always a bed to be had and the facilities are modern and clean.

Joyful high five at Monte de Gozo

15.1 Monte del Gozo A H

Galician: *Monxoi* "Mount Joy"

A Xunta (500, €6): , 981-558942, 1pm, all year, rooms of 8 in various buildings

A Monte do Gozo (Polskie) (par, 40, don): , Rúa das Estelas, 981-597222, May-Oct, run by Polish volunteers

H Santiago Apóstal (€60/60): , c/San Marcos 1, 981-557155

A huge modern monument was erected on the hill's center with images of Pope John Paul II and Saint Francis. A sculpture by Spanish artist Jose Maria Acuña depicts two larger-than-life medieval pilgrims pointing the way down the hill. The tiny chapel dedicated to San Marcos offers quiet contemplation, with a snack stand outside in summer. *Continue down paved Rúa do Gozo across the AP-9 highway and enter the outskirts of Santiago in a suburb called San Lázaro along Rúa San Lázaro* *(map p. 246)*.

17.4 San Lázaro contains the Capilla de San Lázaro, the site of a former 12th-century leprosarium. Several albergues are nearby, a 40min walk to the center or 10 minute ride on bus #11. *Turn L onto Rúa do Valiño after Santuario San Lázaro. The road name changes to Rúa dos Concheiros, named for the merchants who lined the streets in medieval times to sell shells to pilgrims. From the roundabout, continue L along the same street, which becomes Rúa San Pedro. Enter the Old City via the Rúa das Casas Reais. At Plaza Cervantes stay R and continue straight through an arch, and enter the grand Praza Obradoiro!*

Santiago de Compostela

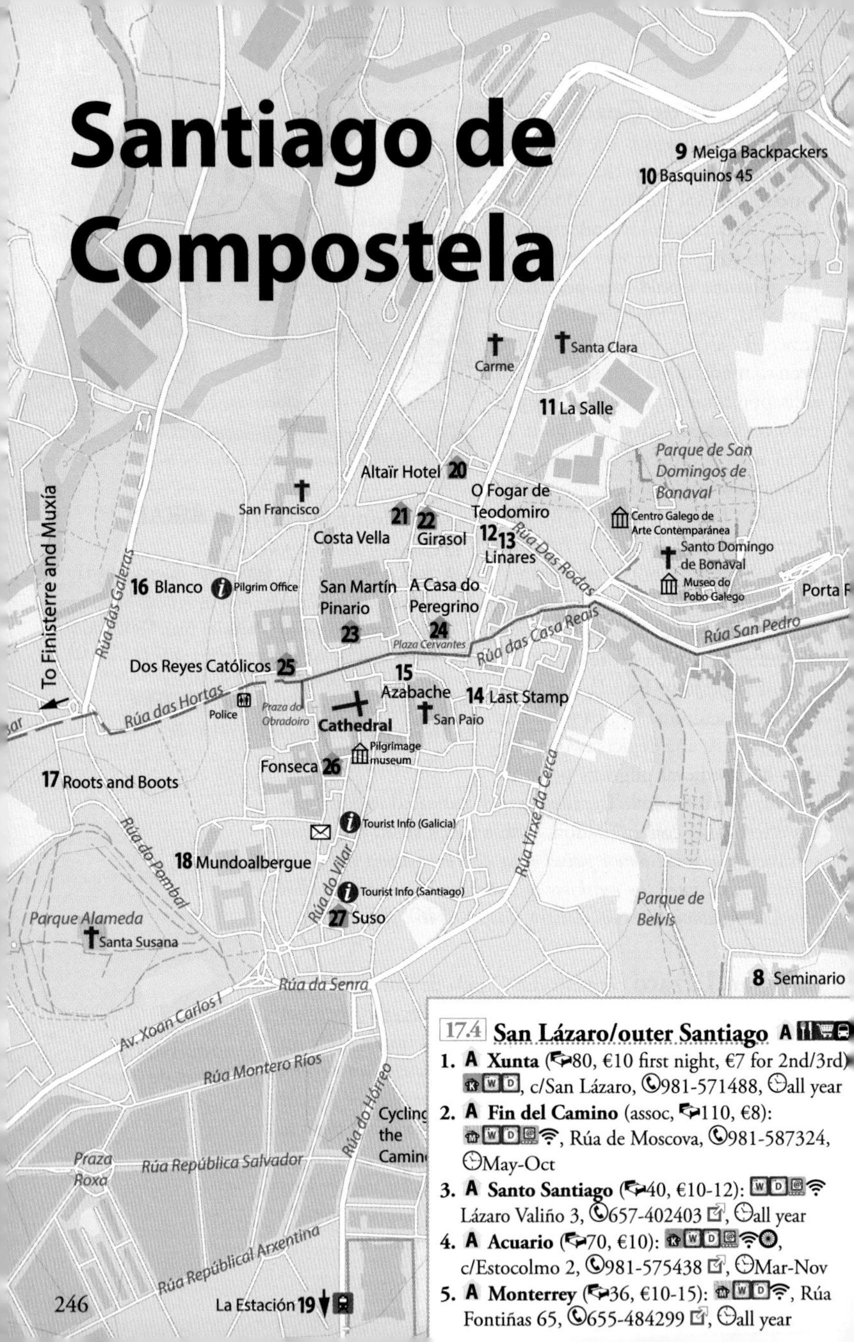

9 Meiga Backpackers
10 Basquinos 45
Carme
Santa Clara
11 La Salle
Parque de San Domingos de Bonaval
Altaïr Hotel 20
San Francisco
21 22
Costa Vella
Girasol
O Fogar de Teodomiro
12 13 Linares
Rúa Das Rodas
Centro Galego de Arte Contemparánea
Santo Domingo de Bonaval
Museo do Pobo Galego
Porta F
To Finisterre and Muxía
16 Blanco
Pilgrim Office
San Martín Pinario 23
A Casa do Peregrino 24
Plaza Cervantes
Rúa das Casa Reais
Rúa San Pedro
Rúa das Galeras
Dos Reyes Católicos 25
15 Azabache
14 Last Stamp
Rúa das Hortas
Police
Praza do Obradoiro
Cathedral
San Paio
Pilgrimage museum
Fonseca 26
17 Roots and Boots
Rúa Virxe da Cerca
Tourist Info (Galicia)
Rúa do Pombal
18 Mundoalbergue
Rúa do Vilar
Tourist Info (Santiago)
Parque de Belvís
Parque Alameda
27 Suso
Santa Susana
8 Seminario
Rúa da Senra
Av. Xoan Carlos I
Rúa Montero Ríos
Rúa do Hórreo
Cycling the Camino
Praza Roxa
Rúa República Salvador
Rúa Repúblical Arxentina
La Estación 19

17.4 San Lázaro/outer Santiago A

1. **A Xunta** (80, €10 first night, €7 for 2nd/3rd), c/San Lázaro, 981-571488, all year
2. **A Fin del Camino** (assoc, 110, €8): , Rúa de Moscova, 981-587324, May-Oct
3. **A Santo Santiago** (40, €10-12): Lázaro Valiño 3, 657-402403, all year
4. **A Acuario** (70, €10): , c/Estocolmo 2, 981-575438, Mar-Nov
5. **A Monterrey** (36, €10-15): , Rúa Fontiñas 65, 655-484299, all year

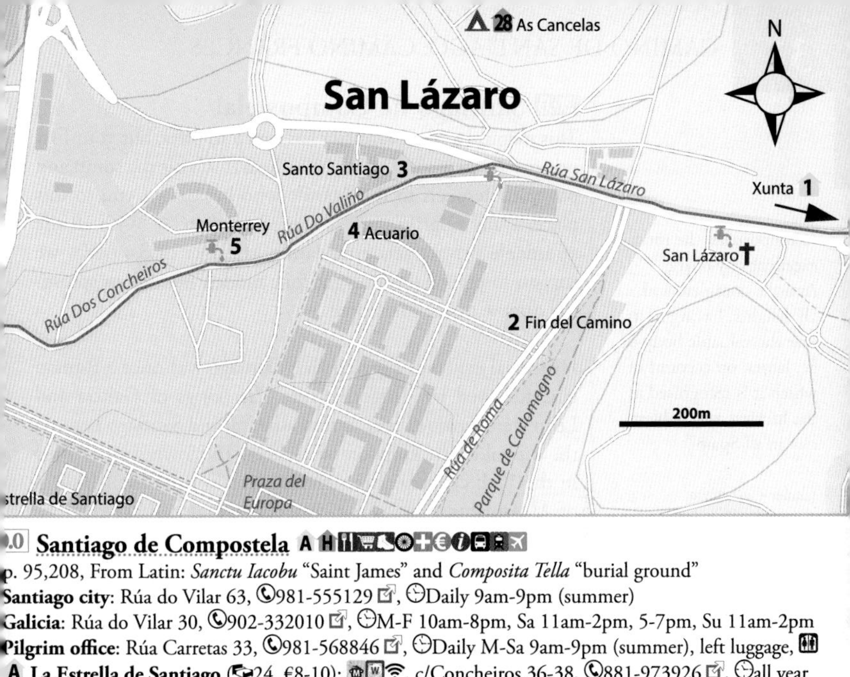

.0 Santiago de Compostela A H

p. 95,208, From Latin: *Sanctu Iacobu* "Saint James" and *Composita Tella* "burial ground"

Santiago city: Rúa do Vilar 63, 981-555129, Daily 9am-9pm (summer)

Galicia: Rúa do Vilar 30, 902-332010, M-F 10am-8pm, Sa 11am-2pm, 5-7pm, Su 11am-2pm

Pilgrim office: Rúa Carretas 33, 981-568846, Daily M-Sa 9am-9pm (summer), left luggage,

A La Estrella de Santiago (24, €8-10): c/Concheiros 36-38, 881-973926, all year

A Porta Real (24, €10-15): c/Concheiros 10, 633-610114, all year

A H Seminario Menor (177, €12/15/-): Av. Quiroga Palacios 2, 881-031768, Mar-Oct, all beds not bunks, some reports of theft, lockers available

A Meiga Backpackers (hstl., 30, €10-13 w/): Basquiños 67, 981-570846, a.y.

A Basquinos 45 (10, €12): c/Basquinos 45, 661-894536, all year

A H La Salle (20, €18/36/59): Tras Santa Clara, 682-158011

A H O Fogar de Teodomiro (hostel, 20, €10-15/-/35): Plaza de Algalia de Arriba 3, 981-582920, 10am all year

A H Linares (14, €22/50/65): Algalia Abajo 34, 981-580443

A Last Stamp (54, €15-18): r/Preguntoiro 10, 981-563525, mid J.-m. D.

A Azabache (20, €14-18): c/Azabachería 15, 981-071254, all year

A H Blanco (20, €18/-/35): c/Galeras 30, 881-976850

A Roots and Boots (hstl., 48, €12-21): Campo Cruceiro do Galo 7, 699-631594

A Mundoalbergue (34, €12-17): San Clemente 26, 981-588625, all year

A H La Estación (24, €14/28/40): c/Xoana Nogueira 14, 981-594624, all year

H Altaïr Hotel (€87/120): c/Loureiros 12, 981-554712

H Costa Vella (€60/81): c/Porta da Pena 17, 981-569530, restored Jesuit house

H Pensión Girasol (€25/45): Puerta da la Pena 4, 981-566287

H San Martín Pinario (pilgrim €23/40 w/): Plaza Inmaculada 3, 981-560282

H A Casa Do Peregrino (€65/75): c/Azabacheria 2, 981-573931

H Hostal Dos Reyes Católicos (-/€190+): Praza do Obradoiro, 981-582200, Parador

H Pensión Fonseca (€35/65): c/Fonseca 1, 981-584145

H Hostal Suso (-/€49): c/Villar 65, 981-586611

H A As Cancelas (tent €15, cabin €65-96): c/35 de Xullo 35, 981-580266

"Compostella, the most excellent city of the Apostle, complete with all delights, having in its care the valuable body of St. James, on account of which it is recognised as the luckiest and noblest city in all Spain."

Codex Calixtinus

20.0 Santiago de Compostela!

This magical and vibrant city has much to offer, but your first priority is likely to head to the cathedral to visit the tomb and pay your respects to the Apostle who has drawn you to this place. Daily pilgrim mass is offered at noon. With all the affordable private accommodation available in Santiago, we suggest foregoing the albergue for a modest pensión or splurging on one of the fine hotels.

Historical evidence suggests that Santiago was once a Roman city, followed by Visigothic rule. The kings of Galicia and León were crowned here at the cathedral and Santiago became the capital of the kingdom of Galicia. The town was fortified in the 11th century after suffering attacks from the Muslims of Al Andalus. Santiago's rich architectural heritage demonstrates its role as the most important city in Galicia through the ages. Santiago's Old City was designated a UNESCO World Heritage Site in 1985.

The long-awaited Cathedral in Santiago de Compostela! (opposite)

Catedral de Santiago

(free, 7am-8:30pm, 981-569327)

Pilgrims first head to the **Praza de Obradoiro**, the large open plaza facing the iconic western façade of the cathedral (featured on the euro coins €.05, €.02 and €.01). Medieval pilgrims gathered here and spent their first night in the city keeping vigil in the plaza or inside at the high altar. Fighting for the best spot was intense and in 1207 got so violent that the church had to be reconsecrated!

Worn finger grooves on the Tree of Jesse in the *Puerta de la Gloria*

Next, pilgrims entered via the west door, through the **Pórtico de la Gloria** by master sculptor Mateo. Pilgrims touched their hand to the Tree of Jesse in the central column. While it is no longer permitted to touch, five finger holes have been worn away from millions of pilgrim hands. The sculpture of Master Mateo also bears the tradition that those who press their head against his will absorb some of his wisdom. Pilgrims would then attend Mass and

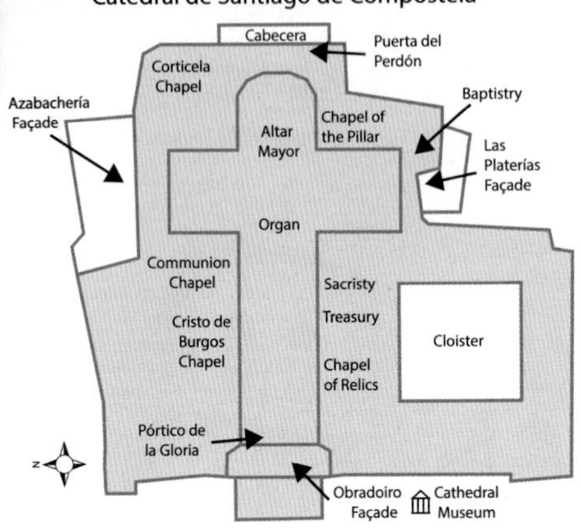

receive indulgences and make their offerings to Santiago and the chapels of other saints. Next the pilgrim would confess to a priest and obtain their **Compostela** (p. 12). Today you'll have to walk a few more blocks to the pilgrim office (and in high season, wait in line) to receive yours, for a donation of €1-2 (confession not required). You can purchase a tube and/or get the document laminated at the shop next door.

The next ritual was to climb the small staircase behind the Altar Mayor (often a line) to touch the **golden statue of Santiago**. Medieval pilgrims would place their hat on his head and their cloak over his shoulders. The statue used to have a golden crown that pilgrims would place on their own head, but the crown has been lost at some point. Today pilgrims usually give the statue a hug or lay their head against his shoulder, to whisper a prayer or message of thanks. Next, pilgrims descend to the **crypt**, with the bones of Saint James and his two followers. One tradition is to leave behind one's walking stick or other memento. Surprisingly, the bones of St. James were misplaced for almost 300 years before being returned to the crypt. In 1589 they were hidden elsewhere in the cathedral to protect from invaders. The bones were rediscovered and returned to the crypt in 1879.

Pilgrim Mass is held at the cathedral daily at noon. Get there at least 1 hour early if you want to get one of the 1,000 seats!

Golden statue of Saint James in the Altar Mayor

During **Holy Years** (when St. James Day of July 25 falls on a Sunday), the **Puerta del Perdón**, the entrance on the east side, is opened and pilgrims can enter and leave through this door, receiving full indulgences (rather than the partial indulgences that an ordinary year bestows). The door is opened with great ceremony January 1 and closed with the same solemnity December 31.

If you're lucky, during the daily noon Pilgrim Mass you will get to see the famous **botafumeiro** in action. Literally the "smoke-belcher," the botafumeiro is the largest censer for spreading incense smoke in the world. Weighing 80kg (175lb) and 1.6m (5ft) in height, the huge censer is swung back and forth from a pulley system above the altar, requiring eight men to get it reaching speeds of 80kph. It is said the censer was installed to cover the stench of all the unwashed pilgrims. The censer is only brought out for special days, though a donation of €300 is said to sponsor an extra showing.

The *botafumeiro* requires eight men to get going.

Pilgrims gather in Praza do Obradoiro in front of the cathedral

Once your pilgrim obligations are complete, you can, like Domenici Laffi in the 17th century, “walk round the church, marveling greatly at everything.” And there is much to marvel at here, one of the largest Romanesque churches in Europe, deceptively austere at first glance but with infinitely fascinating detail.

The Pre-Romanesque 9th-century structure that once stood here was burnt to the ground by Al-Mansur; the bells and gates were carried to Córdoba by Christian captives and incorporated into the Aljama Mosque. (The Christians had their revenge in 1236 when King Ferdinand won them back and had Muslim captives take them to the Toledo Cathedral).

Free Meals at the Parador

In keeping with a long history of providing hospitality to pilgrims, the Reyes Católicos Parador (p. 254) offers free meals to pilgrims with a Compostela. While not as generous as the three nights of lodging and meals offered to pilgrims in medieval times, hey, it's still a free meal. Only the first ten pilgrims in line qualify, so come early. Meal times are 9am, 12pm and 7pm. Bring a copy of your Compostela. Walk downhill past the hotel and into the car parking entrance. There is no seating while you wait, and you are not allowed to bring a backpack inside with you. Free meals are served where the staff of the hotel eat and are modest but tasty with a hearty helping of wine.

The current structure was begun in 1075 and consecrated in 1128. The towers were added later in the mid-18th century and each depicts one of St. James' parents. The Baroque façade was also constructed at this time. Archaeological evidence suggests that a Roman temple to Jupiter may have stood on the same spot.

The southern façade is situated at the **Praza das Praterías** where, in times past, silver jewelry was sold. The portal here is particularly well preserved. The eastern façade features the **Puerta del Perdón**, and the northern façade features an 1122 Romanesque portal.

July 25 is the patron saint day of Santiago, celebrated to the hilt with fireworks over the cathedral!

Inside, the golden **Altar Mayor** features images of Santiago in his three manifestations. Numerous chapels rich in imagery invite visitors to wander and explore. The cathedral is often packed out around the time of pilgrim Mass; consider visiting early in the morning for maximum peaceful atmosphere.

Cathedral Museum: (€4 for pilgrims, ✆902-557812, ⌚Apr-Oct 9am-8pm, Nov-Mar 10am-8pm) One ticket gets you into the crypt, treasury and museum. Maestro Mateo designed the clever crypt underbelly in order to support the weight of the **Pórtico de Gloria** above. Sculptures are displayed amongst the architecture. The highlight of the treasury is a 1544 monstrance showing scenes from the life of Santiago. The museum contains a fantastic collection of medieval tapestries and other historical art. The museum also offers a particularly worthwhile rooftop tour (€10/€12 if combined with the general museum), as well as guided tours of the archaeological excavations (€10) and tribune (€8) both in Spanish.

Santiago has a wealth of other historical buildings and cultural experiences. Many visitors plan an extra day or two to enjoy the sites of this pilgrim city.

Bagpipe player serenades visitors to Santiago de Compostela

Hostal de los Reyes Católicas
To the L when facing the cathedral from Praza do Obradoiro is the sumptuous Hostal de los Reyes Católicas, a 1501 pilgrim hospital commissioned by Ferdinand and Isabella, the *Reyes Católicas* ("Catholic monarchs"). The building served as hostel, infirmary and orphanage. Under Franco, the splendid historic building with its Plateresque door was converted into a Parador, one of a series of luxury hotels throughout Spain using historic buildings.

Monasterio de San Martín Pinario (981-574502)
Just north of the cathedral off Praza do Imaculada is the impressive Monasterio de San Martín Pinario. The Baroque façade is organized like a retablo and features an interesting staircase. The retablo mayor is very fine Baroque including images of Santiago. The ornate *Churrigueresque* altarpiece shows San Martín riding alongside St. James. Part of the monastery serves as accommodations, with good value pilgrim rooms.

Museo das Peregrinacións (Pilgrimage Museum)
(€1.20 pilgrim rate, Tu-F 9:30am-8:30pm, Sa 11am-7:30pm, Su 10:15-2:45pm, *Rúa de San Miguel 4,* 981-581558) Interesting museum dedicated to the Santiago pilgrimage. The museum has a new exhibit at *Praza Praterías 2* including a cathedral model and an interactive video game where you can role-play a medieval pilgrim.

Since medieval times, Santiago de Compostela has been known for its *azabeche* (jet), a black stone made of petrified wood that is used to make jewelry.

Museo do Pobo Galego (Museum of the Galician People)
(Free, Tu-Sa 10am-2pm and 4-7:30pm, Su 11am-3pm, *San Domingos de Bonaval,* 981-583620) This museum features artifacts from Galician history as far back as Celtic times, displayed in a 14th-century convent (Santo Domingo de Bonaval). The museum includes a Gothic chapel where several famous Galicians are entombed.

Be sure to try a slice or two of *Tarta de Santiago*, an almond cake dusted with confectioner's sugar in the shape of the Santiago cross.

Centro Galego de Arte Contemparánea (Galician Center of Contemporary Art, free, summer Tu-Su 12pm-9pm, winter Tu-Su 11am-8pm, *Rúa Ramón María del Valle Inclán,* 981-546619) Next to the Museo do Pobo Galego, this modern art museum shows a contemporary window into Galician life with high-quality exhibits.

Platerías façade of Santiago cathedral

All good things come to an end, and for many Santiago de Compostela is a bittersweet arrival, so jubilantly anticipated but also symbolizing the end of the pilgrimage. We wish each pilgrim satisfying closure and excitement for the next chapter. It's never too early to start dreaming of the next pilgrimage, or lace your boots back up and walk to Finisterre.

Transportation from Santiago

Santiago de Compostela Airport (SCQ) is located in Lavacolla, about 15km outside of Santiago. Empresa Freire (✆981-588111) offers frequent bus service between Santiago bus station and airport daily from 6:20am to 11:50pm (€3, 20 min). A private taxi to the airport costs €20. Numerous airlines offer inexpensive flights to major European cities.

Santiago's bus station (*Plaza de Camilo Díaz Baliño*, ✆981-542416) connects to most of the major hubs of Spain.

Santiago's train station (*Rúa do Hórreo 75*, ✆902-240202) is on the RENFE line; book tickets well ahead for best prices.

32-35 CAMINO FINISTERRE

Glimpse the ocean and seaside town of Finisterre on this pleasant and less populated path

Keep on walking for a less crowded trail, breathtaking ocean views, mysterious shaded forests and the lighthouse at the "end of the world."

An increasing number of pilgrims who reach Santiago keep walking to Finisterre, an additional 90km (3-4 days). Still fewer walk the additional day to Muxía, with its seaside church and Santiago lore. The path is well marked and considerably less populated than the Camino Francés. While services are fewer and farther between, the trek is not very difficult for a seasoned Camino hiker, with undulating hills, thick forests and quaint villages with stone fences. The landscape takes on the enchanting addition of the sea when approaching Finisterre and Muxía.

The original roots of the Finisterre pilgrimage are not decisively known, though many speculate that it may have been a pre-Christian pilgrimage route to the *Ara Solis* at Cabo Finisterre (p. 272). Before Columbus stumbled upon the new world, the western coast of Spain was literally thought of as the "end of the world" (Latin: *finis* end, *terrae* earth).

Pilgrim statue on the way to the Finisterre lighthouse

Today the route to Finisterre is marked with yellow arrows as well as concrete milestones that indicate the distance to the coast. The waymarks from Santiago to Finisterre and from Hospital to Muxía are marked only in one direction (east to west), while the route from Finisterre to Muxía is marked in both directions. It is possible to walk Santiago-Muxía-Finisterre OR Santiago-Finisterre-Muxía. We recommend the latter, principally because of a delightful stretch of uninterrupted countryside between Hospital and Finisterre, though this book gives information for both itineraries. The trail can be walked any time of year, but May through September offer the longest daylight hours for covering the long distances. As in the rest of Galicia, rain is a constant possibility.

This additional trail serves as a kind of "epilogue" to the Camino experience. The act of walking literally until the trail meets the sea can be helpful to shift gears and process the experience. In summer, hundreds of pilgrims gather at the lighthouse of Finisterre to watch the sun sink below the horizon, and some followed a tradition of burning an item of clothing there to signify the end of the journey (no longer permitted). Both the towns of Finisterre and Muxía are pleasant seaside towns with affordable accommodation options if you choose to stay a few days. While the sea is often too wild here for swimming, the Galician food and culture make for interesting exploring.

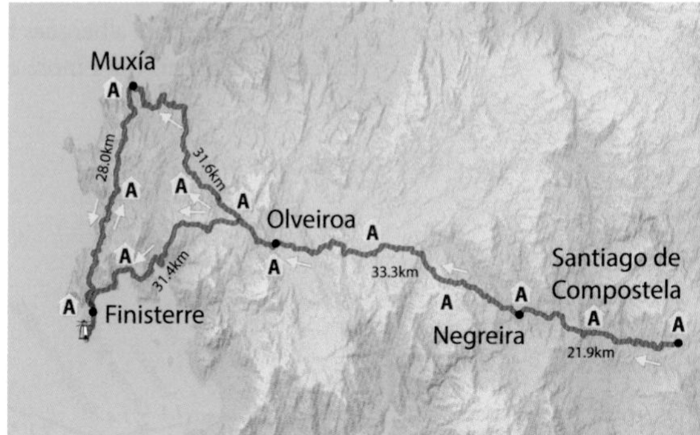

32

SANTIAGO COMPOSTELA TO NEGREIRA

21.9km
(13.6mi)

5-6 Hours
Difficulty:
P 69%, 15.8km
U 31%, 6.1km

A Albergues:
Castelo 10.4km
Negreira 21.9km
Vilaserío 34.2km

Pilgrims enter Sarela on the Camino Finisterre

Walk through eucalyptus forests, picturesque traditional hamlets and over a legendary bridge.

This shortest of Finisterre stages has been rerouted in recent years to eliminate road walking to be about 1/3 on natural paths. Waymarking is generally good, but pay some extra attention compared to the Francés route. The climb after Aguapesada is steep and tiring! There are several cafés en route but few accommodations. The Xunta albergue fills early, but luckily several new private albergues have opened. Continue on to Vilaserío (+12.3km) for a more challenging day.

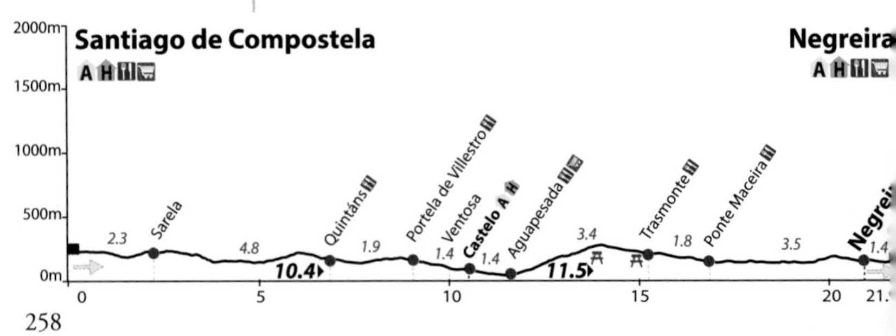

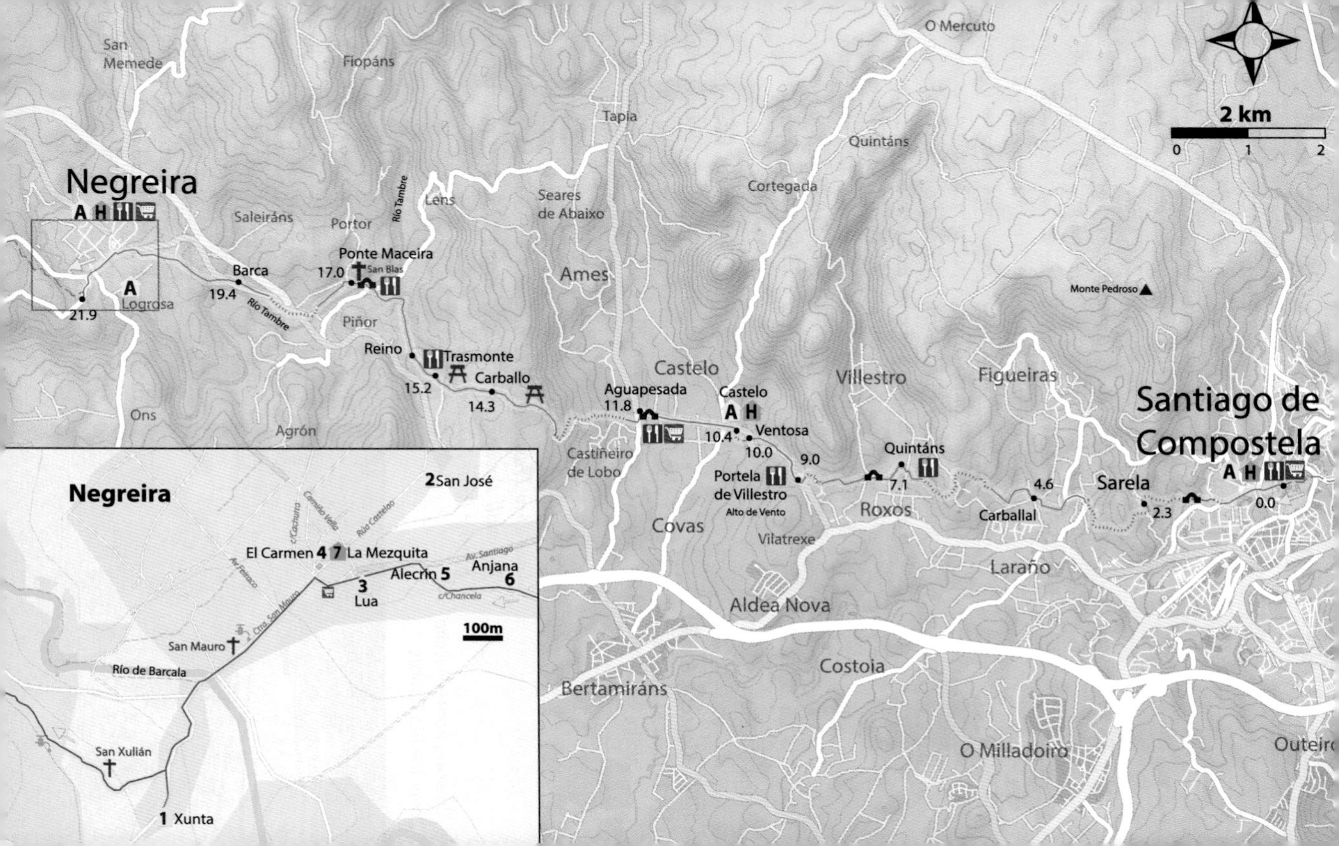

Negreira
A H
San Memede
Fiopáns
Tapia
O Mercuto
Quintáns
Cortegada
Seares
de Abaixo
Lens
Río Tambre
Saleiráns
Portor
Ponte Maceira
17.0
San Blas
Barca
19.4
Río Tambre
A
Logrosa
21.9
Piñor
Reino
Trasmonte
15.2
Carballo
14.3
Ons
Agrón
Ames
Castelo
Aguapesada
11.8
Castelo
A H
Ventosa
10.4
10.0
9.0
Castiñeiro
de Lobo
Portela
de Villestro
Alto de Vento
Covas
Vilatrexe
Villestro
Quintáns
7.1
Roxos
Figueiras
Carballal
4.6
Sarela
2.3
0.0
Santiago de
Compostela
A H
Monte Pedroso
2 km
0
1
2
Laraño
Aldea Nova
Costoia
Bertamiráns
O Milladoiro
Outeiro
Negreira
2 San José
El Carmen 4
7 La Mezquita
Alecrín 5
Anjana
6
3
Lua
Av. Santiago
c/Chancela
Río Castelo
Camiño Vello
c/Cachurra
Av. Fermaco
Ctra. San Mauro
San Mauro
Río de Barcala
San Xulián
1 Xunta
100m

Stone crucero

0.0 *To leave Santiago (map p. 246), go to the cathedral and walk downhill with the Parador to the R and police station to the L. Cross at Rúa do Pombol to Rúa de Poza de Bar. Turn R through green park Carballeira San Lorenzo with huge oak trees and the 1216* ***Convento de San Lorenzo (1.0km)****. Cross a small stone bridge onto a dirt path. When the path comes to a T with a paved road, turn L into* ***Sarela (2.3km)****. Be sure to take a look back at Santiago from this last vantage point. Turn R onto a gravel uphill path partway through town. Join a paved road that goes through* ***Carballal (4.6km)****. Turn R just after town onto a small paved road, turning to dirt. Rejoin the paved road through* ***Quintáns (7.1km)*** *past a rest area near a bridge. Return to dirt trail for a bit until passing* ***Portela de Villestro*** ***(9.0km)****. Follow the paved road over Alto de Vento through* ***Ventosa (10.0km).*** *Pass* ***Castelo (10.4km)*** *with an albergue 500m to the R. Cross a bridge into Aguapesada.*

10.4 Castelo A H
A H **Casa Ríamonte** (6, €13/30/55 w/): , c/Castelo, 981-890356, +500m

11.8 Aguapesada

offers a pleasant halfway stop. *Now the trail begins to climb steeply on a dirt path through eucalyptus often accompanied by song birds. Meet a paved road and continue on it through the town of* ***Carballo (14.3km)****, through agricultural fields past a picnic area up to* ***Trasmonte*** ***(15.2km)****. Continue on the paved road downhill through the hamlet of* ***Reino (15.7km)*** *to arrive to historic Ponte Maceira.*

Crossing Ponte Maceira over the Río Tambre

17.0 Ponte Maceira

(Galician: "Bridge of the Apple"), true to its name, features an attractive 13th-century bridge across the Río Tambre (restored in the 18th century). According to legend, St. James and his followers were fleeing from the Roman army. The saint's crew ran across a bridge at this spot, but the bridge was divinely destroyed after them, leaving the Roman soldiers stranded on the other side. The image of the broken bridge is featured on the coat of arms of the local council. Maceira was also the site of a 13th-century battle between the troops of Diego Xelmérez, archbishop of Compostela, and the fighters of Pedro Froilaz de Trava and his sons Fernando and Bermudo. Today the town is beautiful preserved with traditional mansions lining the street displaying family coats of arms. The cool waters offer an ideal spot to soak weary feet. At the far end of the bridge is the 18th-century Capilla de San Blas with a stone roadside cross.

Negreira wedding

Make sure you have enough supplies to make it to Cee in stage 34, the next full-service town.

Turn L on a 1-lane road after town, which passes under an overpass and continues through agricultural fields to meet and cross the highway through ***Barca (19.4km)****. Cross back over the highway and continue on the road into Negreira, with the turnoff (20.4km) for* ***Logrosa albergue*** *to the L.*

+0.7 Logrosa A H Pop. 54

A H **De Logrosa** (8, €17/30/40 w/): (free), c/Logrosa 6, 981-885820, 12pm all year

21.9 Negreira is a modern town with a full array of services, including some good seafood restaurants and the last full-size supermarket until Cee. The medieval *Pazo del Cotón* is an interesting historical marker with part of the original defensive wall, which adjoins the 18th-century Capilla de San Mauro. A modern sculpture depicts a man emigrating away from Galicia, a very common story in this region with high unemployment. On the far side of town, after the Xunta albergue, is the 18th-century Neoclassic Iglesia de San Xulián with a stone rollo.

21.9 Negreira A H Pop. 7,077

1. A **Xunta** (22, €6): c/Patrocinio, 664-081498, 1pm all year, fills early
2. A H **San José** (50, €12/20/30): c/de Castelao 20, 881-976934, all year, call in winter
3. A **Lua** (40, €10): Av. de Santiago 22, 698-128883, all year
4. A **El Carmen** (34, €10): c/Carmen 2, 636-129691, 12pm all year, same building as La Mezquita
5. A **Alecrin** (40, €12): Av. de Santiago 52, 981-818286, Apr-Oct
6. A **Anjana** (18, €12): c/La Chancela 39, 667-204706, Apr-Sept
7. H **La Mezquita** (€30/50): c/del Carmen 2, 636-129691

33 NEGREIRA TO OLVEIROA

33.3km
(20.7mi)

8-10 Hours
Difficulty:
P 68%, 22.8km
U 32%, 10.5km

A Albergues:
A Peña 7.7km
Vilaserío 12.3km
S. Mariña 20.9km
P. Olveira 31.5km
Olveiroa 33.3km

Colorful garden after Negreira

Traverse tiny villages and beautiful gardens with decorated stone hórreos. Sleep in a traditional Galician building.

This is the longest stage of the Finisterre route, and over two-thirds of the day is on paved roads. Stock up on needed food in Negreira as there are no shops, with only a few cafés and drinking sources en route. For a shorter day, consider staying in intermediary albergues.

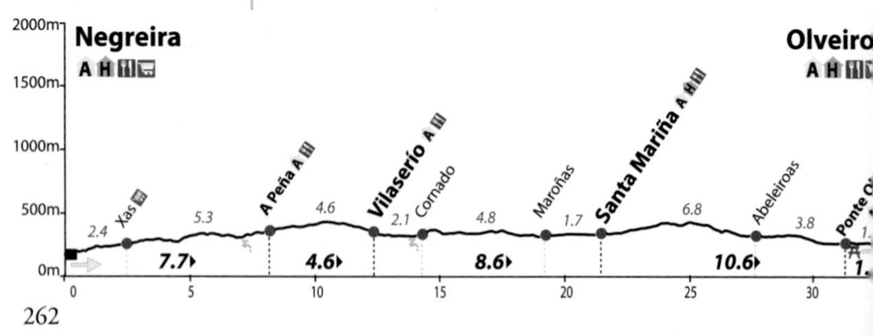

Os Currais
Embalse
de Fervenza
Río Xallas
Antes
A Pereira
Ribadeza
Pazos
O Campelo
A Carballeira
2 km
0
1
2
Os Vaos
Río Xallas
Olveiroa
A H
33.3
Ponte Olveira
31.5 A
Poteliñas
27.3
Lago
30.0 Corzón
Río Xallas
Mallón
San Cristóvo
de Corzón
27.7
Abeleiroas
Bon
Xesús
23.8
Xastro
Gueima
AC-403
Maroñas
19.2
20.9
A H
Santa Mariña
Fontecada
Parada
San Vicente
Cornado
14.4
Corneira
Colúns
AC-403
Pesadoira
12.3
A
Vilaserío
Paraxó
Nantón
Arzón
H
A Picota
Pesadoira
de Abajo
8.4
Piaxe
Portocamiño
7.7
Rapote
Barcala
A
A Peña
6.3
Negreira
A H
Camiño Real
Meiro
Tuñas
Xas
2.4
Pedralonga
0.0
Asenso
Olveiroa
Xunta 1
Hórreo/Casa
2 Loncho
3 As Pias
50m
Santiago
Outes
Sera de
Outes
Arzón
Pontevedra

Graveyard and stone crucero

7.7 A Peña A

A **Alto da Peña** (20, €12): , c/Piaxe 5, 609-853486, all year

12.3 Vilaserío A Pop. 72

A **O Rueiro** (30, €12): , 981-893561, Mar-Oct

A **Casa Vella** (12, €12): , c/Vilaserío 23, 981-893516

A **Municipal** (10 mats, don): basic, mats on floor, far side of town, hospitalera comes from house #39 to request donation

20.9 Santa Mariña A H

A **Santa Mariña/Antelo** (10, €10): , 981-852897, all year

A H **Casa Pepa** (16, €12/-/40): , 981-852881, all year

31.5 Ponte Olveira A

A **Ponte Olveira** (20, €12/-/30): , c/Ponte Olveira 3, 981-852135, all year

A **O Refuxio da Ponte** (10, €10): , 981-741724, all year

0.0 *From the Xunta albergue in Negreira, backtrack to turn up to the church and continue on a paved road to the forest, where it turns into a pleasant forest dirt path with pleasing views of the surrounding valleys. Meet a 2-lane road, turn R onto a narrow paved road at the mini market and continue through* ***Xas*** ***(2.4km)****, where evidently there was a dog wandering about on the wet cement! Leave Xas on a dirt road through field and forest. Skirt the town of Camiño Real and pass through* ***Rapote (6.3km)****.*

Continue on dirt paths to ***A Peña*** ***(7.7km)*** *and* ***Piaxe (7.9km)****, joining a paved road. Soon windmills come into view ahead. Continue through* ***Portocamiño (8.4km)*** *before veering R onto a dirt path. Rejoin the 2-lane paved road until a dirt path to the L leads into Vilaserío.*

12.3 Vilaserío offers a possible early stopping point or rest stop. *Pass the private Vilaserío albergue and continue to* ***Cornado (14.4km)****, where the trail turns to an earthen track to* ***Maroñas (19.2km)****. Return to pavement and pass the Iglesia de Santa Maríña before crossing AC-403 at Santa Mariña.*

20.9 Santa Mariña has a café and two albergues along the highway. *Stay along the highway and turn R to* ***Bon Xesús (22.8km)****,* ***Gueima (23.1km)*** *and* ***Xastro (23.8km)****. Return to dirt paths to* ***Lago (26.8)****, and follow pavement through* ***Poteliñas (27.3km)*** *to* ***Abeleiroas (27.7km)***

Galician hórreo

and turn R at the bus stop. The paved path arrives at a Y in ***Corzón (30.0km)*** *with its Igrexa de San Cristóbal. Take the L fork and continue over a bridge to meet the main road. Turn R on the main road, with a special green lane for walkers. Pass through* ***Mallón (31.0km)*** *and over the Ponte Olveira bridge over the Río Xallas.*

31.5 **Ponte Olveira** has a café and albergue with a green lawn. *Continue on the main road until the signposted L turn into Olveiroa. The Xunta albergue is a short detour R.*

33.3 Olveiroa A H Pop. 129

1. **A Xunta** (46, €6): , 658-045242, 1:30pm, all year, restored traditional buildings
2. **A H Albergue Hórreo/Casa Loncho** (48, €12/25/45): (free), 981-741673, Mar-Nov, small shop
3. **H As Pias** (€40/50-60): , 981-741520

33.3 **Olveiroa** is a charming traditional village said to have more *hórreos* than people. Observe magnificent examples of stone *hórreos*, some of which are beautifully illuminated at night. There is a small Igrexa Santiago as well as a stone *rollo*. There was no shop here at time of research, though Albergue Hórreo sells basic supplies. The Xunta albergue is spread over several sensitively restored historic buildings. A nearby café offers pilgrim *menús*.

Detail of Galician hórreo

34 OLVEIROA TO FINISTERRE

31.4km +3.2km to lighthouse
(19.5mi +2.0mi to lighthouse)

7.5-9 HOURS
DIFFICULTY:
P 42%, 13.3km
U 58%, 18.1km

A ALBERGUES:
Logoso 3.6km
Hospital 5.5km
Cee 19.6km
Corcubión 20.0km
San Roque 22.0km
Finisterre 31.4km

View of Finisterre

Relish a long stretch of earthen path on the wild Galician countryside. Catch your first glimpse of the sea and walk along the beach to arrive at the "end of the earth."

Another long stage, but there are intermediate accommodations options. The day includes beautiful isolated walking through the high Galician countryside leading to stunning sea views. The route splits after Hospital, with the L path going to Finisterre and the R to Muxía (stage 34A). The path to Finisterre meanders along the beach to enter the city. From the Xunta albergue, the walk to the lighthouse is an additional 3.2km each way. Pilgrims gather at the lighthouse for sunset.

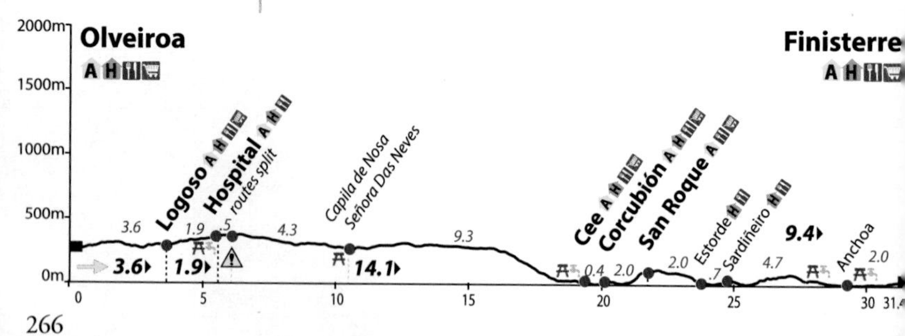

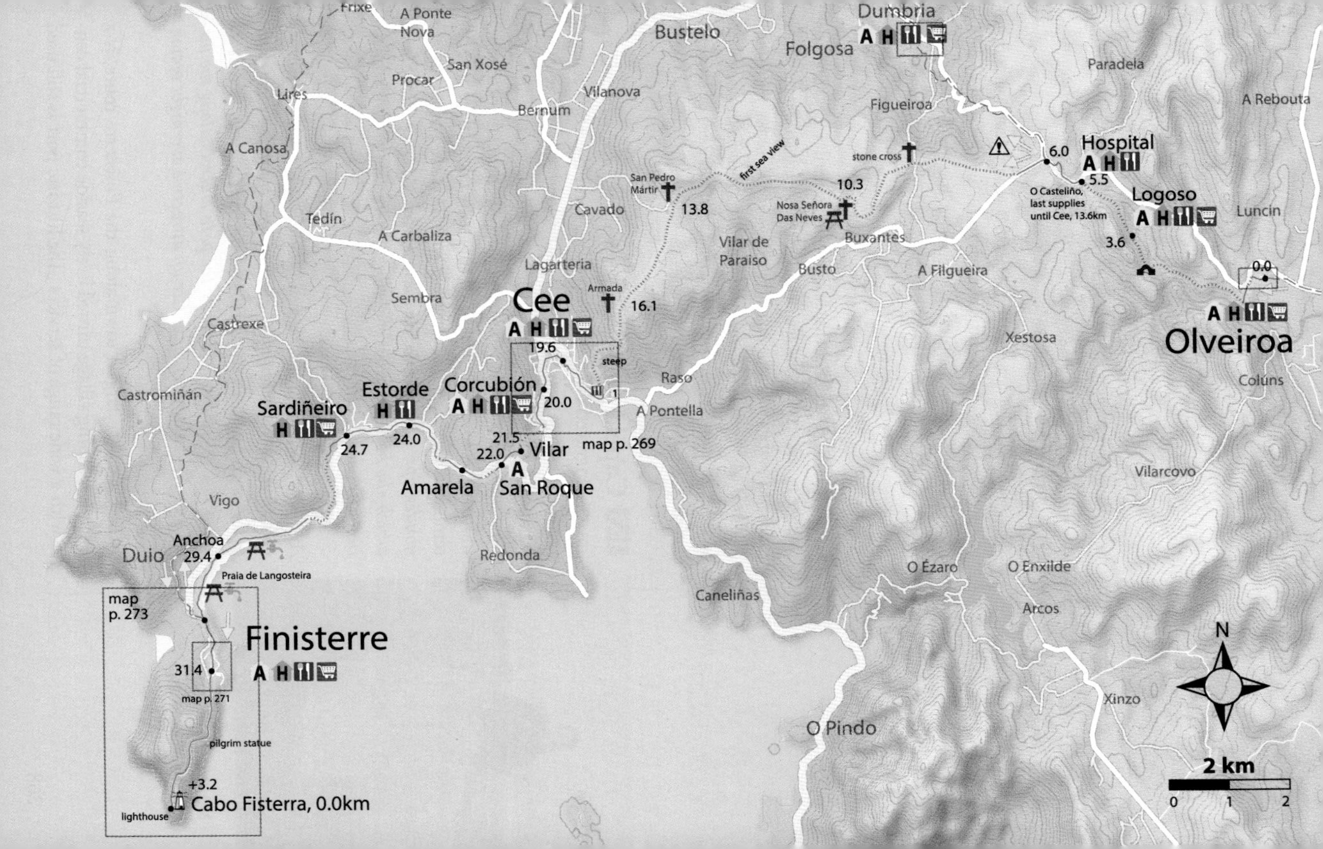
Frixe
A Ponte Nova
San Xosé
Procar
Lires
Bustelo
Vilanova
Bernum
Dumbria
Folgosa
Paradela
A Rebouta
Figueiroa
stone cross
first sea view
6.0
Hospital
O Castelino,
last supplies
until Cee, 13.6km
5.5
Logoso
Luncín
San Pedro
Mártir
13.8
10.3
Nosa Señora
Das Neves
Buxantes
3.6
A Canosa
Tedín
A Carbaliza
Cavado
Vilar de
Paraiso
Busto
A Filgueira
0.0
Lagarteria
Armada
16.1
Sembra
Cee
Xestosa
Olveiroa
Castrexe
19.6
steep
Raso
Colúns
Castromiñán
Estorde
Corcubión
20.0
1
A Pontella
Sardiñeiro
24.7
24.0
21.5
22.0
Vilar
map p. 269
Amarela
San Roque
Vilarcovo
Vigo
Anchoa
Duio
29.4
Redonda
Praia de Langosteira
O Ézaro
O Enxilde
Caneliñas
map
p. 273
Arcos
Finisterre
N
31.4
map p. 271
Xinzo
O Pindo
pilgrim statue
2 km
+3.2
0
1
2
lighthouse
Cabo Fisterra, 0.0km

3.6 Logoso A H

A H **O Logoso** (22, €12/30/40): , 659-505399, all year

5.5 Hospital A H

A H **O Casteliño** (18, €12/20/-): , 615-997169, all year

0.0 *Leave Olveiroa on the main paved road, then turn L over a small bridge onto a dirt path. The trail climbs a beautiful windswept route with low-lying brush, pine trees and views of windmills. Cross a cement bridge to quiet Logoso.*

3.6 Logoso has a café, albergue and small shop all in the same building. The town of Hospital is opposite the road on the R, where a pilgrim hospital was once located. *Meet the main road that leads to Hospital.*

5.5 Hospital has the last services until Cee. *Take the smaller paved road to the R after the café, which crosses the main road and brings you to a large roundabout where the path splits (6.0km). ⚠ Continue L for Finisterre past a monstrous carbide factory. In 500m, turn R onto a dirt path for 12km of heavenly walking in nature.*

Marker for the split: Finisterre or Muxía

10.3 Capela: The path passes a stone *rollo* with a *Pietá* image (engraved CR for *Camino Real*) and the 18th-century Capela da Nosa Señora das Neves ("Our Lady of the Snow Chapel") with a peaceful sheltered picnic area. The water flowing here is said to be particularly beneficial to nursing mothers. A local pilgrimage to this spot takes place in September. *Continue uphill for a first glimpse of the ocean! Pass the nondescript* ***Sanctuario de San Pedro Mártir (13.8km)****, which also has a tradition of healing waters, said to cure arthritis in joints when submerged.*

A 100m detour is marked to the ***Cruceiro do Armada (16.1km)****, a recreation of an ancient stone cross. The view down to the bay is fantastic. ⚠ Exercise caution on the steep, loose track down to Cee. Toward the water the path emerges along the waterfront. New albergues make Cee an attractive overnight option.*

19.6 Cee, the largest town along the Finisterre route, is a charming fishing village turned lively seaside commercial center with a wide range of services. The historic port is still used

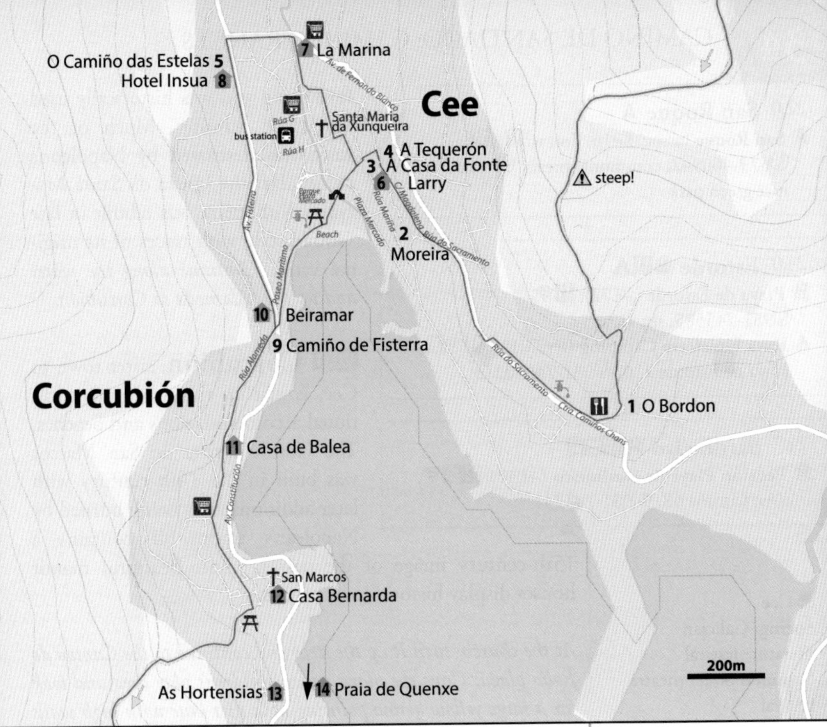

9.6 **Cee** A H Pop. 7,898

A **O Bordón** (24, €12): Camiños Chans, 981-746574, 12pm all year

A H **Moreira** (14, €12/-/30): c/Rosalía 75, 981-746282, Mar-Oct

A **A Casa da Fonte** (42, €10): Rúa de Arriba 36, 981-746663, Mar-Dec 15

A **A Tequerón** (10, €15): Rúa de Arriba 31, 666-119594

A H **O Camiño das Estelas** (30, €12/-/30): Av. Finisterre 78, 981-747575, all year, part of Hotel Insua

H **Larry** (€40/60): c/Magdalena 8, 981-746441

H **La Marina** (€44/55): Av. Fernando Blanco 26, 981-747381

H **Hotel Insua** (€55/70): Av. Finisterre 82, 981-747575

0.0 **Corcubión** A H

p. 1,767, Celtic: "circular bay," free in library, c/Explanada do Porto 17, 981-706163

A **Camiño de Fisterra** (14, €10): c/Cruceiro de Valdomar 11, 981-745040, all year

0. H **Pensión Beiramar** (€30/40): Av. Finisterre 220, 981-745040

1. H **Casa de Balea** (€40/52): Rafael Juan 44, 981-746645

2. H **Casa Bernarda** (€35/65): Párroco Francisco Sánchez 3, 981-747157

3. H **As Hortensias** (€40/50): Lg Praia de Quenxe, 981-747584

4. H **Praia de Quenxe** (€40/45): Lg Praia de Quenxe 43, 981-706457

22.0 **San Roque** A
A **San Roque** (assoc, 16, don w/): , 679-460942, communal meals, 4pm all year, nice green park

24.0 **Estorde** H A
H **Playa de Estorde** (-/€72): , 981-745585, sea views
A **Ruta Finisterre Camping** (tent €12): , Playa de Estorde 216, 981-746302

24.7 **Sardiñeiro** H
H **Pensión Playa de Sardiñeiro** (-/€42): , c/Av. Coruña 68, 981-743741

for fishing and was historically used for whale hunting. Much of the town was destroyed by Napoleon's troops, but the Igrexa da Santa Maria da Xunqueira was rebuilt in late Gothic style with traces of its original vault. *Continue along the water and up Rúa Alameda to Corcubión.*

20.0 **Corcubión**, sister town to Cee, is just up the road with additional accommodations and beaches. The Gothic Igrexa de San Marcos was built in the 14th century with later additions after being burned by Napolean's troops. It contains a 15th-century image of the patron saint. Beautiful manor houses display historic coats of arms.

Cee
Spring: Galician literature festival
Summer: Street theatre festival
Sunday is market day.

Corcubión
April 25: San Marcos, celebration of patron saint

At the church, turn R up the steps and continue to the Campo de Rollo plaza. Cross the plaza past a children's play area and look for a large yellow arrow pointing up a dirt lane with high walls on either side. Follow this path out of Corcubión, which joins a paved road and leads through the hamlet of ***Vilar (21.5km)*** *to* ***San Roque (22.0km)****. Return to the road and continue onto an earthen path. Pass through* ***Amarela (22.7km)*** *and continue on a 2-lane paved road through Estorde and Sardiñeiro.*

24.0 **Estorde** and 24.7 **Sardiñeiro** are both along the beach with restaurant and hotel options. *Leave town on a dirt footpath with elevated views of the sea, which rejoins the main road and then departs again to pass along the shore. The rest of the way into Finisterre can be walked on the sidewalk or by taking your shoes off and walking along the sandy beach. The beach* ***Praia a Langosteira*** H *stretches about 2km prior to the entrance to Finisterre, passing the town of* ***Anchoa (29.4km)****. The Finisterre Xunta albergue is located in the center near the harbor and next to the bus station.*

Barefoot pilgrims enjoying the sandy beach

Finisterre has drawn mystics and :ers to its rocky shores for thousands of s. The Romans named it *finis terrae*, "the of the earth" and, staring out into the anse of wild ocean from the lighthouse Monte Facho, it's easy to see how it may e felt that way. Celtic pagans built an al- to the sun (*Ara Solis*) at Finisterre, and r Christians developed their own rituals ınd this place. From the town to the thouse is 3.2km, and numerous foot- ıs crisscross the peninsula's hilltop lead- to interesting natural and religious sites.

s fishing village has grown as a tourist tination with many accommodations as as seafood restaurants, mostly located r the vibrant historic port.

charming historic center has twisting ets perfect for exploring. Visit the

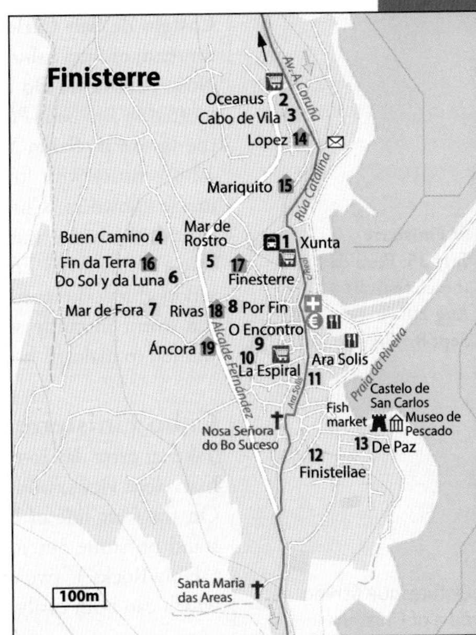

31.4 Finisterre

Pop. 4,983, Latin: *Finis Terrae* "the end of the world," (also Fisterra, Finisterra)

1. **Xunta** (36, €6): c/Real 2, 981-740781, 1pm all year, Finisterre completion doc.
2. **Oceanus** (€12): Av. A Coruña 33, 609-821302
3. **Cabo da Vila** (28, €12/-/30): A Coruña 13, 981-740454, all year
4. **Buen Camino De Sonia** (42, €12): c/Atalaya 11, 981-740771 all year, sauna
5. **Mar de Rostro** (23, €12): Alcalde Fernández 45, 637-107765, Mar-Nov
6. **Do Sol y da Lua** (18, €10/-/30): c/Atalaya 7, 981-740655, all year
7. **Mar de Fora** (11, €10): Rúa Potiña 60, 686-939079, all year
8. **Por Fin** (11, €10): c/Federico Ávila 19, 636-764726, Apr-Nov
9. **O Encontro** (5, €12-15): c/El Campo 7, 696-503363, Apr-Nov
10. **La Espiral** (12, €12/30/38): c/Fonte Vella 19, 607-684248, all year
11. **Ara Solis** (16, €10-12): c/Ara Solis 3, 638-326869, all year
12. **Finistellae** (20, €12/30/35): Manuel Lago País 7, 637-821296, Easter-Oct
13. **De Paz** (26, €10): Víctor Cardalda 11, 981-740332, all year, call in winter
14. **Hospedaje Lopez** (€15/25-30): c/Carrasqueira 4, 981-740449, sea views
15. **Hostal Mariquito** (€30/42): c/de Santa Catalina 44, 981-740044
16. **Pensión Fin da Terra** (€27/38 shared bath): (free), Atalaia 30, 981-712030
17. **Hotel Finesterre** (€40/50): c/Federico Ávila 8, 981-740000
18. **Hostal Rivas** (€25/35): c/Alcalde Fernández 53, 981-740027
19. **Áncora Hotel** (€28/37): c/Alcalde Fernández 65, 981-740791

Castelo de San Carlos, which has been transformed into a museum of local fishing culture. The 18th-century **Capela do Nosa Señora do Bo Suceso**, featuring a Baroque retable, is located in *Ara Solis Plaza*. On the way to the cape you'll pass the **Igrexa de Santa Maria das Areas**, originally built in the 12th century with funds from Doña Urraca, containing an image known as "Christ of the Golden Beard." According to legend, the image was sculpted by Nicodemus and was on a ship coming from England when a huge storm began. The sailors threw the statue into the ocean to ballast weight and the storm instantly stopped, apparently because the image wanted to make its home in Finisterre.

Finisterre
July 25: Festa da Praia (beach festival)
Aug 20: Fin do Camino
Sept 8: Virxe do Carme

Cabo Finisterre

Take an extra day to explore Monte Facho further, which has marvelous views, wild beaches and interesting historical sites. On the west side of Monte Facho, a series of massive rocks stand on stone outcroppings, known as the **Piedras Santas** ("Holy Rocks"). Two of these are known as the *Abalar* stones, which can both easily be moved back and forth if pushed on

Picturesque fishing port of Finisterre

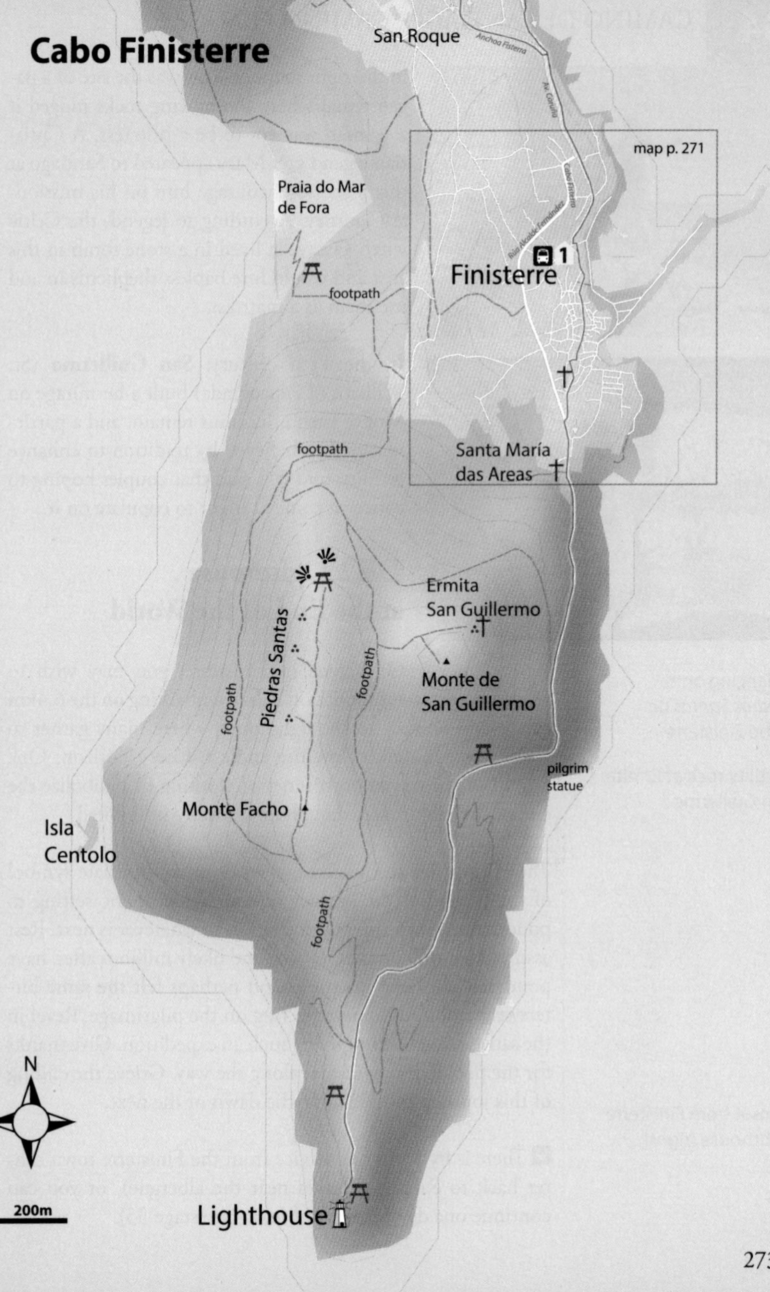
Cabo Finisterre
San Roque
Av. Coruña
map p. 271
Praia do Mar de Fora
Finisterre
1
footpath
footpath
Santa María das Areas
Ermita San Guillermo
Piedras Santas
footpath
footpath
Monte de San Guillermo
pilgrim statue
Monte Facho
Isla Centolo
footpath
N
200m
Lighthouse

in the right manner. This was the site of a pagan ritual where the moving rocks judged if a woman was apt to be a priestess. A Christian legend says Mary appeared to Santiago at this place to encourage him on his missionary journey. According to legend, the Celtic witch Orcavella lived in a stone tomb in this area and would lure hapless shepherds in and use them as a mattress.

In the 11th century, **San Guillermo** (St. William of Penacorada) built a hermitage on Monte Facho. Its ruins remain, and a particular rock is believed by tradition to enhance fertility, and it is said that couples hoping to conceive come at night to copulate on it.

0.0 Lighthouse at the End of the World

Balancing on *Piedras Santas* on Cabo Finisterre

Fertility rock at Ermita San Guillerme

On arrival in Finisterre, you may wish to check into an accommodation before embarking on the 6.4km round-trip journey to the lighthouse, where many gather to watch the sun sink below the endless watery horizon. One pilgrim ritual was to burn shoes or clothing to symbolize the end of the pilgrimage, though now strictly prohibited.

The setting sun at Finisterre serves as an appropriate symbol of the ending of the journey and an atmospheric setting to ponder the return trip and transition to whatever is next. Rest assured that millions before you, and likely millions after, have pondered the same questions and perhaps felt the same bittersweet emotions upon reflecting on the pilgrimage. Revel in the satisfaction of completing such an expedition. Give thanks for the people you have met along the way. Grieve the ending of this journey and welcome the dawn of the next.

Sunset from Finisterre lighthouse (right)

There is frequent bus service from the Finisterre town center back to Santiago (leaves near the albergue), or you can continue one day further to Muxía (see stage 35).

process your Camino experience for a few days, author Tracy unders offers her house near Muxía, called *A Casa Do Raposito* 'ouse of the Little Fox), as a post-Camino retreat on a donation sis. Arrange in advance: ✆981-730842

The end of the road at kilometer 0.00 before the Finisterre lighthouse

34A

OLVEIROA TO MUXÍA

31.6km
(19.6mi)

7-9 Hours
Difficulty:
P 50%, 15.8km
U 50%, 15.8km

A Albergues:
Logoso 3.6km
Dumbría 9.7km
Muxía 31.6km

Rooftop crosses at Iglesia San Martiño

Walk through rolling countryside, delight in magnificent sea views and visit the holy rocks on Muxía peninsula.

This route is only marked thoroughly in one direction, from Olveiroa to Muxía, so if returning from Muxía this way be extra aware of reversed arrows and surroundings. This route is less popular than the route to Finisterre (stage 34) and feels more remote and wild. Dumbría has an impressive new albergue that gets very little use. Walk out to the Muxía church at sunset for a fulfilling end to the day.

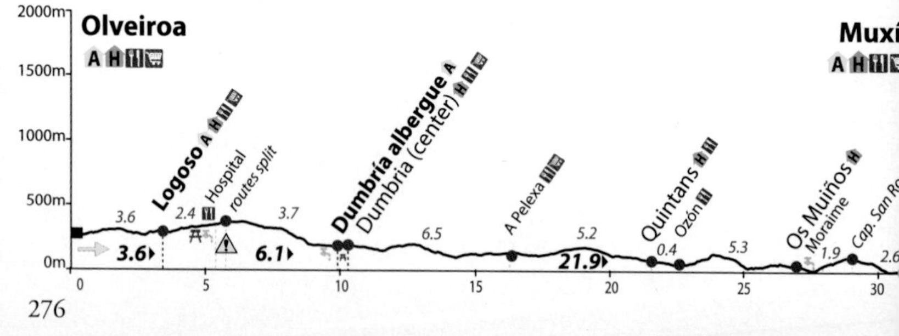

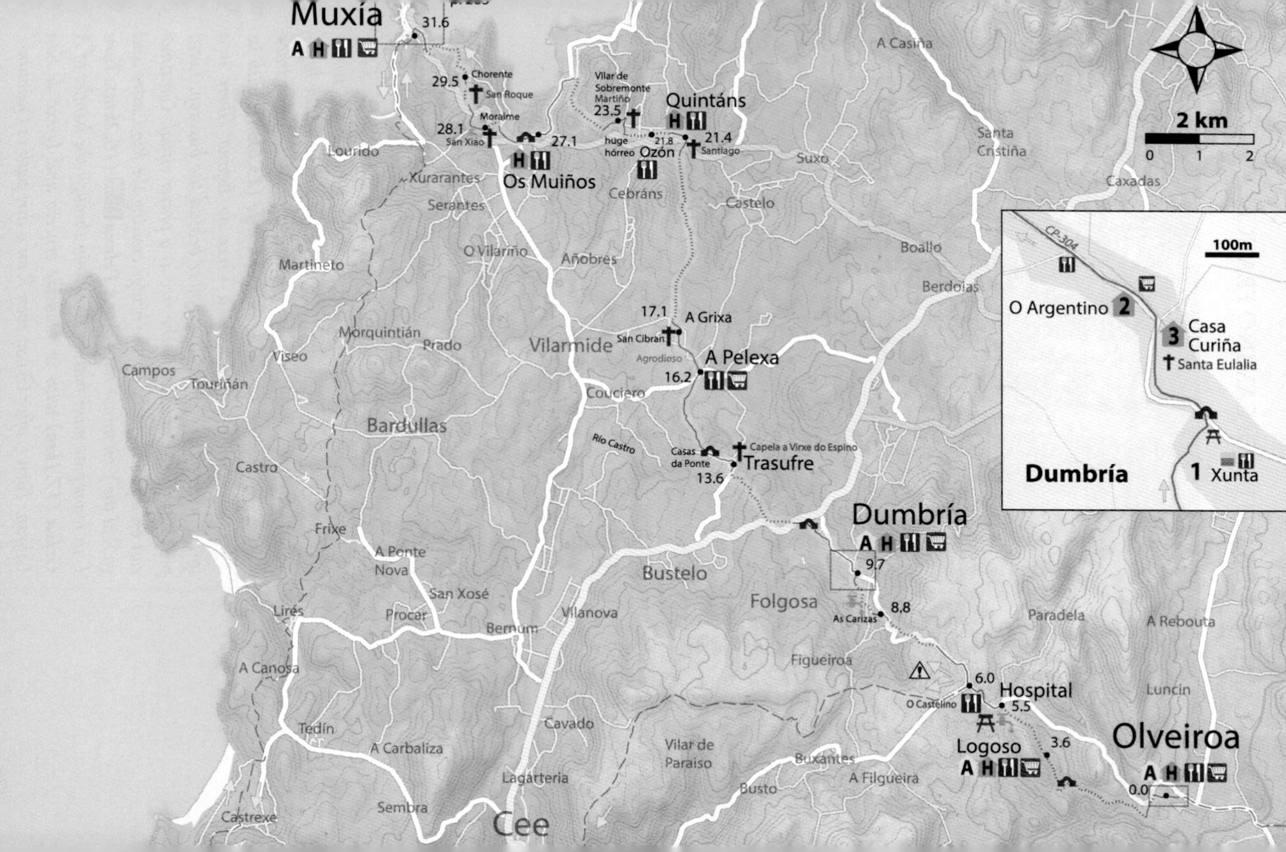
Muxía
31.6
29.5
Chorente
San Roque
Moraime
28.1
San Xiao
27.1
Os Muiños
Vilar de Sobremonte
Martiño
23.5
huge hórreo
21.8
Ozón
Quintáns
21.4
Santiago
A Casiña
Santa Cristiña
Suxo
Caxadas
2 km
0
1
2
Lourido
Xurarantes
Serantes
Cebráns
Castelo
Boallo
Berdoias
O Vilariño
Añobres
Martineto
17.1
A Grixa
San Cibrán
Agrodioso
A Pelexa
16.2
Vilarmide
Morquintián
Prado
Campos
Touriñán
Viseo
Couciero
Bardullas
Río Castro
Casas da Ponte
Capela a Virxe do Espino
Trasufre
13.6
Castro
Dumbría
9.7
Frixe
A Ponte Nova
Bustelo
Folgosa
8.8
As Carizas
San Xosé
Procar
Bernum
Vilanova
Lirés
A Canosa
Figueiroa
Paradela
A Rebouta
6.0
O Castelino
Hospital
5.5
Luncin
Tedín
Cavado
Vilar de Paraiso
Buxantes
A Carbaliza
Logoso
3.6
Olveiroa
0.0
A Filgueira
Busto
Lagarteria
Sembra
Castrexe
Cee
CP-304
100m
O Argentino
2
3
Casa Curiña
Santa Eulalia
1
Xunta
Dumbría

Ubiquitous eucalyptus forest before Muxía

0.0 *For the description from Olveiroa to the* ***trail junction (6.0km)****,* *see p. 268.* ⚠ *From the split after* ***Hospital****, take the R option along the road then turn off to the L onto a dirt path. Follow this path through* ***As Carizas (8.8km)*** *to Dumbría.*

9.7 Dumbría A H

Pop. 1,000, Celtic: "fortified town"

1. A **A Conca** (Xunta, 26, €6): , next to municipal pool to L of Camino, 981-744001, 1pm all year, at pool
2. H **O Argentino** (-/€30-40): , 981-744051
3. H **Casa Curiña** (-/€48-60): , c/Estiman, 981-744024

9.7 Dumbría has a well-designed albergue, funded by the owner of the Zara clothing store chain. *Walk past the albergue into town passing the 17th-century Iglesia de Santa Eulalia. Continue on the main paved road, which crosses over a small bridge and the highway after which it becomes a dirt track up through* ***Trasufe (13.6km)****, with its Capela a Virxe do Espino. There is a spring with purported healing power behind the bus stop. Local people tie pieces of cloth to the tree as a prayer ritual. Continue east on a paved road over the bridge crossing the Río Castro and go R at the Y on minor road into* ***A Pelexa*** ***(16.2km)****. Turn L in town past mini market Agrodosio through the hamlet of* ***A Grixa (17.1km)*** *with its roadside crucero and Igrexe de San Cibran. Turn L after Grixa, then R on a dirt path to Quintáns.*

21.4 Quintáns houses the modest Capilla de San Isideo. *Turn L and leave town on a dirt road. Pass by a massive hórreo with 22 stone supports! Pass* ***Ozón (21.8km)*** *to the Iglesia de San Martiño with a Romanesque apse and ruins of a Benedictine Monastery. After town, take a hard L turn through* ***Vilar de Sobremonte (23.5km)*** *on the road and turn R on a footpath. Come to a paved road close to the sea; turn L into Os Muiños.*

21.4 **Quintáns** Pop. 240
Hospedaje Plaza (€30/40): , Quintáns-Muxia, 981-750452

27.1 Os Muiños: Pass through this village, which has a panadería for provisions. *Leave town on the paved road, then straight on a grassy trail crossing the highway through* ***Moraime (28.1km)****, the site of the Iglesia de San Xiao de Moraime, an influential medieval monastery. Turn R after town and cross the highway onto an small dirt road to pass the* ***Capela de San Roque (29.0km)*** *with a stone crucero in the forest. Continue on the dirt path through* ***Chorente (29.5km)****. The path will emerge on a boardwalk along the sea. Follow the shore into* ***Muxía (31.6km)****,* *p. 284.*

27.1 **Os Muiños**
Galician: "the mills," panadería
Pensión Paris: Os Muiños 41, 981-750616

Huge hórreo after Quintáns

35 FINISTERRE TO MUXÍA

28.0km
(17.4mi)

7-8 Hours
Difficulty:
P 54%, 15.2km
U 46%, 12.8km

A Albergues:
As Lires 13.5km
Muxía 28.0km

Iglesia de Nosa Señora da Barca in Muxía

Roam the wild coastal moors and idyllic countryside on this less-traveled route. Marvel at the seaside church of Muxía and mysterious rock formations.

This is a pleasant and isolated stage, the path winding through forest and village with the sea often in sight. Several cafés provide refreshment. To stay in the Xunta albergue in Muxía and receive a certificate of completion (*Muxiana*, p. 285), remember to **get a stamp in As Lires**. The path is less traveled than Finisterre and has a sense of wild sea and idyllic countryside.

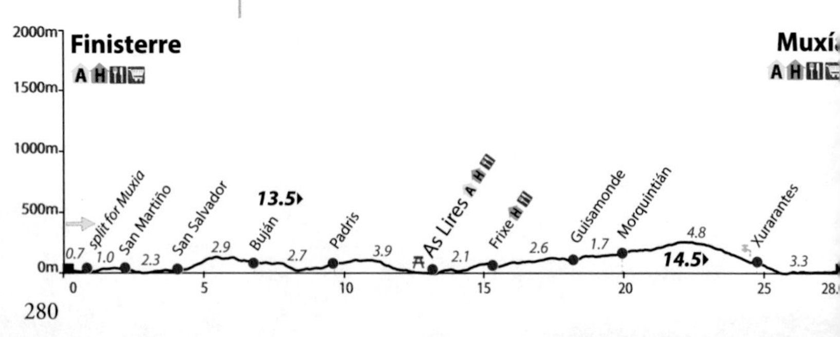

map
p. 285
Muxía
28.0
Praia de
Lourido
26.1
Lourido
24.7
Xurarantes
Os Muiños
Ozón
Quintáns
Suxo
Carñes
A Casiña
Cebráns
Castelo
Serantes
Boallo
Martineto
Vilela
O Vilariño
Añobres
Cabo
Touriñan
Santa
Maria
Morquintián
19.9
Prado
Vilarmide
Sendande
Viseo
Campos
Touriñan
Coucieiro
Guisamonde
18.1
Bardullas
Loalo
Castro
Río Do Castro
Frixe
15.6
A Ponte
Nova
14.2
Praia de
Nemiña
Ría de
Lires
Vaosilveiro
Río Do Castro
San Xosé
Dumbría
Bustelo
Folgosa
Procar
13.5
As Lires
Get a stamp!
Bernum
Vilanova
Canosa
11.7
Tedín
Cavado
9.6
Praia de
Rostro
Padrís
A Carbaliza
Lagartería
Vilar de
Paraiso
Buxantes
Busto
A Filgueira
7.9
Suarriba
Sembra
Cee
Xestosa
Buján
6.9
Raso
A Pontella
Corcubión
Castromiñán
4.0
San Salvador
Castro
Vigo
3.7
Hermedesuxo
Escaselas
2.9
Anchoa
San Martiño
1.7
Praia de
Langosteria
Redonda
O Ézaro
O Enxilde
Caneliñas
Arcos
Hotel
Arenal
1.1
Praia de
Mar do Fora
0.0
Finisterre
map
p. 271
N
O Pindo
2 km
0
1
2
map
p. 273
Cabo Finisterre

Finisterre or Muxía? The choice is yours

0.0 *From the Finisterre Xunta albergue, walk up Rúa Catalina past the Concello and post office (maps p. 271 and p. 273). Continue along the main road and turn L on Aldea San Marín de Abajo at a bus shelter after the sign for Hotel Arenal (a Camino marker reads San Martiño, the next town, 1.1km). Stay straight through lower* ***San Martiño (1.7km)*** *past a housing development and then through upper San Martiño. Pass cornfields until going through* ***Escaselas (2.9km)****; turn L at a crossroads. Continue straight through* ***Hermedesuxo (3.7km)****, which has a stone crucero. At the crossroads, take the diagonal R into* ***San Salvador (4.0km)****, past Hotel Dugium. At the far end of town, the road turns to dirt and continues straight past an hórreo. Wind through a eucalyptus forest before passing through Rapadoiro and back onto an earthen track to* ***Buján (6.9km)****. After town, turn R on a paved road past a lumber factory into the forest. Continue on dirt through* ***Suarriba (7.9km)****, then turn L on a track with views of the sea. Meet the paved road to walk uphill, then turn L onto a dirt road with many yellow arrow markers at* ***Padrís (9.6km)****. The trail is paved through* ***Canosa (11.7km)****, then turns off to the L on dirt. Cross a small bridge to enter As Lires.*

13.5 As Lires A H - get a stamp!

Pop. 165, Galician: "the lyres"

- H **Casa Raul** (-/€40-60 w/shared bath): , ©981-748156
- H **Casa Lourido** (€30/40): , ©981-748348
- H **Casa Luz** (€30/40): , ©981-748924
- A H **As Eiras** (22, €12/45/55): , ©981-748180, popular cafe
- H **Casa Jesus** (-/€54): , ©981-748393

13.5 As Lires is such a small town that the accommodations have no street addresses—ask around if you have trouble finding one. ⚠ **Make sure you get a stamp from café As Eiras**. The Xunta albergue in Muxía requires this stamp to prove you didn't arrive by bus. There is a stone crucero and Igrexa San Esteban. *Walk through Lires on the main road, then turn off onto a smaller road that will turn into a dirt path. Cross over a new bridge—look to the L to see the stepping stones that until recently pilgrims used to ford the river.*

*Enter tiny **Vaosilveiro (14.2km)** and continue on the dirt path that meets with a paved road. Turn L and then a quick R to cross the highway and pass through the outskirts of **Frixe**, **(15.6km)**, with Romanesque Iglesia de Santa Leocadia onto a dirt path. A sharp L downhill goes into **Guisamonde (18.1km)** on the paved road. Follow the paved road past a crucero and water fount (non-potable) into **Morquintián (19.9km)**, with its Romanesque Iglesia de Santa María. Continue on the paved road until it comes to a T. Turn R (ignoring the old cement maker), then turn off to the L on a dirt path. Continue through forest into **Xurarantes (24.7km)**. Turn L in town on a paved road curving around the forest. For the fastest way into Muxía, continue on the road. If you'd like to visit the attractive beach of **Praia de Lourido (26.1km)**, follow the markers straight on a dirt path that will turn to sand. There is not a clear path here so walk toward the water, and turn R to rejoin the main road.*

Enter Muxía via the sidewalk along the main road. To go directly to the albergue, turn R at the sign on Rúa Os Malatos and follow signs uphill through town to the albergue. To head to the church and seaside promenade, take the main road. The Camino is not well marked through town (map on p. 285).

15.6 **Frixe**

Casa Ceferinos (-/€50): Frixe 11, 981-748965

O Camiño dos Faros (The Lighthouse Camino) is a new 200-km route along the Costa da Morte between Finisterre and Malpica. The route features views of the spectacular rugged sea coast, numerous historic lighthouses, and picturesque fishing villages. The route is still under development and not thoroughly marked, but GPS tracks are available for download. Accommodations are only in hotels and guesthouses.

More information at **caminodosfaros.com**

Muxía coast line on the western side

View of Muxía from Monte Corpiño

28.0 **Muxía**
Pop. 6,634, Archaic: "the monks"

1. **Xunta** (32, €6): , c/Enfesto, 610-264325, 1pm all year
2. **Da Costa** (8, €12/-/34): , Av. Doctor Toba 33, 676-363820 , all year
3. **Muxía Mare** (16, €12/37): , Rúa Castelao 14, 981-742423 , all year
4. **@Muxia** (41, €11): , c/Enfesto 12, 609-615533 , all year
5. **Delfín** (20, €10): , Av. López Abente 22, 622-345358, Mar-Nov
6. **Arribada** (38, €12-15/40/55): , c/José María del Río 30, 981-742516 , all year
7. **Bela Muxía** (52, €15/-/50): , r/da Encarnación 30, 687-798222 , all year
8. **La Cruz** (€45/65): , Av. de López Abente 44, 981-742084 , with sea views
9. **A de Loló** (€80/90): , Rúa Virxe da Barca 37, 981-742422
10. **Apartamentos Praia do Capitán** (-/€70): , c/Virxe da Barca 43, 981-742337

28.0 **Muxía** is a picturesque fishing town located on a small peninsula, known for its fish and handmade lace, but best known as the home of **Nosa Señora da Barca** ("Our Lady of the Boat"), housed in a rustic church built over the rocky shore mere meters from the crashing waves. Legend has it that Mary appeared here in a stone ship to deliver a message to a discouraged Saint James. She informed him that he had been successful and should return to Jerusalem, his mission in Spain complete. She also gave him the image of herself displayed in the church. The second Sunday in September is *La Festa de Nosa Señora da Barca*, one of the most important celebrations in Galicia. Thousands come from far and wide to visit the church, dance, sing, eat *caldareta* (fish stew) and parade the virgin through the streets. Sadly, the church building was severely damaged by fire after being struck by lightning on Christmas day in 2013.

The large rocks outside the church are said to be the remains of her boat—*Pedra dos Cadris* represents her sail, the kidney-shaped *Pedra do Timón* the rudder and *Pedra da Abalar* (a rocking stone similar to those in Finisterre) represents the hull. The rocking stone was used in pre-Christian times to determine the guilt of an accused party, and it continues rocking even after being broken during a storm in the 1970s. One legends says that when thieves were trying to rob the church, the stone rocked back and forth so loudly that the neighbors awoke and chased away the thieves. There is also the *Pedra dos Namorados* where couples come to declare their love.

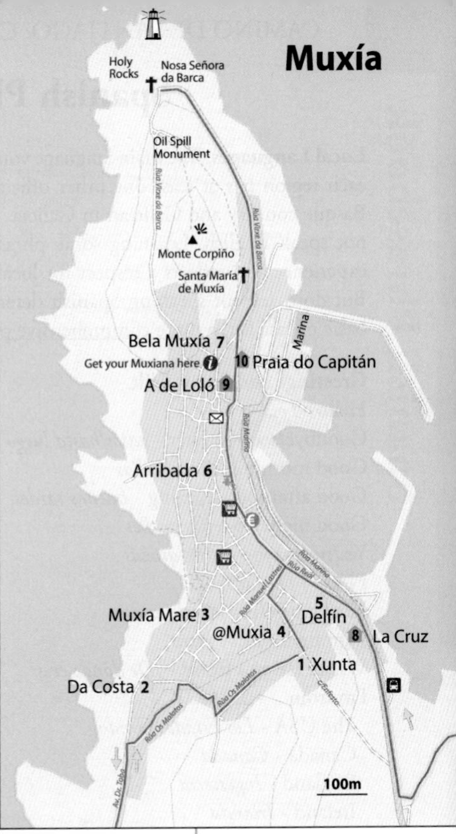

Walk out to the sanctuary via a very pleasant promenade on the northeast side of the peninsula passing the 14th-century Marine-Gothic style **Iglesia de Santa María de Muxía**. Return by walking up the hill behind the church past the monument remembering the tragic Prestige oil spill of 2002. Walk up to the top of **Monte Copino** for an elevated view. This return path is known as the *Camiño da Pel* ("Way of the Skin") because pilgrims would wash themselves in a nearby fountain before entering the church.

Be sure to stop by the helpful **Tourist Information** (981-742563, M-F 10am-2pm, 4-8pm; Sa/Su 11am-1pm, 3-5pm; summer M-F 9am-9pm, free internet). Present your credencial to receive the *Muxíana*, a decorative certificate of completion similar to the *Compostela*. The *Muxíana* is also available at the Xunta and Bela Muxía albergues.

Transportation Muxía to Santiago: Bus services at 6:45am and 2:30pm M-F, Sa 7:30am and 2:30pm, Su 7:30am and 6:45pm, confirm by calling Hermanos Ferrín, 981-873643. For more options, take a bus to Cee, which has more buses per day to Santiago.

Spanish Phrasebook

Local Languages: The main language you'll hear on the Camino is Spanish, though each region has at least one other official language, such as Basque (*Euskara*) in Basque country and Galician in Galicia. Many local people along the Camino do not speak English. Learning some phrases in Spanish will greatly enhance your experience and reflects a respect for local culture that is often much appreciated. But don't let not speaking Spanish deter you from the Camino. Below is a very basic phrase list; a more comprehensive phrasebook is available on our website.

Greetings and Small Talk

Hello - *hola*
Goodbye/see you later - *adiós/hasta luego*
Good morning - *buenos días*
Good afternoon/evening - *buenas tardes*
Good night - *buenas noches*
Yes/no/maybe - *sí/no/quizás*
Please - *por favor*
How are you? - *¿Cómo estás?*
I am fine. - *Estoy bien.*
Where are you from? - *¿De dónde eres?*
I'm from... - *Soy de...*
The USA - *Los Estados Unidos*
Canada - *Canadá*
England - *Inglaterra*
Ireland - *Irlanda*
Australia - *Australia*
South Africa - *Sudáfrica*
Thank you - *gracias*
You're welcome - *de nada*
Excuse me - *disculpa*
Nice to meet you. - *Mucho gusto.*
I (don't) understand/Do you understand? - *(No) Entiendo/¿Entiendes?*
Do you speak English? - *¿Habla Inglés?*
I don't speak Spanish- *No hablo Español*
Please speak more slowly. - *Por favor, hable más despacio.*
One minute, please. - *Un momento, por favor.*
Walk well/happy trails -*Buen camino!*
What time does it open/close? - *¿A qué hora abre/cierra?*
Where is (are) the...? -*¿Donde está(n) ...?*
bathroom - *los servicios*
hospital - *el hospital*
a hostel – *un albergue*
Where can I find water? - *¿Dónde puedo encontrar agua?*
Do you have wifi? - *¿Tiene wifi? (wee-fee)*
Password - *contraseña, clave*

Problems - *problemas*

I'm lost. - *Estoy perdido.*
Help! - *Ayúdame!/Socorro!*
Call the police! - *Llama a la policía!*
Call a doctor! - *Llama a un médico!*
I need a doctor/dentist. - *Necesito un doctor/un dentista*
Go away! - *Véte!*
Leave me alone! - *Déjame en paz!*
Medicine - *medicamentos*
Pharmacy - *farmacia*
Medical center/clinic - *centro de salud*
Blister - *ampolla*
Fracture/sprain - *fractura*
I'm sick. - *Estoy enfermo/a...*
I'm allergic to - *Tengo alergia a...*
Penicillin - *la penicilina*
Bee sting - *picadura de abeja*
Beg bugs - *los chinches*
Pain - *dolor*

Web Index

Every guidebook is out of date by the time it goes to print. We have done our best to ensure that the information contained in this book is accurate. However, things change, so the most up-to-date information about this guidebook is on our website, **www.caminoguidebook.com**. There you can find:

- **Updates** to this book, including changes in route, accommodations, contact information, availability, etc.
- **Relevant websites** (those marked in text)
- **GPS files** of every route in this book, free to download to your personal device (GPS or smart phone) for foolproof navigation
- **Planning information:** Gear selection, fitness and training, biking and horses, blister prevention, foot care, bedbugs precautions, maps, navigation, GPS, Google Earth, smartphone apps
- **Travel Information**: Visas, transportation (flights, buses, trains, taxis), medical care and health insurance, tours and tour operators, luggage transfer
- **Advice:** Confraternities, alternate itineraries, budgeting, albergue etiquette, phone and internet providers, families with children, Leave No Trace principles, camping, dietary restrictions, winter walking
- **Inspiration:** Photos of each stage of the Camino, descriptions of other pilgrimage trails around the world, blog entries

Acknowledgements

The work of producing a guidebook of this depth involves many more people than simply the authors. Thanks to our parents, who are always supportive of our work and willing to lend a quiet place to work and help out with childcare. Thanks to Barcelona native Rebecca Moyano Gonzalez for proofreading the phrase book (available online) and offering valuable suggestions. Thanks to all who have supported and enriched the pilgrim experience by contributing to the general body of Camino research and reflection through confraternities, online forums and social networking. Thanks to the many hospitaleros who have volunteered their time to care for the wayfarers and strangers who happen upon their door. To our children, thank you for reminding us to take childlike wonder in the world around us. Any mistakes in the text are solely the fault of the authors. If you find errors in the book or have updated information, please contact us at **info@caminoguidebook.com**.

To all supporters and contributors: *eskerrik asko, grazas, gracias* and thank you!

About the Authors

David Landis and Anna Dintaman

Anna Dintaman and **David Landis** are a husband-and-wife team with over 10 years of experience working with walking routes in the Mediterranean and Middle East. Both avid hikers and bicyclists, their experience ranges from backpacking Patagonia and Nepal to hiking in the Alps, Andes and Appalachian mountains to cycling across the United States. They have shared a deep love of the Camino since they each separately took a 500-mile journey on the Camino Francés in 2009. In 2007, David cofounded the Jesus Trail, a hiking trail that connects sites from the life of Jesus.

David and Anna coauthored *Hiking the Jesus Trail*, an in-depth hiking guide to pilgrimage sites in the Galilee. They are also involved in developing various pilgrimage and walking routes in the Middle East. David and Anna take pride in doing all their own research, writing, photography, maps and layout and design. They enjoy introducing their children to the joys of walking, the outdoors, and experiencing other cultures.

Feedback, comments & corrections welcomed: info@caminoguidebook.com

facebook.com/caminoguidebooks
instagram.com/caminoguidebook
twitter.com/caminoguidebook
pinterest.com/caminoguidebook

Village to Village Press, LLC specializes in publishing hiking guidebooks and supporting trail development projects, especially with an emphasis on pilgrimage along the Camino de Santiago and in the Middle East and Mediterranean regions.

We offer a range of services in the publishing process including writing, editing, layout and design, photography, and web/social media integration. We specialize in consulting services for trail, tourism and community development including:

- Trail development strategy and implementation
- Communications strategy
- Non-profit project management
- Practical travel resource development
- Tourism product branding
- Public relations and marketing

www.villagetovillagepress.com